THE HEART OF RELIGION

by the same author

EARLY INDIAN RELIGIOUS THOUGHT

THE HEART OF RELIGION

P. D. MEHTA

COMPTON RUSSELL
ELEMENT

First published in Great Britain 1976 by
Compton Russell Ltd.,
The Old Brewery, Tisbury, Wiltshire
and printed in England by
The Compton Press Ltd.

ISBN 0 85955 029 X

CONTENTS

PART FOUR
THE HOLY LIFE

PREFACE

. . . and then at last Mother Earth gave birth to man: a creature conscious of self, a religious being.

If he lives only as an economic, social and political animal, he remains sub-human. But if he tends the religiousness within him he matures as a whole and fulfilled human.

The nature of man's fulfilment and the growing pains involved in living the everyday life religiously are considered in this book. Parts of it may give cause for shock and pain to some, but for the unbiased reader it may open a door to the vision of reality and the understanding of life. The passages which deal with the importance of the knowledge of the nature of things, the so-called conflict between religion and science, the state of the wholly purified mind and the unusual modes of awareness and 'knowing' by 'being', may suggest fresh avenues of research in such fields as epistemology, psychology, education and the social order.

I am deeply indebted to several friends for generous help in various ways: to Jo Corble, Norman Fraser and Marita Llinares for typing the manuscript; to Betty Duke-Woolley and Beryl Jenks for assistance with the Index; and to Lester Halhed for preparation of the diagrams. Encouragement and strong support have come from Klaus and Rut Bahlsen, Ingrid Brooke, Dr. Fritjof Capra, Patricia Chown, Betty Duke-Woolley, Victor Duret, Norman Fraser, Beryl Jenks, Dr. I. B. Horner, Christmas Humphreys, Juan Mascaró, Silvia Mehta, John Moore, Rosemary Monk, the late H. J. Newlin, Sidney Penry, Dr. Irmgaard Schloegl, Valerie Tompkins, Geoffrey Watkins, and many other well-wishers and supporters, both known and anonymous.

To each and every one I tender my grateful thanks. Lastly, my thanks are due to the publishers and printers for their care and attention in the production of this book.

P.D.M.

London, January 1976.

ABBREVIATIONS

A.	Anguttara Nikāya
Ait. Up.	Aitareya Upaniṣad
Ānand. Ser.	Ānandāśrama Series
B.G.	Bhagavad Gītā
Bhāg.	Bhāgavata Purāṇa
Bibl. Ind.	Bibliotheca Indica
Bṛh. Up.	Bṛhadāraṇyaka Upaniṣad
Chānd. Up.	Chāndogya Upaniṣad
D.	Dīgha Nikāya
Eng.	English
Exod.	Exodus
Gen.	Genesis
Jer.	Jeremiah
Lam.	Lamentations of Jeremiah
M.	Majjhima Nikāya
Maitr. Up.	Maitri Upaniṣad
Matt.	Matthew
Rev.	The Revelation
R.V. or RV.	Ṛg-Veda
S.	Saṁyutta Nikāya
SBE.	Sacred Books of the East
Śvet. Up.	Śvetāśvatara Upaniṣad
Tait. Up.	Taittirīya Upaniṣad
Up.	Upaniṣad
Vin.	Vinaya Piṭaka
Vism.	Visuddhimagga

The reader will notice that the initial letter of certain key words is sometimes printed as a capital and sometimes not. It is hoped that it is soon appreciated that the capital is found wherever it is necessary to distinguish a word being used in its transcendental sense.

All Biblical quotations are from the Authorized Version except where indicated otherwise.

PART ONE
THE THEME: ITS NATURE AND CONTEXT

CHAPTER ONE
THE THEME

WHENEVER the creative activity of the spirit effectively meets the urgency of the human situation there is a true renewal for all who are quickened by it. They become New Men and usher in a New Age. Such were Lao Tzu, Kṛṣṇa, the Buddha, Zarathuśtra, Moses, Jesus, Muhammad, and many others of whom history has but a dim record. Each of them made the needed response to his own unique situation and communicated religious truth in a form which was outstandingly marked by its originality.

Although each teacher effected renewal during his lifetime only within the limited sphere of his local culture, yet so powerful was the influence of his exemplary life and the spirit manifesting through him, so profoundly true his teaching, that the gospel survived his death by many centuries and overflowed widely beyond the bounds of the land where the urgent situation originally arose. For thousands of millions of people, the word of the great teachers preserved in the scriptures of the world has been the bread of life. Most people somehow feel in their bones what the great teachers saw perfectly, that the spirit is the root of everything. If a man's whole being may be likened to a tree, its root is the spiritual part. If this root be healthy, a man can understand the problem confronting him; but if his inner being is afflicted, his prime need is to mend his own spirit. In all human affairs the root crisis is spiritual and personal, manifesting itself outwardly as a material or cultural or social or international or any other crisis.

What is the situation today?

Science, which as a cultural pursuit was formerly known as natural philosophy, has risen to a status of prime importance in this century and is now the dominant force in the life of the world. Materially, it has enabled man to establish a technological age. It has put within his grasp manipulable power great enough to destroy all life and even to turn this planet, the Earth our mother whom he knows not how to honour, into a dazzling explosion bright enough to give some distant astronomer in a distant age a passing thrill. Contrariwise, man could use this vast knowledge and power in the service of the good, if only he understood what is the real good; and he could use it not only to fulfil the unfolding pattern of his own being but also to serve the other children of mother Earth, the animals and the plants and the very soil on which he lives. He is lord here; it is his bounden duty to exercise dominion, which means not inhuman, destructive exploitation but the parental responsibility of nurturing and sustaining with loving wisdom.

Modern science has radically changed the conception of the nature of things. Matter no longer has the meaning it had until the last century, so much so that the old-fashioned use of the word materialism or materialistic in many a modern context is a misuse. So too, deterministic, causal conceptions, whilst operative in various contexts, now have to coexist with, if not be superseded by, indeterminacy, which nevertheless does not mean chaotic lawlessness. The universe is not just a mechanical engine. It is more like a living organism.

Sufficiently radical changes in the conception of the nature of things necessitate corresponding changes in both thought and action in other fields. To cite but one example from the past, the first Roman Catholic theology, that of Saint Augustine of Hippo in the early fifth century, accepted and utilised the scientific conceptions of Democritus and Plato. Aristotle disagreed with these. Arabian and Jewish scholars, who took for granted the physics and philosophy of Aristotle, so influenced Catholic scholars after the Muslim entry into Spain that the Roman Church was deeply shocked by the acceptance of Aristotelian as against Platonic science by men like Abelard and Albertus Magnus. Nevertheless, eight and a half centuries after Saint Augustine, Saint Thomas Aquinas, a pupil of Albertus Magnus, having mastered Aristotle's physical and psychological writings, made use of them for his *Summa Theologica*, which was accepted finally by the Roman Church as the basis of its theological position.

World exploration during the past five centuries has introduced countries and cultures to each other. Applied science has completed what exploration initiated and has forcibly intercommunicated the world. Yet there is no community of man. There is an instrument for unification, but no organic comity of nations. Fissiparous forces are operative everywhere. All nations, great or small, strong or weak, developed or underdeveloped live in suspicion, fear and unhealthy rivalry with each other and fall into war with sickening regularity. Wars and fears of nuclear war are in fashion. So too are brain washing and genocides and the suppression of religion and a sensitive way of life in some parts of the world.

Science has provided knowledge and technical means for a sufficient production of food and goods to satisfy human needs – needs, not greeds. Yet nowhere are there people free of anxiety; in several countries there is a shortage of necessities; and everywhere, incontinent man squanders his life-energy and material resources in brutish excitements. Improved mechanical devices and a rising flood of gadgets and inventions afford the untrained masses a leisure which spells boredom with all its attendant ills and gives rise to problems due to the accelerating pace of modern life, to increasing regimentation, to the diminution of individual creative or recreative activities, to increased noise and to shriller advertisements.

Where national management, aided by modern techniques, has raised a façade of material ease and affluence, standards of conduct, socially and commercially, have deteriorated. So have standards of living – using the word 'living' in the true sense – while the standard of expense, the cost of living, has risen and continues to rise steeply. What has happened is that the exploitation of man by man and the demoniacal drive to satisfy greed and vanity have found new methods of expression, cloaking themselves under a new economic jargon: fools never see that they are the most helpful friends of knaves. Larger and larger numbers of people live more self-indulgently and heedlessly now than was possible a generation or two ago. Despite seeming welfare there is dissatisfaction and frustration. An old way of life, felt to be irksome or unjust, is being rejected, partly under the influence of a vague, blind hope for a better future. But the new way that is coming into being also lacks understanding of purpose and meaning in life and it is certainly devoid of moral skill. Serious indeed is the breakdown of moral codes in various spheres, with consequent sickness of the soul, violently invaded by licence, frustration, hate, and all the evil progeny of sin. Thus crime is now an established and increasingly successful business and it is freely admitted that the affluent state offers the conditions for this. Meanwhile, the majesty of the law suffers increasing discomfort, order stumbles more frequently into the arms of chaos and licence pretends to be freedom.

At the same time it must be recognised that quite remarkable advances have been made in this century materially and socially, in the fields of health and education, in organising relief for suffering at home and abroad and in cultivating a more humane and intelligent approach to various problems. Yet all this on the credit side is too light a counterweight to the debit side, for both individual suffering and an endless succession of large-scale crises and wars are ever-present facts.

This age witnesses the dissolution of formal religion. Hordes of dull-minded people, either intoxicated by easy affluence or sensual gratification or reacting with hate against frustration and miserable circumstances, have lost interest, if they had any, in religion in any shape or form. Added to this is the confusion and painful perplexity produced in many thoughtful and devoted people through suffering which they cannot understand or through the discrediting of several old religious ideas and beliefs by modern science and psychology or by secular philosophies mulishly hostile to all religion. The official custodians of hard-pressed organised religions, unable to create faith afresh by being living exemplars here and now, try to save formal faith by actually stooping to the use of worldly techniques rampant today – compulsive persuasion by advertisement, by cunning psychological methods, by holding out the bait of spiritual powers and hierarchic positions and by all the other paraphernalia of exploiting men's inclinations and minds. Clerical intellectuals rehash outworn ideas in pseudo-scientific jargon or in psychological garb in order to keep abreast of secular knowledge. The great theologians spin out webs of discursive thought in answer to mounting modern criticism, quite forgetting that discursive thought is but the sepulchre of personal, living realization and that at best it has only a temporary stimulating effect. Thought never added a cubit to spiritual stature. To heal the fresh outburst of disease new medicine is needed. The eternal verities are undoubtedly eternal verities, but the scriptural word which they ensoul has to be uttered with power in a new tongue after the march of centuries, else the old word fails to energise the living present, as is the case today.

Consequently, so many people, religious, irreligious and non-religious, suffer from a growing spiritual malaise. Man as a true human is essentially a religious being and only secondarily a political, social and economic animal. Wheresoever and whensoever his religious nature is thwarted he is ill, miserable and on the downward path and every aspect of his total life bears the scars of this thwarting.

Thus the present situation is charged with an urgency, poignant and dangerous. The lack of true communion between man and man, the new conception of the nature of things and the control of power of undreamed-of magnitude, and the serious threat to survival more because of the decline in living the holy life than the possible misuse of nuclear or some similar power, all cry out for a reassessment of relationships, values, goals and ways of life. The majority of people, apathetic and incompetent, will tend to stay in their ruts, going through the motions of formal religion. But those who are not idle and fearful, who honestly direct every energy to understanding religious truth for themselves, will see that a true reappraisal is possible only if the heart of religion is a glowing reality throughout their whole lives.

Today's human problem is less a problem of doing and much more a problem of being, less of activity and more of rest, less of the sound and fury of achievement and expansion and much more of silence. Far more important than freedom from poverty, disease and other worldly troubles is freedom from worldliness, freedom from greed, hate, delusion and aggressive egoism, freedom from lack of self-knowledge and freedom from ignorance of the reality of the Transcendent and of the ways for its realisation here-now. Imperatively, man's problem is to abjure the pursuit of wealth and power – always a lunatic and criminal pursuit when premature – and instead to grow in love and wisdom and develop the skills to express them in perfection. Until such love and wisdom have flowered, wealth and power will inevitably be misused and plunge man into sin and suffering.

How may the pure flame of religion be rekindled today? There are missionaries all over the world who devote themselves to the propagation of the particular faith to which they belong. But no local culture of the past, no formal garb of the existing great religions, Christian, Buddhist, Hindu or any other, can effectively meet today's world need. There are many liberal spirits who work for the unification of all religions. But no syncretist nor eclectic 'universal' religion will save man from suffocating in his spiritual vacuum. There are well-intentioned good persons, around whom grow new cults and whose adherents believe that they have the panacea for the world's ills. But they will not provide the Bread of Life, for their philosophies and theories and the practical disciplines they recommend are like alluring shallows detracting one from the mid-stream course of meaningful living.

None of the above make, or can make, the needed response to the unique present.

That response which would rekindle the pure flame of religion today could come only from those who have themselves realized the Transcendent. The founders of the great religions of the past were such men. They all –Kṛṣṇa, Zarathuśtra, Buddha, Christ – announced a second advent. Certainly a teacher appears again and again, but never as a repetition of a past form which was a creative fulfilment for that specific living situation. Never again will Kṛṣṇa, Zarathuśtra or Jesus come back as persons recognisable as Kṛṣṇa, Zarathuśtra or Jesus, for the movement of the spirit is non-repetitive, invariably unique in every manifestation of its single essence. The teacher of today will draw afresh from the timeless spring of truth and he will fill a new cup fashioned by the need of the new world age. Whoso has the heart to lift the cup to his burning lips will be healed and, then only, live.

Are the earnest ones then to light their candles and search for the world teacher? Are they to watch for the new dawn when a World-Saviour will come from on high and give a world teaching upon which, as a foundation, will be constructed the edifice of a world religion?

Great teachers inspire and transform their devotees by the influence of their living presence. This presence is a silence; this influence is formless and unconditioned. To the light of reality the living presence awakens the sleeper in the dark: the dark whose substance is thought-speech, whose drive proceeds from the egoistic misconception of self, whose binding power is the burdensome conditioning by the past and by environment. Of necessity, the Perfected Holy One must speak to his listeners. The words are treasured. The words continue through time, commentaries are written and conflicting interpretations lead to fierce argument. And so for the simple souls who hunger and thirst there is but stale bread and sour wine. Formal religion is fossilized religion. The church and the temple and the sacred tomes and the postures of piety may thrill and elevate and comfort and entrance. Yet all too often they are monumental impediments to Truth. They cover the living heart of religion with a vast rubble heap of illusions, mere pieces of death. Leaving death to the dead, let the true man go to the living heart.

This is one of the keynotes for today, that each man shall individually search out the living heart of his own free will and in his own way. Unquestioning acceptance of authoritarian teaching marks the impotent. Let there be unceasing vigilant investigation of that which is. So shall each man see the truth.

That wonderful arc in human history extending over two millennia which saw the emergence of the founders of the great religions, each in his own sphere, will not repeat its old shape. The mechanical repetition of an expended pattern would prove but a monotony. Life discards the obsolete. Renewal is rebirth. Therefore the world will not witness the rise of a new world-embracing religion and the establishment of a world-wide Church which will either oust or absorb all other religious organizations. Nor will it see any existing religion do so, despite all militant evangelism, an activity characterizing the immature. A religious totalitarianism may prove an even greater evil than any of the secular ones.

This does not mean that the day of the Holy Ones is over. They have appeared through the ages and will continue to appear, whether they are recognised or not. As in all past instances, whatever the Holy One of today or tomorrow will teach will be the expression of his individual realization of the Truth. The Truth is the spirit-parent of the Word of all the great teachers. In him who keeps the word, which means in him who lives the holy life, there arises the stainless vision of the Truth. He enters into the measureless communion which is the realization of the Transcendent. He is the living word.

What such realization means and what is involved in such realization is at the very heart of all religion. It is the main theme of this book.

CHAPTER TWO
THE APPROACH TO THE THEME

IMMEDIATELY the question arises: can the Heart of Religion be communicated through the medium of thought or speech?

As long as we are self-conscious, we are as opaque matter obstructing the light. When we are reduced to our no-thingness, the Transcendent is there. In this experiencing of the Infinite we are unself-conscious. We do not know God, but God knows us. We cannot know God for our kind of knowing is incapable of grasping the Infinite; the knowing by the Infinite of us is other than what we can mentally perceive. The Beloved who truly gives her self to love, 'swoons'. The Lover 'knows' her.[1] Recovering from the swoon which is the unself-conscious state, a conception grows, for the natural tendency of the surface mind, the conscious verbalizer, is to set limits to the infinite and formulate a spatio-temporal experience out of the spaceless and timeless experiencing. Strange are the results of such conceiving.

Truly, experiencing the immeasurable is indescribable. The Unknown, the Infinite, cannot be crammed into the known and finite mould of thought-speech. Thinking-speaking about the Transcendent only forges mental images of the imageless – a game of make-believe like the fantasy-play of an imaginative child. The Living Experiencing is Truth in the religious sense; it is the real knowing of God. The images made by the mind, the verbal formulations set down in a book, even in Holy Writ, however stimulating or inspiring, are but expressions of conceiving and bringing forth, excrescences of the ineffable Reality. They are but a tomb of the Truth. Man, the Living Immortal, must rise out of this tomb, leaving in it merely a bundle of clothes, an astonishment to the unawakened.

Form, nevertheless, must not be despised. Its very limitations are the goads that move us to Transcendence. Thought itself can serve the purpose of laying bare the fact that all images are but idols; and speech itself can sound the alarm that deflects us from the rape of truth. If thought-speech be pure, the human dialogue can lift our eyes to the stars. Then, if it is possible to empty the mind of all its images, its illusions and delusions, the divine dialogue can take place, for the emptied mind, spacious and silent, does not hinder the experiencing of the Transcendent. This

[1] Gen., 4.1. 'And Adam knew his wife Eve and she conceived.'.

unclouded vision is shapeless and formless. It is not finite. After the unself-conscious experiencing in which the total mind was wholly silent, the surface mind again sets up the self-conscious experiencer. The verbalizing faculty intrudes upon the beatitude of silence; finite images of the imageless Infinite materialise the unclouded vision; and thus the word of scripture comes into being.

The act of conceiving and the act of verbalizing must be as pure as possible. What sullies the purity is our conditioning; the conditioning of the psycho-physical organism through natural evolution for over a thousand millennia, and the cultural conditioning by the particular society in which we are born and bred and educated. The great teachers were those who, to the highest degree possible in their circumstances, had grown free of their conditioning. This freedom is pre-eminently marked by the fact that each saviour or enlightened one outgrew the tradition in which he was brought up and the disciplines in which he was trained, without seeking to deliberately oust or destroy the faith and religious practice of his own fellow men.[2] His teaching, nevertheless, inevitably shakes, even cracks, a fossilized old order. But for his true listeners, the Word which he utters is the Bread of Life, for he who has rightly outgrown his conditioning is a creator. His Word is the affirmation of the living experiencing of the Transcendent. Such speech is prophecy, prophetic speech. It inspires, it moves, it fecundates; but it cannot communicate, meaning that it cannot hand over, the Heart of Religion to the listener. Each man has to realize the Transcendent for himself, even as the new-born babe has to breathe for himself in order to live as an individual. Such realization is possible if the quickening light of spiritual insight plays upon the Word, for thus there is revelation of living truth.

This living truth – religious truth – is not a doctrine or belief or mental cognition or intuitive perception or verbal statement. It is the unself-conscious, immediate awareness of the here-now. It is the actual state of fully awake BEING, without separatively perceiving being as self and the environment as not-self, without interpreting the Infinite Reality as an idea, shape, form, sound, touch, smell or feeling. Let Reality BE. Let there be no disturbance of the Silence, of the Peace of God which passes understanding. Just live that Life Eternal. That is the experiencing. That is the 'substance' of Religious Truth. It is totally lived by Whole Being. Springing out of that timeless ineffable into time – and into experience and event – the mind, if holy, will give expression to prophetic speech.

[2] Matt., 5.17. 'I am not come to destroy but to fulfil'.

The holiness of the mind depends on spiritual insight, and insight depends on purity of mind and heart. Thus, religious understanding is not superficial verbal understanding nor simply *sensibilité*. It is a 'knowing' by at-one-ment, by a 'soul-union' which transcends intellectual ideation and intuitive grasp. The perfection of the subsequent verbalization depends first upon the purity of the mind, and this purity is none other than the freedom from all the conditioning by natural evolution and by socio-cultural influences, and next upon the training and skill of the intellect.

If then, there is scholarship as well as religious understanding the theme of this book can be approached seriously and fearlessly. The Heart of Religion is not a matter for critical analysis or engaging exposition. It has to be lived with our total being. Reader and writer together embark upon a genuine enquiry, a wholehearted honest experimenting, a ceaseless searching. There is no end to this, no final answer; for all ends are dead-ends, all man-declared finalities are denials of the non-finite Transcendent. Our enquiring and experimenting and searching is simply our love-gift to Life Abundant; through motiveless outpouring of this gift there is measureless discovery of the Unknown.

Being serious means, therefore, that neither reader nor writer may embark on this voyage with any ulterior motive. A defined motive is no other than a fixation by the mortal in terms of the limited and the particular. Thus we merely tread the wretched round of mortality and miserably fulfil the mortal motive, predestined, an illusion whose sad fate is death. How can ever-dying mortality compass or reveal ever-living immortality?

Many a high-sounding motive may lure the unwary writer: to expound the true meaning of Holy Scripture; to comfort the sorrowing; to enlighten those in darkness; to serve God; to love one's neighbour; to save man from destruction; to exalt the true faith; to leave the world a better place than one found it; to show the underlying reality of the world's religions; and so on. Can we not see that they are all rooted in self-ness, delusion, pride, conceit, ignorance, hate, power-lust and greed? That they are all modes of exploitation of man by man? And yet, if a writer writes because care-free thought-less love carries him on the crest of a creative life-wave, might not all pure motives find sweet and unpremeditated fulfilment?

So let every calculated motive be eschewed, and let reader and writer approach the Heart of Religion as beggars, stripped, dispossessed. Our greatest qualification[3] when we approach the Unknown is that we know nothing. The mind is empty. The attention is blind – waiting to be shown; deaf – waiting the Word; bisexed and unprocreative – waiting the immaculate conception and virgin birth; lame – waiting the leading of the divine hand. In this clean state of primordial New-ness, we may beg for our Daily Bread in all seriousness.

The mind is empty. The attention glows, white hot. This emptiness does not mean the blankness of total ignorance. We do still have our knowledge through the experience of our whole past in the form of technical skills, intellectual perceptions, aesthetic faculties and any other forms that make up our psychological content. But whereas in the past we felt we possessed knowledge, when in actual fact we were possessed and imprisoned by beliefs and ideas and in short our total experience; whereas in the past we were in the unenlightened state, the state of *avidyā* as taught in India, we have now the felicity of completely dying to the past and to every flickering mortal moment. So the attentiveness lives im-mortally at white heat, unbound by the psychological movement of sense impressions, perceptions, conceptions or ideas through the whole of chronological time. This is the enlightened state, the state of *vidyā* of the Indians, the state of creative emptiness, of the Void which is filled with the perpetual flashing of the Plenum. This is the state of freedom. This is the open mind, the mind that is unbiassed and unprejudiced, the mind whose light is never darkened by any preconception or assumption.

With this mind, serious, one can fearlessly approach the Heart of Religion. We can now be true scholars, that is true disciples, which means true learners. The true learner is a ceaseless discoverer of the new, not just a modifier, however brilliant, of the past. Unto him, the infinite Unknown continuously moves into a temporal beatitude of the known. He, the bereaved beggar, holds out a bottomless bowl, an invisible fiery ring of adoration through which the endless stream of divine beneficence flows. He is aflame with enlightenment. To him, in love with Truth, transcendent wisdom is an open book, and his blind attentiveness fills the world with streaming light. He, true scholar, neither clings to ideas or beliefs or doctrines, nor does he impose them on any man. Free of self-ness, with its endless conflict of grasping vainly for self-perpetuation against the implacable destruction-regeneration wrought by the death-rebirth of the becoming process, he is free of fear.

---

[3] Evans-Wentz, *Tibetan Yoga and Secret Doctrines*, p. 61:

A foolish man proclaimeth his qualifications;
A wise man keepeth them secret within himself;
A straw floateth upon the surface of water,
But a precious gem placed upon it sinketh.

From *The Precious Rosary*, Stanza 58.

Let reader and writer, thus prepared, study the religions of the past, and study religion which is now present, never forgetting that for the study of religion, the spirit demands a renunciation by intellect which is not required by any worldly study. The holy books of the world which state the word of God or Truth or Wisdom or Love, will remain stumbling monuments painfully bruising us, unless we read them with the eye and the heart with which we read, must read, the wordless holy book, the Book of Life in which indeed, 'Day unto day uttereth speech, and night unto night showeth knowledge.' (Psalms, 19.2.)

He who reads the Book of Life, only reads. Reading, he understands. Out of his understanding arise the verbal forms which express his comprehension. His Word of Wisdom is his compassionate response to his children hungry for truth. How significant is his final word – AUM[4] – for this sound has no meaning in terms of thought-speech. The reader of the Book of Life freely relinquishes the verbal forms of comprehension. He does not fix them; he does not commit the sinful folly of attempting to organise Truth into a final system. Finalities are corpses. Therefore he transcends all fixations of thought.

Let the child learn of his Father. As the theist may say, 'God shines His face upon his Son' – and are not reader and writer his Sons? Like sparks of light arise the forms of comprehension, and vanish away into that Void, 'dark with excessive bright'[5] whence they flashed. Mind like a sensitive plate suffers the imprint, but, alas!, ignorance mistakes the picture for the living beloved and lust and hate exploit the mistake. So steps in satanic authority armed with set beliefs, conclusions, doctrines and dogmas, and with sanctions of heaven and hell, to bind man – man, who is born free! – and to twist his mind into the tortuous mould of congealed thought. Yet, though hedged in by this dark and cruel tangle, the wise Word born of Compassion shines by its own living light. He who is serious and fearless will, scatheless, blunt the wounding edge of bondage. He will see light.

[4] Svet. Up., 1.13,14, Praśna Up., 5. 1-7, Māṇḍūkya Up., 1-12.

[5] Milton, *Paradise Lost*, 3.380.

CHAPTER THREE
THE AFFIRMATION AND THE PROMISE

SCATTERED through the scriptures of the world are affirmations of a great realization. The poet-seer Pragātha sings in the Ṛg-veda:

We have drunk Soma and become immortal;
we have attained the light; the gods discovered.
Now what may foeman's malice do to harm us?
What, O immortal, mortal man's deception?

Ṛg-veda, 8.48.3

Aspiration to this realization of immortality, to this attainment of light and this discovery of the gods, is hymned by Kaśyapa the son of Marīci:

O Pavamāna, place me in that deathless undecaying world,
Wherein the light of heaven is set and everlasting lustre shines.
Flow, Indu, flow for Indra's sake.
Make me immortal in the realm where dwells the king, Vivasvān's son.
Where is the secret shrine of heaven, where are those waters young and fresh.
Flow, Indu, flow for Indra's sake.
Make me immortal in that realm where they move even as they list,
In the third sphere of inmost heaven where lucid worlds are full of light.
Flow, Indu, flow for Indra's sake.
Make me immortal in that realm of eager wish and strong desire,
The region of the golden Sun, where food and full delight are found.
Flow, Indu, flow for Indra's sake.
Make me immortal in that realm where happiness and transports, where
Joys and felicities combine, and longing wishes are fulfilled.
Flow, Indu, flow for Indra's sake.

Ṛg-veda, 9.113.7-11.

The Ṛṣi Bṛhaddiva the son of Atharvan declares:

Bṛhaddiva, the foremost of light-winners, repeats
these holy prayers, this strength to Indra.
He rules the great self-luminous fold of light, and
all the doors of light hath he thrown open.

Thus hath Bṛhaddiva the great Atharvan spoken
to Indra as himself in person.
The spotless sisters, they who are his mothers, with
power exalt him and impel him onwards.

Ṛg-veda, 10.120.8,9.

In the Avestā, Zarathuśtra affirms:

When I beheld Thee in my very eyes, then I realized Thee in my mind, O Mazdā, as the First and also the Last of all Eternity, as the Father of Vohu Mana (the Good Mind), as the true Creator of Ashā (Holiness), and Lord over the actions of Life. Yasna, 31.8.

Then did I realize Thee as the Most Bountiful One, O Mazdā Ahurā, when the Good Mind encircled me completely. He declared to me that silent meditation is the best for attaining spiritual enlightenment. Yasna, 43.15.

Him will I seek to turn towards us with hymns of adoration, for now in truth have I beheld him clearly in my mind's eye. Knowing through Ashā of the Good Spirit in word and deed, I can now see Mazdā Ahurā Himself, so let us treasure up His praises in Garo Demāna, the House of Heavenly Song. Yasna, 45.8.

Lao Tze writes in his Tao-Teh-King:

The greatest virtue is in simply following Tao, the intangible,
inscrutable.
Inscrutable, intangible, and yet containing forms.
Intangible, inscrutable, and yet containing things.
Profound and obscure, but having an essence, a veritable essence
in which is consistence.
From eternity until now its nature has remained unchanged.
It inheres in all things from their beginnings.
How do I know of the origin of things?
I know by Tao. No. 21, 'The Empty Source'.

The Buddha declares:

Bhikkhus, there is a not-born, a not-become, a not-made, a not-compounded. *Bhikkhus*, if that unborn, not-become, not-made, not-compounded were not, there would be apparent no escape from this here that is born, become, made, compounded.

Udāna, 80.

Nibbāna does exist, the way leading to *nibbāna* exists and I exist as adviser. M., 3.6.

So I, *bhikkhus*, being liable, because of self, to birth . . . ageing . . . decaying . . . dying . . . sorrow . . . stain, seeking the unborn . . . unageing . . . undecaying . . . undying . . . sorrowless . . . stainless, the uttermost security from the bonds, *nibbāna*, won the unborn, the uttermost security from the bonds, *nibbāna*. Knowledge and vision arose in me: unshakeable is freedom for me, this is the last conditioned state, there is now no more re-becoming. M., 1.167.

Victorious over all, omniscient am I,
. . .
For I am perfected in the world,
a teacher supreme am I,
By myself all-awakened,
Become cool am I, *nibbāna* attained.
To turn the *dhamma*-wheel
I go to Kāsi city,
Beating the drum of deathlessness
In a world that's blind become. M., 1.171.

Give ear, *bhikkhus*; the deathless is found, I instruct, I teach *dhamma*. M., 1.172.

In the Old Testament we read:

And Enoch walked with God: and he was not; for God took him. Gen., 5.24.

Noah walked with God. Gen., 6.9.

I have seen God face to face and my life is preserved. Gen., 32.30.

And God said unto Moses, I AM THAT I AM. Exod., 3.14.

And Moses went up unto God, and the Lord called unto him out of the mountain. Exod., 19.3.

And Moses went into the midst of the cloud, and gat him up into the mount: and Moses was in the mount forty days and forty nights. Exod., 24.18.

And the Lord spake unto Moses face to face, as a man speaketh unto his friend. Exod., 33.11.

And he (Elijah) arose, and did eat and drink, and went in the strength of that meat forty days and forty nights unto Horeb the mount of God. I. Kings, 19.8.

And it came to pass, as they (Elijah and Elisha) still went on, and talked, that, behold, *there appeared* a chariot of fire, and horses of fire, and parted them both asunder; and Elijah went up by a whirlwind into heaven. II. Kings, 2.11.

Be still, and know that I am God. Psalms, 46.10.

The Lord is my shepherd; I shall not want.
He maketh me to lie down in green pastures: He leadeth me beside the still waters.
He restoreth my soul: he guideth me in the paths of righteousness for his name's sake.
Yea, though I walk through the valley of the shadow of death, I will fear no evil: for thou art with me; thy rod and thy staff they comfort me.
Thou preparest a table before me in the presence of mine enemies: thou anointest my head with oil; my cup runneth over.
Surely goodness and mercy shall follow me all the days of my life: and I will dwell in the house of the Lord for ever. Psalms, 23.

Whither shall I go from thy spirit?
Or whither shall I flee from thy presence?
If I ascend up into heaven, thou art there:
If I make my bed in Sheol, behold, thou art there.
If I take the wings of the morning,
and dwell in the uttermost parts of the sea;
Even there shall thy hand lead me,
and thy right hand shall hold me. Psalms, 139.7-10.

In the New Testament we find:

I and my Father are one. John, 10.30.

I am the way, the truth, and the life. John, 14.6.

Believe me that I am in the Father, and the Father in me.
John, 14.11.

And now I am no more in the world . . . and I come to thee.
John, 17.11.

And when he (Jesus) had spoken these things, while they beheld, he was taken up; and a cloud received him out of their sight.

Acts, 1.9.

I knew a man in Christ above fourteen years ago (whether in the body, I cannot tell; or whether out of the body, I cannot tell: God knoweth;) such an one caught up to the third heaven.
And I knew such a man, (whether in the body, or out of the body, I cannot tell: God knoweth;)
How that he was caught up into paradise, and heard unspeakable words, which it is not lawful for a man to utter.

II Corinthians, 12.2-4.

Pythagoras taught:

And when, after having divested thyself of the mortal body, thou arrivest at the most pure Aether,
Thou shalt be a God, immortal, incorruptible, and Death shall have no more dominion over thee.

Vv. 70 & 71 from *The Golden Verses of Pythagoras and Other Fragments*, selected and arranged by F. M. Firth.

Repeatedly in the Upaniṣads the great seers affirm their realization of the Atman, their knowledge of Brahman. Śvetāśvatara, Śākāyanya, Sanatkumāra, Satyakāma Jābāla, King Pravāhaṇa, Jaivali, Ajātaśatru the king of Kāśī, Raikva, Śāṇḍilya, Naciketas, Uddālaka Āruṇi, Pippalāda, Yājñavalkya the prince of Yogis, and many others, had realized union with God, or, to use that remarkable Upaniṣadic phrase, had become Brahman. Śvetāśvatara affirmed:

I sing the songs of olden times with adoration: may my own songs follow the path of the sun. Let all the children of immortality hear me, even those who are in the highest heaven. Śvet., 2.5.

I know the spirit supreme, radiant like the sun beyond darkness. He who knows him goes beyond death, for he is the only path to life immortal. Śvet., 3.8.

Pippalāda declared:

Thus far, in truth, I know that supreme Brahman.
There is naught higher than It. Praśna, 6.7.

Sanatkumāra said :

Where there is the Infinite there is joy. There is no joy in the finite. Only in the Infinite there is joy; know the nature of the Infinite.

Where nothing else is seen, or heard, or known, there is the Infinite. Where something else is seen, or heard, or known, there is the finite. The Infinite is immortal; but the finite is mortal.

The Infinite is above and below, north and south and east and west. The Infinite is the whole universe.

I am above and below, north and south and east and west. I am the whole universe.

Atman is above and below, north and south and east and west. Atman is the whole universe. Chānd., 7.23-25.

I am the Alone, the attributeless. I am the Lord taking away sin. I am the quiescent, the endless, the all-full and the ancient. I am neither the agent nor the enjoyer. I am the changeless and the decayless. I am of the nature of pure enlightenment. I am the one and everlasting bliss. Adhyātma, 68 & 69.

Then Kumāra Kārttikeya asked his father to expound the realization of Atman.

And Śiva declared :

I am of the nature of Parabrahman . . . I am the I that has given up 'I' . . . I am beyond the reach of mind and speech . . . I am Atman and Sadāśiva (the ever auspicious one) . . . There is none other than Brahman, and that is I . . . I am Brahman that is Sat (Being or Truth), and bliss, and the ancient . . . I alone am the Adiśesa (primeval time), without name and form, of the nature of bliss . . . I am of the nature of the All-Void . . . I am the unconditioned, the permanent, the Unborn . . .

Tejobindu, chapter 3.

Śrī Kṛṣṇa affirmed :

I am the abode of Brahman, the Immortal, the Inexhaustible, of eternal righteousness and unending bliss. B.G., 14.27.

I am seated in the hearts of all B.G., 15.18.

Because I am beyond the perishable, and even beyond the imperishable, in this world and in the Veda I am proclaimed the Spirit Supreme. B.G., 15.18.

al-Hallāj affirmed :

> If ye do not recognize God, at least recognize His signs. I am that sign, I am the Creative Truth (*ana'l haqq*), because through the Truth I am a Truth eternally. Kitāb al-Tawāsīn.

Muhammad declared :

> God ! There is no God but He; the Living; the Eternal; nor slumber seizeth Him nor sleep; His, whatsoever is in the Heavens, and whatsoever is in the Earth ! . . . He knoweth what hath been before them and what shall be after them; yet naught of His knowledge will they grasp save what He willeth. His throne reacheth over the Heavens and the Earth, and the upholding of both burdeneth Him not; and He is the High, the Great !
>
> The Quran, Sura 2, verse 256.

> This is God your Lord. There is no God but He, the Creator of all things; therefore worship Him alone – and He watcheth over all things.
>
> No vision taketh in Him, but He taketh in all vision : and He is the Subtile, the All-informed.
>
> The Quran, Sura 6, verses 102 & 103.

* * *

Many are the forms of the affirmation. What of the promise ? In the Bṛhadāraṇyaka Upaniṣad, Yājñavalkya says :

> He who is free from desire, whose desire finds fulfilment since the Atman is his desire, the powers of life leave him not. Being one with Brahman, in Brahman he abides.
>
> When all desires that cling to the heart disappear, then a mortal becomes immortal, and even in this life attains liberation.
>
> While we are here in this life we may reach the light of wisdom; and if we reach it not how deep is the darkness. Those who see the light enter life eternal : those who live in darkness enter sorrow.
>
> 4.4.6,7,14.

The Aitareya says :

> He (Vāmadeva) having ascended aloft from this world . . . became immortal, yea, became immortal. 5.4.

The Kaṭha Upaniṣad says:

He who has understanding,
Who is mindful and ever pure,
Reaches the End of the journey
From which he never returns. 3.8.

Then Naciketas, having received this knowledge declared by Death, and the whole teaching of Yoga, attained Brahman and became free from passion, immortal. And so may any other who knows this in regard to the Atman. 6.18.

The Kena Upaniṣad:

When known by an awakening, It is conceived of, truly it is immortality one finds. 12 (or 2.4.)

The Kauṣītaki Upaniṣad:

Having reached That, he becomes immortal as the gods are immortal. 2.14.

The Muṇḍaka Upaniṣad says:

He, verily who knows that supreme Brahman, becomes very Brahman . . . He crosses over sorrow, he crosses over sin. Liberated from the knots of the heart he becomes immortal. 3.2.9.

In the Bhagavad Gītā, Śrī Kṛṣṇa declares:

He who serveth me unfailingly by the yoga of devotion, he, crossing beyond the qualities, is fit to become Brahman. 14.26.

Though ever performing all actions, taking refuge in me, by my grace he obtaineth the eternal, changeless abode.

Merge thy mind in me, be my devotee, sacrifice to me, prostrate thyself before me, thou shalt come even unto me. I pledge thee my troth; thou art dear to me.

Abandoning all other spiritual paths, come unto me alone for shelter; sorrow not; I will liberate thee from all sins.

18.56,65,66.

Zarathuśtra's promise:

Whoever comes after the follower of Ashā (holiness), his dwelling in future shall be the light.

To him who is His friend in spirit and action, Mazdā Ahurā will grant Perfection and Immortality, and out of His abundance Ashā as well, and through His own overflowing strength His Might and Majesty, and the firm support of His Good Mind.

Yasna, 31.20,21.

In the New Testament:

> For the wages of sin is death; but the gift of God is eternal life through Jesus Christ our Lord. Romans, 6.23.

> He that hath an ear, let him hear what the Spirit saith unto the churches; To him that overcometh will I give to eat of the tree of life, which is in the midst of the paradise of God.
> ... He that overcometh shall not be hurt of the second death.
> ... To him that overcometh will I give to eat of the hidden manna, and will give him a white stone, and in the stone a new name written, which no man knoweth saving he that receiveth it.
> Revelation, 2.7,11,17.

> He that overcometh, the same shall be clothed in white raiment; and I will not blot out his name out of the book of life, but I will confess his name before my Father, and before his angels.
> Him that overcometh will I make a pillar in the temple of my God, and he shall go no more out: and I will write upon him the name of my God, and the name of the city of my God, which is new Jerusalem, which cometh down out of heaven from my God: and I will write upon him my new name. Revelation, 3.5,12.

> ... If a man love me, he will keep my words: and my Father will love him, and we will come unto him, and make our abode with him. John, 14.23.

The Buddha's assurance:

> Going along in accordance with what is enjoined, having soon realized here and now by your own superknowledge that supreme goal of the Brahma-faring for the sake of which young men of family rightly go forth from home into homelessness, you will abide in it. M., I. 172.

> Now it may be, Poṭṭhapāda, that you think: 'Evil dispositions may be put away, the dispositions that tend to purification may increase, one may continue to see face to face, and by himself come to realize, the full perfection and grandeur of wisdom, but one may continue sad.' Now that, Poṭṭhapāda, would not be accurate judgment. When such conditions are fulfilled, then there will be joy, and happiness, and peace, and in continual mindfulness and self-mastery, one will dwell at ease. D., I.196.

* * *

What do these affirmations mean? Can we know their meaning with our minds? Our minds are finite, and our words are ghostly echoes of the silent sound that sings the glory of the Transcendent Real. Truly, the awe of the Lord is the beginning of wisdom. Our awe is an intensity of love-longing. So, we stand our ground in the presence of that Majesty, unbetrayed by feet of clay. Uplifted with awe, we tremble with the passion of self-giving, not daring to ask anything yet with heart all tremulous for our ravishment by the fire of divine love. Then we are given the divine eye which sees without mediating light. We are made wise. And we know. And we are silent.

So it is, beyond the highest heaven. But here on earth we must use words. Touched to purity by the flame of truth, we may converse together with the humility born of the vision that gave us the knowledge of the ignorance of our minds. The intellect is in bond to desire. It invents the ways and means to serve its master. Desire springs dually; and the conscious desire is in discordant play with its unconscious twin. Desire is conflict, and desire blinds seeing and deafens hearing. Our senses are rendered untrue. We have taken leave of good sense in all our living here. So our body is bruised, our heart is pierced.

But this very intellect when hurt, distressed, rebels against its tyrant desire. It discovers the great delusion, self-ness. It discovers that all its proud knowledge, its cunning techniques and its alluring skills are a fabric made of illusions. In that discovery itself is its purification and its release. Now, there is intelligence. Now, the senses, pure and free, are the instruments for maintaining perfect relationship between all the parts of the unity sensuously experienced as the multiplicity. Seeing the One is the Many and the Many are One, division-making intellect is transformed into intelligence which understands, without intellect losing a single one of its own special powers. For now it is the Atman, God the Unknown Immanent, that sees by means of the eye and hears by means of the ear, cognizes by means of the intellect and understands by means of intelligence. And knows with the heart. Then the Affirmations are Light, Truth, for the words have vanished like ghosts before the shining dawn which heralds the rising sun. And YOU are that sun.

The Truth which is the affirmation is not the words. The Living Substance which is the affirmation is not this, not that – *neti*, *neti*, as Yājñavalkya said. The Nirvana renders all existential manifestation, all perceptions and feelings, all words and symbols, *anattā*, not the Transcendent Real. Eat the bread, which is the Body, and drink the wine, which is the Blood, in remembrance – in remembrance only – of Me, the Living One, the One whose name must never be taken in vain.

There is the WAY, which is itself enlightenment, which is itself realization of the Transcendent. The Truth, Life Eternal, shows its face in him who knows all the ways of the self, and thus knowing, stands beyond all self-ness whilst still embodied in a unique self. He can say truly, 'I am the way, the truth, and the life.' Of this WAY there is no chart, no instruction, no symbol, no word. But this WAY is reflected here as many ways, ways which are charted, taught, described. Not by blindly obedient following of any of these ways, for all blind following is unhappy folly leading to a dead-end, but, by ceaseless, open-minded enquiry into these ways, we get free of them all and become the WAY, of which each one of us may truly say, 'I am the WAY'.

He who has become the WAY is the intelligent one with unerring insight. The slave of desire, however trained, cannot conduct the open-minded enquiry into the charted ways leading to a defined goal as described in the scriptures of the world. Intellect, without going through the fire, merely makes new, illusory patterns kaleidoscopically. But by watching the intellect at work, by becoming aware of its servitude to desire, the released insight of intelligence uncovers the WAY through the examination of the ways.

Thereupon we know the meaning of the Affirmations. And also the meaning of the Promise, for we are now the very substance of that Promise.

* * *

The open-minded enquiry is free of the constraints of authority. Our investigation is for seeing truth, not for accepting or rejecting the verbal statements in the scriptures. When we see the truth in the words, there is a seeing (in the present tense), a state of awakenedness continuously giving rise to our passing feeling-thought-speech-action process. This present, living seeing does not die and become a seen (in the past tense), for then the thought-speech which last expressed the live seeing becomes a fossil, a *verbal* doctrine, dogma, belief or conclusion, a theological or philosophical system, a construct of mere knowledge. It ceases to be active love and enlightening wisdom. God, the Plenitude in the Void, becomes invisible; we cease to breathe the divine air, the Holy Spirit, Vāyu of the Ṛg-veda. Instead, we are chained in the posture of mock worship to our stocks and stones, to our idols, whether of brass or of the stuff of man-made concepts.

But religious truth is the immediate, living seeing, in the here-now, and not a collection of fossils of thought. And yet, even as material fossils will yield the secret of a living story to the open-minded investigation of the intelligent, unprejudiced scientist, so too will the word of scripture yield a life-giving fragrance to the religious man who seeks rightly. The important point to bear in mind is not to look for another bundle of explanations or ideas labelled 'the true interpretation of the scripture' or 'the revelation of the secret doctrine', although explanations, ideas and statements will, of necessity, be present, or else there can be no speech or writing. Our task will essentially consist in seeing the false in the true and the true in the true. The false in the true is the misinterpretation or wrong application of the Word; the true in the true is the pure understanding and its right expression in action of the word. The Word itself represents the true. How shall we know for certain that we hold a misinterpretation or have right understanding? Intellectually, we can never know for certain! Any knowing is but a temporary mental construct. Everything changes. Out of our ignorance and fear and our pathetic passion for security, we look for and cling to anaesthetizing postulates such as the unchanging goodness of God or the eternal bliss of Brahman. How can we postulate anything about the Unknown, or about that which transcends all that we know? We use the phrase, 'eternal verities'. It is a telling phrase. It makes an impact on us. But can we 'know for certain' the content or meaning of 'eternal verities'?

Religious truth is an inexhaustible well-spring. As we keep on seeing, in the present, our minds keep on producing intellectual formulations. Our task is to sift them and not to hold on to them. Seeing the false in the true enables us to let go of falsity. By seeing the true in the true we have understanding. Where there is pure understanding we do not cling to the verbal formulation but let it go. Both ways, we are purified; both ways, we are in constant pure action with the activity of seeing here-now and living by it.

Material techniques, cultural disciplines, aesthetic skills, scientific methods, social advances and the organized routine of everyday life both individually and collectively, are all based upon the past, the accumulation of experience and knowledge, the transmission of tradition and the acceptance of authority. Not so the flash of genius, or of insight into truth. Worldly truth is a continuous modification of the past, but the flash of the Transcendent is the entry of the Unknown into our mortal sphere. It does not merely modify us. It transmutes us, it makes us new. As long as intellect merely accepts the word of scripture, as long as mind merely submits to conditioning by authority, even the authority parading as the voice of God, the lightning of the Transcendent is withheld from us by the fog of our conditioned being. Remove this fog by totally open-minded enquiry and the immortal, not-worldly light makes our eye single and fills our whole being.

Thus, the disciplines of the theologian, historian, linguist or any scholar, valuable as they are in their own special, limited contexts, inevitably fall short in the unconditioned sphere of the immortal Transcendent, which is the 'context' of religious truth. The scholar investigates the word of truth and holds on to the word. The truly religious man sees that the truth cannot be 'investigated'. He utilises the word in order to lay bare the nature of his own mind and then lets go of the word. When bare, empty, the light of the Eternal illumines him. The scholar who has been touched by the Transcendent has at least some qualification for approaching the Heart of Religion, for when he is thus touched, his mind is in abeyance, so to say, as if in a mindless state, and so does not interfere with his understanding-through-being.

Clearly, then, our enquiry cannot be restricted to conventional scholarship. We will not, for instance, compare religions in the usual sense. The limited, the mortal, can be compared with something else which is also finite. The Heart of Religion is the Infinite. Comparison has no place here. The finite study labelled comparative religion is an intellectual pastime. The Truth-seeker studies it in order to free his mind of it. This is no condemnation of the study of compared religion. Indeed, the comparative religionist may find that the fruits of his labour have been thankfully utilised in these pages.

Again, we will not be concerned with any particular thesis, which has to be consistently presented and logically proved. Logic has its proper function in the sphere of intellectual or verbal comprehension and for constructing communicable thought. The limited and particular, the mortal and finite has to be logical if it is to serve us. Where the immortal and infinite is concerned, sanity cannot confine the a-logical truth of Awakened Being within the strict limits of conventional logical structure. At the same time, the sane mind, whole and pure, in unison with religious truth, will not affront the logic demanded by intellect, provided that intellect has not been dulled by authority or by conditioning. The mind must be free; and the free mind must enquire freely. The searching must be unhampered by any predetermination.

So, if we approach our theme as a whole, we may see the varied unfoldings of the religiousness of mankind. The word of the different scriptures presents wide disagreements and also intimate harmonies. All these throw light on each other. And if only our eyes have been well washed by the tears of our heart's longing for Truth, we shall see its wonderful richness displayed in the variety of its expressions, and we may understand any and every religion all the better for it.

Intellect is arrogant and immodest. When critical, it rends and ravishes. Wisdom is meek and chaste. When understanding, it heals and unifies. The open-minded enquiry is a wise enquiry, reverent and grateful. One of its faithful servants is doubt, the humble but searching doubt of truth-seeking. It challenges all authority, but not with the insolent self-assertiveness of the ignorant. The First Noble Truth of Buddhism, for example, states that birth (*jāti*) is sorrowful (*dukkha*), old age or decay (*jarā*) . . . death (*maraṇa*) is *dukkha*. This statement is taken at face value. So too is the belief in reincarnation by the faithful of the Buddhist and Hindu world. Millions of Christians accept literally the teachings of the Immaculate Conception and Virgin Birth, and the Resurrection and Ascension of Jesus. Are such beliefs true? If there is truth hidden in them, what is that truth? Is it what has been popularly believed through the centuries? Again, it is not rare to come across such statements as, 'dangerously near to pantheism', 'oriental fatalism, . . . negativity, . . . nihilism', 'but this is Gnosticism, . . . Gnostic heresy', etc. What value is there in such statements in addition to telling us something about the mind and character of those who make them? One more example will suffice. The founders of some great religions are presented as perfect and holy men who triumphed over temptation and lived sinless lives, and who had supernatural powers and performed miracles. In short, they are presented as stylised pictures of perfection and, in at least two cases, as embodiments of deity. Is this true? Just what does such a picture signify? How does it arise? And what value has it? Our concern is Truth, the Heart of Religion. So the open-minded enquiry must be serious and fearless, utterly free. Religion is not the exclusive preserve of the established great religions of the world, still less of the organized churches claiming authority to lay down what is or is not religious truth. This is especially true of the Heart of Religion. Whatever purifies and perfects a man, relates him fully to life and allows the realization of the Transcendent, is Religion.

Whoso can re-tell the holiness of the old scriptural word in terms of realization, effectively serves his age and milieu. Such is the saint, the poet-seer, the yogi, the mystic. If he is one who spontaneously lives the truth, if he is the embodiment of wisdom and the heart of love, if he is one who utters the New Word and makes the New Affirmation, then a new World-Teacher is in our midst. It is necessary for our enquiry to be sensitive to that fact, to be watchful and be able to see if indeed in our own day any enlightened being walks the earth. More, it is imperatively necessary to understand his teaching, for this teaching, which will bear the stamp of originality, will be wholly relevant for today's human situation. Mere preoccupation with 'the glorious past' is nostalgia for the dead. The true glory is no other than the actual light of the living present. If this is missed, harping on the glorious past is the hall-mark of our own dullness; and that dead past will be a burden which crushes our spirit in fact however fondly we may delude ourselves that it refreshes us.

To make the significance of the great teachings of the past concerning the Heart of Religion come alive in modern terms is not, therefore, the whole of our task. Every epoch has its own limitations. Whilst eternal verity is eternal verity, its expression always suffers the constraints of the age in which it is affirmed. When the world situation ushers in a new age, the old constraints, the old opportunities and even the old significances change. This is pointedly true today as perhaps never before, which makes it so necessary to see the new emergence which is significant now, and to see its intimate relationship with modern life. This new emergence will in course of time radically alter the whole ambit of the long established great religions. This ambit is so vast that we must deal in our enquiry mainly with those elements which constitute or bear upon the Heart of Religion.

CHAPTER FOUR
THE INJUNCTION AND THE MANDATE

At first sight the gates are barred.

Śrī Rāma says to Hanuman :

> Never should the Upaniṣads be imparted to an atheist, an ungrateful person, one intent on vicious actions, one having no devotion to me, or one who loses his way in the cave of books. On no account should they be given to one devoid of devotion.
>
> Muktikopaniṣad, 1.47.

The sage Śvetāśvatara says :

> This highest mystery in the Vedānta which has been declared in a former age should not be given to one whose passions are not subdued nor again to one who is not a son or a pupil. Śvet. Up., 6.22.

The seer Śākāyanya says to King Bṛhadratha :

> Let no one declare this most secret doctrine to anyone who is not a son, who is not a pupil, who is not of a tranquil mind.
>
> Maitri Up., 6.29.

Śrī Kṛṣṇa says to Arjuna :

> Never is this to be spoken by thee to anyone who is without austerity, nor to one without devotion, nor to one who desireth not to listen, nor yet to him who speaketh ill of me. B. G., 18.67.

Jesus says in his Sermon on the Mount :

> Give not that which is holy unto the dogs, neither cast ye your pearls before swine, lest they trample them under their feet, and turn again and rend you. Matt., 7.8.

Dionysius the Areopagite writes :

> And I pray, let no uninitiated person approach the sight; for neither is it without danger to gaze upon the glorious rays of the sun with weak eyes, nor is it without peril to put our hands to things above us. On the Ecclesiastical Hierarchy, Cap. 2.1.
>
> These things thou must not disclose to any of the uninitiated, by whom I mean those who cling to the objects of human thought, and

imagine there is no super-essential reality beyond, and fancy that they know by human understanding Him that has made Darkness His secret place. The Mystical Theology, Chapter 1.

From the Prologue to *The Cloud of Unknowing*, edited by Evelyn Underhill, Fifth Edition, pp. 39-41:

> In the name of the Father and of the Son and of the Holy Ghost! I charge thee and I beseech thee, with as much power and virtue as the bond of charity is sufficient to suffer, whatsoever thou be that shall have this book in possession, either by property, either by keeping, by bearing as a messenger, or else by borrowing, that in as much as is in thee by will and advisement, neither thou read it, nor write it, nor speak it, nor yet suffer it to be read, written, or spoken, of any or to any but if it be of such one, or to such one, that hath by thy supposing in a true will and by an whole intent purposed him to be a perfect follower of Christ not only in active living, but in the sovereignest point of contemplative living the which is possible by grace for to be come to in this present life of a perfect soul yet abiding in this deadly body....
>
> Fleshly janglers, open praisers and blamers of themselves or of any other, tellers of trifles, ronners and tattlers of tales, and all manner of pinchers, cared I never that they saw this book. For mine intent was never to write such thing unto them, and therefore I would that they meddle not therewith; neither they nor any of these curious, lettered, or unlearned men. Yea, although they be full good men of active living, yet this matter accordeth nothing to them.

From *The Supreme Path, the Rosary of Precious Gems* of the Tibetan Master, Gampopa, of the Kargyutpa Sect:

> The Perfect Wisdom having been found within oneself in virtue of the *guru*'s grace, it would be a cause of regret to dissipate it amidst the jungle of worldliness.
>
> To sell like so much merchandise the Sublime Doctrine of the Sages would be a cause of regret. The Ten Causes of Regret, Nos. 7 & 8.

Supreme Teachers laid down the injunction: the Heart of Religion was to be withheld from the vicious, the ungrateful, the unsubdued; from those without devotion, austerity, tranquillity; from 'dogs' and 'swine'; from those who were not sons or pupils; from the curious, and from both the lettered and the unlettered.

Who, then, were those worthy to receive the teaching? Śrī Rāma says to Hanuman:

> O Māruti, it is only after thorough testing that the Upaniṣads should be imparted to a disciple giving service (to a *guru*), to a well-disposed son or to one devoted to Me, following good observances, belonging to a good family, and being of good intelligence.
>
> Whoever studies or hears the one hundred and eight Upaniṣads attains Me. Muktikopaniṣad, 1.48,49.

Śākāyanya says to Bṛhadratha:

> To one who is devoted to none other (than his teacher), to one endowed with all (good) qualities, one may give it. Maitri Up., 6.29.

From the Prologue to *The Cloud of Unknowing*:

> If it be to those men, the which although they stand in activity by outward form of living, nevertheless yet by inward striving after the privy spirit of God, whose dooms be hid, they be full graciously disposed, not continually as is proper to very contemplatives, but now and then to be perceivers in the highest point of this contemplative act, if such men might see it, they should by the grace of God be greatly comforted thereby.

Out of compassion, the truth is withheld, for the truth sears. It sears all; but whereas the searing moves the unfit to evil, and to spreading destruction, it purifies and heals the worthy one. Out of reverence and love for the truth, it is withheld, for truth is a tender flower. How easily its beauty is shattered, when the organizer congeals it into an inflexible, rigid doctrine. How easily its fragrance is lost, in the incense of the rituals and the smoke of the crude fantasies of the conventionally pious.

The Truth is hidden: one. The holy of holies in the temple is an empty space, the void which is the unknown mystery whence flash forth appearances – gods, angels, oracles, whatever you will.

The scripture is twofold: exoteric and esoteric. The exoteric is the outward teaching of the priest, the external observances and beliefs of the populace. Based on the exoteric arise the palaces of theological thought, the petrified illusion of 'truth' authoritatively asserted and automatically accepted by the senseless, that is, by those who seeing, see not, hearing, hear not. The exoteric is a vast prison. For have we not offended God, scandalized truth? Must we not, then, serve our sentence? It happens, however, that the inhabitant of this prison is himself the trinity of judge, prisoner and jailer.

The prisoner could become free by virtue of the esoteric. No power can prevent him. It is he himself who prevents himself because he cannot, in his present condition, understand the esoteric and apply it. Unwisely clinging to the destitution of greed he covets the riches of freedom. Meek poverty is the riches of freedom. But on this he casts a harsh eye. So he seeks a teacher who will show him the way to break out of his prison, quickly and violently, but yet allow him to wallow in his present condition. In other words, this deluded, greedy one wants to grab the best of both worlds. The inexorable law of life leads him to a self-professing teacher, lewd-lipped, selling the way out. Round such teachers grow petty cults. The teacher fattens; and teacher and pupil move deathwards. The indignant retort is: 'but I did get such and such desirable results.' Let us always remember: 'get' and 'desirable results' are absent from the fulness of truth.

All worldly criteria are invalid where the truth of religion is concerned. So the true teachers lay down certain pre-requisites: devotion to Me – endowed with good qualities – being of good intelligence. The pupil has to discover the meaning and content of these qualifications. He has to learn to grow in virtue, soul strength, by freeing himself from the lustful acquisition of virtue. Lust bars out intelligence, defeats insight; and so the esoteric teaching remains a closed book to a man because of his own incapacity to look or to listen, however much he may read the word of the mystic doctrine or study the instructions of the great teachers or practise the techniques of yoga.

We have to change our condition radically. This change has nothing to do with the existing 'order' of society outside ourselves; it has everything to do with the existing disorder in our own minds and hearts. By virtue of such a change we can understand esoteric teaching.

* * *

Can we obtain a glimpse, in the religious context, of the nature of the teacher, the pupil and of the master-disciple relationship? What can we learn from an actual example?

In ancient India the brahman *guru*, who was as a spiritual father and preceptor, taught a brahman youth the initiatory verse, instructed him in the *sāstras* (the books dealing with the knowledge of various subjects)[1] and conducted the necessary ceremonies up to that of the investiture of the sacred thread which was performed by the *ācārya*. The *ācārya* was the spiritual guide or teacher who instructed the brahman youth in the

[1] See Nārada's recital to Sanatkumāra, Chānd. Up., 7.1.2.

Vedas, in the law of sacrifice and religious mysteries. The *ācāryas*, such as Drona, were also masters of the arts of war and peace which they taught those of their pupils who were of royal blood.

In the great Indian Epic, the Mahābhārata, (12.328.41), it is stated that the number of pupils should not exceed five. The pupils were known as *antevāsins* since they lived in or near the guru's household, which was an *āśrama*,[2] or hermitage, snuggling on the edge of the woods, not too far from the village bounds. Usually it was an austere, simple home by a stream, set amidst peaceful surroundings : the influence of nature was never underestimated in India. Pupils and disciples of the guru came to be called *chelas*, a term popular to this day. The brahman child began his education at the age of 8. This education was called the *brahmacarya*; it was the state of chaste, religious studentship. A child of the *kṣatriya* (the military or governing) caste began at 11, and the *vaiśya* (the trading or agricultural) caste at 12. This limit could be extended to 16, 22 and 24 years respectively; but after that a youth lost his right to recite the Sāvitrī verse,[3] and could not be accepted by a guru as his chela or by any householder as his son-in-law, for he could not offer sacrifice.[4]

The Sacred Laws as codified by Manu, Āpastamba and others lay down in great detail the rules to be observed by the chela regarding his food and drink, clothing and lodging, daily duties as a resident member of the guru's household, mode of study, and his personal conduct towards all. The guru is enjoined to reprove and, if necessary, to chastise an errant pupil :

> If the pupil commits faults, the teacher shall always reprove him.
> Threatening, fasting, bathing in (cold) water, and banishment from the teacher's presence are the punishments (which are to be employed), according to the magnitude (of the fault), until the pupil leaves off (wrong-doing). Āpastamba, 1.2.8.29,30.

> (As a rule) a pupil shall not be punished corporally.
> If no (other course) is possible, (he may be corrected) with a thin rope or thin cane.
> If (the teacher) strikes him with any other (instrument), he shall be punished by the king. Gautama, 2. 42-44.

The guru is to the chela as a father to his son and it is his duty to instruct him lovingly :

[2] *lit.* a place of mortification.
[3] R.V., 3.62.10.
[4] Manu, 2.36,38-40; Āpastamba, The Sacred Laws of the Āryas, 1.1.1.18,21.

> Loving him like his own son, and full of attention, he shall teach him the sacred science, without hiding anything in the whole law.
> And he shall not use him for his own purposes to the detriment of his studies, except in times of distress.
> A teacher who neglects the instruction of his pupil no longer remains a teacher. Āpastamba, 1.2.8.25,26,28.

> A man destitute of sacred knowledge is indeed a child, and he who teaches him the Veda is his father; for (the sages) have always said 'child' to an ignorant man, and 'father' to a teacher of the Veda.
> Of him who gives natural birth and him who gives (the knowledge of) the Veda, the giver of the Veda is the more venerable father; for the birth for the sake of the Veda (bears) eternal (good) both here and hereafter.
> Let a man consider that (he receiveth only bodily) existence when his parents begat him through mutual affection and when he was born from the womb (of his mother).
> But that birth which a teacher acquainted with the whole Veda, in accordance with the law, procures for him through the Sāvitrī,[5] is real, exempt from age and death. Manu, 2.153,146-8.

> Created beings must be instructed in (what concerns) their welfare without giving them pain, and sweet and gentle speech must be used by (a teacher) who desires (to abide by) the sacred law.
> He, forsooth, whose speech and thoughts are pure and ever perfectly guarded, gains the whole benefit which is conferred by the Vedānta.
> Let him not, even though in pain, (speak words) cutting (others) to the quick; let him not injure others in thought or deed; let him not utter speeches which make (others) afraid of him, since that will prevent him from gaining heaven. Manu, 2.159-61.

The term *āśrama* (place of mortification, as in *atyāśramin* in the Śvetāśvatara Upaniṣad, 6. 21, and in the Maitri Upaniṣad, 4. 3.) is used also to denote each of the four stages in the life of the brahman : student, householder, anchorite and wandering mendicant. In the last two stages the brahman becomes more and more free from all worldly attachments, so that he is fitted to enter his 'home', *astam*, as the realization of the Transcendent was designated as early as in the Ṛg-veda, 10.14.8. 'The

[5] R. V., 3.62.10.

entire history of mankind does not produce much that approaches in grandeur to this teaching,' declared Deussen.[6]

When the chela completed his twelve year pupillage, his guru, the brahman anchorite, advised him to marry a girl fit for his family and dear to him, live the life of the householder, the *gṛihapati*, for twenty five years, and then become an anchorite.[7] Now he in his turn could act as a guru and take chelas. Thus the guru was in most cases a man approaching his fiftieth year. Twenty five years later he could take the final step and become a wandering mendicant, not as a nuisance to society but as one from whom flowed spiritual wisdom and blessing.

Strong, healthy bodies and trained minds, skills that were needed for a citizen's life in the world as brahman, or as king or administrator or warrior, or as merchant or agriculturist, sound morals, and the realization of the Supreme as the spiritual goal of life, these were the objectives of both guru and chela.

The guru had insight. He understood his chela. The relationship between a guru and his chela was as a father to a son, as a whole person to a whole person, individual and unique. The chela's education was essentially religious and personal. It was a living relationship, not a mere contract for a fee. Neither guru nor chela had any problem of breadwinning; the chela begged in the village, and in accordance with the socio-religious custom of the day the pious villagers supplied the daily necessities. Safe set beyond all worldliness, the guru was free to educate the chela; he was under no constraint to produce a breadwinner, a factory hand or an office worker. Free of brutal competition, of the stresses and strains of a city life, the chela learned in the atmosphere of the leisured dignity of nature and of the deep love and understanding from his guru. There was little, if any, tension in the air between guru and chela. The guru was blessed with an eager and tractable group of five or six chelas, to each of whom he could give full attention. He had no syllabus to wade through within a set time, no anxieties connected with examination results, no promotions to covet. He was not cursed with personal ambitions or with any brutish drive for 'self-expression'. Education was his true vocation.

The guru appreciated the significance of speech and the importance of the mastery of language. Discursive thinking is an exercise of the faculty of speech.[8] Since mind and speech interdepend, the guru taught

[6] Paul Deussen, *The Philosophy of the Upaniṣads*, p. 367, T. & T. Clark, 1908, trans. by A. S. Geden.

[7] Nāradaparivrājaka Up., Chap. 2.

[8] M., I. 301.

the chela the sacred Vedic texts: the correct pronunciation of the words; their derivation and meaning; the metre and authorship of the verses; the facts and legends about the *ṛṣis* who composed the hymns; and the correct intonation of the verses in order to produce the right effect upon both speaker and listener. In this manner the thousand and twenty eight hymns of the Ṛg-veda were first learned by heart. In due time the chela learned all he had to learn from his guru. He now knew his *dharma*, his own way of religious living, verbally. He was proficient enough to think about it, discuss it and expound it as a body of knowledge, and perform the necessary religious rituals. He could now marry, bring up his own children, and after they were launched in the world he could become a hermit, a *vānapraśtha*, and enter upon the contemplative life, in his turn taking chelas if he wished. The contemplative life was indispensable for the personal realization of the profundities, intellectually, that is verbally, gathered during his studentship.

* * *

With very rare exceptions, educators in our day and age are not contemplatives in the deep sense, although they may be religious men in the social, worldly sense, in that they accept and are conditioned by the verbal teaching of the faith they profess, and observe its external instruments of grace.

As part of his task, the guru fulfilled the role of the priest in the pulpit and in the performance of his conventional duties, of the schoolteacher and of the housemaster. He also stood *in loco parentis* in fuller measure than a modern university tutor. But the guru's essential task was to put his chela in the way of realizing the Transcendent, a task quite beyond all that the priest or housemaster or tutor does or can do. The significance and implications of this point can be appreciated by those who have truly experienced the Transcendent. It cannot be appreciated by those who are 'lost in the cave of books', as Śrī Rāma said,[9] or by those who do not live the holy life.

Not all gurus were capable of putting their chelas in the way of realizing the Transcendent. Only the great teachers, the *mahā-gurus* or *mahā-ṛṣis*, could do so. Those chelas who were to develop in such wise as to become teachers gave evidence of this in their tender years. The great *ṛṣis* who were the composers of the Vedic hymns, the great authors and teachers of the *āraṇyakas* and the Upaniṣads, the *arahants* and

[9] See p. 30.

bodhisattvas, Buddhas and Christs, were *mahā-gurus* who were perfected, holy men.[10]

The guru's training of the chela in the days of his studentship was the lesser task. The chela was conditioned according to an ideal pattern of character and proficiency. But if the chela showed signs of steady devotion to the guru and of a consuming passion to discover truth, if on being tested he gave proof of his worthiness to receive the esoteric truth, then the guru undertook the greater task: he helped the chela to release himself from his conditioning; to understand the self in him and the ways of the self; to become free of all delusion; to change totally and become the complete human, that is, the Perfected Holy One; and to realize Transcendence. The conditioning in youth aimed at producing a good man in the best worldly sense; the freeing from the conditioning released the immortal.

At this stage the guru was the psychologist in depth. Guru and chela now dealt with the inner depths of being. The outward mask had to come off for the free *brahmaputra*, the son of God, to emerge. Here it must be clearly understood that the guru's psychological work was not directed towards reconciling a patient with the community in which he lived, or recirculating a worldling into society. It was directed towards freeing the chela from all worldliness, and also from all intellectually conceived and wilfully imposed unworldliness or other-worldliness. The spiritual life is life in freedom, neither enslaved by worldly values nor conditioned by a thought-out unworldliness, which is only a self-projection.

Furthermore, guru and chela had to realize freedom from the whole realm of the psyche by discovering the 'emptiness' of the psyche. The Supreme is not found, not even to be sought, by 'you' or by 'me'. The Supreme IS. Any still centre to which I am led, or whatsoever I find in my innermost depth, is of my making, and hence not the Supreme, the Immeasurable, God, Atman or Brahman. If we say God or Truth is the centre, then that centre is everywhere – the Plenitude. If we say Brahman or Reality is the boundless sphere or the All, that boundless sphere is nowhere – the Void. These are but words, symbols that may stimulate the psyche. Reality, the religious truth, transcends all the temporal manifestations to which we can give names.

Such realization implies a complete disentangling from the no longer needed word of scripture; it also implies a transmutation of one's own

[10] Perfected, holy men arose in several lands: China, Iran, India, Egypt, the Semitic lands and Europe.

being. Only the worthy chela, strong and capable, was fit for the esoteric teaching concerning truth. The word of the esoteric is no other than the word of the exoteric. It is the chela who, transformed, understands the truth beyond mind. The *mahāguru* knows the word or the symbol for its true temporal worth, for he is under no illusion regarding the truth it represents. He does not misuse the exoteric word. He handles its power for his esoteric psycho-spiritual activity.

We can understand, therefore, why the great teachers laid down their injunction against the indiscriminate dissemination of the deep teachings and disciplines. Not only would the disciple come to grief, but society too would suffer, perhaps disintegrate, because all that we, as worldly people in and of the world, strive for and believe in as good, worthy, true, beautiful, leading to happiness and progress, all of it is negated or put aside where the realization of the Transcendent is concerned. Jesus used stronger language than the teachers of the Upaniṣads and the Gītā in calling those unfit to receive the inner teachings dogs and swine,[11] when he laid down the injunction to withhold the truth.

The young brahman on leaving his guru to take up his priestly duties may be likened to a graduate in divinity entering upon his ministerial duties in his parish.[12] Consider, however, the gulf between a doctor of divinity and a Ruysbroeck or St. John of the Cross or St. Paul or Jesus. So, too, there was a gulf between the trained brahman and a Prajāpati Parameṣṭhin or a Yājñavalkya or a Kṛṣṇa or a Buddha. The great teachers, in all lands, do not pass on information or condition us according to a predetermined pattern. They awaken us into the enlightened state; they liberate us into the Unconditioned.

* * *

Those who designed the great rituals of Brahmanism knew that the psyche could be suggested or represented by physical symbols. They knew that symbols could be appropriately chosen and used for widely differing ends, evil or good. In past millennia, intellectual analysis played a much smaller part than it does in our own age. The folk felt through, rather than thought into, the deeps. Religious ritual thus had an important, perhaps the most important, place in the life of the community. Hence the mastery of correct ritual procedure stood at the centre of the young brahman's training.

[11] Matt., 7.6.
[12] The reader must remember we are considering *ancient* India.

All ritual worship lies within the sphere of the conditioned. The worshipper, though comforted, uplifted or even inspired by the drama played with symbols, remains bound within the circle of mortality, that is, of the conditioned. But the original designers of ritual worship as found in the great religions of the world had deep insight. They used certain symbols to help one to break free of the bondage to all symbolism. The church spire points to the limitless beyond. The emptiness of the adytum is the unknown no-thing, the numinous self-existent without which the knowable conditioned cannot be. The ordinary worshipper does not enter there: only the one representing the Supreme may make the approach.

The voluminous ritual treatises of Brahmanism known as the Brāhmaṇas give detailed instructions[13] for the construction of the place of worship and for all the different ceremonies, interspersing the instructions with suggestive ideas. They are clues to a better understanding of oneself. Inner meanings are more often revealed in the Upaniṣads which form the concluding chapters of the Brāhmaṇas; but even here much remains hidden. Hence it was necessary to go to a teacher, one who had realized the Transcendent. His words took the disciple thus far; his influence, through his personal presence and the attention (not mere thought) which he gave his disciple – a spiritual induction, so to say – took him further. The actual liberation into the Unconditioned had to be realized in silent aloneness.

Learning by hearing the spoken word was *śravaṇa*. The practice of bodily postures, *āsanas*, and of various breathing exercises, *prāṇāyāma*, induced freedom from restlessness. Keeping the body quiet and poised, the chela meditated upon what he had heard. The guru then questioned him regarding his reflexion, *manana*, and gave further instructions in accordance with the teachings laid down by the ancient seers. The practice of the *yamas* and *niyamas*, the virtues, restraints and daily observances, formed the chela's character and pattern of religious living. Furthermore, the chela was taught to be in rapport with nature by living in gentle, contemplative union with it. The Earth, for example, was always reverenced as the gracious, loving mother, and the life-process by which she sustained one was gratefully acknowledged.

Such upbringing and education conditioned the chela in accordance with a predetermined conception of holy living. It made him receptive to the powerful influence of the religious rituals in which he participated.

[13] In the case of the Hebrew Pentateuch the instructions given to Moses are attributed to the Lord Himself.

In the hands of great ceremonialists these rituals produced profound psychological effects. Trained to meditate, the attention of the skilled celebrant was wholly concentrated upon the psycho-spiritual significance of the ritual. It was the power of the concentrated thought of the celebrant and of the devout feeling of the participants which made the 'atmosphere' of the ceremony, exerted the influence for uplift and inner vision in the congregation, and made the ritual a veritable sacrament, a ceremonial magic. The actual presence and benediction of the invoked and worshipped deity was deeply felt. Such magic was essentially a communion with the divine and with nature. The esteem in which the efficacy of the sacrificial ritual was held was expressed in superlative terms by some of the greatest Upaniṣadic Teachers.[14]

Nididhyāsana, profound meditation, set the seal on the foregoing. Reflexion, *manana*, is a thought-speech activity. Verbal patterns are formed. Should fresh evidence or further reasoning show that a different verbal pattern better represents the matter under consideration, the old pattern is set aside. But this intellectual activity does not stir, even though it may evoke a flash out of, the deeps of the mind. Mind is a receptive-responsive sensitivity of the psycho-physical organism, the existential man. Its obvious and outward manifestation is intellectual (*manasic*) activity. The deep nous, *buddhi*, does not stir or function as intellect does, that is, as a maker and breaker of verbal patterns, all of which are the result of stimuli reaching the brain via the sense organs. When the whole being is still and attention is intensely alert, nous, *buddhi*, 'thrills'. If this 'thrilling', formless and indescribable, finds intellectual expression later on, the word of scripture emerges as the inspired utterance, *udāna*, or the creative idea. Thus arise the teachings of saints and seers within the fold, be it the Hindu, Jewish, Buddhist, Christian or any other fold.

This realization of religious truth is only a conditioned one because it has been led up to by hearing and by reflexion upon an accepted doctrine, and by means of a laid down method of development. *This* profound meditation, called meditation with seed, only serves to intensify from within the conditioning that has already been imposed from without.

But where the realization of unconditioned freedom is concerned there is a new *śravaṇa* and *manana*; and there is quite a different *nididhyāsana*, a meditation without seed, that is, a contemplative union with Reality in which self-ness is not.

[14] Bṛh. Up., 6.3.7-12.

The guru now imparts the great utterances, *mahāvākyas*, to the chela. They are affirmations of the fact that beyond conditioned existence there is unconditioned being. Where formerly the chela worshipped God as the Transcendent Other (than himself), regarding the path of holy living, the *brahmacarya*, as a way leading to a distant divine goal where, in short, the 'I' was here in time and space and matter, a mortal entity separate from the timeless, infinite, immortal Thou, the chela is now told: 'I am Brahman', *aham brahma'smi*; 'That art thou', *tat tvam asi*; 'That am I', *tadasmi*. Hearing these spoken words with his ears is only the beginning of the new *śravaṇa*. Yājñavalkya said to Paiṅgala[15] that the chela's own investigation into the meaning of the *mahāvākyas*, the esoteric truth divulged to the worthy chela, was *śravaṇa*. The implications of designating a 'hearing' as an 'investigation of the meaning' of First and Last Utterances, in the context of religious truth, should be understood.

This investigation is not an out-turned searching for facts or an accumulation of verbal statements or the extraction of some intellectual principle such as some scientific law of nature or a psychological insight. The striking feature of this investigation is the quietening and not the stirring up of the intellect. The quieter the mind becomes, the more readily does the verbal statement, 'That thou art', yield up its secret to the attentive disciple. This investigation is inward communion. It changes the disciple's ordinary mode of awareness into a mode of 'spiritual' knowing, which is devoid of verbal content. The quiet attentiveness of the disciple is remarkably like the act of listening. One is simply in the state of listening; one is not listening *to* anyone or *for* anything. In this state, one may, 'hear a sound of gentle stillness'.[16] The changing and changed mode of awareness is the 'hearing', which may, after the event, be given a verbal expression by the discursive mind. In this *śravaṇa*, what begins as a hearing proceeds as such and culminates as a ceaseless listening state. What is 'heard' in this state is the *śruti*, the 'directly heard' spiritual truth which the Hindus claim for the Vedas, the Zarathuśtrians for the *Gāthās*, the Muslims for at least parts of the Quran, etc. *Śruti* is called revelation by Christians.

Both *manana* and *nididhyāsana* are involved in such *śravaṇa*. The new *manana* has no element of ordinary intellectual activity which expresses itself as positive verbal statements. Its chief feature is a clearer and clearer seeing that all the gathered knowledge, the heap of beliefs and convictions, the accumulation of meritorious or virtuous actions, are

[15] Paiṅgala Up., 3.2.
[16] I. Kings, 19.12.

all a conditioning within which one is imprisoned and that they are all empty of Reality. They are but constructs of the mind, a *māyā* or make-believe that these ephemeral phantoms are the substance of truth. Such reflexion lays bare the nature of the mind and exposes the ways of the self in us, ways which are forces for the perpetuation of a mythical self-centre to which our egoistic, desirous thought fearfully clings.

This reflexion, passive and alert, is a denuding process. It dissolves away all the creations of fancy, all the theologies and the philosophies which are the cloud-palaces of thought-speech upreared by man whilst he is impure and unfree. This is one of the deep meanings of Śiva as destroyer. He is Saturn. Śrī Kṛṣṇa declared, 'I am time laying desolate the world.'[17] And in this passive, non-karma-generating activity of reflexion, the binding continuity of time itself, and hence of birth and death, are resolved into the timelessness of the pulse of eternal life. Hence the Upaniṣadic affirmations, '. . . become immortal, yea, become immortal.'[18]

This kind of transcendental reflexion is part of that profound contemplation, that *nididhyāsana* where one is the Alone: the Alone, wholly silent, is the beatific, embodied Truth, Eternity hearing its own Silence.

Manana reveals that the early reflexion which was part of the young chela's training, which made him proficient in doctrine and ritual and the orthodox practice of the religious life, and which built him into a pre-conceived pattern of thought-out goodness, was a self-centred, ego-assertive acquisitive process which derived its driving force from the pleasure principle. Who would strive for goodness or truth, who would serve God or man, supposing he were assured that the goal reached is not happiness or peace, the worthwhile or the desirable? *Manana* and *nididhyāsana* show him that saintly man in the world though he be by the best of worldly standards, he has so far but sweated for a personal reward – a case of, 'my desire, O Lord', not of, 'Thy will, O Lord' – and that he has been sculptured into a static block labelled, 'the holy man'. When he sees how the pleasure principle has dominated and moulded him, he also sees that the pleasure principle is in fact the pleasure-pain principle. It is the depriver of freedom and the creator of our shadow self; it is the sorrow producer, the progenitor of sin and death. Now he can understand the Buddha's Noble Truths about *dukkha*, the ill state, in which he teaches that all conditioned existence is pain and misery.

[17] B. G., 11.32.
[18] See above, pp. 15, 21, 22.

To see this is distressing and shattering. Therefore, do not broadcast the esoteric truth to any but the fit. Therefore, also, 'For he that hath, to him shall be given : and he that hath not, from him shall be taken even that which he hath.'[19]

Serious dangers may attend the imparting or investigation of the *mahāvākyas*; dangers of pride and conceit, of misinterpretation and terrible evil-doing, of moral and intellectual wrecking, even insanity and suicide. Should one steer clear of the dangers, there is enlightenment and the realization of truth. The guru's silent participation in the chela's *manana* can be a protection. His 'spiritual induction' can help to launch the chela into the uncharted abyss. The limit of *manana* and the *nididhyāsana* confined to the sphere of conditioned existence is the limit of Speech and Mind. The chela's transcendent *nididhyāsana* liberates him into the Unconditioned Infinite, into, 'THAT from which Speech and Mind return, not having found.'[20]

The open-minded investigation of the *mahāvākyas* frees one from the limiting effects of all socio-cultural conditioning. The power to exercise deep insight is one of the hall-marks of spiritual growth. The mind which is free of illusions and delusions, of the beliefs, criteria and evaluations imposed by our society and culture, is now animated by an extraordinary energy, an invincible power. It is a winged horse. The free spirit rides his Pegasus with joy. It is like Apollo the Sungod riding his horse-drawn chariot; it is like the Zarathuśtrian 'Light-rayed, immortal Khurshed (the Sun-god) of the heavenly horses whom we praise'; it is the power by which Yājñavalkya goes up to *āditya-loka*, the realm of the Sun-god.

This realm is still the realm of manifestation or the potentiality for manifestation: of archetypes or archetypal ideas; of distinctive consciousness, for Pegasus is still *your* Pegasus. It is still the realm of māyā (the-play-of-the-universe-maker), where there is latent *tṛṣṇa* (the longing-thrill for existential being), where there is death, and where there is sin in a transcendental sense, that is, in an a-moral sense, of necessity, for without division-making or duality-producing there is no patterning, no relationship-making, no manifesting.

The work of chela and guru together ends with the ending of the investigation of the *mahāvākyas*. This is the end of *manana*, symbolized by the sacrifice of the horse, the *aśvamedha*. *This* sacrifice does not kill any animal. This sacrifice means the sanctification of the mind. The

[19] Mark, 4.25.
[20] Tait. Up., 2.4;2.9; Tejobindu Up., 1.20; Śāṇḍilya Up., 2.4.

sanctifying process, the sacrifice or making sacred, is a living process of transformation through 'dying' into the New Birth, a true Rebirth.

With the fulfilment of the *aśvamedha* there is present the *puruṣa*, the Alone, the Person that is higher than the 'unmanifested' (the formless states of consciousness),[21] the last limit higher than which there is the No-thing, the Ain-Soph of the Hebrews, the Tao of Lao-Tze, the Brahman of the Upaniṣads.[22]

The transcendental *nididhyāsana* liberates one from the conditioning by natural evolution, a conditioning built into brain and nerves and into the psycho-physical organism called man.[23] Now there takes place the supreme sacrifice, the *puruṣamedha*, in what is called the *asaṁprajñāta samādhi*.[24] This is Brahman, the desert of the Godhead, the Nirvana, the Divine Dark, the Father in Heaven (*abba* = the Unknown Origin), the Voidness or *śūnyatā* where self-ness is not.

To see the Heart of Religion, it is essential to understand *śravaṇa* or hearing, *manana* or reflexion, and *nididhyāsana* or contemplative union.

* * *

The *mahārṣis* who hymned the Ṛg-veda and the *mahāgurus* who were the great teachers of the Upaniṣads were liberated beings. The word *ṛṣi* means a singer, *mahārṣi* a great singer. The *mahārṣis* were not merely great poets inspired by religious vision, the *mahāgurus* merely great theologians or philosophers. Singers of the Song of Eternal Life, the *mahārṣis* knew the truth by being the Truth. Poets, however great, do not live holiness as the *mahārṣis* and *mahāgurus* did. Poets, like Dante, have written far more wonderful poetry than any of the *ṛṣis* did; but in the case of the *mahārṣis*, their very being was the silent poetry which purified the minds of devotees and eased their vision of Reality.

It should be clearly understood that the great *ṛṣis* and gurus were not speculative philosophers. Experiencing the Unknown takes place in the silence of the Alone, where there is no mental-verbal disturbance. The Holy Ones sang the Psalm of Life out of compassion for deaf mortality. Their most effective quickening influence upon their beloved disciples was through their silent presence. Their concern, the Truth which is Religion, a timeless pulse of Being lived in every incalculable moment, was beyond the reaches of speech and mind. This Truth is Love. This

[21] See below, pp. 371 *ff*.
[22] Katha Upaniṣad, 3.11.
[23] See below, pp. 217 *f*.
[24] See below, pp. 350, 362.

Truth is Creation. In irreconcilable contrast, the whole of theology, philosophy and science lies within the sphere of speech-thought. It is the product of intellectual curiosity and mortal needs. But the Great Teachers were those who had crossed this restless sea in their ship of Truth to the shoreless Infinite.

Clearly, then, the meaning of the words 'teacher' and 'teaching' in the context of the Heart of Religion is quite different from their meaning in any worldly context. The Teacher did not take the disciple through a course of instruction at the end of which a certificate of proficiency was given to each successful candidate. It is important to bear this in mind. In the worldly context, in which a chela is trained to become a brahman priest who has to attend to his specific duties towards his flock, there is a course of instruction by the guru. Not so, where liberation into the Unconditioned is concerned. Here it is a living interplay, not a formulated method nor a laid-down path. Indeed, here there is only learner and learning, for only in the state of learning can there be experiencing of the Unknown, whereas teaching can be only of the already known, and hence no longer transcendent. In this living interplay, the erstwhile teacher, the 'father' and his 'son', the disciple, are both in that ineffable communion where the son may receive a double portion[25] of his father's glory. In the freedom of the unselfed state, well may the *mahāguru* say, 'Let us keep watch together, this immortal hour.'

Such were the great teachers who laid down the injunction against the improper dissemination of sacred knowledge.

The esteem in which sacred knowledge was held is expressed in many passages. For example, the Code of Manu lays down in chapter 2:

110. Unless one be asked, one must not explain (anything) to anybody, nor (must one answer) a person who asks improperly; let a wise man, though he knows (the answer), behave among men as (if he were) dumb.

113. Even in times of dire distress a teacher of the Veda should rather die with his knowledge than sow it in barren soil.

114. Sacred Learning approached a brahman and said to him: 'I am thy treasure, preserve me, deliver me not to a scorner; so (preserved) I shall become supremely strong.

115. 'But deliver me, as to the keeper of thy treasure, to a brahman whom thou shalt know to be pure, of subdued senses, chaste and attentive.'

[25] See II Kings, 2.9.

Admission into the Mysteries, or participation in sacred rites or initiations in various cultures the world over, was conditional upon solemn vows of secrecy, with the threat of dire sanctions against violation. Nevertheless, some of the sacred teachings were divulged in one way or another. For instance, Aeschylus, 525-456 B.C., who was born in Eleusis, the centre of the worship of Demeter, was accused of revealing the secrets of the Eleusinian mysteries, briefly mentioned by Aristotle[26]. Eustratius, a late commentator of the 12th century, quotes from Heraclides Ponticus that Aeschylus was acting in one of his own plays where there was a reference to Demeter. The audience suspected revelation of inviolable secrets and rose in fury. Aeschylus saved his life by fleeing to the altar of Dionysus in the orchestra. When he was charged with this crime before the Areopagus, his plea that he 'did not know that what he said was secret', was accepted and he was acquitted. Eustratius adds that the real cause of leniency by the judges was his prowess at Marathon.

There are many hints in Vedic literature which reveal the meaning of esoteric teachings. In the Ṛg-veda the name of Soma represents[27], materially, a terrestrial plant and the exhilarating juice extracted therefrom, and spiritually, a celestial plant[28] and a god. The Soma sacrifice was a main feature of the ritual of the Ṛg-veda. The Soma juice was extracted and the devotee who quaffed it felt so exhilarated and invigorated that he was moved to actions normally beyond his natural powers. It was claimed for the drink that it could cleanse the heart of sin, destroy falsehood, promote truth and confer immortality.

But a preoccupation with the physical aspect blinds one to the spiritual significance of Soma. There are several pointers to this significance in the Ṛg-veda. For example :[29]

> One thinks when they have brayed the plant, that he hath drunk
> the Soma's juice;
> Of him whom Brahmans truly know as Soma no one ever tastes.

The unequivocal affirmations that the true Soma is never tasted, shows that the Vedic ritual symbolizes the inner religious life, the states of mind and the process of purification which culminate in enlightenment and communion. The scriptures are concerned with man's fruition as a

[26] Ethics, 3.2.
[27] As Haoma does in the Avestā.
[28] R.V., Book 9, hymns 38, 61, 63, etc.
[29] R.V., 10.85.3.

religious being, not with botany. The draught of immortality is distilled in the deeps of the soul, not in a brewery. Soma leads to sanity, to perfect well-being. Bibbery does the reverse. The scriptures uphold abstention from all narcotics and intoxicants.

Treatises on haṭha-yoga and several of the Upaniṣads contain strange statements regarding the breathing practices[30] known as *prāṇāyāma*, such as the retention of the breath for forty-eight minutes or more, and even of the cessation of breathing. But there are also some revealing statements in the Upaniṣads:

> The avoidance of being impressed by the phenomenal world (as if it were the real or absolute instead of being only the relative) is said to be expiration (*recaka*). The awareness, 'I am Brahman' (*aham brahma'smi*) is inspiration (*puraka*). The constant retention of this awareness without any agitation is the retention or cessation of the breath (*kumbhaka*). Such is the practice of the enlightened. The ignorant merely close their nostrils or suffer from nose-ache.
>
> Tejobindu Up., 1.31.

> Taking his stand on himself when Brahman is seen, rejecting everything caused by ignorance of the Atman, is expiration. Absorbing the wisdom of the scriptures is inspiration. Keeping oneself in the knowledge of Brahman is retention of the breath.
>
> Varāha Up., 5.56-58.

With regard to the yogic physical postures, we have these:

> Being firm in the unshaken spiritual wisdom constitutes posture (*āsana*). Maṇḍalabrāhmaṇa Up., 2.2.5.

> That should be known as posture, in which one can meditate uninterruptedly on Brahman, with ease and without fatigue.
>
> Tejobindu Up., 1.25.

For penetrating insight into the inner meaning of the Bible, works such as the Zohar[31] should be studied, and the study vivified and made fruitive by calm, sustained meditation. Revelation comes through fruitive meditation, or contemplative prayer, in which the purified, emptied mind is open and ready to receive the truth. The revelation of the meaning of esoteric teachings is not the result of speculative thought,

[30] See also M., 1.243 *f*.

[31] *The Zohar*, translated by Harry Sperling and Maurice Simon, 5 vols., The Soncino Press, 1933.

it is not merely intelligent interpretation, nor an imaginative flash or inspiration. This revelation is present when the mind is free of conditioned thinking, and is still and silent.

The day of the sharp division between the exoteric and the esoteric is over. The authoritarian, hierarchical order of the past and the rigid limitation of all that was appropriate and permissible to each according to his station in life has given place, broadly, to a socialistic, democratic relationship between man and man.[32] Whoso has the urge to do so is free to investigate, experiment and learn. The sources of knowledge, such as books, cultural and religious organizations, personal research, are all available to him. What is possible for him depends upon his own stage. A child can take in a biblical or *purāṇic* story, not the *Summa Theologica* or the *Timaeus*, the doctrine of *śūnyatā* or the *brahma-sūtras*. But if any man is animated by the pure passion to make the open-minded enquiry into Truth, what is there to obstruct his enquiry and prevent his discovery of God? This we shall find out as we proceed. We start as the child in darkness, under threat from evil. If our enquiring is ceaseless and pure, we awaken as a child of light, innocent and free of conflict. In the exoteric form, 'Suffer little children, and forbid them not, to come unto me: for of such is the kingdom of heaven.',[33] Jesus embodies a profound esoteric truth. Yājñavalkya presents it thus:

> Let a brahman,[34] having shaken free of (the burden of) book-knowledge, choose to live as a child. When he becomes free of both learning and childlikeness, he becomes the silent one. Shaking free of both sound and silence he becomes a brahman.[35]
>
> Bṛh. Up., 3.5.1.

For the sake of those hungering and thirsting after righteousness, for those burning with the pure passion for Truth, out of infinite compassion for suffering man, for the sake of the welfare and happiness of all, the Great Teachers pronounced the mandate to share this treasure of treasures freely with all who would and could take it.

[32] It is true that about a third of mankind is dominated by a small number of authoritarians who believe they can forcibly change the masses into their conception of what man ought to be. As history has repeatedly shown, Life exterminates these authoritarians. But the cost in suffering to mankind is terrible. Man is a slow learner.

[33] Matt., 19.14.

[34] That is, a brahman by birth.

[35] That is, a brahman in fact, which means, according to the Vajrasūcī Upaniṣad, a man who, whatever be the caste to which he belongs by birth, has realized Brahman.

Śrī Kṛṣṇa says to Arjuna:

> He who shall declare this supreme secret among my devotees, having shown the highest devotion for me, without doubt he shall come to me.
> Nor is there any among men who performeth dearer service to me than he, nor any shall be more beloved by me on earth than he.
> B. G., 18.68,69.

Zarathuśtra declares:

> He who expounds to the wise the *mānthra*, the Holy Word, is indeed blest. Yasna, 51.8.

The Buddha says to his first sixty perfected ones:

> Walk, *bhikkhus*, on tour for the blessing of the manyfolk, for the happiness of the manyfolk, out of compassion for the world, for the welfare, for the blessing, the happiness of *devas* and men.
> Mahāvagga, 11.1.

Some forty years later, shortly before his death, he says at the Kutāgāra Hall:

> Therefore, *bhikkhus*, ye to whom the truths I have perceived have been made known by me, having thoroughly made yourselves masters of them, practise them, meditate upon them, and spread them abroad, in order that pure religion may last long and be perpetuated, in order that it may continue to be for the good and happiness of the great multitudes, out of pity for the world, to the good and the gain and the weal of *devas* and men. D., 2.119.

The living Jesus, the Son of Man, says to his twelve apostles before sending them forth:

> Go not into the way of the Gentiles, and into any city of the Samaritans enter ye not:
> But go rather to the lost sheep of the house of Israel.
> And as ye go, preach, saying, The kingdom of heaven is at hand.
> Heal the sick, cleanse the lepers, raise the dead, cast out devils: freely ye have received, freely give. Matt., 10.5-8.

The Risen Christ, the Son of God, says to the eleven:

> Go ye into all the world, and preach the gospel to every creature.
> He that believeth and is baptized shall be saved; but he that believeth not shall be damned. Mark., 16.15,16.

CHAPTER FIVE
COMMUNION

ALL the world is in communion; for communion is relationship and everything exists in relationship with everything else. Even as a man in profound slumber rests in unknowing communion so lives this intensely active universe.

Look at the speeding galaxies keeping tryst, or colliding cataclysmically in preparation for new emergence. See the stars in their courses spelling out Life's story, or suns and circling earths in intimate play bringing forth nurslings of immortality.

Is not that high peak in communion with highest sky? This boulder with the curve of earth which cradles it? That hard headland with the surging seas surrounding it? Or this roaming river with its bed and banks? Both the moving and the unmoving are in communion: the atom's vibrant nucleus with its attendant electrons, and the speechless furniture with the motionless room.

In endless variety the play of life holds hidden revelation. The flower is in communion with the stalk from which it hangs; the falling leaf with the wind which makes it dance; the maiden with her lover and the mother with her babe. Quiet pigeons on a jutting ledge commune with the night, and the stars speak with each other in the pulsing dark and utter wisdom to the listening ear, while the trees which swayed with laughing gladness in the day now rest in silent worship, and man communes with woman.

But just as there is the communion which is beauty and joy, there is also the communion of terror and pain and death: the lion's jaw with the antelope's neck; the live bull's head with the senseless abattoir; the executioner's sword with the soft, full-blooded throat. And the redemptive communion of Socrates with his cup: and Jesus with his cross.

The familiar harmonies of daily zest fill our life-span: the cook communing with his salt and the carpenter with his wood; the pianist with his piano and the scholar with his book. And also some strange and tortuous things we see when the clock communes with anxiety and time with sorrow. And does not the Devil commune with God? The practising saint with his lust? And the zealous saver of souls with evil?

All the world is in communion, fed with sacrifice, the great sacrifice which is the ever-turning wheel of universal becoming.

Through him who is whole and pure the world awakens out of unknowing communion into perfect communion. The world does not know it; but he is alight. In the darkness, he is the light of the world. And his awakened state is the timeless communion of the Nameless Unknown with all the world through him the star of truth, the heart of love.

To be thus, is man's religious fulfilment.

BEING IN COMMUNION – this is the Heart of Religion.

* * *

In the distant dawn of his emergence, man, like the very creature out of which he evolved, was in unknowing communion. Adam and God were on speaking terms with each other – a teaching which calls for deep contemplation. Child-man was receptive-responsive directly, and in simple terms, for mind was fresh and innocent. It did not work upon itself. So man lived in delight.[1] With growing self-consciousness, his mind turned inward and talked speculatively. It produced conceptions, and alas! fixed them. It exercised discriminative choice in favour of pleasure against pain. Thus the natural, unknowing wholeness of man's being was split asunder. He was now in the state of 'sin' and he lost pure delight. In his mind there appeared the darkness of confusion; there appeared the conflict of good with evil, of the 'is' with the 'ought to be', of fact with fantasy.

And so it is today. Only when the mind clearly knows itself for what it is, does it cease to sunder the unity of being and to obtrude upon the silence of eternity. Then sin ends with redemption and conflict cools into peace.

Wrapped in unknowing communion in his infancy, man enjoyed his golden age. In our present dark age, recorded as history, there have appeared redeemers and enlightened ones. Theirs was not an unknowing communion, nor was their awareness of truth a knowing by a self-conscious mind. Whilst they lived, theirs was the perfect communion. So, in the timeless now, they are the restorers of communion for us.

Mysteriously, man always hears the call or sees a picture of the long-lost Eden. He does not understand this pull at his heart, for its meaning is twisted by the usual condition of the mind. Yet through scores of thousands of years some men experienced revelations which gave them an ineradicable conviction of the reality of the Transcendent and inspired them with a hope and a faith in a way of life which led to a

[1] The name Eden means delight.

heavenly goal where this High God was no idle dream, was not only a pious aspiration but an eternal home and an ever present felicity.

These realizations of communion, dimly understood but intensely experienced, were treasured as the spiritual heritage of the race. The long waves of life followed each other. In our present tide, the established great religions all affirm the Transcendent, the Ways thereto, and the Life Abundant which is the fruit of treading the WAY. In wonderfully rich and beautiful forms have these Affirmations been made, for through the many millennia man's power of speech has flowered. This is the difference between the half-dumb Acheulean of a bygone aeon and us today.

This speech is the language of poetry, for poetry can tell of the silence, of the unity. But when speech is the noise of argumentative intellectual discourse, it is the language of duality, of confusing division.

The great secret, the hidden mystery, the inmost esoteric truth of the spiritual realization which is the ineffable communion, is the Silence. And all the utterances of scripture culminate in and dissolve into the Silence. This Silence is the Great Peace, the 'peace of God which passeth all understanding', the peace to which Jesus referred when he said, 'Peace I leave with you, my peace I give unto you: not as the world giveth, give I unto you'.[2] This Silence is the Nirvana of the Buddha, the 'other shore' to which one has crossed over, the *samādhi* of the Buddhist and the Hindu, the 'meditation' of Krishnamurti, the 'secret yoga sleep' of the Upaniṣads.[3]

This Silence is the pristine, timeless state of unconditioned Mind. Mysteriously, it contains the movement of the disturbed mind, the *māyā* which is spatio-temporal existence. The realization of this Silence is therefore no escape whatsoever from the storm and stress of the stage-show of Reality. It is the whole and perfect being in communion.

* * *

What moves? What makes a noise? How are we cut off from the silence? What rocks the communion?

'As it was in the beginning, is now, and ever shall be'. Such is Nature's being in communion: a flexible, variety-displaying movement and action in accord with law. If an atom of chlorine and an atom of sodium are moved into intimate proximity with each other, they will unite to

[2] John, 14.27.
[3] Varāha Up., 4.16. Maṇḍalabrāhmaṇa Up., 2.5.

form common salt. Neither atom has any choice in the matter. If a bar of iron is heated at one end, the molecules of iron vibrating at a higher frequency will make adjacent molecules vibrate at diminishing frequencies down towards the cold end. The molecules can exert no choice.

Atoms and molecules remain unchanged unless and until constrained by forces. The play of forces is duly measurable; scientific laws are obeyed and man can predict the products and their quantities and properties. Inanimate nature does not seem to display or allow of choice by will or deliberation. Whatsoever happens cannot happen otherwise. Whatsoever happens is right. The 'harmony' is inevitable. The communion can never be anything but a communion. And inanimate nature manifests spectacular intensities, and unimaginable vastnesses and minutenesses: but no pleasure or pain, joy or sorrow; no in-turning or outgoing; no I or thou; no mind, no psyche.

Yet these self-same inanimate atoms, aggregating in certain ways, form cells which display self-motivation, self-healing and self-reproduction, which are characteristics of living matter. They can learn – and the ability to learn is a sign of mind. In cells we see the cycle of birth, growth, decay and death. Whereas inanimate atoms display no choice but react according to the forces at play, living matter, even in early and simple forms such as the *coelenterata*, displays the power to delay a response; matter is no longer purely automatic; there is an interplay between an obvious outwardness and a hidden withinness. And then through scores of millions of years nerves and brain emerge, and the receptivity-responsivity of living things, that is, mind or psyche, experiences and expresses pain and pleasure, joy and sorrow; a sense of me and mine, of friend and foe; of the herd, tribe and clan; of safety and danger; and of self-consciousness and self-preservation. With these last two there begins the whole story of separativeness; of being cut off from whole reality; of the egoistic misperception of our real being as a separate entity which is not so much in relationship with but is struggling for survival at the expense of other entities; of being in constant conflict with malign forces in a hostile universe. And this separative self-consciousness is the parent of the fundamental fear that its continuity will be snapped and death will overwhelm it in everlasting oblivion.

With the uprising of separative self-consciousness with its inevitable accompaniment of fear and conflict, the golden age of unknowing communion in Eden's carefree delight comes to an end. Neither 'Adam' nor 'Eve' was 'born' or 'grew' or 'matured'. They knew not time, and time's infliction of selfness and striving, of anxiety and sorrow. They knew no dis-ease. But they changed. The life-force, the 'subtle serpent', seduced them. They began to distinguish in their conscious minds the two elements composing the pleasure-pain mechanism of their living, organic being; that is, they grew in the knowledge of 'good' and 'evil'. Whatever promoted organic life, judged by pleasing sensation, was good; the opposite was evil. 'Adam' and 'Eve' – their names represent man in his childhood, long ago – feared and rejected death because they did not understand it. LIFE (*prāṇa*) for them was only biological. So they chose pleasure by preference. The mind stored up the multitudinous impressions life made upon them, remembering the pleasant ones and trying to forget the unpleasant. But the suppressed impressions found nourishment and fruitful breeding-ground in the hidden depths of the mind.

Man started in the state of *avidyā*, an ignorant creature, unenlightened. Naturally, his dawning intelligence was incapable of right understanding. If he could have remained in a steady state of unenlightenment, free from the conflict of adaptation with adaptability, he would have remained a fixed animal species. But the possibility of exceptional development, coincident with structural physical changes, especially the brain, lay within him. So, through being 'seduced', he lost his unknowing communion and bliss, his unconscious immortality in Paradise. Living in the misery of conflict after his expulsion from Eden, he felt lonely in his hostile universe. He turned to his own mind – proud, ambitious, possessive, greedy, vengeful, aggressive and confused as it was, his Mephistopheles – for succour in his battle with life. He was quite ignorant of the fact that the talking mind – the thinker and his thought – was now the slave of the pleasure principle, and, worse still, he could not see that the pleasure principle was in fact the pleasure-pain principle.

This dark mind, carrying time's heavy burden of the accumulated memories of our age-long past is the noise maker, the sorrow maintainer. It insulates us from the Silence of heaven's own music. And all these memories, and conflict and sorrow, are built into our very nerves and brain and our whole organism. They constitute our conditioning by natural evolution. They are part of our living heritage transmitted through uncounted ages.

* * *

But Life transcends our human failure, just as it transcends any and every success. 'Brahman is Life (*prāṇa*)' – the Transcendent is Life – says the Chāndogya Upaniṣad (4.10.4).

The psycho-physical organism is not merely what we know of it, or imagine we know of it, with our conscious minds. Its latent potentialities defeat the imagination. The organism which is named 'man' is contained and wholly subsumed within the Transcendent. The reality of the Transcendent flashes into our life again and again, even as day dispels the darkness of night. But, just as a man who refuses to come out of a deep, underground cave remains in a rhythmless dark, so too he who curtains his eyes against the Transcendent Light.

How separate an entity is each of us? What substance is there to our egoistic misperception of our true being?

Earth is mother. Sun is father. We are here by virtue of Earth and Sun, and all that they have done for some five thousand million years or so in order to bring us forth. And we, we have not only forgotten but also we positively deny our undeniable factual relationship and oneness with our Parents. Our Mother Earth bore us; she bears with us though we spit upon her and stain her virgin purity by denying that we emerge out of her side. And when our little spark is cinder she will silently enfold us again, totally, in her all-enduring, uncomplaining heart.

Rebellious and errant children that we are, we have run away so far and for so long that we do not know our Parents for what they really are, nor do we know what wondrous possibilities are the heritage they hold for us. Are sun and earth, and for that matter the entire universe, only vast energy sources, only phenomena of light and heat and electricity and magnetism, only radiation and matter and all that little bit which we have so far discovered and dubbed 'material' and which constitutes our proud 'verified scientific knowledge' and our chatty philosophies? Is mind or spirit, God or Brahman or the Absolute something quite different from, and to be set over and against, 'matter'? Or is this separation and conflict something imposed by our dark minds, a mere assumption, an arbitrary assertion, with no warrant in truth? Might it not be that what we name as earth and sun, what we name the universe, holds within itself every new temporal manifestation through the immense rhythms of the evolutionary process? And that the eternity of the timeless, unitary withinness will unfold its beauty in countless forms of endless variety through unmeasured time?

Our knowledge today is but a tiny fragment still, an almost invisible speck of dust in the universe. Yet it has made such an astounding break through our ignorance-barrier that it has dematerialized matter. Matter IS immaterial energy. To our minds as they are, energy is still a mystery; and how energy 'becomes' matter is still a mystery. We rely upon and use mathematical equations to describe observable 'material' phenomena and to produce 'material' phenomena by applying what we deduce from mathematics. How far, or how different, is such mathematics from mind?

Today we have come to this edge. Our today is a million-year-old day. Today, we who peer over the edge, trembling before the abyss, are still not in communion. Hence our tormented souls, our troubled bodies; our fears and hates and wars; our gods and our devils in deadly conflict, and our own selves the lacerated victims, the terrible field of that sorrow and destruction.

Will tomorrow, then, a million-year-old tomorrow, be the day of divine knowledge? Shall we strive for enlightenment tomorrow and achieve communion, earn our Sabbath, rest in Nirvana? Vain thought and devilish desire of an ignorant egoist of confused mind! The Infinite, the Transcendent, is not an object, not a goal, to be grasped or won. It IS. We do not awaken to it as to *an* experience or *a* state. But by being fully awake to *what is*, here and now, by taking up the cross (to use Christian terms), and not letting go or running away from it, the eternity of the here-now is embodied in every fleeting moment of time and the divine glory blazes in the transience of the cross. Communion is, where there is complete attention.

Such attentiveness is a power of the mind, of this very mind which can be, and so often is, dark and confused, ill, the sorrow-producer. Energy, or primordial nature, which became atoms and molecules, grew to life as cells and evolved into self-knowing as man. Sun and Earth, primordial nature itself, 'knows' through us. We the evolutes of fundamental energy are not just the cast-outs of primordial nature but integral portions of her. We are her, she is us. She is all that we can name or perceive. She, the one and only 'body', is the inanimate stone, the living plant and the thinking man. Primordial energy is Mind. It is the Unborn, the Unmade, the undying Spirit, God, and whatever else our discoveries will reveal and our unfolding vision show us. All these, perceived by our senses and mind as a multitudinous variety, exist in real and ever-changing patterns and relationships. He who sees with perfect insight the separate patterns as well as their complete inter-relationships, sees the one reality and understands the one unity.

We have become so hypnotised by the variety, so obsessed by the demoniacal activity to assert separate selfness, that we have become almost wholly blind to this unity, even though we may intellectually, but with heart benumbed, give assent to it. Yet if we sit by the still waters, communing, and drink of the draught of the well-spring of Life, the bitter wound of separation we have inflicted on the Divine Body which is nature is healed and we are restored to the unity which is bliss.

Where there is complete attention, there is Silence, communion. Through the vast tides of time, the world put itself forth as perfected men again and again. They, the first fruits of humanity, by immergence into the Silence, unified themselves with this-nature, perceived by the senses and named by speech-mind, and also with that-nature, beyond ordinary perception, which they named the One God, the One, the Reality, and so on. The Few knew the oneness of this-nature and that-nature.

But this unity, realized in the experiencing of communion, defied the power of the mind to express it in speech. Mind, the mind of everyday use and activity, is but our organic receptive-responsive sensitivity utilizing our speech faculty. So the verbal forms in which we have our precious heritage of Their Teachings suffers from the defects inherent in speech, which also means the gaps in knowledge.

The Way to that-nature lay through this-nature. When the darkening shades of the 'knowledge of good and evil' ended the timeless shining of the golden age, mind made increasing acquaintance with this-nature. Mind saw, heard, tasted, felt, and remembered this-nature as so many bits and pieces. Thus the conscious mind. In its sleeping deeps were strange forces and stirrings – the influence of that-nature upon the whole being – activities of man's withinness which he neither comprehended intellectually nor understood through communion.

Sometimes in sleep came intimations of that-nature, intimations that aroused longings too poignant for mind to grasp for an unimaginable fulfilment. And sometimes came intimations, when awake, which fixed in him an ineradicable conviction, shot through and through with wordless wonder and beauty, with deathless hope and sublime exaltation, with awe, and with passionate love, of the Immortal Transcendent, the Last Answer to his First Question: I – who? whence? whither? why? Child-man did not, because he could not, put it in such language. Language, which is a communication-tool of mind, develops through time, like mind. But the whole being – man, mankind – is wholly influenced, timelessly, by the one unity, the eternal that-which-is. Child-man used his own language, largely composed of symbols and ritual worship, and less of words and abstract conceptions.

Sun and Earth, man's parents and continual preservers, the starry heavens and endless space, taught man his early lessons with terrible severity as well as with exquisite tenderness and joy. His school was this-nature. Tempest and flood, volcano and earthquake, shook him, hurt him, terrified him, destroyed him. Beast of prey, insect, reptile and his own kind heaped anxiety and sorrow upon him. Disease, drought, hunger and thirst assailed him. Man's Parents were harsh. It could not, and can not, be otherwise, for this is how they are. This is how, through their own issue, man, they come to knowledge, and with knowledge, control and change by deliberation and choice, a growing power and activity of the withinness.

Happy lessons also there were, and in rich variety, so much so that the lure of ephemeral happiness – pleasure, success – has blinded man to truth. It has ranged him on the side of pleasure against pain, perpetuating in his psyche a state of conflict between pleasure and pain with no prospect of the resolution of the conflict.

Hence his most fervent aspirations were escapist, couched as preferential choice in favour of one of the terms of a duality against the other. Against the fact of sorrow, insecurity, conflict and death, he arrayed his longing for bliss, security, peace and immortality. Seeking escape from the undesirable to the desirable, he struggled with might and main for his mind-created goals. Thereby he only perpetuated conflict. The spirit world of his imagination was peopled by dark and evil powers arrayed against the gods of light, by Titans and demons, by the shades of the ancestors, by all kinds of beings. It was important to communicate with them and cement alliance with the desirable powers through placatory rites and sacrificial ceremonies, for this was the insurance of security and happiness in the hereafter.

But, through the millennia have arisen the Few. To worship the gods, to be good and pious, was not enough. They were in anguish because it seemed to them that death lorded it over all life. They saw sin, they saw suffering which they could not explain except by attributing it to the will of the gods or the malice of demons. Had life any purpose, any meaning? Were there the Immortals, or were they a figment of man's imagination? Many were the earnest questions they asked, to which the discursive, logical mind could frame no certain nor satisfactory answer. Deep was the distress of their souls. But they were great souls. They were the noblest children of their Parents, though Sun and Earth knew not how they created them so. Stirred to the depths by a divine discontent, they chafed at the infuriatingly restrictive limitations life had imposed upon them. Passionately they felt that if only they could burst through the thorny bounds of ignorance, fling away the fetters of mortality and triumph over the lord of death, they would assuredly win the beatific experience of the Immortal and realize here-now that freedom and serenity which is ineffable bliss. That indeed would be fulfilment.

They 'succeeded'. They realized the Silence. On immergence into the Silence, they entered the sea of liberation, Nirvana, the kingdom of heaven. The without had given no final answer. The within by itself knew the humiliation of defeat. But when the without – the sense activities and the discursive mind – was in a pacified condition, and the very depth of the withinness, unresisting and wholly open, throbbed in perfect rhythm with the without, separative self-consciousness vanished and there was no separate entity, the 'I', to obstruct the total harmony. Being in communion, the Real was realized.

In this state of communion, the discursive mind which is the noise maker is silent. When out of communion, the talking mind never stops its incessant chatter, except in profound slumber. This chatter is mainly verbal; when not verbal, it consists of a succession of sense-impressions, visual or auditory or tactile or olfactory or gustatory; it also includes the restless confusion of memories and indulgence in anticipations. All this chatter centres round the 'I', the ego-self, in our ordinary waking and dream states. In profound slumber self-consciousness is perforce cut off. It is a temporary death – the death which holds within itself the mystery of regeneration, not death the destroyer. Here we are restored to communion. But this is an unknowing communion, a communion without attention.

When, not asleep bodily, the discursive mind stops talking, and attentiveness is at its intensest; we are wholly awake, and silent. This is the communion which is the transcendental realization of Truth, the Infinite, God, which 'you' experience as an egoless being and not as a separate self-conscious self. This is the One Source which is the Living Root of all religion. Here, all the Teachers are one. Out of this unitary truth there grow and poliferate the different religions.

After the transcendent experiencing, back in ordinary consciousness, Those who realized were aware that no discourse, spoken aloud as audible speech or spoken silently as thought, could contain or could express unerringly this experiencing. Their whole being was saturated with bliss, with peace, with love, with enlightenment, with deathlessness. And they saw with clear sight that the words and conceptions associated with man's escapist longings, named bliss or love or immortality, were not the Real which they had experienced, or rather, which the Real had manifested through their experiencing.

Wisely, they affirmed that the Real was not this, not that. But since the love-call of their disciples who hungered and thirsted could not be denied, many an Affirmation of the great religions of the past took the form it did. The 'sons', the worthy ones ready for the esoteric teaching, understood and profited. The perfected holy one was himself present to correct and help them. Thus for them there was no intrusion by the sorrow of time, of psychological and not chronological time, upon the bliss of eternity.

But there were many others who were in thrall to the sorrow of time. Driven though they were by the pain of being out of communion, they could not shake free from the shackling demands of intellect, from the craving for a verbal construct that would lay down a logical doctrine and point to a goal to be reached by a mortal person in time. So, alas!, devoid of the Realized Being's wisdom and skill and inspiring presence, the lesser teachers spoke learnedly: God or the Transcendent was the other than oneself; union with the Transcendent or fellowship with God was the goal at the end of a way; there was a method, a discipline, a practice of holy living which constituted the way. The words symbolizing the goal, such as Brahman or God or Truth or immortality or peace or bliss were taken in their conceptual meanings by their followers, that is, as the opposite of the other component of a duality, namely the devil or falsity or death or turmoil or sorrow, thus sowing the seeds of the errors and confusions bedevilling all theologies.

Nevertheless, the pure Heart of Religion throbs through the bruised body of scripture. It is for each man to listen, to watch, to understand and to be in communion.

PART TWO(a)
THE FEW: THE HOLY ONES: THE PAST

CHAPTER SIX
THE DIVINE DIALOGUE

LET there be no illusions regarding the nature and the spiritual stature of the Great Teachers. They who could help disciples to realize the Unconditioned and awaken to the Transcendent were themselves in living communion with the Supreme. In the Scriptures can be read the signs of the Holy Ones, for the inward, real experiencing of communion is exoterically expressed in several of the great affirmations.[1]

'Enoch . . . was not; for God took him.' 'Elijah went up by a whirlwind into heaven.' It is not said that either of them suffered physical death. 'Vāmadeva . . . having ascended aloft from this world . . . became immortal, yea became immortal.' And several centuries later it is said of the ascension of Jesus that, 'When he had spoken these things, as they were looking, he was taken up; and a cloud received him out of their sight.'

Joseph and Moses see or speak with the Lord face to face. Moses and Elijah go up into the mount of the Lord, forty days and nights. The 'mount of the Lord' of the Old Testament has its counterpart in the Zarathuśtrian *Ushidaraena*, the Hindu *Meru*, the *sahasrāra cakra* of Kuṇḍalinī-yoga, the *brahma-loka* of Buddhist meditation. The Buddha and his great disciples can spend seven days and nights continuously in the deep *samādhi* or communion called the cessation;[2] and they can visit and converse with Brahmā the Creator. Zarathuśtra sees God with his eyes, knowing him in Truth to be the Wise Lord of the Good Mind and of good deeds and works. Lao-Tzu knows the origin of things by knowing Tao.

The author of the Creation hymn in the Ṛg-veda is named Prajāpati Parameṣṭhin, which means Supreme Lord of Creatures. So too the name Elijah means God Himself. The name Bṛhaddiva,[3] given to the *ṛṣi* who affirms he has thrown open all doors of light and has spoken with the god Indra as himself in person, means belonging to the lofty sky, heavenly or celestial. The name alone, however, is not the sole indicator of him who knows communion. His exemplary life and his teaching prove the name.

[1] See above, pp. 15 ff.
[2] M., 1.94.
[3] R.V., 10.120.

Very significant is the presentation of the teachings in the form of the divine dialogue. In several Upaniṣads, a short question is asked, the answer to which is put into the mouth of one or other of the three Persons of the Trinity. In the Maitreya Upaniṣad, Maitreya is answered by Mahādeva, the great god Śiva; in the Kaivalya, Āśvalāyana by Brahmā, the Creator; in the Ātmabodha, the teaching is given by Nārāyaṇa, the Supreme Being; in the Subāla, by Brahmā. How shall we understand these and many similar examples?

Various are the approaches to the Supreme Communion in silent aloneness. When the heart grows still with the touch of Beauty, when self so surrenders that Passion meets Love as the river meets the sea, when the mind is so free of all images that Truth shines shadowless, or when the votive act flows into the heart of infinite Grace, there are no gates to bar the Way. Before the complete immergence into the Silence there is a state of discriminative consciousness characteristic of the holy one's approach on each separate occasion. It influences the form or nature of the consciousness which will emerge after the Silence. The Silence itself is devoid of both discriminative consciousness and unconsciousness, for here Awareness and Being are identical. As the emergence out of the Silence proceeds, that Awareness-Being suffers limitation into form, a form distinguished by attributes traditionally associated with one or other of the divine Names which are the springs of power and benediction in the scriptures of the world. This mode of consciousness is the fount of inspired teachings which the holy one presents in the shape of the divine dialogue. Every sentence of this prophetic speech is the milk of deep prayer and the bread of contemplation for his disciple.

The named divinities are products of man's mind, temporal and unreal, labels, so to say, of the immortal real. Merely to read the letter of the scriptures easily misleads the reader into regarding the named divinities as independent personal Beings, other than him who is in communion. If he who reads has known a loosening of the bonds, better still the dissolution of the limitations imposed by separative self-consciousness, he will be free of the confusion-making conflict between the 'I' and the 'Thou'. Then he will not mistake the named divinity as *a* Transcendent Being wholly other than the self-conscious 'I'. Then too he will become aware, provided his thought processes do not interfere, of the living meaning hidden in the words of scripture : 'I am that I am'; 'I am Brahman'; 'the Tathāgata (the Buddha) is a name tantamount to Truth (*dhamma*), tantamount to Brahman', and again, 'the Tathāgata is the *dhamma*-become, the *brahma*-become'; 'I am the way, the truth and the life'; 'I am the truth – *ana'l haqq*'; 'I am the I that has given up I'.

The supreme communion is not the communing of an 'I' with a separate 'Thou'. In the supreme communion there is a vanishing of the opaque barrier of separative self-consciousness. Phenomenally, the separate psycho-physical organism which bears the Teacher's name is there, a tangible, living man visible to all. But with the vanishing of self-consciousness, he who erstwhile was conscious as 'I am myself and not you' is no longer conscious in those terms, nor in the terms 'Thou *and* I are one'. He is *in the state of* I AM – the one and only I AM which is the one, total, absolute reality. He does not know – in the ordinary sense of a perceiving subject knowing an observed object – that he is in the I AM state when the I AM shines unobstructedly through him.

Thus the supreme communion is in actual fact the disappearance of all that dismembers the Unity. There is no separative consciousness of discrete particulars to sunder the unity of the I AM. Here the word 'I' is not a personal pronoun, nor does it represent a blown up self-become-superself by union with a God born of man's imagination. In this communion where self-ness is not, the word 'I' may be spoken of as transpersonal: 'I am the I which has given up I' as Śiva said to Kumāra the Kārttikeya.[4]

[4] Tejobindu Up., 3.3.

CHAPTER SEVEN
MOSES

It is said that he who was drawn out of the water killed a man of the land of bondage. When Pharaoh heard of this and was angered, Moses fled into Midian (= Contention) where Reuel (= God is friend) later called Jethro (= pre-eminence), was priest. Moses sat down by a well where the seven daughters of Reuel came and drew water, and filled the troughs to water their father's flock. Shepherds came and drove them away; but Moses stood up and helped them and watered their flock. When the seven daughters told this to their father, he asked where Moses was, and why had they left him, and instructed them to call him, 'that he may eat bread'. So Moses came, and Jethro gave his daughter Zipporah (= little bird) to him for a wife; and their son was Gershom (= a stranger there). Moses then kept the flock of Jethro. One day he led the flock to the back of the wilderness and came to the mountain of God, Horeb (= waste). And here, 'the angel of the Lord appeared unto him in a flame of fire out of the midst of a bush; and he looked, and, behold, the bush burned with fire, and the bush was not consumed. And Moses said, I will now turn aside, and see this great sight, why the bush is not burnt. And when the Lord (Yahweh) saw that he turned aside to see, God (Elohim) called unto him out of the midst of the bush' (Exod., 3. 2-4). And God (Elohim) announced that he was the God of the father of Moses, the God of Abraham, Isaac and Jacob. The Lord (Yahweh) declares he has seen the affliction of his people in Egypt, and avows his intention to deliver them out of the hand of the Egyptians and bring them to a land flowing with milk and honey. For this purpose he wants to send Moses to Pharaoh to bring the children of Israel out of Egypt.

But Moses fears. 'Who am I', he says to God (Elohim), 'that I should go unto Pharaoh, and that I should bring forth the children of Israel out of Egypt?' (Exod., 3.11) God assures him of his divine support. But Moses says: 'Behold, when I come unto the children of Israel, and shall say unto them, the God (Elohim) of your fathers hath sent me unto you; and they shall say to me, What is his name? What shall I say unto them?' (Exod., 3.13).

And God (Elohim) reveals his inner nature (Exod., 3.14,15): 'I AM THAT I AM (*ehyeh asher ehyeh*): and he said, Thus shalt thou say unto the children of Israel, I AM (*ehyeh*) hath sent me unto you. And

God (Elohim) said moreover unto Moses, Thus shalt thou say unto the children of Israel, the Lord (Yahweh, *which comes from the same root as* Ehyeh), the God (Elohim) of your fathers, the God of Abraham, the God of Isaac, and the God of Jacob, hath sent me unto you'.

Such is part of the account as given in Exodus of the experiencing of communion by Moses. The form of the divine dialogue is distinctive of Judaic monotheism.

God! The incomprehensible mystery! The sublime and awful majesty! The terrible one, distant and unknown! Whose face to see spells Love and Death! Whose voice to hear makes you a Son of Destiny and changes the pattern of the life of man for aeons!

YHWH (Yahweh) is his name. When a man sees him on his throne, the glory of the Divine King touches the mortal with immortal light, and his eye will shine undimmed for six score years. And if the Lord speaks unto him, he is invested with the mandate no mortal monarch may dare gainsay without peril.

Were a man to ask, 'Who is the Lord God of Israel?', the answer is 'Mi'. And if he ask, 'What is the Lord?', the answer is 'Eleh'. He who has not stood in the Light of the burning bush knows not that the hidden No-thing, through wisdom, emanated itself as Elohim. And Elohim is the Name Divine by which is told the unity of Mi, the hidden Subject, and Eleh, the hidden Object. It is the unity which is Pure Action, in which the disjunction of Subject and Object and the closing of the gap are in ceaseless rhythm – Creation's dance in endless Eden – bliss endless, for YHWH cannot sin though he may tempt, to try the temper of his fibre, man whom Elohim made in his own living image.

Moses tended the flock of Reuel in the wilderness. In the waste, a man can awake out of isolating loneliness into unselfed aloneness. Then he stands on holy ground. Heart's longing sets aflame the soul. And Moses sees and hears – this the disjunction – and also IS – this the closing of the gap. Disjunction there is, for each man cannot be unaware of himself as himself. For him in this state, there are 'others' – and this is his multitudinous loneliness. And union there is, for whoso tends the flock within his own being, watering it at the well of wisdom, is freed from the sight and sound of otherness. Then, YHWH alone IS, sounding the name of Transcendent All-Being, Ehyeh, I AM, the unitary unselfed Aloneness of Moses, the man of God, who was drawn out of the waters. And so can it be for you and for me, for each one of us is drawn out of the waters of the Mother – the mother of flesh at whose breast we fed, and also the All-Mother, Eve, the mother of all living.

So Elohim is YHWH the maker of Heaven and Earth. Without his dividing-unifying Action there is no world, no history. And YHWH is Ehyeh, I AM. Without this transcendent realization there is no Sabbath, the Eternal Rest in which is rooted all Action which is Creation. While the bush burned, Moses was taken up into, and became, I AM. So too is it with you or with me, when the bush burns.

Rightly did the Teachers who wrote the Torah choose the dialogue form.

Moses feared to look upon Elohim and hid his face! There are those whose tradition imposes a constraint: God is the Transcendent Who, wholly other than me the creature, the what. When my 'I-ness' is dispelled by the light of vision or the fire of adoration, and for the first time the barrier between YHWH and me vanishes, I am afraid to look, and to acknowledge that there is no disjunction between *that* Elohim and *this* me. This is the closing of the gap. But it breeds in me a responsibility: to take the children of Israel out of bondage. Who is Israel? And who are Israel's children? Israel is God who strives to redeem man and restore him to perfect relationship with his Source; Israel is he, a man, who strives with God, who perseveres with God; Israel is he who rules with God. With the first realization of Elohim, I, the man, am become an Israelite. So in my everyday human life the guiding hand of Elohim must never be obstructed. A difficult task! Furthermore, I am now related to all mankind, to all the children of Adam. And they have now a claim on me: to help release them from *bondage* to the delights of sense – the forbidden fruit – for they raise before one's eyes the dark cloud that hides the face divine. A dread responsibility!

So Moses feared. What would happen when the gap opened again – and open it must – and he be exposed to his not impregnable state? He bore a burden of guilt – the man he had killed in the land of bondage – and he feared. He feared his own inability – he was not eloquent, he said unto YHWH.[1]

This is the first occasion on which Moses is taken up into the I AM state. It is the uncharted abyss, empty of everything that a mortal knows. Deep in his psyche is the de-grading hidden force of his shortcomings, of the incompleteness of enlightenment. He is diffident; he hesitates. And YHWH is angered – which means that *Neshamah*, the divine, innermost spark of the soul in Moses, beyond Sin, waxes hot with shame at the weakness of *Nephesh*, the natural soul. YHWH is angered, for

[1] Exod., 4.10.

Gevurah or *Din*, the power of stern judgment and punishment is part of his very being. And the decree has gone forth: Israel shall be redeemed and the oppressor humbled. But YHWH is also the Lord full of mercy, *Hesed*, and of compassion, *Rahamim*.[2] So he promises Moses the help of his elder brother Aaron[3] who 'can speak well'.

The brothers meet – in the mount of God![4] Can two separate men meet thus? When you have ascended to the mount of God there is no 'you'. And when your brother too has there ascended, you will not find 'him'. The unity of YHWH is not of space and time, not of event or person. *There*, is no seeking. Space and time and event and person are measured, moving, mortal. But in YHWH is no death! YHWH is still, silent, the Sabbath. To 'meet' in the mount of God – a spiritual induction[5] – and the unity of YHWH – unblemished. The brothers 'met', and 'kissed' – Love's seal on the service of God. This service begins when men are ripe: Aaron is 'fourscore and three years old', Moses 'fourscore'.

The shape of your life is determined by the peak on which you stand. Your standing-ground is your inmost awareness, which is your point of Transcendence. All your feeling and thought, speech and action, is the expression of that awareness. Your standing-ground changes. Whilst you are ignorant, disobedient, sinful, you are a pawn of fate, a tool of evil. Your peak is submerged in darkness. But if you care with pure passion, your peak is bathed in light. You stand on holy ground, on the peak which is God's, not yours. And on this peak you are showered with transcendent blessing. This is the immortal. But you, the shape and life which is the ephemeral body-mind, are part of mortality. Body-mind is the stuff of duality, conflict, wear-and-tear. Its movement through time and space is doomed to include error, fading-away, disintegration. So the organism necessarily perishes, whether your standing-ground is submerged in darkness or bathed in light. So, 'he' who bore the name Enoch or Moses or Elijah or Jesus, died.

But if you do ascend into the mount of the Lord and stand on the peak which is God's, the transcendent blessing showered on you will so shape your life and influence on earth, that men will not forget God. And your name will be a deep bed, a long bed, for the overflowing stream of God's abundance for ages to come. Do not, then, weep for the mistakes you

[2] Exod., 34.4,7. See also G. G. Scholem. *Major Trends in Jewish Mysticism*, pp. 211 ff.

[3] Aaron = enlightenment; the illumined one.

[4] Exod., 4.27.

[5] See above, p. 40.

may make – only the self-conceited cannot endure to be in the wrong. YHWH is beyond right and wrong – each and every one of us must dig his own grave – or else be guilty of the pride of Lucifer.

Once the mission begins, Moses is constantly led by God. The occasions come when he is 'in the mount forty days and forty nights',[6] when YHWH 'spake unto him face to face, as a man speaketh unto his friend',[7] when 'he was there with YHWH forty days and forty nights; he did neither eat bread, nor drink water . . . and . . . when he came down from Mount Sinai . . . he did not know that the skin of his face shone because he had been talking with God'.[8]

Thus Moses was transfigured, and in and through him there was the full realization of the I AM state.

And yet, this Moses could be stirred to such fury when he heard the Israelites singing and saw the calf – mere image – before which they danced, that he broke the two tables of the testimony which were the work of Elohim, and upon which was graven the writing of Elohim; and he took the calf and burnt it in the fire, ground it to powder, and strewed it upon the water and made the Israelites drink of it. And thereafter, three thousand of them were slain by the sons of Levi according to the word of Moses.[9]

And this very man of God could even disobey YHWH ! In the desert of Zin the Israelites chided Moses because they had no water. Then YHWH told Moses to take his rod and speak to the rock which was before the eyes of the people. But Moses took the rod and smote the rock twice instead of speaking to it. The waters flowed abundantly. But YHWH said to Aaron and Moses, 'Because ye believed me not, to sanctify me in the eyes of the children of Israel, therefore ye shall not bring this congregation into the land which I have given them. This is the water of Meribah;[10] because the children of Israel strove with YHWH, and he was sanctified in them.'

When the end came, 'And Moses went up from the plains of Moab unto the mountain of Nebo, to the top of Pisgah, that is over against Jericho'.[11] And YHWH showed him the Promised Land, the Land unto which he was not allowed to enter because of his disobedience by the waters of Meribah.

[6] Exod., 24.18.
[7] Exod., 33.11.
[8] Exod., 34.28,29 (RSV).
[9] Exod., 32.15-20,26-28.
[10] Numbers, 20.12,13. Meribah = strife.
[11] Deuteronomy, 34.1. Jericho = the place of fragrance.

CHAPTER EIGHT
PRAJĀPATI PARAMEṢṬHIN

HEAVEN endures constant. Earth changes her garb whensoever Heaven's light enfolds her. Heaven's light is invisible. 'Tis Earth which refracts the unknown light and drapes herself in flashing colours for our soul's delight.

The Communion is timeless and measureless. In its heavenly state it is eternally silent. When Earth nestles in Heaven, man sings of the Silence – a Song of Creation – and Creation itself, like Heaven, is constant, invisible, unknown.

It matters not when a man lived. A thousand ages ago, if Heaven touched him, he stood in silent wonder. And afterward, perhaps he made a sound – his hymn of Creation. That sound was a call, for whoso cared, heavenward. Or perhaps he saw a bird or a beast, a rock or a tree – and this became the sign of the Holy.

The tides of time flowed on. Heaven endures constant. But Earth grew older, and richer in colour. And man her child, grown to power of speech, was drawn more often to more intimate Communion. The benediction of Heaven is the same a hundred ages ago as it is a thousand ages ago. It is ever the same. Only Earth, and man, had changed and grown.

Prajāpati Parameṣṭhin sings his Song of Creation :[1]

Then was not non-existent nor existent :
  there was no realm of air, no sky beyond it.
What covered in, and where ? And what gave shelter ?
  Was water there, unfathomed depth of water ?
Death was not then, nor was there aught immortal :
  no sign was there, the day's and night's divider.
That One Thing, breathless, breathed by its own nature :
  apart from it was nothing whatsoever.
Darkness there was : at first concealed in darkness
  this All was indiscriminated chaos.
All that existed then was void and formless :
  by the great power of Warmth was born that Unit.
Thereafter rose Desire in the beginning,
  Desire the primal seed and germ of Spirit.

[1] R.V., 10.129.

Sages who searched with their heart's thought discovered
the existent's kinship in the non-existent.
Transversely was their severing line extended :
what was above it then, and what below it?
There were begetters, there were mighty forces,
free action here and energy up yonder.
Who verily knows and who can here declare it,
whence it was born and whence comes this creation?
The gods are later than this world's production;
who knows then whence it first came into being?
He, the first origin of this creation,
whether he formed it all or did not form it,
Whose eye controls this world in highest heaven,
he verily knows it, or perhaps he knows not.

No mere philosophical speculation this! The *ṛṣis* of the Ṛg-veda were singers of the songs of eternal life. They who had realized Transcendence composed hymns and uttered speech that was the poetry of the spirit, pure prophecy. Theirs was eternity. Not for them to produce the speculations of philosophic genius or to wrest the knowledge of nature's craft through science and numbers – for that is the realm of the mortal. Knowledge is a burden you acquire. And when you come to the end of your lane you die. Eternity is Realization's light when Transcendence suffuses you the unselfed. And when you come to the end of your lane you too will die – and thereafter, a star in the heavens which declare the glory of God – but you will have sung the hymn of Creation whilst here on earth.

Prajāpati Parameṣṭhin prophesies Transcendence. 'Then' – or 'in the beginning' as in the Upaniṣads[2] – is the timeless. No duration here. No non-being, no unmanifest held in suspense, prior to precipitation into space-time event. No consciousness in the oblivion of sleep that waits the awakening wherein subject and object will start up, twinned, discriminate. 'In the beginning' always speaks of un-mattered spirit. No geometry, no count! No cause, no effect, no accounting! No law! For the freedom of the unconditioned is not subject to constraint nor loosened into impotence by licence.

'In the beginning' represents you yourself in the I AM state, in the actual transcendent experiencing.

[2] Bṛh. Up., 1.4.1, 10, 11, 17; 5.5.1. Chānd. Up., 4.2.1, 2. Tait. Up., 2.7. Ait. Up., 1.1.1. Maitr. Up., 5.2; 6.6, 17. Subāla Up., 1.1

Then! Transcendence free of existent and non-existent, thing and no-thing! No death, no non-death, for death cannot feed in the absence of the existent and non-death can subsist only in the non-existent. 'No sign was there, the day's and night's divider'. When you are bodily awake, and enter the Silence, and permit discriminative consciousness to sink to rest, there is no 'day' for you, and the existent is mantled in the dark folds of non-analytical awareness. In this awareness you do not name anything.[3] The 'night' is the impenetrable No-thing, the unshining womb of the twins, discriminative consciousness and that which we earth-creatures call unconsciousness, which is but the 'sleep' of discriminative consciousness, even as discriminative consciousness is the bonding, the form-ing, of unconsciousness.

But the prophet's Transcendence, this realized Awareness-Being of Prajāpati Parameṣṭhin, is the uttermost depth which is other than existent and non-existent, death and non-death, day and night. The living man breathes air. When in Supreme Communion, there is only THAT ONE, *tad-ekam*, of which the Holy One, the living man, is as it were the point of the shining of Transcendence. THAT ONE needs not to 'breathe air'. THAT ONE's eternal IS-ness is self-subsistent. THAT-ONE means no 'other'.

In the supreme communion the manhood is taken up into the Godhead. The Godhead is THAT ONE. Mysteriously, the Holy One also is THAT ONE – a Unity born by the power of *tapas*. Here we must understand *tapas* not as 'warmth' or 'heat' or 'austerity', but as perfect attentiveness – the pure, absolute attentiveness in which there is no separate subject attending nor object attended. Prior to that glowing attentiveness which bursts into infinite blinding light, the communion is in 'darkness', the mystical No-thing. The *tapas* hots up to burst into all-pervading all-comprehending light. Thus we may experience the meaning of Agni, Lord of Fire, the meaning of the Zarathuśtrian *āthro puthroahurahe mazdāo*, Fire the Son of Ahura-Mazda. Above all, we may, if we have sufficiently reverent intelligence and clarity, begin to respond to that awe-ful statement, *aham brahma'smi*, I am Brahman.

'Thereafter rose Desire, *kāma*, in the beginning, Desire the primal seed and germ of spirit, *manas*.' The Unit born of the power of *tapas* is the self-existent One: Father-Mother in unity; all the gods, yet unborn, in their togetherness; Heaven-Earth, *dyaus-pṛthvī*, still conjoined but destined to fall apart, for the 'universe' – you yourself in your totality, I myself in my unitary reality – is the child of necessity, of 'duty', *dharma*.

[3] cf. Gen., 2.19,20.

The *kāma* that mortals know is not that divine *kāma*, the creative action which is a power of transcendent love, the love that is a release, indestructively, of two in eternal play. The 'wisdom gone beyond', divine wisdom, holds the unseparate two as a non-duality. When the longing for self-discovery, for *beholding* the mystery of self-existing Being, stirs the unmoving wisdom to motion, the unitary Being, which is Awareness-Being, opens apart. And space and time spring forth together with mind, *manas*, and all the gods[4] stand in shining array in that first dawn of the cosmos, new-born.

So the poet-seer of the Ṛg-veda affirms to himself : 'Yes, I am, indeed, Prajāpati Parameṣṭhin'.[5]

Thus does Creative Love open the eye of absorbed Vision to the nature of the multitude which is the unitary One. Thus also, Creative Love preserves the open way between Father and Mother, between Heaven and Earth, between the 'waters above' and the 'waters below'.[6]

But when the living man steps down into his lone self-ness, his 'worldly' state, the living Vision of Light fades, for *manas* takes charge and locks the thrilling light into the fixed forms of faded memory. The words remain, to spring to new Vision and new Words with renewed communion.

How *can* the gods know, and declare, whence it was born and whence comes this world's creation? For I, Parameṣṭhin, am the living chalice which holds all the gods in their togetherness, and the life of each of the gods pours into the world through the open channel which is me, Prajāpati : but I was not, when Transcendence shone as Awareness-Being! Only through *manas*, the maker and preserver of variety, the variety which engenders the *kāma* that mortals feel, can I be a perceiving subject who sees an other, the object. GOD cannot know GOD, for GOD IS. And the absolute IS is devoid of 'knowing'. In Transcendence there is REALIZATION, but no 'knowing'. So the 'wisdom gone beyond' necessitates Silent Emptiness, the complete stilling of the activity we call 'knowing'. And then, Wisdom speaks Truth.

The Truth in the Vedas transcends all 'polytheism', all 'sacrificial ritual of a nature-worshipping primitive people', all 'philosophical speculations or gropings after spiritual truth'.[7] Remain a spectator, a groper, and see if you can compose the songs of the Veda. Be a Holy

[4] Agni, Varuṇa, Indra, Soma, etc.
[5] Lord of creatures, Supreme Being.
[6] Ait. Up., I.I.2.
[7] These are the usual terms of description of the Hymns of the Vedas.

One possessed of poetic gift and animated by prophetic insight, and see if you can prevent yourself from making the Affirmations of Transcendence.

The Vedas are essentially the expressions of the transformations of mind and consciousness experienced in the living process of the fruition of Holiness, starting with the first *metanoia*, the lovely dawn-vision of holy living (represented by the goddess Uṣas), onward through the upholding of righteousness (Varuṇa), the triumph of spiritual victory (Indra), the utter purification of the soul by the Lord of Fire (Agni), the inspirational flight of the alone to the Alone (Soma) in supreme communion and the blazing forth of the light of realized Transcendence (Āditya, the Sun in the unclouded heavens). Such is he who has 'realized the Atman', as above. Such is Brahman. And the realized Transcendence authorises the Holy One to affirm *aham brahma'smi*.

The Veda cannot be read by mere intellectual genius. It has to be seen by Vision; it has to be heard by Revelation. And this is true of all Scriptures.

CHAPTER NINE
THE TEACHERS OF THE UPANIṢADS

ATMAN and Brahman, names for realized Transcendence, fill the Upaniṣads:

'In the beginning this (world) was Atman alone in MAN-FORM (*puruṣa-vidhaḥ*).[1] Looking around he saw nothing other than Atman. He said first: 'I am', Thus arose the name 'I.'[2]

MAN is Transcendence thinking. Not discursive talking, not form making, this thinking is instantaneous creating: Power-Action here-now; Word being Flesh without start, without end, but with finish. Its 'heart-beat' is Love, its 'brain' is Wisdom. MAN, male-female, the Celestial Co-equal, is the Thought, the Living Image, the Fair Form of Perfect Measure, of the Transcendence.

That MAN is the measure of all creation.

This man, male and female, the Earth-child, in his holy state is the integration of seer and lord and producer and worker. And he can measure all things rightly. In his worldly state he is in confusion and conflict, the generator of sin, the agent of evil, the victim of sorrow. And he measures all things falsely, for Heaven and Earth and all therein can never fit into the measure of self-ness.

In his holy state, in communion, *this* man IS *that* MAN.

Transcendence – measureless, formless – holds within itself all forms and the measures of all things. Transcendence flows into and through Celestial Man, and thus the Created Universe subsists. Whilst the flow is free, Heaven and Earth are in union. This is the bliss (*ānanda*) of Brahman being realized in and through the Holy One, the Earth-child in the pure state. And the measure of each thing fits into the measure of all creation.

In the silent emptiness of communion, spoken of as 'In the beginning', the Holy One presents the realizing of *ātman* as being in MAN-FORM, *puruṣa-vidhaḥ*.

* * *

Atman is transcendent awareness. 'Who am I?' asks the saint-seer. Looking within, veil after veil of conceptions and states of consciousness disappear. Mind remains: not your mind or my mind, but mind-only,

[1] Usually translated as 'in the form of a person'.

[2] Bṛh. Up., 1.4.1.

empty of all thought-forms, transparent, universal; an order of life-energy (*prāṇa*) which is, as it were, non-finite, self-shining 'space' (*ākāśa; rocanā divaḥ*, ethereal space). This is an order of being or existence which, fecundated by Transcendence, holds the archetypal 'forms' and 'forces' of all that is. Of these forms, MAN-form is the chief for us humans. But here, MAN-form is the ALL-form and not exclusively the counterpart of the earthly human being.

This MAN-form has no shape nor size nor continuity, for it is a birth-less-deathless, potentiality unconstrained by space-time, cause-effect, or by change. This non-finite, immeasurable ALL-form, uni-form, fecundates 'dim or coloured space', *rajas*, a firmament or 'ground', and becomes the multi-form, the universe as apprehended by our bodily senses and brain. Now we are in the sphere of energy-exchanges (to use a modern, scientific term) and we measure distance and time and acceleration, and we name it matter, or energy-mass, inanimate and animate. All separate forms in the world derive from ALL-form. Each of us, a man form, is related to MAN-form.

Are there three orders – Transcendence, mind-only and the natural world?

There is but One Total Reality. Each one of us is aware of only a fraction of it at any moment. The name we give to this Total Reality as fragmentarily apprehended by our usual waking consciousness, is 'the objective world' or 'the natural order'. In subtler, quieter states, we apprehend inner depths of mind to which we are not usually awake. When such awakening reaches a peak point, we give the name Mind-only, or Pure Mind,[3] to this same Total Reality. When all separative self-consciousness has completely dissolved, and the One Reality is unobstructed by the fragmentary 'me', we name it Transcendence.[4] What we are in fact doing when we give these names is to indicate our own different modes of awareness of the one and only Order. They may be three modes, or more, or less. It is convenient, however, for the purpose of communication, to talk in terms of, say, three orders. We constantly cognize multiplicity and differences. We are aware of the unity only rarely. This is due to our constitution, for even to continue to exist from day to day demands constant discrimination between all that supports life and all that destroys it. The differences make the relativity within the Total Reality; the one-wholeness is its absoluteness.

For the Holy Ones of the Upaniṣads, Brahman or Atman, realized

[3] Mind regarded as the ultimate Reality.
[4] Or, the One, the Godhead, the Absolute, the Infinite, etc.

Transcendence, is 'THAT, from which speech and mind return, not having attained.[5]

Speech functions in the natural order which is characterized by finitude and particularity, by birth and death. It is the voice of the brain.[6] Speech and mind are not entirely confined to the finite, to the stream of the finite which is the sum and substance of our usual daily life. For, without being false, speech has the strange power of contradicting finitude simply by uttering the word infinity. But whereas with all finites the brain has, or produces, a thought-form (visual, auditory, tactile, etc.) corresponding to the word, the mind is quite unable to produce any thought-form (which of necessity would be finite and particular) corresponding to words such as infinity, absolute, eternity, God and so on. Nevertheless, there is that extraordinary experiencing by men, because of which they have used just such words. There is in fact a link, a relationship, though we have not as yet discovered its nature or its rationale, between the formless, non-finite, im-measurable depths of mind – the speech-less mind, empty of thought-forms – and the finite, everyday world in which speech-mind is so active. Our ignorance of the nature of that link is one reason why it is convenient to refer to Mind-only as an order on its own; all that we know and can explain in terms of energy-exchanges throughout the natural universe does not apply to it; the 'energy', *prāṇa*, of Mind-only, is a mystery.

In relation to this im-measurable Mind – the deepest, awesome mystery of the psyche – the natural world and all our ordinary speech-mind formulations – beliefs, ideas, acquired knowledge, etc. – seem to be illusory, *māyā*vic. Speech has already resolved into complete silence before the sensitivity to Mind-only has fully blossomed. And if speech cannot touch the flame of Pure Mind, still less can it attain the Light of Transcendence, Brahman.

But let us not fall into the trap of imagining that Mind-only, or Pure Psyche, is the ultimate Real. Even in the im-measurable profound of Mind, out of which all creation emerges – emerges, not 'begins', for beginning-ending, birth-death, belong to the natural order of the universe – there is duality: positive-negative, or male-female, 'power' or 'energy', held in restful tension till Motion's first thrill sets going the cosmic dance; and there is self-awareness,[7] though quite beyond the

[5] Tait., 2.4; Sāṇḍilya, 2; Tejobindu, 1.20; 3.8, 38. Maitreya, 1.9.

[6] cf. the Buddhist teaching: the *bhikkhuni* Dhammadinnā, one of the Buddha's distinguished nuns, says to the layman Visākha: 'Initial thought and discursive thought is activity of speech'. M., 1.301.

[7] The *samprajñāta samādhi* of the *yogi*. See below, p. 361 n. 41.

gross bodily or personal self-awareness of everyday life. It is this last vestige of self-consciousness which finally dissolves in the actual realizing of Transcendence, a realizing by the Total Reality and not by any 'me', because 'I' have completely let go the 'I'. And in relation to Transcendence, the deepest depth of Psyche, Mind-only, is also illusory, *māyā*vic.

Neither the natural world nor Mind-only is a total illusion, as some have said. Transcendence, Mind-only and the universe are all just one Total Reality. They are in eternal relationship, else the realization of Transcendence could never have taken place. In the liberated Holy One there is no illusion, for in him is wholly fulfilled the prayer (Bṛh. Up., 1.3.28):

Asato mā sad gamaya	From the unreal lead me to the Real
Tamaso mā jyotir gamaya	From darkness lead me to Light
Mṛtyor māmṛtam gamaya	From death lead me to Immortality.

The archetypal MAN-form contains within itself all the archetypal forces and forms, to which men have given innumerable names, such as *suras*, *asuras*, *devas*, Archangels, Angels, the gods and goddesses of the various pantheons, Truth, Goodness, Beauty, and so on. MAN is Transcendence thinking – not one thought nor many thoughts – but the unconditioned pulse of Creative Power, which that saint-seer, the *yogi* in communion, verbally formulated as *puruṣa-vidhaḥ*. The Holy One, by being unseparate from that unconditioned Supreme, *is* the Awareness-Being termed Atman, because that which you and I ordinarily call mind is absorbed, 'eaten up', in the process of emergence into Atman.

Atman is the eater-up of the mind. 'Self' and 'Soul' are inadequate and misleading translations of Atman, especially because those terms evoke a sense of 'entity', which precisely Atman is not. Yājñavalkya says to Kahola Kauśītakeya: 'The Atman is that which transcends hunger and thirst, sorrow and delusion, old age and death'.[8] And to King Janaka: 'This great unborn Atman, undecaying, immortal, fearless, is Brahman'.[9] Prajāpati says to Virocana and Indra: 'The Atman which is sinless, ageless, deathless, sorrowless, hungerless, thirstless – 'tis that which should be sought out'.[10]

What is this unborn, unageing, undying, sorrowless, thirstless, hungerless, sinless and beyond delusion? A power? A postulated entity named

[8] Bṛh. Up., 3.5.
[9] Bṛh. Up., 4.4.25.
[10] Chānd. Up., 8.7.1.

God? A delusive fancy? Or is it the awareness which is realized Transcendence when you yourself are in the holy state? The Varāha Upaniṣad,[11] having affirmed the identity of Atman and Brahman, speaks of the Atman as, 'Consciousness (*cinmātra*), all-pervading, absolute (or eternal, *nitya*), all-full, blissful, the unity'. The Sarvasāra Upaniṣad says: 'Brahman is . . . absolute consciousness . . . differenceless, pure, noumenal, the true, the indestructible.'

It should be clearly understood, therefore, that the terms Atman and Brahman essentially represent that transpersonal awareness which is present during the experiencing of Transcendence. They do not stand for merely a deity or personal God or anything postulated by thought and speech. Atman or Brahman is indeed 'THAT, from which speech and mind return, not having attained'.

The Holy One realizes Atman through MAN-form, for he himself, one specific man-form, is directly related to MAN-form, the primordial MAN, the Thought which is the Original Conception, or, the Sacred Word, *aum* or the *śabda Brahman*.

* * *

Person is a sacred word. The Upaniṣads do not hesitate to use their own suggestive methods, even if quaint, to enlighten the devotee:

> Because, before (*pūrva*) all this, he burned up (√ *uṣ*) all evils, therefore he is a person (*pur-uṣ-a*).[12]

Atman is devoid of all evils. They manifest only in 'all this', the existential world as experienced and cognized by us in our impure state by our tainted discriminative consciousness. 'All evils', *sarvān pāpmana*, are all evil states of mind. Out of the 'heart' comes evil. Evil mentation is the evidence of the sick heart and the diseased mind.

'He burned up all evils'! Burning is affected by *tapas*, pure attentiveness, which by its intensity generates that 'psychical heat', *agni*, which burns up all evil-mindedness in the Earth-child. It is as if a transmutation of mind takes place.

He who has burned up all evil-mindedness is now the pure one. In this state he, the Holy One, knowing that THAT Holy One is realized on earth through him, is named *puruṣa*, Person. A Person is one in whom

[11] 2.21. cf. the Buddha's phrase (M., I. 329 and D., 2.223): Consciousness (*viññāṇa*) which is attributeless, endless, shining (or accessible) everywhere.
[12] Bṛh. Up., 1.4.1.

the second and third orders – Mind-only and the natural man after his 'baptism by fire' – are in harmony. The purified man-form is the triumphant manifestation of MAN-form. And in this holy state of First Personhood, the full significance of MAN is realized.

This MAN – Transcendence thinking – is creation – a simultaneity of Life-Death, where Life *and* Death are immortal complementaries. Since Transcendence is Life (Brahman is *prāṇa*, Life, as the Chāndogya Upaniṣad says, 4.10.4), Death is in fact other-Life. Life and other-Life are in eternal interplay – creation – a constant fecundation of male-female, positive-negative. So heaven endures constant and Earth's subsistence is displayed by the ever-changing garb of Beauty. But that Beauty is of Heaven. In Earth is the becoming process, which is sorrow as long as my mind is evil. When pure, that supernal Beauty shines through the Person here on Earth.

The Person, unlike the body, is not mortal, not finite, and has no 'personality'. In human terms I never 'know' that Person. When my separate human personality, that illusory phantom which is a sorry disharmony of conflicting attributes and disorderly change, is utterly empty of evils, the One Infinite Person shines unhindered. God is *deva* = Shining One, *āditya* = Unbound, Whole. My 'personality' is in truth Person-usurper; a false idol raised up by my ignorance, egoism and vanity; a skin-bag-full of ills. Burn away! And in the Wholeness which is free of all separativeness, *puruṣa* the Person affirms 'I AM' in blissful silence. Gone is my dark shadow-self, the demon that plagued me through time – psychological time, the container and breeder of fear and conflict and untold sorrow. The I AM is the Alone, the light which flickers not, the light named *Savitṛ*, the sun that shines by day *and* all through the night.

Psychological time! But this is in play with chronological time which exercises such dominion over the life span and processes of the organism. When the live body moves under nature's compulsion, the Holy One feels the earth-tremor as a disturbing activity, a disequilibration out of Heaven. The jolt to the communion thrusts isolating loneliness intrusively upon the Whole Aloneness. And there is fear.

> He was afraid. Therefore one who is alone is afraid. This one then thought to himself: 'Since there is nothing else than myself, of what am I afraid?' Thereupon, verily, his fear departed, for of what should he be afraid? Assuredly it is from a second that fear arises.[13]

[13] Bṛh. Up., 1.4.2.

What is this fear? It is a two-way fear: one way, before Atman realization; the other, in the returning to discriminative consciousness, as mentioned in the previous paragraph. With respect to the former, the realization of Atman means that the Holy One must step out of his space-ship of mind into spaceless-timeless eternity.[14] To plunge out of the last vestige of the familiar into the Unknown is the moment of Truth, the total unselfing possible to the Holy One, the moment of Death in its immortal resplendence, the unknowable other-Life. So there is 'fear'. It is quite unlike fear when a rock in a raging sea shivers your ship, or when the child of your heart is ailing, ailing. Recall the waking up when you dream you are falling through space! The panicky clutching for safety! The fear of the nowhere, the nothing!

Only he in communion who has crossed into nowhere from the point of no return has feared divinely. How strange this fear is! The Holy One giving himself wholly to the Unknown, suddenly trembles. 'Quick! Grasp that Supreme-to-be-known, and fear shall be no more.' But Death stands shining invisibly: 'Truth is no object of desire. Unseizable is Transcendence. Naked, plunge!' The Holy One, taken up into THAT ONE, realizes Death the other-Life as no other than Life. Heaven endures constant. And fear is not.

Yājñavalkya affirms:[15]

> That Atman is not this, it is not that (*neti, neti*). It is unseizable for it is not seized. It is indestructible for it is not destroyed. It is the Alone, associateless, unattached, for it does not attach itself. It is unbound. It does not tremble. It is not injured.

The Atman is not finite, particular, limited, personal or impersonal. It is, like Brahman, trans-personal. It is not created, mortal. Mind or consciousness cannot grasp it. It cannot be possessed – no man can say *my* Atman – it cannot be seized. It is indestructible, for that which is not put together by mind or by energy-matter cannot be pulled apart into pieces or annihilated. It is neither an existent, that is, an appearance out of something more fundamental, nor a non-existent. It is Transcendence; devoid, therefore, of agitation, imbalance, sorrow or any need. It is fearless. Like Brahman, it is *satyasya satyam* – the Real-ness of Reality, Be-ness of Being, Very God of Very God.

Atman realization is the secondless, one-only. Transcendence is non-

[14] See also pp. 350, 361, 371 f. in connection with the *samāpattis* of infinite *ākāśa* and *viññāṇa* and the samādhis termed *saṃprajñāta* and *asaṃprajñāta*.

[15] Bṛh. Up., 3.9.20; 4.2.4; 4.4.22; 4.5.15.

finite, unconditioned: energy (*prāṇa*) pure and absolute. Form, finite and conditioned, appears as the Holy One emerges out of Atman: a second, an other, a separate self-consciousness. And again, a startle of fear! 'Assuredly it is from a second that fear arises.'

But if I, once again in Earth, am wholly attentive to what actually is here and now, the other-making obtrusiveness of self-consciousness disappears. The 'observer' vanishes. There is no second, no fear.

* * *

Transcendence, Heaven and Earth, are in timeless conjugation. The Holy One's awareness of this, in communion, he translates as world-creation. In ancient days, this was spoken of in the common terms of common creatures, exoterically; the Few learned and discovered the inner meaning.

> He, verily had no delight (*sa vai naiva reme*). Therefore one who is alone has no delight (*na ramate*). He desired a second. He was indeed as large as a woman and a man close conjoined. He caused that very being (*evātmānaṃ*) to fall (√ *pat*) into two parts. From that arose the Sovereign Lord (*pati* = husband) and the Lady (*patnī* = wife). Therefore this: 'oneself is like a half-fragment' as Yājñavalkya used to say. Therefore, this void (*ākāśa*, mind-space) is filled with the Feminine. He (the Sovereign Lord) conjugated with her (the Lady). Therefrom were produced beings with intelligence (*manuṣyā*).

In the static undivided there is no creative action. Wisdom by itself is non-moving; it lives only through love. Without wisdom, joy of love degenerates into destructive lust. But when poised by the power of wisdom, joy of love is the bliss of creative action – Desire Divine, free of binding consequence, the blissful state of peaceful union, timeless and deathless, the true meaning of *kāma*, Eros.

Creative action is play (√*ram*), and play means interplay. Where Transcendence and the shining void intermingle, there rises the stir which is Desire. Mystery! Mystery can never be known intellectually by analysis, for mystery cannot be dismembered. But the pure one, *puruṣa*, can participate in Mystery, with loving action which is unifying understanding.

In timeless conjugation, Life/other-Life, the male-female, rest in the undifferentiated unity of unmoving action. When the mystery arises,

Desire is the power that draws the severing line between male and female, and each awakens to differentiated self-existence in a unity of creative interplay with the other. And so the whole universe – psycho-spiritual and psycho-physical – is put in motion. Life is movement.

This Male, the Sovereign Lord, and this Female, the perpetual Feminine, are all-powerful archetypal forces. The conjugative union of this Lord and Lady is the primordial marriage made in Heaven, and from it flow all the archetypes that man has named. It is the well-spring of 'energy' (*prāṇa* the River of Life, *Oceanus* that encircles the world), which underlies the divine sanctifying that upholds Heaven and Earth, the Great Sacrifice spoken of in the Upaniṣads and other scriptures, the emanation (*visarga*) which is the action (*karma*) that causes the birth of 'beings',[16] that is, of the archetypes named *devas*, gods, angels.

Puruṣa, the Holy One realizing Atman, is Lord-Lady in silent stillness. On seeking Self-Awarenes when moving out of Atman, Lord and Lady separate. They 'fall apart'. Desire stirs. And Eros acts and creates the Universe, psycho-spiritually, a universe which is a psycho-spiritual cosmos, in that middle order, Mind-only.

Thus have arisen the cosmogonies of past ages. Emerging as they do out of a religious consciousness, they have inevitably taken shape, in part, as theogonies; and thence religious minds proceeded to construct corresponding anthropogeneses. The creation myths of the world are replete with this wonderful *māyā*, these charming illusions which are the colourful shadows of the One Reality.

The Upaniṣad proceeds:[17] 'He knew, "I, indeed, am this creation, for I emitted it all from myself." Thus, he became creation. He who knows this as such comes to be in that creation of his.' The significance of the teaching is clear. In Atman-realization, the state of pure Awareness-Being, there is no differentiation. In the returning to ordinary discriminative consciousness, differentiation sets in. The brain of the Holy One, in accordance with its conditioning during studentship by the socio-cultural heritage of the day, produces the conceptions and thought-forms of the 'spiritual' or 'psychic' world. He 'emits it all out of himself', he 'becomes it', he 'is it'. Thus the shapes of the hosts and forces of the celestial and archetypal worlds are all the creation by the Holy One, and not creation by a postulated *entity* named God. They are his conditioned interpretations, the many mind-forms which are born out of his primary MAN-form which is the ALL-form.

[16] B.G., 8.3.
[17] Bṛh. Up., 1.4.5.

A little further on in the same Upaniṣad[18] we see evidence of the conditioning influence of the socio-cultural environment of that age:

> Verily, in the beginning this (world) was Brahman, one only. That, being one, did not flourish. He created further an excellent form, the *kṣatra* power, even those who are *kṣatras* (rulers) among the gods (*devas*), Indra, Varuṇa, Soma, Rudra, Parjanya, Yama, Mṛtyu, Iśāna....
>
> Yet he did not flourish. He created the *viś* (the commonality), those classes of gods who are designated in groups, the Vasus, Rudras, Ādityas, Viśvedevas and Maruts.
>
> Still he did not flourish. He created the Śūdra order, Pūṣan. Verily this (earth) is Pūṣan the nourisher, for she nourishes everything that is.
>
> Yet he did not flourish. He created further an excellent form, *dharma* (Justice, or the rule of the sacred Law). This is the power of the ruler, namely *dharma*. Therefore there is nothing higher than *dharma*.... Verily that which is *dharma* is Truth.

Returning from Brahman realization, the sage-seer peoples the archetypal world with celestial counterparts to his own material world, where society consisted of the brahmans, the rulers and warriors, the traders, and the workers. Archetypal forces are, however, very real in so far as they dominantly influence man's psycho-physical life. The mind-projected forms, the 'ethereal bodies' of gods, demons, angels, etc., which fill the pantheons of the various cultures which have arisen in the world, are a wonderful revelation of the psychological understanding of those who raised and maintain these cultures. To be released from domination by – that is, to outgrow, intelligently and gracefully – all the gods and demons, is to find true liberty. But the immature and violent discarding of this psycho-spiritual heritage usually means subsequent slavery to devils instead of a becoming cooperation with the angels. The ubiquitous tragedy, however, is that people being what they are – ignorant, fearful, violent, stupid, and self-oriented – the authority of the gods and submission to the angels has all too often wrought untold, useless suffering for men and animals alike. To cite only two examples: blood-sacrifices on holy (!) altars, and carnage in holy(!) wars.

* * *

[18] Bṛh. Up., 1.4.11-14.

The originality of the form in which the divine dialogue is presented in the Kaṭha Upaniṣad throws a revealing light on the nature of such dialogue. Naciketas goes to the home of the Lord of death. He says :

> This doubt that there is in regard to a man deceased : 'he exists', say some; 'he exists not', say others – This would I know, instructed by thee.

Then Death gives the answer. And Naciketas realizes Brahman and becomes free from passion, free from death.

What does it mean to go to the home of Death? And be taught by Death? In the silent aloneness of the supreme communion, there is the cessation of all discriminative consciousness. All speech and thought, all particular and limited mental activity, is in repose and there is a suspension of the mortal mode of consciousness.[19] In this enstasy, which is neither a trance nor a state of ecstasy, the Holy One has 'died' to the known world. Alive, he 'knows' death. He himself is now the 'Lord of death'. Then there is manifest on earth the realization of the immeasurable Unknown, the unborn, undying, fearless, sorrowless Atman. Afterwards, the teaching given by the Holy One is the fruit of this communion, known as the dialogue with Death.

But Death the Teacher is Death the other-Life, Consummator and Perfector. It is the divine dark, the abyss which is the firm ground out of which streams all creation by the action of the beyond-knowing. How then shall Death-Lord (*Yamarājñaḥ*) answer the question of Naciketas?[20] 'Even the gods had doubts as to this of yore – choose another boon instead of the answer to this question,' begs Yama. And he offers the choicest of worldly gifts in addition to his previous gift of the knowledge of the heavenly fire, and the attainment of the infinite world and the partaking of immortality. Naciketas stands unswerving, for 'there is none like thee, O Death, who can answer'. All the offered wealth, be it of earth or dignities, of pleasures or intellect or skills, cannot compare with the pearl beyond price, the answer to *this* question. And only Yama, prime mortal who found the way to the immortal and was given lordship over the highest of the three heavens,[21] could answer rightly.

Out of the abyss, Death the other-Life points his finger to his twin, Life. The pointing is the Way. Life, the answer, is the invisible Un-

[19] See below, pp. 343 f., 350, 383 ff.
[20] Naciketas = the unknowing or non-thinking one.
[21] See R.V., 10.13.4; 1.35.6; Macdonell, *Vedic Mythology*, p. 172.

known, omnipresent. 'Give me your worldliness, die to your selfness,' says Death, 'and my immortal twin will suffuse you with Transcendence here-now.'

This is Yoga.

CHAPTER TEN
THE BHAGAVAD GĪTĀ

Kṛṣṇa, Lord of Yoga (*yogeśvara*), proclaims[1] to Arjuna:

> I am the abode of Brahman the immortal and imperishable, and of eternal truth (*dharma*) and of pure happiness.

Who is Kṛṣṇa? Who, Arjuna? And whose gift is the Bhagavad Gītā?

He who writes scripture is no reporter; nor versifier nor professional theologian. He is Author, one who affirms realized Transcendence. Kṛṣṇa Dvaipāyana Veda-Vyāsa,[2] the composer of the Gītā, revealed in his poem the realization of Transcendence in his own being. The Song of the Goal, the Way and the Fulfilment is couched in the form of the divine dialogue between the warrior-prince Arjuna and his charioteer Kṛṣṇa of the race of Yadu – Kṛṣṇa, worshipped through the centuries as the manifestation of Viṣṇu Himself.

Arjuna typifies Everyman: in his un-whole state, an unhappy mortal, confused in mind with regard to Reality and ignorant of the art of living in accord with his own pattern of being; healed, he is the selfless agent skilfully fulfilling his true destiny (*dharma*). Kṛṣṇa typifies the one in whom all evilmindedness has been burnt out, the Person (*puruṣa*), the Supreme Person (*puruṣottama*), Perfect Man who is God walking awhile 'midst mortals.

Veda-Vyāsa as the living man in the world is himself Arjuna.[3] In the I AM state, as the purified Holy One in whom was manifest realized Transcendence, he is Kṛṣṇa.[4] Did not the Lord Himself announce,[5] 'Of the children of Vṛṣṇi I am Kṛṣṇa; of the sons of Pandu I am Arjuna; among seers in silence I am Vyāsa; among poets I am Uśanā'? Only the lips kissed by the Fire of the Immortal can sing a Bhagavad-Gītā!

This Song of the Lord is called an Upaniṣad. In those Upaniṣads cast in the form of the divine dialogue, the answer is usually ascribed to one or other person of the Trinity; in the Gītā it is given by Kṛṣṇa, God in his wholeness beyond human compassing, presented in MAN-form. In

[1] B. G., 14.27.
[2] Dvaipāyana = island-born. Vyāsa = arranger or compiler.
[3] Arjuna = white, clear; the colour of day, or lightning, or dawn, or milk, or silver.
[4] Kṛṣṇa = black; dark blue, the colour associated with ākāśa, mind-space.
[5] B. G., 10.37.4.

the Kaṭha Upaniṣad, the transcendent truth is voiced by the Lord of Death; in the Gītā, by the living God. Was the Gītā, by any chance, composed close in time to the Kaṭha Upaniṣad? Two visions, complementarily, of the same treasure?

In Veda-Vyāsa the sense of Transcendence became quenchless light. His vision in the I AM state was the vision of the One Total Reality, revealed through the words of Kṛṣṇa and Arjuna.

Kṛṣṇa affirms:

> There are two *puruṣas*[6] in the world, the perishable and the imperishable. The perishable is all things in creation. The imperishable is the Still (*kuṭasṭha*, rock-seated).
> But the highest *puruṣa* is another. It is called the Supreme Atman which, pervading all, sustaining the three worlds, is the immortal Ruler.
> Since I am beyond the perishable and even beyond the imperishable, therefore in the world and in the Veda I am proclaimed the Ultimate Person (*puruṣottama*). 15.16-18.
>
> I am the Father of this universe and the Origin of the Father (*pitāmaha*; the Great Father, the Unnameable Transcendent). I am the Mother and Nourisher of this Universe. I am the One that should be known; the purifier; the sacred syllable AUM; the Ṛg, Sāma and Yajur Vedas. 9.17.
>
> I am the Atman seated in the heart of all things. I am the beginning, the middle and the end of all that lives. 10.20.
>
> When day[7] comes all that is made manifest streams forth from the unmanifest; and all that is manifest dissolves into the unmanifest when night[7] comes.
> But indeed, beyond the unmanifest there is another, a timeless unmanifest, which lives eternally when all else (within time's web) passes away.
> That Unmanifest is called the indestructible. It is called the last bourn (*gatiṃ*, goal). They who reach it return not. That is my supreme abode. 8.18,20,21.
>
> I am the abode of Brahman, the immortal and imperishable.
> 14.27.

[6] The psycho-physical personality, and the PERSON (see above p. 82 f.)
[7] The day and night of Brahmā the creator.

Arjuna's avowal:

> O Thou Supreme Brahman, Supreme Abode, Supreme Holiness, eternal divine *puruṣa*, primeval Deity, unborn, the Lord.
> Thus have all the Ṛsis acclaimed thee; also the divine Ṛṣi Nārada, and Asita, Devala and Vyāsa. And now you yourself tell me this.
> 10.12.13.

Kṛṣṇa's utterances present the One Reality in all its possible forms: as Supreme Being; as Immortal Ruler; as Father-Mother (the Lord-Lady that brings forth the universe; the demiurge); as the Origin of the Father (the Unknown Infinite); as Creator and Creative Power (AUM); as Brahman (the Origin of the Father; the absolute Awareness-Being); and as Atman (the transpersonal Awareness of Totality; Brahman's 'Self'; the one and only 'I'). Veda-Vyāsa, *mahāṛṣi* of the Gītā, had realized the full meaning of 'I', *ahaṃ*. It means the One Total Reality which cannot be denied after the obscuring sense of isolated selfhood is dissolved. Then indeed *ahaṃ* is the unabandonable. All the Teachers, including the Buddha, freely used the word *ahaṃ*, I; and they used it with affirmative Power by virtue of their full awakening to the Transcendent Real. Through the words he puts into the mouth of Kṛṣṇa, Veda-Vyāsa silently proves Transcendence realizing itself through him the human poet-seer.

The Truth which Kṛṣṇa affirms, Arjuna sees and confirms. When the Holy One is in the I AM state, during which there is perfect suspension of perception and feeling, the psycho-physical being undergoes a transformation. Transfiguration is a word used in this connection, for even the bodily appearance is different – 'shining' – as it was said of Moses, the Buddha, Jesus and of other Holy Ones. On returning to ordinary everyday consciousness, the impress of that harmony of Transcendence, Pure Mind and the natural man may give rise to expression in thought and word of the experienced Reality. And the natural man confirms in verbal form that Seen Revelation, that Heard Truth. Veda-Vyāsa as the living man in the world expresses this Voice and Vision through the words he puts in the mouth of Arjuna.

Kṛṣṇa teaches, 'He who serves Me unfailingly by the yoga of devotion (*bhakti*), he, crossing beyond the qualities,[8] is fit for Brahman-immerging' (14.26); and he declares, 'When he truly sees all (apparently) separate

[8] *sattva*; rhythm, harmony, essence, goodness, purity. *rajas*; motion, passion, the disturbing quality. *tamas*; darkness, gloom, inertia, ignorance, error.

existing beings as rooted in and proliferating out of the One, he becomes Brahman' (13.30). 'He who serves Me' – Me, the revealed as well as the inexpressible One Reality. Whoso is aflame with the pure passion for Me, is fit for immergence into Transcendence. This pure passion which lights up the night and shines through the day is man's love divinised. This is *bhakti*. The qualities of *sattva*, *rajas*, and *tamas* are the threads with which the web of bonded existence is woven, by you, by me. Love divinised unweaves the web, and you and I, made pure, are ready for the freedom of the unconditioned.

Bhakti has a twin, *jñāna*, knowledge, the pure awareness which is Being. Whoso is quite purified, in whom love divinised burns steady and bright, who truly sees, and who knows with the knowing which is Being that the Many are the One Only, he verily 'becomes' Brahman. Timelessly, the veiling mists obscuring the perfect, holy union of Transcendence, Heaven and Earth have vanished for the time being. When the breath of Grace is stilled – for none may take that air too long – then again *sattva* and *rajas* and *tamas* impose their disequilibrating activity upon the Still One, and the Brahman-become constricts again into a seeing subject observing objects.

That Indestructible Unmanifest, the last bourn reaching which there is no return, 'is my supreme abode' says Kṛṣṇa. And he also says, 'I (*puruṣottama*, the Ultimate Person) am the abode of Brahman' – Brahman the Indestructible Unmanifest, the non-finite, the immeasurable, the absolute. How can this be? How can each be the abode of the other? It *is* so! Realization is in the living content of man's actual experiencing; it is the plenitude beyond count. Comprehension of this, by him in whom evil-mindedness is burnt out, is of the nature of attuned vibration, not distorting the Truth. But it cannot definitely grasp, and so limit, Whole Reality. Clearly, Realization is beyond explanation. Yet it has a core of strange logic, or else comprehension and Realization would each be separate for ever in lone darkness. This logic makes paradox true; and this logic has the elasticity of the living, whereas the purely formal verbal structure has the rigidity of the inanimate. Each to its own place.

Veda-Vyāsa knew all this. So he spoke inspiring words, magical words, about the Numinous and the Unknown in both its aspects – that which comes to one in the condition of Revelation, the I AM state when 'Arjuna' is rapt into 'Kṛṣṇa', and that which remains the Unknowable, the Transcendent Mystery. And he also knew this truth about himself, the man in the world, in relation to Transcendence, namely, the truth that is fully told in the words, 'I do not know'.

If I can confess quite honestly, 'I do not know', I am beyond the conflict between pride and humility, between conceit and modesty; I am truly meeked. Then, I can stand in adoring awe (the 'fear' of the Lord) before the Transcendent Mystery, asking for nothing whatsoever, letting God be God. When I, contained here and now by Mother Earth, chastened, can say with the simple assurance of the innocent, 'I do not know', my heart is freed of heaviness (*tamas*), and Mother Earth takes me into the land of Light (*sattva*) and lays me at the feet of the Holy. Then only, I the son of man grow into my full Manhood. And when the Wisdom-Love of my Father-God overfills my heart and radiates into his Kingdom, the universal Glory of the One Transcendent Real, then Transcendence has blazed into Self-Awareness through 'me'. Only the light will shine. The 'me' will remain invisible; and will die, consummated. What bliss! Do we see the 'body' of the sun? Or light?

To know the fact of 'I do not know' is the healthy root for true faith. Belief-empty, I am faith-full. Where there is no web of illusions and fixed ideas spun out by sense-brain activity, Pure Mind shines. These are not mere words. Come clean, and you will *be* the Light.

The shining of Pure Mind is the source of right comprehension – what comprehension is permitted to us. The mystery of Kṛṣṇa's revelations that the Indestructible Unmanifest is the abode of Him the Supreme Person and that he in turn is the abode of the Indestructible Unmanifest, is the mystery of the Container and Contained. Transcendence 'resists' Transcendence. The Primordial Energy, immeasurable, undifferentiated, interplays with itself, giving rise to vortices of energy, measurable because of the production of differentiation. Cosmos appears where no cosmos was. No categories – space, time, etc. – apply where the Primordial is concerned. They are co-terminous with Cosmos. Yet Cosmos and the Primordial are an identity! This ancient esoteric tradition is obviously beyond intellectual grasp. But it energizes the perfectly silent-minded one in the I AM state. It may help the un-egoistic, willing learner to sense the inseparability, in whole truth, of the Primordial and Cosmos, God and man, spirit and matter. The Contained is the Container and the Container is the Contained. Let the mind, calm and pure, remain intensely alert, and restful, and it will absorb knowledge which is beyond analysis, but has perfect clarity.

If this calm and clarity prevail unperturbed, one will understand Kṛṣṇa when he says:

> I am life immortal and also death; being and non-being am I.
>
> 9.19.

All-consuming Death am I and the source of all things to come.

10.34.

In the I AM state, Life and Death the other-Life are realized as the immortal complementaries through Veda-Vyāsa. So too are being (the manifest) and non-being (the unmanifest), which are the interchanging states of all that is, of all the world. Being flows into non-being and we who are in being name it death. Non-being flows into being and we who are in being name it birth. Birth and death are names given in both cases by us who are in being, from the standpoint of our natural being. Whilst we are in being there is, within limits, identifiable entity, which is lost when being flows into non-being. Being is particular, non-being is universal or 'common'. The one universal non-being, undifferentiated, comes to birth as the many individual beings, differentiated. It is essential to understand this in order to understand the becoming-process and the meaning of *punabbhava*, again-becoming, mistakenly pictured as re-incarnation, as the continuity successively in space-time of an identifiable entity, called soul or person or character or whatever you name it, which in fact has identifiability as a particular entity only as a nominal (verbal) association with the manifestation of finite being. Again-becoming, *punabbhava*, as a continuously changing process not composed of permanent identifiable entities, is true; this was taught by the Holy Ones, possessed of insight; but the re-incarnation picture of it, made by the populace, is a distortion of the original teaching.[9]

When sense and speech-thought activity is stilled, birth-death interpretation by that living being is absent. Pure Mind (or Mind-only) is sensitive to the wholeness of being and non-being, manifest and unmanifest, particular and universal. Kṛṣṇa, that is, the man Veda-Vyāsa in the state of immergence into the profound beyond discursive mind, states this as 'I am life immortal and also death; being and non-being am I'. The other statement, 'All-consuming death am I and the source of things to come', tells us of the fact of the streaming movement of being into non-being and non-being into being, the *saṃsāric* movement or becoming-process of all the world.

The Lord, that is, the wholeness of being and non-being, is the one and only transmigrant. The transmigrating is the constant interchanging of states[10] within the One Lord.

* * *

[9] See also below, p. 157 f.

[10] If the analogy helps, consider the interchange of states in the following process: water (visible and tangible) – boil – steam (invisible and intangible) – condense – water – boil – steam, and so on, interchanging constantly.

Through the ages men have believed in angels, demons, spirits, gods, *devas*, *suras*, *asuras*, and so on. For many people, such beliefs are inherited from their elders, or they are the progeny of dreams, fears, ignorance and superstition: for our purposes, let us omit consideration of this aspect. For some people, however, they are symbols for an awareness of that which eludes exact verbal expression: this, we may try to understand.

Transcendence fecundates Mind-only, *ākāśa*, which thus holds the archetypal forms and forces of all that is.[11] *Ākāśa* is dimensionless and immeasurable. The archetypal forms and forces are thus shapeless and indescribable, and yet possessed of the potentiality for differentiation.

When the Holy One is in the Silence, in perfect communion, he is one with *ākāśa*, the Void which is the Archetypal Plenitude. Whilst in communion, he does not know this Archetypal Plenitude in the manner that a seeing subject knows an observed object. The impress of *ākāśa* during this speechless-thoughtless Silence upon the psycho-physical organism may afterwards be interpreted in ordinary waking consciousness by brain-mind, by speech-thought. This interpretation can be made only in terms of forms, sounds, etc., that is, in terms of the material and faculties of our psycho-physical organism and its life and experience. Thus it is unavoidably a somewhat maimed interpretation. It is as if an integrating dimension were excluded, as if we attempt to understand the three-dimensional world in terms of a two-dimensional being and consciousness. We cannot pack a cube into a square! But by virtue of realizing communion, we can, on returning to two-dimensional consciousness, simply affirm that there is THAT which is over and above our two-dimensional world, and in which our limited world is wholly though inexplicably subsumed.

The interpretation in ordinary waking consciousness is an analytical differentiating activity, as if a prism had refracted the one beam of white light into the several colours of the spectrum.

One of the forms produced by this interpretative activity is given all the names comprised in the angelic and demonic orders. My psyche being what it is, my qualities (such as kindness, austerity, etc.) being what they are, my body being what it is and my imagination functioning as it does, the angelic and demonic hosts are described in the way I do describe them. My angels and demons are the symbolic portraits (not 'true to life' photographs) of archetypal forces, of 'cosmic energies' beyond my ability to describe exactly or to bend to my will.

[11] See above, pp. 78 ff.

Besides these angels and demons representing universally operative archetypal forces, there are my own angels and demons, namely, my own psychical energies manifesting constructively or destructively, for good or for evil. To these, the archetypal forces are related. It is a fact of human experience that meditation or prayer or any mode of communion with the archetypal forces (of which our deep-rooted sense – sense, not mere concept – of God or the Holy or a Supreme Power are examples), produces results in the psyche of the communicant: occasionally even bodily results. Sometimes, one is aware of these archetypal forces even without taking any deliberate steps to commune. It is wise to remember that meditation or deep prayer intensifies the 'good' and the 'evil' in us alike. But whenever a Holy One is in true Silence, the human and the angelic world, in their perfection, are joined in action which is pure beneficence.[12]

Angels, gods, *devas*, etc., are terms representing archetypal forces or cosmic energies which are constructive; their opposite numbers, the demons, the disruptive. If we are sensitive to the living nature of the Cosmos we see these energies as 'anabolic' and 'katabolic', and as maintaining a functioning balance, more or less, throughout the living universal process. They are not good or evil in a narrow, moralistic sense, but their effects on us may be pleasant or painful. Thus the one, formless, non-descript, measureless power in *ākāśa* finds expression in numerous forms, degrees and qualities when it works through the psyche. Angels and demons may be thought of as modes of release of power out of *ākāśa* (Mind-only).

All the great religions of the world have their angels and demons. In Judaic mysticism, Metatron, the transfigured Enoch (after his being taken up into the seventh heaven by God), identified with Yahoel (or Yaho,[13] an abbreviation of YHWH), is placed by God on a throne next to the Throne of Glory. He remains in the position of the highest of all created beings. The names of Michael, Raphael, Gabriel, Uriel and others are known the world over. In Christian belief, Christ is regarded as the King of the angels, and in Buddhism the Buddha is called the Teacher of both *devas* and men. The Buddha declares[14] that he has fared and abided in all the realms of the *devas* except that of the *devas* of the Pure Abodes, for had he done so he could not have come back to the world of men. Again both the Buddha and Christ are said to descend

[12] See below, pp. 337 f., 377ff.
[13] See G. G. Scholem, *Major Trends in Jewish Mysticism*, pp. 67-72.
[14] M., 1.82.

into the nether regions to preach and to redeem. The psycho-spiritual worlds of Hinduism, Zarathuśtrianism, Islam and Judaism, and also the Greek, Celtic, Teutonic and other pantheons are filled full with their gods, angels, demons and whatever spirit-forms they cared to shape.

What does the Gītā say? Kṛṣṇa reveals:

> Of the Ādityas[15] I am Viṣṇu, of luminaries the radiant sun. I am Marīci[16] of the Maruts....
> I am Indra, chief of the gods. Of the senses I am the mind, and in living beings the light of consciousness.
> Of the Rudras[17] I am Śankara,[18] of Yaksas[19] and Rākṣasas[20] I am Vitteṣa (Kuvera, lord of wealth). Of Vasus[21] I am Pāvaka[22]....
> Of priests know me as the divine priest Bṛhaspati, of warriors Skanda[23]....
> Of speech I am AUM (the sacred syllable)...
> Of all trees I am the Aśvattha, the tree of life... 10.21-26.

And the Blessed Lord reveals much more in the same strain.

Whose names are these? They are the names of the hosts, and of the rulers of the hosts, of the realms of light and darkness. Kṛṣṇa thus affirms the containment of the archetypal world of Mind-only in the One Total Reality, in his own Whole Being. The revelation is awesome. Kṛṣṇa is at one and the same time the Creator, Sustainer and Nourisher, and also the Disrupter and Death-dealer. He identifies himself not only with all the archetypal forces but also with the channels of communication between those forces and the psyche, as when he says, 'I am Uccaiḥśravas of horses, nectar-born, Airāvata of lordly elephants . . . Vainateya of birds' (10.27,30). Uccaiḥśravas and Airāvata are the horse and elephant of Indra, and Vainateya (also known as Garuda) is the bird (part eagle, part man) on which Viṣṇu rides. The animals and birds, ornaments and tools, weapons and musical instruments associated with *devas* and demons, gods and angels symbolize the psychical modes or intel-

[15] The gods of the celestial light.

[16] One of the seven *mahārṣis* and chief of the Maruts, the storm gods who ride in the wake of Indra the thunderbolt wielder.

[17] The howling or roaring gods of storm and destruction.

[18] Śiva, the auspicious one.

[19] A class of supernatural beings attendant on Kuvera, lord of wealth.

[20] Goblins or evil spirits; a sort of Titans or enemies of the gods.

[21] Eight deities attendant upon Indra.

[22] Pāvaka is one of the eight deities of note 5, namely Fire, Anala, an epithet of Agni.

[23] The god of war.

lectual faculties through which archetypal forces and we ourselves interact.

Now with rare exceptions each one of us mistakenly believes that *I* think or *I* feel, as if the 'I' were a wholly exclusive, immutable entity. In fact, just as 'my' body is only a particular, changing patterning of elements out of the world store of matter, 'my' thought is a particular and very changeable patterning of the mental energy of universal mind. At the same time, because I am I at any and every passing moment even though *not* as an immutable entity, 'my' thought, feeling, mood, response, etc., is distinctive of 'me' at that moment. And yet, notice how 'I' fall in, generally, with the thought and mood of the company in which I am at the moment – having 'taken on' the psychical atmosphere so to say – but equally fall in with a different, even opposite, thought and mood of another company on some other occasion. (Mob influence is a well-known and sometimes dangerous phenomenon.) As with the everyday psychical atmosphere, I am influenced, even more powerfully so, by archetypal forces, especially by those which are the root-influence which shaped my religious heritage.

What safeguard, then, is there against being ruined by the demonic or disruptive forces? The archetypal energies do not choose. They are like electricity: touch a live rail and you will be killed; safeguarded by proper insulation you can use it beneficially. The indispensable safeguard against evil is pure morality, and a strong, sensible, balanced mind. Immense energy, in the measurable sense of the physicist as well as the immeasurable 'energy' of Mind-only, is condensed in concrete form in the living man, a mind-body organism. A man's own bodily constitution, sensitivity, character, training and mental development – his whole 'pattern' – is the apparatus for the functioning of archetypal energy, and the nature of its expression through him. This power can be rightly utilized by a man only if he is pure – free of ambition, vanity, greed, hate, delusion, egoism, selfness – and if he is capable of that total attentiveness which is free of isolating self-consciousness.

In the pure state, he is not trapped by the prevailing psychical atmosphere, he is not the victim of the 'psychological weather conditions'. Imperturbable, in *upekṣā,* he is at home in and with *ākāśa,* and can be taken up into the I AM state – 'Arjuna' merges into 'Kṛṣṇa'. So, Veda-Vyāsa the living man as Arjuna, 'sees' and 'knows' Kṛṣṇa (Veda-Vyāsa unseparate from the One Reality) as Indra, Viṣṇu, Marīci and so on by means of the psychical modes or mental faculties symbolized by the horse, elephant, bird and so on. This is not fancy, not speculation. It is actual experiencing when the wheel of imagination is stilled and the religieux has transcended the whole of the discursive mental process.

Indra, Skanda, Airāvata and so on are names for specific modes of activity of MAN, *puruṣa*. You yourself have in you, and are, Indra, Āditya, Zeus, Apollo, Aphrodite, Artemis, Michael, Gabriel, God the Father, the Holy Spirit, the Eternal Virgin-Mother, Viṣṇu, Śiva, and the entire host, 'good' and 'evil', without exception. Whatsoever name there is, is the relative, a portion of the ever-transforming being of the One Total Reality. To see with insight, and really to understand, any and every manifestation or energy represented in these names, is to be freed from bondage to them or illusion in regard to them. Then, the unnameable One, the Unknowable Truth, 'shines' through you the unresisting, transparent medium in the form of a living man.

Veda-Vyāsa, in silent communion, thus understands the revelation. But now comes the awful, terrifying part when he desires to see the 'Form' of the Supreme I AM. The I AM has no form! The creative magic, *māyā*, of the I AM, which itself is the Transcendence beyond being-becoming, releases the vision of the universal becoming-process to Veda-Vyāsa (as Arjuna, *a* living man). But no individual living man can see the universal becoming-process by means of his own ability to see. I cannot see beyond my own horizon – and how infinite is the whole beyond! Yet in Silence, the Grace of Communion shuts 'my' eyes. Kṛṣṇa, the embodied Grace, grants me the 'Divine Eye'. This is the Third Eye – the all-seeing eye of the Auspicious, Benign One, for none can endure that awesome Vision were he not filled and sustained by the Comfort (Strength) and Sweetness of the All-Merciful.

Only for him whose morality is perfect, whose mind is infinitely resilient and therefore invincible and imperturbable, empty of selfness, only for him can the Third Eye open. What Kṛṣṇa does to Arjuna – the granting of the Divine Eye – is one meaning of the phrase 'spiritual induction' used in this book.

What Veda-Vyāsa sees of this Form is put in words in the mouth of Sanjaya and of Arjuna:

Sanjaya says:

> When Kṛṣṇa, the God of Yoga, had thus spoken, O king, he appeared then to Arjuna in his supreme divine form.
>
> And Arjuna saw in that form countless visions of wonder: eyes from innumerable faces, numerous celestial ornaments, numberless heavenly weapons;

Celestial garlands and vestures, forms anointed with heavenly perfumes. The Infinite Divinity was facing all sides, all marvels in him containing.

If the light of a thousand suns suddenly arose in the sky, that splendour might be compared to the radiance of the Supreme Spirit.

And Arjuna saw in that radiance the whole universe in its variety, standing in a vast unity in the body of the God of gods.

Trembling with awe and wonder, Arjuna bowed his head, and joining his hands in adoration he thus spoke to his God.

11.9-14.

Arjuna says:

I see in thee all the gods, O my God; and the infinity of the beings of thy creation. I see god Brahmā on his throne of lotus, and all the seers and serpents of light.

All around I behold thy Infinity: the power of thy innumerable arms, the visions from thy innumerable eyes, the words from thy innumerable mouths, and the fire of life of thy innumerable bodies. Nowhere I see a beginning or middle or end of thee, O God of all, Form Infinite!

I see the splendour of an infinite beauty which illumines the whole universe. It is thee! With thy crown and sceptre and circle. How difficult thou art to see! But I see thee: as fire, as the sun, blinding, incomprehensible.

Thou art the imperishable, the highest End of knowledge, the support of this vast universe. Thou, the everlasting ruler of the law of righteousness, the Spirit (*puruṣa*) who is and who was at the beginning.

I see thee without beginning, middle, or end; I behold thy infinite power, the power of thy innumerable arms. I see thine eyes as the sun and the moon. And I see thy face as a sacred fire that gives light and life to the whole universe in the splendour of a vast offering.

Heaven and earth and all the infinite spaces are filled with thy Spirit; and before the wonder of thy fearful majesty the three worlds tremble.

The hosts of the gods come to thee and, joining palms in awe and wonder, they praise and adore. Sages and saints come to thee, and praise thee with songs of glory.

The Rudras of destruction, the Vasus of fire, the Sādhyas of prayers, the Ādityas of the sun; the lesser gods Viśve-Devas, the two Aśvins charioteers of heaven, the Maruts of winds and storms, the Ūsmapās spirits of ancestors; the celestial choirs of Gandharvas, the Yakṣas keepers of wealth, the demons of hell and the Siddhas who on earth reached perfection : they all behold thee with awe and wonder.

But the worlds also behold thy fearful mighty form, with many mouths and eyes, with many bellies thighs and feet, frightening with terrible teeth : they tremble in fear, and I also tremble.

When I see thy vast form, reaching the sky, burning with many colours, with wide open mouths, with vast flaming eyes, my heart shakes in terror : my power is gone and gone is my peace, O Viṣṇu !

Like the fire at the end of Time which burns all in the last day, I see thy vast mouths and thy terrible teeth. Where am I ? Where is my shelter ? Have mercy on me, God of gods, Refuge Supreme of the world !

The sons of Dhṛita-rāṣtra, all of them, with other princes of this earth, and Bhīṣma and Droṇa and great Karna, and also the greatest warriors of our host, all enter rushing into thy mouths, terror-inspiring with their fearful fangs. Some are caught between them, and their heads crushed into powder.

As roaring torrents of waters rush forward into the ocean, so do these heroes of our mortal world rush into thy flaming mouths.

And as moths swiftly rushing enter a burning flame and die, so all these men rush to thy fire, rush fast to their own destruction.

The flames of thy mouths devour all the worlds. Thy glory fills the whole universe. But how terrible thy splendours burn !

Reveal thyself to me ! Who art thou in this form of terror ? I adore thee, O god supreme : be gracious unto me. I yearn to know thee, who art from the beginning : for I understand not thy mysterious works. 11.15-31.

Kṛṣṇa says :

I am all-powerful Time which destroys all things, and I have come here to slay these men. Even if thou doest not fight, all the warriors facing thee shall die.

Arise therefore ! Win thy glory, conquer thine enemies, and enjoy thy kingdom. Through the fate of their Karma I have doomed them to die : be thou merely the means of my work.

Droṇa, Bhīṣma, Jayad-ratha and Karna, and other heroic warriors of this great war have already been slain by me: tremble not, fight and slay them. Thou shalt conquer thine enemies in battle.

11.32-34.

Sanjaya says:

When Arjuna heard the words of Kṛṣṇa he folded his hands trembling; and with a faltering voice, and bowing in adoration, he spoke. 11.35.

Arjuna says:

It is right, O God, that people sing thy praises, and that they are glad and rejoice in thee. All evil spirits fly away in fear; but the hosts of the saints bow down before thee.

How could they not bow down in love and adoration, before thee, God of gods, Spirit Supreme? Thou creator of Brahmā, the god of creation, thou infinite, eternal refuge of the world! Thou who art all that is, and all that is not, and all that is Beyond.

Thou God from the beginning, God in man since man was. Thou Treasure supreme of this vast universe. Thou the One to be known and the Knower, the final resting place. Thou infinite Presence in whom all things are.

God of the winds and the waters, of fire and death! Lord of the solitary moon, the Creator, the Ancestor of all! Adoration unto thee who art on all sides, God of all. All-powerful God of immeasurable might. Thou art the consummation of all: thou art all.

If in careless presumption, or even in friendliness, I said 'Kṛṣṇa! Son of Yadu! My friend!', this I did unconscious of thy greatness. And if in irreverence I was disrespectful – when alone or with others – and made a jest of thee at games, or resting, or at a feast, forgive me in thy mercy, O thou immeasurable!

Father of all. Master supreme. Power supreme in all the worlds. Who is like thee? Who is beyond thee?

I bow before thee, I prostrate in adoration; and I beg thy grace, O glorious Lord! As a father to his son, as a friend to his friend, as a lover to his beloved, be gracious unto me, O God.

In a vision I have seen what no man has seen before: I rejoice in exultation, and yet my heart trembles with fear. Have mercy unto me, Lord of gods, Refuge of the whole universe: show me again thine own human form.

I yearn to see thee again with thy crown and sceptre and circle.

> Show thyself to me again in thine own four-armed form, thou of arms infinite, Infinite Form. 11.36-46.

So Arjuna sees Kṛṣṇa's celestial forms and the whole universe in its variety standing in the body of the God of gods. The becoming-process, the mysterious ways of divine power and the infinity of the divine form are burning splendours, awesome and terrible to behold, beyond the strength of a mortal to endure. When Arjuna says, 'Reveal thy self to me! Who art thou in this form of terror? I yearn to know thee who art from the beginning, for I understand not thy mysterious works', Kṛṣṇa answers, 'I am all-powerful Time which destroys all things, and I have come here to slay these men. Even if thou dost not fight, all the warriors facing thee shall die . . . Thou shalt conquer thy enemies in battle'.

Indeed, Time lays desolate all the worlds. For Time is age, decay and death. But Time is also the sowing of the seed, its germination and sprouting, growth and fruition. There is no manifestation without Time and Death the other-Life, which means Life in movement (*rajas*) not Life the Timeless.

But Life in movement is Life the Timeless activating and lavishly expending its energy (*prāṇa*) in eternal Beauty – Beauty for the Third Eye, the Divine Vision, but for the conditioned mortal an unendurable terror, 'Like the fire at the end of Time . . . the princes of the earth . . . and the greatest warriors . . . rushing into thy mouths, terror-inspiring with their fearful fangs . . . caught between them, their heads crushed into powder'.

The link which unites Death to Life, Eternity to Time, is Wisdom-Love. It is selfness, ignorance and sin which wishes the Truth, the what-is, to be otherwise. Inevitably, the Will of the Divine, Lord of omnipotence, brings everything to fulfilment in Its Way. Not for me to obstruct, or presume to improve. The Way of the Unknown is the Best Way. The Love of God brings me through numberless life-generating deaths to Death, *the* gift of God, in which the 'I' is liberated into the Infinite Unknown.

Thou art dearly beloved of Me – this was Kṛṣṇa's plighted troth to Arjuna. Will I, Arjuna, prove my Love and 'die' into Kṛṣṇa?

Veda-Vyāsa sang of the One Total Reality in rich measure. Kṛṣṇa declared he was Transcendence, he was *ākāśa* the cosmic power and container in its wholeness, and he was the great wheel of life, the becoming-proces which is the natural order. Such was the realization by the Holy Teacher, Kṛṣṇa Dvaipāyana Veda-Vyāsa.

* * *

Through the ages, the many have constantly battled for the assertion and preservation of separate selfhood. The Few, seeing selfness as the very root of evil, extirpated this root. Urged and sustained by their Vision of Transcendence, they too battled, the epic battle sung in the Mahābhārata. Strange was the composing and reciting of this 'poem', this allegory-myth, vaster than the vast.[24] Stranger still was the narrating of the fighting to the blind king Dhṛtarāṣṭra, by his charioteer Sanjaya. For through the favour of Veda-Vyāsa, he received divine vision to see the events whilst they were actually taking place and relate them to his sovereign.

Set in the very midst of the battlefield, between two great armies, is delivered the teaching embodied in the Gītā.

In the field of the soul in deadly strife blooms the lone immortal flower of life. You are the field. And the flower is YOU. And you yourself are the singer of the flowering of Transcendence in you.

* * *

To enquire, to investigate and to learn is characteristic of at least some human beings. The Holy Ones of old India, enquiring 'Who am I?', were led to Atman-realization; enquiring 'What is Ultimate Reality?', they were led to Brahman-realization. It must be clearly understood that the questions lie wholly within the religious (not speculatively philosophical) context; the investigations are carried out by the religious mind; and the findings are the culmination of the transformation of the religious consciousness, a culmination which is realized Transcendence. They are not enquiries, investigations and findings by the worldly-minded in the social or scientific context, confined to everyday practical life.

The 'subjective' approach culminated in Atman, or Awareness-Being, the 'objective' in Brahman, or Awareness-Power. But in Transcendence there is no differentiation between Power and Being. Indeed, Awareness, Being, Bliss, Power and so on are human words used simply for the convenience of human conversation reaching out into the fullness of communion. Whether the approach be subjective or objective, the emergence of Atman or Brahman equally necessitates the complete

[24] It consists of over 90,000 verses, more than seven times the Iliad and Odyssey combined. Its traditional author is the poet-seer, Kṛṣṇa Dvaipāyana Veda-Vyāsa, the grandfather of the heroes of the Epic. He taught it to his son Śuka and to his pupils, one of whom, Vaiśampāyana, at the bidding of Veda-Vyāsa, recited it to King Janamejaya, who was a great-grandson of Arjuna, and thus five generations removed from Veda-Vyāsa.

denudation[25] of the mind, which then becomes utterly pure, empty and transparent. Hence there is that supreme realization by the *puruṣa*, the Holy One in the state of revelation: Atman and Brahman are identical; the One Total Reality, Infinite, Unknown in its essential IS-ness, is the ultimate meaning of the word 'I'. And THAT is the I AM.

Whenever we talk of Being or Awareness in the ultimate sense, this Being or Awareness is trans-personal: personal and impersonal are integrated and transcended. Hence that wonderful mystery: the Infinite embodied in the finite, and each and every finite an inseparable but unique part of the Infinite. In other words, the One is the Many, the Many are the One. Behold! The universe of sense and mind and spirit, of matter and form and life, is the glory of God, and is in the glory of God! Behold, with eyes shut in reverent love, the Glory that is God-Being needs not the universe for its shining! It is Grace that lights the universe, that the blind may see, the deaf hear, and the dead quicken. Do we ask, how can such wonder enfold you and me? It is a question of one's mode of Awareness of the eternal that-which-is. Awake! And be silent! And stay so still that time's poisoned dart born of self-ness can never touch the timeless beatitude! And then the pulse of desire, and the march of psychologic time, will be in step with the unmoving feet of God!

In Transcendence there is no differentiation of objective and subjective. If Brahman were to utter the word 'I', that 'I' is the meaning of Atman. Whosoever, pure in mind and heart, realizes Brahman or Atman or the One Total Reality as the one and only 'I', has realized freedom from all self-ness. He, objectively regarded by us as a particular self, an identifiable person, he, who in everyday life will refer to the living organism that goes by his name as 'myself', he is, in fact, the unselfed one. An egoless being, he has ceased to obstruct the peaceful flow of Universal Life or to disturb the harmony of Universal Being.

[25] See below pp. 366 ff., 371 ff.

CHAPTER ELEVEN
GOTAMA THE BUDDHA

How are the Teachers regarded by the folk? How are they known by their intimate disciples? And what did they affirm regarding themselves?

'The Lord is perfected, wholly Self-awakened, endowed with right knowledge and conduct, well-farer, knower of the worlds, incomparable charioteer of men to be tamed, teacher of *devas* and men, the Awakened One, the Lord. He makes known this world with the *devas*, with Māra, with Brahmā, creation with its recluses and brahmans, its *devas* and men, having realized them by his own super-knowledge. He teaches *dhamma* that is lovely at the beginning, lovely in the middle, lovely at the ending, with the spirit and the letter; he proclaims the Brahma-faring wholly fulfilled, quite purified. It were good to see perfected ones like these.'[1]

Such is the public reputation of the Buddha, voiced by brahman householders in town and village. The folk, with simple faith, 'noise it abroad'. But who amongst them knows in depth what it means to be the perfected Awakened One, the Teacher? When a king's chaplain, Jānussoni, asks the young brahman Subha,[2] 'Has the recluse Gotama lucidity of wisdom?', the answer is, 'But who am I, sir, that I should know whether the recluse Gotama has lucidity of wisdom?' And with intuitive penetration beyond his young years he immediately adds, 'Surely, only one like him could know whether the recluse Gotama has lucidity of wisdom.' Only one like him could know! A pearl of wisdom for the religious, for the serious scholar and critic with a conscience.

And when we turn to one like him, to the perfected *arahant*, Kaccāna the Great, we are told[3] that the Teacher is one who has 'become vision, become knowledge, become the truth, become Brahma; he is the propounder, the expounder, the bringer to the goal, the giver of the Deathless, *dhamma*-lord, Tathāgata'.

Affirmations true to the mystery! To understand them needs a sensitivity which presses through the unbroken shell of logic and lights up the beyond. When the mind is silent, there is perfect participation in

[1] M., 1.285,401; D., 1.224-5.
[2] M., 1.175; 2.208-9.
[3] M., 1.111, 195; 3.194; A., 5., 266 ff., 256 ff., etc.

the mystery. Know truth by union, and you are unafflicted by the pain of description's distance.

The Buddha tells his *bhikkhus* significant facts about himself. His pure conduct in thought, speech and action is that of the perfect saint; he calls it the observation of 'the mere details of minor morality'.[4] He discards whatever is unessential for living the holy life, *brahmacariya*: this, and not self-torture nor harmful self-denial, is right asceticism. He often refers to himself as an *arahant*, for the living of the holy life leads to *arahant*ship, worthiness, and he declares that, 'the *bhikkhu* who is an *arahant*, who has destroyed the cankers, lived the life, done what was to be done, laid down the burden, won to the goal, burst the bonds of becoming and is freed by the fullness of gnosis, cannot transgress nine standards : a *bhikkhu* in whom the cankers are destroyed cannot deliberately take the life of any living thing; cannot, with intention to steal, take what is not given; cannot indulge in carnal intercourse; cannot intentionally tell a lie; cannot enjoy pleasures from savings, as of yore when a householder; a *bhikkhu* in whom the cankers are destroyed, cannot go astray through desire; cannot go astray through hate; cannot go astray through delusion; cannot go astray through fear'.[5] His mind is free of the cankers (*āsavas*) of sense-pleasures, of (craving to become such or such, and in fact of all) becoming, of ignorance and of speculative views. Thus freed, he knows that unshakable freedom of mind is his, that the holy life is faultlessly lived, that there is no re-becoming for him and that he has done with bondage to the succession of conditioned states (*jātis*).[6] Fully enlightened, he is the unconditioned one. And this is one of the deep meanings of the terms *brahma*-become (*brahmabhuta*: of one 'substance' with Brahman), and *dhamma*-become (*dhammabhuta*: of the 'element' or very essence of *dhamma*, truth, 'thing').

In an intimate discourse[7] revealing his quest for 'the good . . . for the incomparable, matchless path to peace', the Buddha identifies the goal with *nibbāna* (Nirvana), the unconditioned Awareness-Being designated as the unborn, the unageing, the undecaying, the undying, the unsorrowing, the unstained. And he affirms that he himself has realized it. Since he won it 'through many toils', and seeing that the folk, 'slaves of passion, cloaked in the murk of ignorance and consumed

[4] D., 1. 4-12.
[5] A., 4. 370; D., 3. 133.
[6] Vin., 3.5; A., 2.211; 4.179; M., 1.23; and in many other contexts.
[7] M., 1. 160-175.

with lust and hate', would not understand, he hesitates, he is disinclined, to teach the *dhamma*. Moved by the entreaty of Brahmā Sahampati[8] on behalf of the few who care for Truth, his disinclination vanishes; unhesitatingly he proclaims, 'Opened for those who hear are the doors of the Deathless'.

'Hearken, *bhikkhus,* the deathless is found.' These words of Life he spoke in the opening sentences of his first sermon. There were five who listened, and who, exhorted and instructed by the Blessed One and going in accordance with what was enjoined, soon realized here and now the supreme goal of the holy life – *nibbāna* the deathless.

When the psyche is pure, cleaned of all defilements, the mind is empty of all confusions and illusions: it is transparent. Sensitivity is perfect. Intelligence – the ability to see the truth of things – functions unhindered. Such a person is not liable to delusion[9] and the still mind shines with the light of consciousness, the awakened state. Transcendence fecundates pure mind. The awakened one is the focal point of its action in the world. Religious truth can be taught by him. He, the blameless teacher (doctor),[10] is the Healer of the mind. A doctor of the body need not himself have a perfect, healthy body; he can prescribe a remedy for another person which well might relieve that person of his physical ailment. But the Healer of the mind is a true and effective doctor (teacher) only if he is pure and enlightened.

It was written[11] of the teacher who heals the mind: 'The Good Friend is one who is wholly solicitous of (your) welfare . . . (and) it is only the Fully Enlightened One who possesses all the aspects of the Good Friend.' Speaking of the characteristics of the friend who is sound at heart, in short, of the good friend,[12] the Buddha says, among other things, 'he lays down even his life for your sake . . . (and) he reveals to you the way to heaven'. To Ananda he says[13] that because he (the Buddha) is 'a friend of what is lovely and righteous, beings liable to rebirth (*jāti*) are delivered from rebirth, beings liable to old age . . . sickness . . . death . . . grief and mourning, sorrow and suffering and despair are delivered' from all these.

To help release mortals from the conditioned state into the freedom

[8] The Creator of the world.

[9] The Buddha claims to be such: M., 1.83.

[10] See the Lohicca Suttanta, D., 1. 224-234.

[11] Vism., Ch. 3 para. 61-2, by the scholar-saint Buddhaghosa who flourished about a millennium after the Buddha.

[12] D., 3. 187-8.

[13] S., 1.88.

of the unconditioned is the holy power which the great teachers wield. Liberation is psychological not physical. No one, including the Teachers, is free of bodily decrepitude or decay, and death. It is the psyche, the mind which knows and travails because of the experience of pain, death, evil, sin and all other ills, which can be freed by being purified and seeing the truth of things. In freedom, the Holy One comes upon the reality which is named God or the Transcendent. Through him, that reality operates. Thus he is the Friend who reveals in his own living person 'the way to heaven'. But even as the stars in heaven are useless to the sailor who does not observe carefully, and if observing does not understand and act intelligently, so too is the Holy One to those who will not look, who do not listen, who cannot understand, who are impotent to act.

There are accounts of psychic wonders performed by the Buddha or by one or other of the great *bhikkhus*. But the Enlightened One deprecates such performances,[14] and indeed expressly forbids them.[15] Unperceiving, credulous folk are much impressed by an apparent suspension of natural law, especially when it is in favour of their own wishful fantasies. They enjoy having their sense of wonder absurdly gratified, or their intelligence astounded by the magical. Yet the traditional scriptures of the world are filled with miracles and wonder-workings, with statements about unusual powers such as levitation, making oneself invisible, going through mountains, and so on. Enthralled by such statements, the thoughtless miss their illuminating psychological import and fail to perceive one of the true powers of the Holy Ones: the power to show us the road to freedom from selfness. The lure of developing psychic faculties exercises a strange fascination for the immature, power-lusting dilettante. No serious disciple dabbles in them; certainly he does not exploit them. So, the Buddha lays down his injunction against their vain public display.

For the sensitive and intelligent ones, nevertheless, miracles and wonders are significant and helpful, for they are not unrealities in their own proper context.[16] Indeed, the very existence of anything at all in the universe is a miracle, the occurrence of any event a wonder, any explanation notwithstanding.[17] So the Buddha, himself a master of

[14] D., 1.214.
[15] Vinaya, 2.112.
[16] Mainly, psycho-spiritual.
[17] Consider the history of explanations: e.g. compare the explanations of the falling of objects from a height as given by Aristotle with those by Galileo or Newton; of the causes of diseases as given by primitive witch-doctors with those by modern physicians; etc.

yogic powers, tells Udāyin,[18] 'a course has been pointed out by me for disciples, practising which disciples of mine experience the various forms of psychic power'.

The Buddha often speaks of the exercise of three of his own supernormal powers. He directs his mind to the

(1) knowledge and recollection of former habitations (*pubbenivāsā*) and of many a past *jāti* (birth; conditioned state) . . .
(2) knowledge of the passing hence and arising of beings – mean, excellent, comely, ugly, well-going, ill-going, according to the consequences of their deeds . . .
(3) knowledge of the destruction of the cankers (*āsavas*). He understands as it really is: the ill-state, *dukkha*, its arising, its stopping, and the course leading to its stopping; the cankers, their arising, their stopping and the course leading to their stopping. Knowing and seeing, his mind is freed of the cankers of sense-pleasures, of becoming, of ignorance and of speculative views. Thus he knows freedom and he understands that the succession of conditioned states is ended, brought to fulfilment is the holy life (*brahmacariya*), done what was to be done, and there is no more becoming such or such . . . Ignorance dispelled, knowledge arises; darkness dispelled, light arises, even as he abides diligent, ardent, self-resolute.

The importance of this statement is obvious, referring as it does to cardinal tenets in Buddhist (as well as in Hindu) teachings: the operation of karma, the *pubbenivāsa* and the recurrence of innumerable *jātis*, and the liberation from bondage to this round into freedom through enlightenment.

What is not immediately obvious is the implication of the situation in which the Buddha directs his mind as above. He does it after entering the fourth *jhāna*, a profound state of attentiveness or meditation characterised by perfect purity, equanimity and mindfulness. The *jhānas* (and the *samāpattis*[19]) are mistakenly called trances, and are incorrectly evaluated. They are, in truth, states of communion, culminating in realized transcendence in the state so unimpressively described verbally as 'the cessation of perception and feeling'. It is in fact the deathless state, in which psychological and chronological time have completely coalesced. Such Awareness-Being is the 'unageing and undecaying'. Timelessness is not forgetting or ignoring of time; it is the living pulse of eternity in which time has no unidirectional movement

[18] M., 2.18; see also D., 1.80; M., 1.22, 34; etc.
[19] See below, pp. 371 ff.

(from 'birth' to 'death') but is undisruptive and all-transforming. This is *nibbāna*, the end of all ill. There is no subject-object separative consciousness in this fully Awakened state, in which Mind-only functions freely in and through the purified one (*puruṣa*). Existing in time and space, finite, the Holy One is the bridge with the timeless infinite for any who walk the Way.

This is what the Blessed Lord *does* in supreme communion. And he can do this because of what he *is*. He is *brahmabhuta* and *dhammabhuta* because of constant mindfulness and morality (*sīla*) so perfect that he is freed of all conditioning – the conditioning which is the inborn heritage of evolutionary bodily descent from the animal, and the imposed conditioning of the socio-cultural heritage. Such Holy Ones are indeed 'the givers of the deathless' for they are 'incomparable charioteers of men to be tamed'.

CHAPTER TWELVE
JESUS THE CHRIST

JESUS said (Matt., 13.57), 'A prophet is not without honour, save in his own country, and in his own house', when the folk were offended in him by his wisdom in the synagogue and his mighty works. What weariness it was to him to live in the parental home with his brothers and sisters! They thought him 'mad' or 'possessed' – that was how the folk jeered at the Old Prophets, even Elias. Compassionate grief lies hid in the words (Mark, 3.33-5), 'Who is my mother, or my brethren? And he looked round about on them which sat about him, and said, Behold my mother and my brethren! For whosoever shall do the will of God, the same is my brother, and my sister, and mother.' He said this as the family tried to call him away when he was speaking to a multitude. Some there were in that multitude, 'friends', who 'went out to lay hold on him: for they said, He is beside himself' (Mark, 3.21-2), and 'scribes which came down from Jerusalem' who said, 'He hath Beelzebub, and by the prince of the devils he casteth out devils'. Later on, the Elders of Jerusalem, they who wielded religious authority over the people and were soon to demand his crucifixion, declared, 'He hath a devil and is mad; why hear ye him?' (John, 10.20). On the eve of the Supreme Sacrifice, Caiaphas, the high priest, and the chief priests, elders and the council condemned him for blasphemy.

But other folk there were who said, 'These are not the words of him that hath a devil. Can a devil open the eyes of the blind?' (John, 10.21) And again, there were 'many of the people (who) believed on him' (John, 7.31). Bartimaeus the blind beggar addressed him, 'thou son of David' as he was going out of Jericho (Mark, 10.47-8). So did two other blind men (Matt., 9.27). In the country of the Gadarenes, two men (Matt., 8.29; one man according to Luke 8.26) possessed of devils called Jesus 'thou Son of God'. Others (Luke, 4.34, 41), too, possessed of devils, used this same epithet, and also 'the Holy One of God'. Some men said he was John the Baptist; some Elias; and others Jeremias, or one of the prophets (Matt., 16.14). Pontius Pilate, the Roman governor, declared, 'I find no fault in this man' (Luke, 23.4). Clearly, the folk were divided. Those whose vested interest was religion – common[1] folk – were his enemies. The suffering folk and those with simple faith saw the light. When Jesus died on the cross, the veil of the temple was

[1] Used in the rare sense of 'impure'.

rent and there was an earthquake; and the centurion in charge of the soldiers present said, 'Truly this was the Son of God' (Matt., 27.54; Mark, 15.39).

His disciples were a strange group, at times short of understanding (Matt., 15.17;16.9,11), at times afraid (Luke, 24.37. Matt., 14.26; 17.6). Yet they affirmed Jesus was the Son of God, especially when a miracle by the Master revived their drooping faith. One memorable occasion there was, however, on which Simon Peter knew him through divine inspiration for what he was. In the coasts of Caesarea Philippi, Jesus asks his own chosen disciples, 'Whom do men say that I the Son of man am?' They answer, 'Some say that thou art John the Baptist: some, Elias; and others, Jeremias, or one of the prophets.' Jesus asks, 'But whom say ye that I am?' And Simon Peter's voice rings out, 'Thou art the Christ, the Son of the Living God' (Matt., 16.13-16) – words that live as the undying echo of the thunder of eternity.

It was for this that they condemned him. For when the High Priest asked him, 'Art thou the Christ, the Son of the Blessed?', he answered, 'I am' (Mark, 14.61-2). The simple truth! But the simple truth is not for souls soiled by the sin of Adam. Had he not said before to the Jews, 'Before Abraham was, I am?' (John, 8.58). And 'I and my Father are one'? (John, 10.30). And had he not said to Martha before he raised her brother Lazarus from the dead, 'I am the resurrection, and the life: he that believeth in me, though he were dead, yet shall he live: And whosoever liveth and believeth in me shall never die. Believest thou this?' (John, 11.25-6). And had not Martha answered, 'Yea, Lord: I believe that thou art the Christ, the Son of God, which should come into the world'? (John, 11.27). How could the Establishment take all this, and more besides?

Jesus said (from John, 6,8,10,14 and 15):

> I am the bread of life . . .
> I came down from heaven . . .
> Whoso eateth my flesh, and drinketh my blood, hath eternal life . . .
> I am the light of the world . . .
> I am the good shepherd; the good shepherd giveth his life for the sheep . . .
> My sheep hear my voice, and I know them, and they follow me: And I give unto them eternal life . . .
> I am the Son of God . . .
> I am in the Father and the Father in me . . .
> I am the true vine, and my Father is the husbandman.

And he also uttered deep words unheard by mortals, for they knew not how to listen.

Say these words to yourself in the dead of the night – and face your soul. If the darkness stays heavy, if fear stabs the heart, if confusion scatters the mind, then the soul is sick. But if the night shines with knowledge, if the heart is at peace and the mind is whole, then you yourself are the Son of the Blessed.

'Thou art the Christ, the Son of the living God.' Did Simon Peter, Simon bar-Yona, know and understand what was granted him in a flash of divine revelation?

This man, Jesus, was MAN. His name – YHShWH – contains the divine name YHWH. If not for the containment of YHWH in YHShWH, YHWH is but an abstraction, a timeless potency which never actualizes. It is unfleshed, bloodless. But the purified Holy One, Jesus, is the containing vessel, a 'swelling' in space-time, a Person; a Personality, within which is the mysterious Void, pure Mind, the unconditioned divine. In their wholeness – the Personality interwoven with the Void – is to be seen the MAN, the second Adam, the sinless Adam who is the means of inflow and outflow of Transcendence.

The Void, or Mind-only, is an 'emanation', as it were, or an 'energy', a 'potential', a 'field', a 'container' – all dimensionless, immeasurable – of Transcendence. These words may, when we are quiet, give a 'feel' of the reality; but none of them define or can give rise to a conception of this Void or No-thing. It is, however, a 'power'. In this Void (and we have to say 'in' although it is dimensionless and immeasurable) Transcendence 'resists' Transcendence – a resistance which is a creative interplay of Itself with Itself. In the act of such interplay is set up limitation, as if Transcendence implodes and densifies, giving rise, inescapably dualistically, to manifestation which is visible-invisible, light-dark, positive-negative, male-female, good-evil, constructive-destructive, awake-asleep.

YHWH in action is YHShWH.

After Peter said those fateful words, Jesus declared that, 'on this rock' he would build his church. But when he went on to prophesy a little later how he would be killed and raised up,[2] Peter (whose name means rock) rebuked him : 'Be it far from thee, Lord: this shall not be unto thee.' To which Jesus said : 'Get thee behind me, Satan : thou art an offence unto me : for thou savourest not the things that be of God, but those that be of men' (Matt., 16.21-3). Peter was the obstruction to

[2] This is an example of the constructive-disruptive, making visible-invisible action of Transcendence.

the fulfilment of the supreme destiny of Jesus. Peter was for Establishment. He was blind to the significance of Death the other-Life. He was for making images, as when he suggested setting up tabernacles (Matt., 17.4; Mark, 9.5; Luke, 9.33) after witnessing the transfiguration. Transcendence eluded him. He became the foundation stone of that which immures the free spirit, the intangible and invisible but ever-present Truth. He could not but deny his Lord, thrice, in the hour of all hours. By martyrdom – awesome majesty of the Compassion (*Raḥamim*) of Transcendence, mediating Mercy (*Ḥesed*) and Righteous Judgment (*Gevurah* or *Din*) – came his redemption.

It fell to the lot of Judas to be the means of the right consummation. Manifestation is mortal. The earthly containment of YHWH had to end. But it had to end in a manner which made plain the identity of Death, Love and Life, and which transparently showed the transcendence of the Transcendent through the negation of limitation and finitude and bondage : a negation whose mode is a catharsis of the soul by means of violence on the body; or a liberation of the Void, the inner sanctum, by the disruption of the outwardly observable 'swelling', the form. So Judas obeyed Jesus when he was told by his Master, 'That thou doest, do quickly' (John, 13.27). Judas did not obstruct the destiny of YHSHWH. He guided, in the night, the forces of this world to where the sinless containment of YHWH was. Then followed the final stages of the drama.

But whoso is the instrument of pain and tragedy to another, even if divinely ordained, must himself suffer. Judas hanged himself. He is remembered as the betrayer, by the uncompassionate. Did he 'betray'? He was the son of Doom. Could the son of God have triumphed but for the son of Doom?

'Love ye one another as I have loved you' was the one commandment (John, 15.12) of Jesus, his very own. Commune with those words: 'as *I* have loved you'.

How does embodied Transcendence 'love'?

* * *

Yehouda[3] returns
and stands at the door[4]
of the unseen Light.

[3] Judas.
[4] The darkness which enshrouds.

We await this moment of Love
receive thou Me
is the message of the Silence.
On the instant
Yehouda is within
and the Darkness is at-oned with the Light.
The ever-recurring miracle.

* * *

Tragedy and conflict in the relatively arid lands of the Near East! The crucifixion of Jesus, of al-Hallāj; the flight from Mecca of Muhammad, and his participation in war; the bitter opposition between the 'followers of the Lie' and Zarathuśtra, and the Prophet of Iran's death, according to legend, by the assassin's spear; the murmurings of the Israelites against Moses, against God, and their battles with enemies – the list is sadly long. The affirmation by these Teachers of Authority invested in them by God did not free their lives or missions from powerful strains.

In contrast to this, the Buddha and his *arahants* seem to have escaped violence on the whole. They enjoyed the favourable milieu for religious living and teaching which Āryāvarta (India) and its peoples offered. The Buddha rejected the idea of a personal creator God and of an immortal soul. He spoke of himself as the fully enlightened one, perfected, living the holy life, and as one who had realized the supreme goal of Nirvana, and he asserted that all dispensations other than his own were void. Yet neither he nor his *arahants* were persecuted or molested by the laity, though occasionally rudeness was shown them prior to or during a discourse, or on an almsround.

Jesus affirmed he was the Son of God. Śrī Kṛṣṇa revealed himself to Arjuna as incarnate God, the Ultimate Person, *Puruṣottama*. The Upaniṣadic Teachers summed up their supreme realization in such statements as 'That art thou (*tat tvam asi*)', and 'I am Brahman (*aham brahma'smi*)'. Zarathuśtra and Muhammad each declared he was the Prophet or the Sent One of God. Not one of the Great Teachers had any illusions regarding himself or his mission in the world.

PART TWO(b)
THE FEW: THE HOLY ONES: THE PRESENT

CHAPTER THIRTEEN
KRISHNAMURTI

WHEN Time's discord bruises Life, the light of Heaven dims. Groping and crying in the dark, man sickens with fear and sorrow. Enfeebled, he cannot be wise or virtuous, but becomes the slave of authority – of the leader, the system, the ideology, the church, the book, the guru, the popular idol. Such authority loads him with the chains of creeds and beliefs – verbal vapours – and confines his life to the treadmill of custom and convention. Slave holder and slave are wretchedly alike: ignorant, dull, inept, emasculated. Neither can see that the worm-eaten staircase in their house of dereliction is no way to heaven.

When the primal liberating vision of Truth fades, man blurs Life's Fact with some foolish fiction. In strut the self-appointed stony custodians of this fiction, authoritarians who bandage your eyes, and torture you if you say you are unable, either to see what they assert you ought to see, or to believe without question what you are ordered to believe. When at last the times decay and men groan for the lifting of the darkness, there arises one in whom the white-hot pulse of Life bursts through and shatters the gloom.

Springtime again, exulting in new creation! Be simple, and see – Heaven's Light enfolding Earth! And hear – Time conversing with Life, intoning timeless Silence!

There is at least one amongst us, NOW, who is the living flame.

* * *

Time's discord for Krishnamurti is the burden of the past: the past as enforced conformity to a way of life, as a frozen spectre chilling the warm present. So the mind is dulled and confused, made arthritic, filled with vain sorrow and preyed upon by that vampire, fear. Life then is just a grind of mere existence: no sun, only a glare of cunning artifice; no perfume of the flower in ecstasy, only a cheap scent hiding foulness.

The past in itself is no burden. The living moment, even as the living universe, has its 'breath-rhythm'. If one is perfectly attentive, the *shape* of all that happens in the mind during the 'inbreathing' and 'outbreathing' vanishes into voidness in that still and silent pause after the out-breath. The next breath is a new breath, fresh. Spirit, Life, is no old thing, nothing re-cognizable, nothing fixed or permanent or having continuity. It is new, newness itself, creativeness itself. Hence the Spirit or Life in action spells creative renewal, a new-ing, not a modifying or reconditioning of the old. Intellect cannot trap this in the petty mould of thought, but Wisdom understands it. This renewal means a complete dying to the shape of the past. No part of this shape is held back in the mind through pleasure-lust, greed, fear, anger, hate, desire and stupidity, or through imperfect attention. This does not mean that we annihilate the past, for in fact the immediate now is the living emergent out of the past and the past, changed and transformed, is the actual present. But it does mean that you, the perfectly attentive one, are free and pure. Thus the past, in itself, is no burden.

If, however, we do not attend fully with a completely open mind to what is present now both within ourselves and outside ourselves – and such attentiveness is accompanied by appropriate action where necessary – various portions of the stream of impressions made on the mind by the living present as it becomes the dead past are held back. All these, the accumulated memories, constitute the burden of the past. By not dying wholly to the past, which means by not being fully awake and alive to the present, we become less capable of perfect attention to the factual now. Thus the mind becomes increasingly dull and sluggish. The dead past, mummified[1] or fossilized,[2] is preserved (with slight modifications) through the centuries. To all this we conform slavishly. Or, we rebel against it in the wrong way. For we who are self-centred, violent, ignorant, unskilled, confused and frightened, smash up what was previously established by people like ourselves, and invariably give rise, out of our conceit, to another artificial, sterile philosophy and practice which leads us only to another misery and oppression and destruction in place of the old, sooner or later. All violent revolutions are rooted in hate, all intellectualist welfare schemes in greed; grounded in delusion, they are all roads to perdition.

The mind filled with the dead stuff of the past becomes, as it were, constipated, and we who are alive now – in truth only partly alive – are out of step with the rhythm of Life. We accumulate the outworn lifeless forms because we believe they will protect us in the present

[1] As for instance the conventional conceptions and stylized pictures of the Teachers.

[2] As for instance the dogmas, the rituals, the systems of belief or thought which are regarded as unalterable truth, and the fixed codes of social procedure and behaviour in daily life.

against trouble and danger. Out of fear of Life, the half-alive put their trust in the dead for safety! We forget, or rather we refuse to face the fact, that Life offers no safety or security, and that to live means to live dangerously, to be 'vulnerable', that is, fully sensitive to the whole Life-process. This heavy burden of the past is the negative aspect of the male father figure, expressed as spiritual authority, rigid tradition, fixed ideas, beliefs and convictions, as a regressive clinging to outworn and stupid or even harmful ways, and as a stifling conditioning imposed by our socio-cultural heritage. Such is time's discord bruising Life.

If the wings of that Heavenly Bird, the Spirit of Man, are wounded, how can there be ecstatic flight in unconditioned freedom through the pathless realm of Truth? How mournfully man plods in the stony rounds of repetitive thought and daily custom as if in a funeral procession! The secret longing of his heart is for Life, for the kingdom of happiness which is his birthright. But alas! he is frustrated, enclosed in time's discord. Must he remain imprisoned?

Krishnamurti's whole life-work has been devoted to setting man unconditionally free. It is his avowed purpose. Will it find fulfilment?

* * *

Behold the man who wants to set us unconditionally free! But wait. Can we really see him? And rightly understand him? Has it not been the pathetic illusion of presumptuous mortals through the centuries that they know their Lord and Master, the Holy One? Why, surely! Were they not the Teacher's very own chosen ones who saw him face to face and lived in his presence day after day? Are they not devoted and world-renowned scholars who spend their lives in painstaking research and then tell us the very truth in all its veracity? Who dares to challenge their authority or impugn their credibility?

Are you and I, lifelong neighbours, so short-sighted as to believe that you know me the living person as I really am and that I know you the living person as you really are? Rather, is it not the fact that there is an image of you in my mind and an image of me in your mind, and that each image is distant from the truth of the living reality? Even more, that although we ourselves fabricated this image, it is a blur to our own sight and a puzzlement to our comprehension? It takes an expert jeweller to discern and evaluate a perfect gem. One needs the Third Eye, the Divine Eye, to see the Holy One. Only he who is cleansed of the smears of his conditioning can perceive the Free One.

This does not mean that the ordinary man, oneself, is wholly devoid of the sensitivity that enables him to apprehend that here is a man who is the living truth and goodness and wisdom. But one must steer wide of the folly of demanding the measure of the immeasurable. If we examine with an open mind all the presentations by devotees, intellectuals, evangelists, historians, enemies, theologians, poets and rhapsodists and many others, of Jesus or Zarathuśtra or the Buddha or any of the Holy Ones, we will see that each description is but the image of the Teacher in the conditioned and clouded mind of the writer. The living reality which was, or is, the Teacher, is ungraspable, untraceable, beyond all formulation by mind and speech. Produce your yardstick if you still want to measure the Infinite. If Grace will smile at your misdemeanour, you will discover that the best use of your yardstick is to crack it over your own skull. After that, one can look at a realized being with a sane eye.

The Buddha knew he was the Enlightened One; Jesus knew he was the Son of God. What Krishnamurti is in himself, he alone knows; or perhaps he knows not, if he cares not to know. If the light of heaven illumines our eye, we may confess and bear witness to what we see: that he is the unconditioned one, a free human through whom Transcendence realizes itself, making him a light and benediction for the world.

* * *

If direct clearsightedness be not ours, there are signs we may read and facts we may consider.

All the Great Teachers outgrew the limitations of their own tradition and gave an outstandingly original presentation of the One Truth as the answer to the critical challenge of their particular time and circumstance. They came and taught not to destroy but to fulfil. In every case the fulfilment was in terms of the transcendent answer to the worldly malaise, material and psychological, of the day. The relative can be healed only by the absolute. The light and bliss at the heart of the living stream of the becoming-process shines and thrills only by virtue of the Unborn, the Not-becoming, the Undying. So Moses liberates the Hebrews from Pharaoh's earthly bond by reinstating them in covenant with YHWH. Śrī Kṛṣṇa Himself, the Immortal, comes forth whenever there is decay of *dharma* amongst mortals, for the protection of the good and the re-establishment of holy living (*dharma*). Zarathuśtra dispels the confusion of the many gods with a clear monotheism. Lao-Tzu's answer to the disharmony of the conditioned world, political and social, is the unconditioned Tao, the inconceivable and inexpressible. The Buddha's resolution of *dukkha* (the ill which is the relative, the contingent and conditioned) is Nirvana, the absolute. The Cross symbolizes the Power which brought Adam Qadmon (the Heavenly Man) into being: the Cross of Jesus is that same Transcendent Power in its function as redeemer of the fallen Adam, restoring him to his Heavenly State, the one-ness with the Father; and then the Law is crowned with Grace.

Not one of the Great Teachers allowed this Truth to be soiled by the lure of establishing any earthly Utopia, or his life-energy to be wasted in inventing techniques and systems for dealing with the muddlement and evil of the world's politics, economics and unregenerate everyday life at their own level. Each of them saw with unerring insight that man the world over is himself the prolific spawner of ubiquitous ugliness and suffering, and that there is only one way to redeem the world situation: the way of purity and truth, wisdom and love; the way of the unselfed, of the transformed man. It is each man's personal responsibility to realize this. Each man is an individual in the making; that is, unfragmentary within himself, potentially, and undivided from the whole world. The Teachers knew that no man should, or can, be compelled to be pure and true, wise and loving. So they used all their skill for the release of the New Man, the finest flower in the garden of the spirit. They were the Awakeners of man. The Buddha said: 'I go to Kāsi to sound the drum of deathlessness'.

Now the formless realization of Transcendence needs the medium of thought and speech for the sake of communication. The prevailing conceptions of the nature of things, born of the science and material techniques of the day, influence the forms of thought and speech, both ordinary and learned, in general use. They underlie any thesis or description, whether factual or imaginative or philosophical. Soaring abstract thought has firm roots in the ground of concrete reality.

For very early man, God was man-like, or animal- or bird-like. From the pre-Christian millenium onwards when man's speculations led him to propound that the 'elements' of which the world was composed – earth, water, air, fire and ether – consisted of invisible, indivisible, indestructible atoms, his theologies invested God with invisibility, unitariness and eternity, whereas prior to his atomic theories the gods were spirits inhabiting trees, animals, hills, streams, fire, thunder, stars and so on in great variety. This is not to exclude the fact that early man was also capable of abstract philosophical conceptions of a supreme Being or Power possessed of attributes like mercy, knowledge, goodness and so on. The logical conceptions which are the substance of his theologies are bounded in their form by his ideas of the nature of things. Things are indeed the materials for the expression of his awakening to the mysterious NO-THING.

Spirit and matter were usually regarded as being quite different from each other, until the end of the nineteenth century. God (Supreme Spirit) was uncreated. Self-existent and immortal, He was the principle of absolute good. God created the invisible and indestructible atoms which combined together in various ways and produced the forms of matter as sensed and experienced by us. Matter was the principle of evil in so far as it obscured our vision of God and hindered us from living the wholly pure life. The forms perished, the atoms remained throughout time, recombining to produce forms again and again, until God's will withdrew them into his own eternity, and time and motion and manifestation vanished, and only Spirit (and all 'saved' immortal souls) rested in timeless Sabbath. Such, or similar, conceptions prevailed through the millenia.

In our own twentieth century, science has opened up a new world – the world within the atom – a world so extraordinary that it has brought about radical changes in our conceptions of nature and of nature's 'laws'. The interconvertibility of matter and energy, the technical means at our command to transmute at least some of the chemical elements previously believed to be immutable into other elements, the ability to predict through mathematical analysis and research, and subsequently to confirm by experiment, the existence of 'particles' which have no mass (no 'stuff'), the introduction of the 'uncertainty principle' (due to Heisenberg), the revolutionizing of the mathematical representation of the properties of matter (through the work of Dirac), the questionability of strict causality of classical mechanics and the replacement of exactness by probability in physical science – all this and other similar considerations have quite changed our understanding of 'matter' and the 'physical' world.

Today, the old hard conception of matter born of our sense-experience of it can no longer be held. The rigid frontiers of matter are vanishing. The new cosmologies – the modern creation myths – are being produced by scientists, mainly the astro-physicists. Modern man is deeply interested in discovering the origins and development of the physical universe and understanding its nature to help him understand himself. The physical is the natural – let us not say 'material' in the old sense of the word, for it does not apply to our present subtler and more sensitive understanding of the natural, and would only mislead us.

Side by side with this, as well as with the changes in technology, in the control and use of energies such as heat and electricity, in medicine, communication, transport and in several other spheres, brought about through the growth of experimental science since the end of the sixteenth century, there have been changes in political, economic and social spheres. We have seen the disappearance or at least the diminution of autocracy and feudalism in some parts of the world; the rise of parliamentary democratic systems and the steady passing of power out of the hands of a privileged few into the hands of the people; the emergence of social democracy, of the welfare state, of universal education in several countries, of the humanizing of the law and a diminution of social barriers between man and man. The old order was rigid, characterized by stern authority, hierarchy, fixed customs and beliefs in every sphere of life, especially the religious. The new order is more flexible; in extremity, it wallows in 'permissiveness', a euphemistic term for evil. The new order has new problems and perplexities.

Changes in this century have been more swift and dramatic than in the past. As betokening man's control over natural resources and energies, hardly anything could be more breath-taking than his rocketing away from planet earth, setting foot on the moon and safely returning home to mother earth. Investigations by anthropologists, archaeologists, philologists, comparative religionists and sociologists have led to changes in the attitudes and relationships between men in different parts of the world. Prejudice and contempt for 'lesser breeds' – and all nations, whatever their degree of culture, have been guilty of this offence against humanity – and cruel oppression and ruthless exploitation are slowly diminishing. There is a growing appreciation of other people's culture, however different it may be from one's own, and a fast growing acknowledgement of their human-ness, a human-ness no different from one's own. All this to the good.

At the same time, we have seen the rise and establishment of secular totalitarianisms in the name of the welfare and happiness of the common man. This kind of socialism, authoritarian and restrictive of freedom of thought and action, except as permitted by the ruling body in the state, is rigidly and fiercely anthropocentric. God or Transcendence is banished by the decree of small mortals who do not confess to human fallibility. The totalitarians coexist, in a strained way, with the non-totalitarians. Both groups use terms like democracy, freedom, welfare, justice, etc., each group having its own private definitions of such terms. Neither group can quite eliminate fear, anxiety, mistrust, hate, mental disease, armaments, war and suffering in some form or other in their own lives. Both groups, however, live in harmony in certain cultural spheres, such as music or dancing, and in lighter vein, the circus.

Very significantly, this century has seen the rise of experimental psychology and the rapid expansion in the use of psychological techniques for influencing human behaviour and for dealing with human problems and illnesses. Psychology, science and cultural advances have been powerful influences in the overthrow of the old outlook and way of life, the old secure complacency and the musty conformity with the 'each-according-to-his-station-in-life' social oppression. Today we actually witness disruption everywhere: licence, violence, a mad rush, fear, bestiality; decidedly no freedom, peace, love, well-being, happiness, in the true meaning of those words. And the true meaning is the transcendent meaning, which is also the human meaning and not the sub-human meaning which is the one the multitudes hold.

All these, especially the new conceptions of the nature of 'matter' and of man the psycho-physical being, and the new social consciousness with its accompanying changes in social behaviour and the relationship between man and man, have marked what we call modern progress and reform. Yet the fact remains that the race of man finds itself confused in mind, restless, anxiety ridden, fear driven, in constant conflict and war, the pathetic slave of its passions, greeds, hates and stupidities. If this statement is denied, then produce the men and women, say ten, or even five, who are pure, enlightened and free, the fount of Truth, Love and Peace.

The whole state of the modern world, tense, and intensely needing its right spiritual complement, calls for a fresh burst of the Energy of Transcendence in an original form to match the new world condition and meet it efficiently. There have been many local upsurges of the spirit. But, offshoots as they are from old trees, rooted in one or other of the living great religions, they have only increased the vast number of already existing minor sects. Despite them all, the times are in decay.

Our twentieth century has nevertheless heard a new Affirmation of Transcendence, and it witnesses the surge and the sweep of a great new Life-wave over all that lies in its path. Can man use this power intelligently, *and with love*, this time?

* * *

Stand on a tropical beach on a calm sunny morning and watch the long waves rise and fall: a dance of life, a rhythmic movement, unregimented; and also an inevitable clash when the new-risen wave meets the spent wave moving homeward. The receding and advancing waves are but one water. He is a wise man who attends to the new wave rising and clearly sees the old one retreating, without attempting to prevent either the rising or the retreating wave.

In the religious sphere the old wave carried on its crest ever-to-be-loved figures: Parameṣṭhin, Vāmadeva, Moses, Zarathuśtra, Yājña-valkya, Āruṇi, Śrī Kṛṣṇa, Lao Tzu, Gotama the Buddha, Jesus the Christ, Muhammad, Śankara, Milarepa and others whose names would take too long to tell. They span a mighty arc of history – some four thousand years. They originated great religious cultures in China, India, Tibet, Iran and Western Asia, which powerfully interacted with each other, sometimes concordantly, sometimes discordantly. The Great Teachers fulfilled their missions. But their followers, caught in the cage of the letter of the law and of their personal shortcomings, made the centuries heavy and grey as they raised up and established one rigid organization after another. Despite influences for flexibility and freedom, the conventional expositions of the world's religions are marked by authority, hierarchy and fixed traditions; by the master-disciple relationship and laid down disciplines for treading clear-cut paths to achieve specific goals, all entailing obedience (often unquestioning) and routine observances; by systems of doctrine and dogma and a binding creed, and, sadly, by fierce intolerance between religions and between the various sects of each religion.

These great local cultures of the past had their place and function. They have brought man up nearly to the end of his adolescence, a troublesome and dangerous age on the one hand, but holding rich promise of human fulfilment on the other if only – only if – he will grow wholly and healthily out of his adolescence into full egohood and thereafter, transcending egohood, realize selflessness. In the past, the local rhythms of history occasionally overlapped, stimulated and even fecundated each other through their confrontation – witness the rise of Sikhism after the mutual interaction of Islam and Hinduism – and themselves experienced modification – note for instance the changes undergone by Indian Mahāyāna Buddhism as it experienced the influences of Tibetan, Chinese and Japanese cultures when it spread northwards and eastwards. Today the world is an intercommunicated and interdependent one world as never before, and inevitably those old local rhythms of history commingle. They may come to their transformative ending (Death the other Life – a finishing or perfecting – Τελειος), as a new world-rhythm emerges.

Krishnamurti's creative impulse has set the new rhythm vibrating through the world. For the first time in history our century witnesses one who speaks to all people that dwell on earth. He addresses himself to each and every person as a human being irrespective of his nationality, creed, caste, status and culture. His passionate concern for mankind is not for an intellectual abstraction labelled humanity but for each living man as he really is in himself. For Krishnamurti, the world or all humanity is really you the single person. It is your problem or confusion or sorrow which is the world problem and disorder and misery, for you are the world and the world is reflected in you. You, free and whole, are the living root of a world at peace in which life is zestful and meaningful.

Out of his own realization, Krishnamurti gives the Transcendent answer. His realization is embodied in what he says and writes of truth, wisdom, love, beauty, virtue; of the infinite, the immeasurable, the unknown; of god, man, nature; of life, death, meditation. And of the silence. Understanding himself by virtue of the clarity of an unconditioned mind, he understands his neighbour. Free of the illusion of any utopia, seeing the fact of the immediate situation, sensitive and fully attentive to you as you are, he does not dole out prim platitudes or sentimental consolations in answer to your perplexities or pain. He tries to help you to see for yourself the truth of the matter with a mind that is open and free. In order that the mind may be free and open he sweeps aside all that conditions and distorts it, namely, authority, hierarchy, dogma, doctrine, creed, ritual, ceremonial, belief, tradition and custom. All these are obstructions to seeing truth, to understanding yourself, says he who is a representative *homo sapiens* in the modern era of *homo socialis*. He is no destructive anarchist: pay your just dues, drive your car according to the rules, observe the courtesies, he says. He is a constructive radical: on the foundation of a righteous life, continuously discover the truth for yourself, be awake to the whole of life, be silent and let the benediction of the immeasurable unknown, of truth, of god, come upon you.

Is all this the product of mere brilliance of mind? Or of fruitive realization? If in some blessed and supremely fortunate moment of unselfconsciousness you are suffused by the breath of the Transcendent, and if you remain clean and simple in heart thereafter, not flaunting your experience as a status symbol, not secretly consumed with pride, not lusting for spiritual authority, you will receive a rare gift of the spirit, namely, an active sense of Transcendence. This sense is your light by which you can see whether a man's utterances on Love, Death, Life, Truth, spring from living realization, the authentic source, or whether they are the product of mortal genius. Truth needs no defence. Nor does the Holy One. Consider the teaching of ancient India: see the Atman by means of the Atman. Or savour the words of Lao-Tzu: How do I know the origin of things? I know by Tao!

Krishnamurti never quotes anyone nor leans upon any authority whatsoever, religious or secular, to support what he says. He exhorts everyone to stand on his own feet, to enter into the plenitude of his aloneness which takes him out of the dismal dark of self-enclosed self-pitying loneliness and relates him to all. Here lies a possibility for the emergence of a truly human society instead of a collection of mechanical conformers. Krishnamurti not only rejects the burden of all past religious formulations, not only spares himself and his fellow man arguing or expounding their errors or truths, but also strenuously opposes allowing authority to be invested in him. He is wholly dissociated from the establishment of a new religion or a monolithic world culture around his personality or in his name. A Krishnamurtian sect is anathema to him, for it would only become another divisive force in a world which is already tragically disunited. He bends every energy to release men from bondage and to be unconditionally free, free with the freedom which is not self-indulgence in any shape.

He never lays down a code of conduct, and never pretends to reveal the truth. 'I maintain that Truth is a pathless land, and you cannot approach it by any path whatsoever, by any religion, by any sect.'[3] There are no goals – wishful man's pretty pictures – for Truth has no bounds, no finitude. So there is no one who can lay down a path for you or show you a method for achieving a *summum bonum* called liberation or nirvana or perfection. He totally rejects teachers or gurus and also the teachings of the past, because the whole of the past carried through memory is a crushing load on the mind. All teachers or gurus who lay down paths to which you must conform and creeds which you must believe, are your gaolers. But you, if you care for Truth, can be a learner. If you remain awake and give your full attention to what is actual and immediate, Truth will come upon you and the benediction of the immeasurable will flood you.

[3] *Star Bulletin*, Aug.-Sept. 1929.

Away then with preconceived goals. Away also with the bond of authority-obedience of the teacher-pupil relationship and all disciplines that demand unquestioning conformity. By all means let there be a lively communication with any and every person. If the mind is open, and freely investigating, one can learn unceasingly – thereby conferring teacherhood upon the other person – and there is true discipline. Learning in freedom, the mind is ever young, innocent and vigorous.

Clearly then Krishnamurti is an awakener and liberator, fully belonging to our day and age, responding to today's world, a power for creative renewal, and outstandingly original. He is a world-inclusive springtide of Life, not just another streamlet out of the rapidly expending retreating Life-waves of the past. His advent, the spiritual complement of the new knowledge of the nature of things through science and mathematics, of the new conceptions and structures and functions of world-society struggling for emergence out of the welter of violence and stupidity and fears afflicting mankind today, marks the ending – a consummative transformation let us hope – of an immense cycle of religious flowering for at least forty centuries. His advent also spells the dawn, containing both menace and promise, of a new great cycle.

What is not new – and it can never be old for it lives in the timeless – is Krishnamurti's affirmation of Transcendence, and his salve for the healing of the world, the distillate of understanding and love.

Life's pristine urge shoots up out of earth heavenwards. The wayward winds of circumstance curve it sinuously. In time the urge spends itself and the fountain waters meet earth again. They may form a river, or be lapped by earth lost to the sight of men yet nourishing in silence the everlasting mother. Some men's lives give rise to tides; others', to fresh life.

* * *

Whatever be the titles accorded to the Teachers, whatever be the popular accounts of their character or powers, it must be clearly seen that they were true humans. They have been worshipped as God or the Incarnation of God; declared to be Sons of God, Prophets of God, Sent Ones of God; Enlightened Ones, Liberated Ones, Mahā-yogis, Mahā-gurus, Perfected Holy Ones; and so on, in great variety. It rests with each man to discover the truth hidden in these words and be free of fantasies spun out by conditioned imagination. Especially with regard to the founders of the great religions, the popular conception is one of men who were adorned with all virtues and graces; who could and did perform miracles, converse with God(s) and enjoy the exercise of mysterious powers; who were omniscient. But the populace little understands virtue or grace or omniscience. Still less can the mass of men see holiness where holiness is. If multitudes were indeed clear seeing, the Teachers would not know comparative obscurity in their lifetime, or persecution. Indeed if multitudes were gifted with Vision, religious teachers would be unnecessary. Even as the God of popular worship is the God set up by man in man's own image, so too man's credulous and wishful conceptions of the Teachers are mere idols.

He who longs to read aright the signs of the Holy Ones in the scriptures must enquire with an open mind, capable of clear perception. If he is pure, he can surely sift the true from the false. Blessed is he whose mind is innocent. Thrice blessed is he who sees with the eye made single.

With pure vision, he will see that each and every Teacher, whatever his land or race, is incomparable. Comparison is meaningless in the context of Transcendence. Whoso compares one Teacher with another condemns himself as the ignorant one; all too often as the evil one who foments hate and strife.

These Teachers, the flower of humanity, are the true humans. Who is a hu-man? √*man* means to think. Not the inconsequential, inaudible chatter of the brain, day in and day out, but the creative activity of that 'energy' we may name 'mind-power'. The true hu-man is the happy and good thinker, a creator, the Person (*puruṣa*) who has burned up all evil-mindedness. Mind or conciousness or attentiveness as operating through him is an exceeding powerful force for the true welfare of the world.

The perfect communion of true humans is the full flower of holy living, a living which opens a Way for those who care, for those who are irresistibly drawn to their eternal home.

PART THREE
THE WAY

CHAPTER FOURTEEN
THE WAY

THE way to the eternal home! But the eternal home is nowhere, and it is everywhere. And the way has neither beginning nor ending. With the heart lighted by love and the mind shining with understanding, the way is the way of constant action, the action which is peace and beauty. Moving, it stands still; resting, it spans the world. Like the bud which is here-now, and its blossoming, here-now, the whole way is here-now.

* * *

'There', away from 'here', is the unrealized. As such, it holds pain. The heat of desire impels movement, with toil, in order to arrive there. When reached, 'there' has become 'here'. But then another 'there' appears. The process repeats itself, gathering momentum. Pain accumulates, blocking freedom and denying peace. So it is with the unawakened, seeing but the separateness of beings and things, blind to the links which make the wholeness. When awakened, the freed consciousness sees complete relationship between all, between here and there. Then there is nothing which binds one to vain effort. There is ease and freedom. Peace is active.

The freed consciousness feels no restraint. Its movement from here to there is frictionless. It can move perpetually. There is no energy loss. Its power to see the whole fact transparently keeps it free of pain-generating, illusion-producing misperceptions. It permeates every here and every there. It is everywhere. It is mind-space, *ākāśa,* integrating the here, the there, and the everywhere.

Such is omnipresence.

Each 'before' moves into 'now'. Each particular before, unavoidably set in its particular 'there', constitutes the field for a distinctive event, a space-time point-instant. Each point-instant emerges into the next, reaching 'now'. The emergence is a transformation process, conditioned, as far as a person is concerned, by his volitions, thoughts and actions, as well as by forces external to him, his environment.

The before is related to the now, and the now to the future, as a moving and constantly changing emergent, fraught with pain when the volitions, thoughts and actions are those of an unawakened person. He who is awakened and pure, has ceased to be a source of pain-producing volitions, thoughts and actions. For him there is no grievous burden of memory or anticipation, no heat of desire engendering restless activities. He is not trapped in a futile round of impermanence, of beginnings and endings ('births' and 'deaths') which constitute the cycle of mortality. Instead, he sees the full relationship of before to now, and he plans no future oriented to self. Finely sensitive, he lives fully in the dynamic here-now. Not liable to delusion, freely exercising insight, he sees things and persons as they really are.

Such is omniscience.

The Perfected Holy One, devoid of selfness, is the transparent, unresisting nexus for the inflow and outflow of Transcendence. The life-activity of the Holy One, in awareness and being, expresses in the world in finite forms the non-finite, formless, archetypal energy of *ākāśa,* Mind-only. No worldly criteria, evaluations or judgements have any validity in relation to this life-activity.

Such is omnipotence.

The total becoming-process, that is, the moving and constantly changing emergent on the universal scale, moves from the here-now to the here-now. Whilst we are the children of mortality, we are driven by our ignorance and selfness to rush blindly from here to there, helter-skelter. We have not the vision and skill to move in step with the cosmic rhythm, here-now to here-now, transformatively. Our life is the life of the slave and the victim, squandered in bondage and tears.

The way, then, is that alone which spells release out of the unawakened state into the whole and pure awareness of the here-now. This is the meaning of spiritual fulfilment. It is the foundation of unbroken communion.

* * *

'Show me the Way to Transcendence!'

If you can show me the way to space, I can show you the Way to Transcendence.

'Show me, show me, I *must* find . . .'

Hush! Like space, Transcendence keeps you. Like your living heart, God throbs within. Like the trackless flight of the bird on the wing is the traceless wake of the spirit.

How can there be a way to Transcendence? Transcendence is not *there,* not a finite goal which you or I could re-cognize at the end (dead-end) of a particular path. God that *I* may find is just *a* god, only my concept, merely an idol, predestined smoke of Valhalla's – and my! – inevitable burning.

I the existent, nothingness in manifestation, am but the temporal shade of I WHO AM, NO THING in eternity. This ephemeral form is isolatively self-conscious. An insubstantial concept of itself is produced, named 'I' by self-reference, and 'you' by other living beings. This 'I' is merely a visiting card, lifeless. But if I the living being am an impostor or a thief, or purblind or plain stupid, I always present only a forged visiting card. Evil is the inseparable companion of this 'I'. Then, if you be fool enough, I could be knave enough to pretend to show you the way to Transcendence. If you are content to rot in this rut, you will finally meet death with fatuous complacency. So be wary and consider earnestly and patiently: can there be a way to Transcendence?

I the temporal shade appear in the infinite like a little cloud appears in the erstwhile cloudless sky. I know not how. I only know there is no lessening of the infinite. The infinite sustains me. I change all along the way from birth to death. But the infinite changes not though all change is subsumed in it: and of this I can know somewhat, even perhaps to the utmost stretch of realizing unknowing and being taken into the light. After the fading away of all that was me, the infinite absorbs . . . ? I know not what or how. I only know there is no increasing of the infinite.

In this middle realm which is me, the existential being, there is the achievable and achieved, the knowable and the known. If love and wisdom are in flower, I see that the achieved and known are the past, fossils to which I do not cling. Unencumbered by the memory of the form of past experience, the fruit of the experiencing is the growth of the power of intelligently attending fully to the here-now. To live fully here-now is impossible without dying wholly to the here-now as it vanishes into the past. Where there is the light of life, there are no ghosts.

Only the finite, the mortal, can be known by me the existent. Freedom from the known is indispensable if Transcendence is to realize itself through me, for all my knowing is a fog obscuring the light of the unknown Infinite. But if I never take leave of that good sense which is born of purity – the worldling's commonsense is only a tainted thing – a 'sense' of Transcendence emerges and the ways in which it moves me in my daily life are expressions of the Way of Transcendence through me.

Nestling within that house of God's love, my mother, I knew not me, nor the marvel of the growing of me in her. I knew not I was the one and only, hidden in that dark mysterious plenitude busy with Life's skilled wisdom, the centre of a sweet anxiety and of loving care and concern. I knew not I was the ardently longed-for guest-to-be of unknown hosts, strangers who were in truth closest intimates. And then my mother and I played together in that life-and-death striving which eased her of bodily burden – me, now struggling for life on my separate own in the vast unknown of this world, crying, crying lustily. But I knew not me, nor my mother's pain, nor her joy at my cry. And I knew nothing of my father's happy pride that his again-born self was a new focus of his benevolence and loving-kindness. Only after I grew to mature manhood and loved her who bore our sons, I knew all.

This real and true story of my life – and your life? – is a sacred myth. If you learn with love to read it aright, Revelation will be yours and Transcendence will ever flow through you. This story is a story of the finite. So I could know it. But the myth is the soul of the story, of immeasurable consequence, for it can fly through the bounds of the finite. And in the aloneness of the Infinite there is no burden of acquired knowledge.

This only can I know of Transcendence, namely, that I can never know. Awareness which is Being supervenes when knowledge is stilled. Transcendence sleeps in me the existent, as in all living men, as Immanence. If I give myself unconditionally, the Immanence wakes and stirs into creative action, transforming me the man-beast into the true human. This is indeed the growth and fruition and fulfilment of the existent. Then, Death the other-Life comes as the seal of consummation. But if I do not respond rightly to the indwelling spirit, the Power of the Immanence simply disrupts the existent by means of death the destroyer. He who is wise never prevents Death. Thus, Transcendence and Immanence have free access to each other through the existent. Such is the Way of Transcendence.

This myth is a real and true story of spiritual life.

To give myself unconditionally! Oh, how difficult, dangerous, painful and – blissful! I am as a moth drawn to the light. I must approach rightly or else the light turns into a consuming fire. Absolutely, there is nothing for *me* to gain or achieve or attain: nothing at all in the measure of the existent, for the infinite and immortal cannot be possessed or achieved or attained by the finite and mortal: nothing whatsoever that lies within or has any relation to the context of self. I can have dealings, reciprocally, *with* others. But the One Total Reality deals absolutely *unto* me, for it knows no conflicting duality of a within and a without, and it contains me wholly and inescapably, whereas I am only an infinitesimal within-ness in strain with an unavoidable, boundless and overwhelming without.

Hence, the basic fear and danger afflicting me. I can shrink from the danger, play ostrich to the fear, squander my life as a lotus-eater and cheat the creative Immanence of its awakening. Then, for me the wages of sin, for this is the 'sin against the Holy Ghost'. On my ending, only a dust wandering through the long grey glooms of time

Or, I can see the trend: the emerging of MAN the true human; pure Mind in action, beyond speech and thought; the developing of the receptive-responsive sensitivity till communion is the natural state. And I can also see that the 'I', my visiting card, despoils me of the living existent, the indispensable 'flesh and blood' through which the Word may sound.

If I really see this, and abide by the seeing with unsullied honesty, the 'I' dissolves. Now, Transcendence in full play with Immanence, my own living being is the Way. Remember: Transcendence and Immanence are not-two. I the moth shall not perish then but be transformed into the Light which is the divine Action of the not-two. And in this Action-Light there is no identifiable entity whatsoever. This is a meaning of the *puruṣa-medha* of the Ancient Wisdom.[1]

I the ordinary man am the shadow formed when the Being of God stands in the way of his own eternal light. That light is ever within me and around me. Yet only a shade am I as long as I am unenlightened. Unenlightened I remain as long as I cling to the murk of self. All selfness seared, God is released from the shadow.

Then am I the Rose, the perfect Rose blooming eternally in the desert where no shadows roam. Such is the Way of Transcendence through me.

[1] See also above, p. 45.

CHAPTER FIFTEEN
FRUITIVE DYING

NOTHING for me, the me which is the crucible of ceaseless change, of a swift perishing into a new uprising. The face I present in the new uprising depends upon my skill and success in perishing. The discipline of the way is in learning the art of dying, which negates and reverses my common worldly practice of wearing myself out in order to live.

The way of the world is the way of grasping. Whatever I grasp is deprived of the freedom of life, becomes corpse-like, and in turn clutches me as if with ghost-tentacles. Like a vampire, it sucks the blood of my soul. Ceasing to grasp, I let the pure and rich stream of life flow on unsullied, undespoiled. So I live without fear and sorrow. 'A *bhikkhu* who is without grasping, O Ānanda,' said the Buddha,[1] 'realizes supreme *nibbāna* . . . (and) this is deathlessness, namely the deliverance of the heart from grasping.' The cessation of grasping for any kind of existence, material, mental or spiritual, is deathlessness, the complete ending of isolating selfness, the full awakening of the Immanence.

In the Pali Canon of the Theravādins, a being (*satta*) existing here and now, is thus described by the nun Vajirā :

> Mere bundle of conditioned factors, this!
> No 'being' can be here discerned to be.
>
> Nay, it is simply Ill (*dukkha*) that rises, Ill
> That doth persist, and Ill that wanes away.
> Nought but Ill it is that comes to pass,
> Nought else but Ill it is doth cease to be. S., 1.133

Satta, 'being', is used for a living, intelligent creature, the emphasis in the word being upon a permanent entity held to reside in a perishable frame. Buddhist thought denies that such an entity resides in the existent person and explicitly states that all the components (*khandhas*) which make him up – *rūpa*, form or appearance or body; *vedanā*, sensation, feeling; *saññā*, perceptions; *sankhārā*, mental conformations, volitional activities; *viññāṇa*, discriminative consciousness – are *anicca*,

[1] M., 2.265.

impermanent, relative, perishing; *anattā*, devoid of permanent entity; *dukkha*, the ill.

On one occasion at Sāvatthī, the venerable Rādha approached the Buddha and addressed him thus: ' "A being! A being!" they say, lord. Pray, lord, how far is one called a being?' The Buddha says: 'That desire, Rādha, that lust, that lure, that craving which is concerned with body – entangled thereby, fast entangled thereby, therefore is one called a being.' This formula is repeated again and again, each of the other four components being substituted for 'body' at each repetition. Then he goes on to say that children play with sand-castles as long as they have the desire to do so and are delighted and amused by them. But when they are rid of desire for those sand-castles, 'straightway with hand and foot they scatter them, break them up, knock them down, cease to play with them. Even so, Rādha, do you scatter body, break it up, knock it down, cease to play with it, apply yourself to destroy craving for it. So also with feeling, perception, the activities, consciousness, do you, Rādha, scatter it, break it up, knock it down, cease to play with it, apply yourself to destroy craving for it. Verily, Rādha, the destruction of craving is *nibbāna*.'[2]

At first hearing this sounds as fierce as the words of Jesus, 'If thy right eye offend thee, pluck it out and cast it from thee'.[3] But the Buddha's words, 'apply yourself to destroy craving for it', give us the key. Shapes will always appear; feelings and perceptions and the usual mental phenomena will always arise. If I remain perfectly mindful, free of craving for all these, I offer no obstruction to the interplay of Transcendence and Immanence in and through me the living existent. Under those conditions, this interplay uses up me the temporal being transformatively – this is the 'scatter . . . break it up . . . knock it down . . . cease to play with it' of the Buddha – and the isolative I-consciousness is dissolved away. Thus the living existent is not disrupting vainly, but is actively and intelligently dying to the past, which means the true fulfilling of life.

Each and every one of us dies. Change there always is. But death is the irreversible change, the change which is complete transformation, the other-Life of Transcendence and not a mere reshuffling and repatterning of old pieces of the picture-puzzle of the temporal becoming-process. So the crucial practical question is this: in what manner shall we die? In the manner characterizing the true human or the bestial

[2] S., 3.188.
[3] Matt., 5.29.

sub-human? If, during our lifetime, we have the intelligence, skill and courage to die transformatively to each stage as we emerge into the wholly new – a true *metanoia* – we go through a succession of fruitive deaths. All evil is absent then. There is the consummation of the good. Holiness prevails. Whoso sees, therefore, that oneself may prove to be a means of realization by Transcendence, will take care of this self. He will not wantonly despise and destroy it, nor merely preserve it, nor foolishly indulge it. He will intelligently let it be fully lived through by the embodied Transcendence, which is the invisible, still and vibrant fulcrum of his balancing. He will let self be stripped of selfness. And then this very self will shine like a star as it burns away smokelessly.

* * *

Nothing, then, for me to attain or to achieve, to acquire or to gain. But much to shed: my fancies, ideals, illusions and delusions; my lust for pleasure, possessions, power, knowledge, goodness, liberation, God, Transcendence; my likes and dislikes, attachments and aversions; my ill-will, ill-tempers (masquerading sometimes as temperament), condemnations, hates, ambitions, envy, vanities and wants, emulations; my biases, prejudices, preconceptions, assumptions; my beliefs, convictions, doctrines, dogmas; my misdeeds of thought, speech (constant chatter in particular) and action, and my psychoses and neuroses; my pride and egoism; my preoccupations of mind; my busy-ness and do-gooding. Above all, my self-conceit and selfness.

It is like this: if the house is dirty, I cannot put cleanness into it; but if the filth is out, the house *is* clean. This house of temporal being is a thing of ill. Let it be cleansed and healed and maintained whole and pure. Then I the living existent am the Temple of the Most Holy, the Eternal Home of Transcendence.[4] The temporal being becomes the Eternal Home! For now the moving time of the mortal existent is timeless stillness breathing. With perfect shedding, there is freedom; and all that is good and wonderful – peace and love and the immeasurable Unknown – is present quite naturally.

There is no way to Transcendence but many are the Ways of Transcendence through us. So the task before me is to shed all that makes

[4] 'The body is said to be the temple. The Jīva (the living soul) in it is Śiva (God) alone' – Skanda Up., 10; Maitreya Up., 2.1.

'Know ye not that ye are the temple (ναος) of God, and the Spirit of God dwelleth in you?' 1 Cor., 3.16.

'For ye are the temple of the living God,' 2 Cor., 6.16.

me a thing of ill. And this is the way: tread the path of purity. As I allow myself to be washed clean, I remain quiet: never self-obtrusive, but ever alert, attentive and sensitive. And this is the way: the way of deep prayer or meditation, *dhyāna*; the way of insight, *prajñā*; the way of communion, *samādhi*. Whatsoever is present here-now, placed in my path by Life the Totality, is given whole attention. Nothing is merely accepted or rejected. Meditation, insight and communion are not isolated fragments, specialized techniques for gaining results – sublimely playful self-indulgence! They are a whole life-process, like the beating of the heart and the streaming of the blood, and are operative in every activity throughout the day and the night.

No one can lay down a discipline for me, or set himself over me as a teacher. But if I do care for Truth, I can learn from each and every person. My act of learning unavoidably confers the dignity of teacher upon him through whom I learn. Learning in this manner, in freedom, in love and in pure action devoid of fear, is the real treading of the way, an open, zestful, active way. No seeking, but endless discovering; no searching, but an unconditioned state of search. This is Life in Freedom.

This which is my living path presents the least obstruction to the Way of Transcendence through me. My way is the way of the alone. The Way of Transcendence is the Way of the Alone. If I walk on my way like a man who is a true human, my way becomes one with the Way of Transcendence. The alone and the Alone are the One. My root sin – the ignorance, impurity and incapacity which produces and maintains self-isolation from the Totality – is transmuted into pure virtue, the unity in the One. And the treading of my way makes the way for the Way of Transcendence.

* * *

My way and I are a single movement and not two separate things. I do not 'enter upon the way' (however convenient that figure of speech may be) but am always in it, for it is my way of daily life, it is me myself in process of change, here-now to here-now. 'I am the way' said several Great Teachers. Each person's way is unique. Though it may resemble, even be based upon, the 'way of the Master', any attempt to make it an exact semblance will produce only a counterfeit. My footprints can never exactly match those of another.

Yet all the different ways are also the One Only Way – the way of purity and goodness, love and wisdom, beauty and truth, archetypal names of the Power of Transcendence which energizes me and my way. Transcendence itself signposts each man's way. If I lift up my eyes to the heavens, if my all-absorbing interest, my passion and love, is the Heart of Religion, my way is freed of all separate trace in the infinite light of Transcendence.

To see this happen, and continue to be a living existent, a simple human, calls for courage beyond human. It will be there, if one is unselfed, for this courage is born of transcendent love flowing freely in and through the unselfed. And Love casts out all the fear that is born of the sinful state of separate selfness, and releases and nurtures that other Fear which is the trembling, ecstatic apprehensiveness of Love approaching consummative union.

This Fear – the Fear of the Lord – is a sure-cleaving sword to rend all pride. It is a holy unguent for all the wounds that I suffer. Many a stone on the way is sharp and a long stretch of the way is a *via dolorosa*. The Fear of the Lord – a wide-awake alertness and vigilance, a felt Presence, guiding and commanding, a loving compulsion which to deny is to let my soul be withered – saves me from self and restores me to my right standing, the lowliness below which there is no falling.

Love approaching consummative union! It is here that this Fearful courage is most needed. For here no hold is available: only a winged flight, and this too gives way to the trackless, unmoving rhythm of realized Transcendence, of unitary, non-finite eternity. 'Then was not non-existent nor existent,' says the Ṛg-veda (10.129.1).

Prior to this I need fearless courage to bear the revelation of self-knowledge, of the ways of the self as I tread my way. He who can face his own soul and quietly walk on towards selflessness is the hero. And this is the only living situation in which no sin or evil attaches to heroism. The way is trod *in* the world. Far, therefore, from being an escape from life, it is the most intimate interaction with everyday reality. If I tread the way religiously and not as a worldling, I am changed by the interaction. There is a denuding process in which I am stripped of egoism, vanity, wilfulness, harmfulness, in short, of evil-mindedness and clumsiness. I am the 'loser' all along the way – O Happy Loss! Loss, free of the burden of any gain, for the Infinite is the non-measurable Constant! But I do drink of the poisoned cup of the world's sorrow to the dregs. Then, Transcendence demonstrates deathlessness. For the poison does not kill me the living existent. Only when the hour strikes, 'I' am dissolved into Death the other-Life. Timeless perfection!

But only in the ripeness of Time! And so again courage is needed to save me from the rashness and temerity which want to hustle time, on the one hand, and from timidity and lack of firm-standing on the other.

Thus courage has two faces: fearlessness, facing the mortal sphere of ignorance and sin; and Fear, facing the Transcendent. Neither Fear nor fearlessness survive the crossing of the uncharted abyss. All virtues and values are stripped of form and name and are reduced to no-thingness, their primordial energy, in the void (*ākāśa*), for there are neither virtues nor values in the Infinite. But they re-emerge, enriched by *your* fruition, empowered by *your* realization, as greater psychical and spiritual resource for him who is waiting, poised, to venture the crossing. So you are not useless! And your virtue, through Grace, is of untold worth! You the child of Mother Earth, cosmos-chaos, are a matrix to be inflamed by the Creative Spirit. And if you choose to let yourself be set alight, your virtues and values, as of all the Holy Ones, are the vortices through which the divine life pours and the blessing of Elohim, 'Be fruitful and multiply', is non-procreatively fulfilled, and your path becomes a bridge from Earth to Heaven to carry a million feet.

CHAPTER SIXTEEN
EVIL AND SUFFERING

INTRODUCTION

THOUGH the aeons have seen many a bridge from Earth to Heaven built by the Holy Ones, man has remained earth-bound. He is not yet a Heavenly dweller in his natural domain, the Earth. The scriptures of the world have shown that man's fulfilment lies in the realization of Transcendence. But man is far from such realization. It comes into being only after the resolution of the supreme crisis he can experience. The origins of this crisis, and the mounting pressures and conflicts which culminate in it, are a solemn issue in the religious life and form a central theme of religion – the theme ot evil.

Evil goes by many names: sin, death; the Buddhist *dukkha* or suffering or the ill-state; the Hindu *śoka* or sorrow, *bandha* or bondage; the Zarathuśtrian *akem-mano* or the evil half of the mind. Satan, the Prince of darkness, Ahriman, Māra and many others are the personifications of evil.

Look where we may, there we see suffering: the suffering caused by hunger, disease, homelessness, loneliness, frustration, fear, failure, anxiety, worry, perplexity. There is the pain of growing up; of misfortune or lack of opportunity. We know the ache of love, the agony of hate, the seething misery of jealousy, the wasting bitterness of unfulfilment. We bear the burden of looking after possessions, of shouldering too many responsibilities, of slaving for mere existence. Boredom crushes us. The sharp goad of conscience, the unwelcome necessity for making certain decisions, the cruel thrust of fate, the malignity of circumstance, the trial of separation from loved ones or of being forced into an uncongenial environment – all these cause suffering. There is the sorrow of being misunderstood, unappreciated, ill-treated; the laceration of futile longing for the look that is never given, the word that is never spoken, the letter that never comes; the tearing of the heart by the bad, cruel or faithless husband or wife, by the beloved who will not disengage herself graciously or humanly, by the friend who shuts his eyes or refuses to hear; the sudden stab by the parent who forgets to kiss and the teacher who fails to approve. There is the grief associated with old age and waning faculties; there is the torment of the condemned man in his cell, the oppression by ideologies, the hell of the concentration camp.

There is the acute suffering of seeing others suffer; of one's own inability or helplessness to relieve misery, to right wrongs, to prevent disasters. There is the suffering which must be borne because sin and evil have to be endured till one is able, with help, to deal with them. There is piteous suffering due to our own ignorance, to our own stupidity, to remorse and regret. There is deep suffering due to intellectual travail: what is Truth? Goodness? Justice? Freedom? Peace? Love? What is the Right Way of Life? Who or what is God? Is there, in fact, any God? And if there is God, the God presented by our heritage, how is evil so triumphant, pain and misery so universal? Life seems so meaningless, especially when we know the agony caused by the destruction of the good, the good to which we gave ourselves; by the shattering of our ideals; by the discovery of the inadequacy, even of the falsity, of our sincere beliefs, our deep-seated convictions; by the annihilation of the foundations on which we had built our house of life.

All pain is obvious suffering. But the thorn of suffering pierces every pleasure-bud too, for there is no joyous meeting without the pain of parting overshadowing it, no feasting without its end in sight, no security without bondage, no freedom without uncertainty, no hope without fear and anxiety. There is no terminating of toil without beginning all over again. There is no acquisition, success or achievement for the separate self but that the ego must buy it with death, death the wages of sin.

There is the inconsolable grief of death: the death of a love, a cherished hope, an exalted ideal; the death of the companion since childhood days, of the comrade in the field, of the parent, of the life-partner, of one's own child. The break in the intercourse is a scar on the heart of the living. It leaves its mark for all time. It makes a mockery of pious beliefs. It is like a derisive grin unsanctifying all consolatory doctrines, a shade which steals away the sweet light of life. It harries a man like an avenging Fury, so that he is driven willy-nilly to seek an insurance against the dark hereafter and also against recurring present discomfort. It distracts him into forgetfulness of his true home, the eternal here-now, and imprisons him in a fantastic web of his own weaving, the web of this world and that world, of the world of the flesh and the kingdom of God.

There is, supremely, that agony of the Dark Night of the Soul. No pulse. No God. Only a silent Abyss.

All suffering is a consequence, stemming from various causes and conditions. It follows in the wake of natural calamities such as those due to climatic action or convulsions of the earth itself. In most cases no measures can be taken to forestall them or prevent their occurrence. If there are preliminary warning signs and if time is on our side, we may run away before the calamity overwhelms the region. Again, suffering may follow upon our ignorance of the right technique for operations not involving ethical or humanitarian values; we have to learn our skills by perseverance and by painful experience. And again, suffering follows upon accidents despite all human precautions and care; or upon a snake bite or an epidemic. Suffering of this nature is the practical concern of political and social organization, of technology and medicine and science. It is not the concern of religion as such; but the religious man will naturally do what lies in his power to alleviate suffering.

A vast amount of suffering is due to our own lust, to our feverish pleasure-seeking and self-indulgence, to our greed and our ambition; to our aggressiveness, anger, jealousy, envy, hate, resentment, malice and ill-will; to our vanity, egoistic self-conception and self-seeking; to our own fixed beliefs, ideas and ideals, and the passion (always stupid, sometimes murderous as in the case of authoritarian ideologies and totalitarian policies) to impose these beliefs, ideas and ideals on others; to our own pathetic illusions and sad delusions; to our ignorance of actual fact, material and psychological; and to fear. All such sources of suffering constitute evil.

It is quite easy to see this if I observe my reactions to all stimuli, to my memories and anticipations, to the nature and shape of my fantasies, and the course of my desires. If I am truly discerning, I can clearly perceive that all of them, centring round my 'I-ness', are burning with the fires of greed and hate and delusion. I like the taste of meat, so I kill or am indirectly involved in butchery. I am enamoured of that woman, so I lust after her and I can indulge my passion at least in imagination without let or hindrance. I am attracted by that object, so I want to possess it. I have an aggressive ambition to amass wealth, to rise to fame and succeed in great achievements, so I ruthlessly, cunningly and with stifled conscience, assert my supremacy over others, dominating them by any means or depriving them even of the necessities of existence. I have the passion of the ignorant and conceited to save souls, so I evangelize, militantly; even become a Torquemada. I dislike this person or that thing, so I hurt the person or destroy the thing. I want to be safe and salved, so I act according to my delusion and live as an image, untrue to what I really am. All my passions, desires and thoughts, all ego-centred, arise out of my mind. I am the originator and perpetuator of evil; my evil is the source of suffering for myself and my whole environment.

There is no Evil One – no Diabolos or Satan or Ahriman or Māra – as a being or personal entity; nor is there any metaphysical principle of evil. However convenient a postulated entity or principle may be for talking purposes, the real evil is in me myself, in you yourself, in our own psyche.

It may be said that the above is one-sided. Granting the undeniable fact of evil and suffering, and even granting that I am its originator and maintainer, it may be said that there is the other side of the coin, namely that I am equally the source of good with consequent fulfilment for myself and my environment. This is so within the context of duality, of the ceaseless conflict of good and evil in the worldly sense. But the real good lies beyond my relative good and evil and their conflict. Whilst immersed in this conflict I do not know that real good, and I cannot live the good life in the profoundly religious sense.

This evil, our impure state, is very much the concern of religion.

There is an evil more radical than the evil in our psyche, namely the ill state or evil condition of not being in communion. This is the state of sin, the state in which one is ignorant of Truth, blind to Reality, out of tune with Life, wilfully self-centred, sundered from the Unity. It is the unenlightened, unawake, unwise, ungodly state. It is the loveless state. It stems from ignorance; ignorance not in the ordinary sense of not knowing facts or skills but in the sense of not being sensitive and responsive to the living, changing truth of everything.

Man is in this sorry condition because he could not avoid the plunge into the fallen state. He had to wean himself and reach out to independence by his own efforts. He succeeded in surviving; but the price he paid for survival was suffering. Previous to the growth of his ego-bound self-consciousness, his happiness was a servitude in harmony, his pain was mainly bodily. With the accumulation of experience and memory, the growth of tradition and its transmission down the generations, the mind gathered its worldly wisdom, a set of values and criteria, and skills to satisfy desires and ambitions. Whenever there was frustration the mind suffered.

Now, whereas the body experiences painful and pleasurable sensations, it is the mind which suffers or enjoys those bodily sensations, as well as all the psychological states. The psycho-physical organism is the physical and material experiencer; the mind is the sufferer and enjoyer.

If there were no mind, no receptive-responsive sensitivity, there would be no evil, no sin and no suffering. That which is called evil or sin would be only mechanical process, only action-reaction, destruction-regeneration, with no value judgment attached to it. But mind, growing to awareness of its own incompleteness and inadequacy and its imperfect relationship with others, with the world and with the Transcendent Infinite, aware of having slipped out of the childish comfort of unknowing communion, and aware of the absence of Perfect Communion, sees all this as its root evil. This evil is the greatest concern of religion.

It is the intense awareness of *this* ill-state which causes the most poignant suffering to him who longs passionately for Truth, for God. Without this awareness and its accompanying pain no transcendent realization of Truth, of God, is possible.

It is a mistake to try to get rid of suffering, or to avoid it or prevent it. Suffering is the inevitable consequence of evil. Wisdom lies in understanding suffering and evil. Understanding suffering does not mean avoiding it or preventing it because I fear or dislike it, nor being rid of it by conquest. It means, among other things, that I must see that I cannot separate out the environment, myself, and evil and suffering into water-tight compartments. I and my world are tied together by the whip-knot of evil; and I am lashed with suffering whenever I pretend to ignore that knot, or when I try to cut it or imagine I can cleverly slip through it or outwit it. My neighbour too is knotted, for his world and my world are but one world; and he too is in tears. Suffering is not simply individual suffering, an isolated phenomenon. It is part and parcel of the becoming process, involving each and every person.

* * *

Out of the Great Deep emerges the silent River of Life. Curved downwards below the firmament by the pull of the passion for sentient existence, it falls back on the Rock of Doom. Up spring countless drops, separate lives passionately striving to maintain themselves in wearisome perpetuity.

In the bowls of necessity is played the tragedy of ineluctable Calamity : evil – the World-Woe – the Ill-State.

When a life here, a life there, folds up its energy into itself, it ceases to be dashed on the Rock of Doom. Unburdened of the dead weight of its egoity, it is taken up above the firmament to rejoin the pellucid River of Life.

* * *

THE ZARATHUSTRIAN APPROACH

> The Soul of Creation[1] (*geush urvā*) cried unto God in grief: 'Wherefore hast thou brought me into being? And who shaped me? Wrath and rapine, insolence, aggression and violence sit upon me in my affliction. No one is my protector except thee, O God, so reveal thou to me the strong deliverer.' Yasna, 29.1.

Thus does Zarathuśtra introduce the theme of suffering in his Ahunavaiti Gāthā. When the Soul of Creation asked the question, the Architect of Creation (*geush tashā*) questioned Ashā[2]: 'Who will be the spiritual leader of your creation? When will you grant her a ruler as the good shepherd and the diligent nourisher of the world? Who will be her lord for her joy and bliss, who shall repel the wrath of the wicked?' And Ashā, who wounds not nor is hostile to creation, answers:

> 'I know not one among these heavenly hosts by whom righteous mortals might be led to the Light. He must indeed be the most powerful in uprightness if to his call the zealous shall respond. Mazdā most wise is the Supreme Knower of all actions performed in the past, and indeed of those which will be performed in the future, by *daevas* (devil-worshippers, polytheists and evildoers in general) and by men. Of all these, He himself is the discriminating Lord. Be it with us as he wills.' Yasna, 29.2-4.

The answer comes from Vohu Mano, the Good Mind, one of the Divine Powers of Ahurā-Mazdā, the Supreme Being:

> 'Here in this heavenly sphere, only one such is known to me who alone has listened to our Divine Decrees, and that one is Zarathuśtra Spitamā. He is eager to proclaim the Glory of Mazdā and his Eternal Law in songs of praise to us, so let him be blessed with sweetness of speech.'

On hearing this the Soul of Creation weeps, and says:

> 'Now must I submit to an ineffectual leader, to the words of a man without weapons, instead of him whom I had longed for, a mighty ruler! When, if ever, shall he come into being who will succour me with the might of his hands?' Yasna, 29.8,9.

[1] Literally, of the Ox, *geush*.
[2] Divine Law and Order: Righteousness; Truth; Holiness.

The cry of the Soul of Creation is the cry of each truth-seeker. The wrath and rapine, insolence and aggression on earth is the suffering and evil in one's own being. He who longs for release prays for some power which will authoritatively force the wrong to be made right. But this is the prayer of the unenlightened, for conflict never liberates one. So the answer from the Transcendent is always in terms of the Wisdom that has gone beyond, of the Love that endures and outlasts the world-woe. Quite naturally, the world-soul, like a mortal man, is at first disappointed. The answer is contrary to mortal hopes and expectations. The spiritual answer never can be in terms of the expectations of the calculating, desirous mind. But the open mind allows the true answer to pervade the heart and thus purify and enlighten the whole being of man. God can speak to man only in original terms, unexpected and unforeseeable. When the Unknown is openly present, there is creative renewal.

So the Soul of Creation, reconciled as it were to the message of the Good Mind, proceeds to say:

> 'O Lord of Life, grant unto them (Zarathuŝtra and his disciples) eminence and sovereignty through Holiness and through the Good Mind that thereby they may establish a joyous and blissful existence. I also, O Lord of Wisdom, look upon Thee as the Prime Giver of this gift.' Yasna, 29.10.

In his first sermon[3] Zarathuŝtra declares to earnest listeners the great truth concerning the dual or twin-nature of the mind. There is the *spento-mainyu* (the good twin) and *akem-mainyu* (the evil twin). These twins which constitute the one human mind move a man to good or to evil in thought, word and deed. The evil twin impels him to be a follower and agent of Untruth which produces suffering, the good twin to Truth, which leads to the vision beatific and to belonging to the Divine Powers of God.[4] In the evil twin, *akem-mainyu*, Zarathuŝtra personifies the evil in the psyche.

Zarathuŝtra goes through the agony of doubt and perplexity in his search for the Truth. He says that the *daevas* (the followers of Untruth) also pray to Ahurā-Mazdā with the same fervour as the followers of the Truth for the beatific vision. So he prays that he and his disciples be accepted as the Messengers and Spokesmen of the Lord. The answer is strange: 'We have chosen for you both (the *daevas* and

[3] Yasna, 30.1-11.
[4] Ashā, Xshathrā, Haurvatāt, etc.

Zarathuśtra alike) the good and holy Āramaiti (Devotion, Love).' Here indeed is cause for spiritual distress.[5] How could the Lord grant such favour equally to the opposing groups? 'May she (Āramaiti) be ours', cries Zarathuśtra. He exposes and denounces the followers of the Untruth. But the uncertainty regarding his own rightness and worth, and the sureness of his own foundations, is confessed in poignant words:

> 'The false prophet (Zarathuśtra's opponent) distorts the Sacred Scripture and, in truth, through his evil doctrines, the divine purpose in life as well. He robs me of my holy desire for the possession of the Good Mind (Vohu Mano). So, with these anguished cries of my Spirit I wail to you, O Lord of Wisdom, and to your Divine Law. . . . . Without doubt, followers of the Untruth mutilate my inner life.' Yasna, 32.9,11.

Thus in brief Zarathuśtra expresses the deep spiritual distress of the ill-state of not being in communion.

THE HINDU-BUDDHIST APPROACH

Varuṇa, Lord of the Ethical Order, hates and punishes sin, declares the Ṛg-veda. Fettered by disease and death the sinner suffers for his transgression. To kill, curse, deceive, gamble, cheat, and to indulge immoderately in wine, anger and dice is to sin.[6] There is also sinning against a stranger and the distinction between deliberate and unintentional sinning.[7] The Ṛg-vedic Indians thought it was human to err.[8] They attributed their sins to thoughtlessness and weakness of will; to wine, anger and dice; to bad example and to evil dreams.[9] In addition to the belief that they suffered for their own sins, they thought they could suffer for the sins of others, especially for the sins of their fathers.[10]

The great Ṛṣi Vasiṣṭha prays to the merciful and gracious Varuṇa for forgiveness. Painful as the consequence is, such as disease or death, far more poignant is the severance of the intimate fellowship with the Lord of Heaven. Communion could be restored by oblations and

[5] See also below pp. 165 ff., 197 ff., 265, 356.
[6] RV., 1.41.8, 2.27.16, 7.65.3, 5.85.8, 7.86.6.
[7] RV., 5.85.7 & 8.
[8] RV., 1.25.1, 7.89.5.
[9] RV., 7.86.6, 89.3.5.
[10] RV., 7.86.5, 2.28.9.

sacrifices: confession and prayer[11] by a contrite heart enables Varuṇa's grace to be bestowed on him who was erstwhile the object of Varuṇa's wrath. This bestowal of grace makes him Varuṇa's beloved.[12] Once more in communion with his Lord, Vasiṣṭha stands guiltless and happy-hearted.[13] *Ṛta*, the eternal order and harmony of the universe, again moves unbroken.

The Ṛg-vedic Indians appear to have believed that after death they would either be thrust down into the dread place if they had lived an evil life, or if they had lived a good life they would enjoy eternal felicity. Thus the solution of the problem of pain and suffering, of sin and evil, lay in the observance of all the ordinances laid down for the living of the good life. *Ṛta,* the all-embracing principle and power was supreme over gods and men alike. The gods never departed from the right path. Men could stray, but were saved if they repented and restored themselves to right relationship with the gods.

Such is the simple word of the Ṛg-veda. It remains unconcerned with any extended discussion regarding sin and evil and suffering, but it does affirm that the absence of communion with the Transcendent is sorrowful, an affliction to be remedied.

The symptoms of this affliction, or the forms of this absence of communion, are presented by all the great teachers of India – be they Hindu, Buddhist, Jain or Sikh – as *saṃsāra* (the cycle of births and deaths), old age, decrepitude and decay, sorrow and ignorance.[14] All this was the evil and misery from which they sought, and found, deliverance. The Upaniṣadic teachers present this deliverance as the *tadvanam* or the goal of love-longing, as the realization of Atman or as becoming Brahman; the author of the Gītā presents it as the liberation of the devotee who lives the holy life by the love and grace of Śrī Kṛṣṇa the incarnate Lord; the Buddha presents it as enlightenment or the realization of Nirvana through extinction of greed, hate and delusion. In all cases, the state of communion with the Transcendent[15] is the

[11] Prayers for freedom from sin (*enas*, 'crooked-going sin', in the *Īśā* Upaniṣad 18) are found in RV., 1.24.9; 3.7.10; 7.86.3; 7.88.6; 7.89.5; 7.93.7; 8.67(56).17; 10. 35.3; 10.37.12; AV., 6.97.2; 6.115.1,2,3; 6.116.2,3; 6.117; 6.118; 6.119; 6.120.

[12] RV., 5.85.8.

[13] RV., 7.86.2.

[14] From the Upaniṣads: Śvet., 2.12; Kaṭha., 1.12; Chānd., 3.22.3,4,5; 8.1.5; 8.12. 1; 8.14; Bṛh., 1.2; 1.4.11; 1.5.2; Kauṣītaki, 4.14; Ait., 1.1.4; Tait., 2.8; Maitri, 1.3,4; 3.5; 6.28,34; 7.5,11; also in Adhyātma, 47,48; 55 ff; Subāla, 5; 9; and in the Vajrasūci, Garbha, Nārada-parivrājaka, Yogatattva, etc., etc. Bhagavad Gītā, 13.8. and throughout the Buddhist and Jain scriptures.

[15] Whatever be the name given to the Transcendent: Brahman or God or the Unborn, etc.

supreme good. The forms of thought and speech used suggest that the forms of communion differ from each other, sometimes considerably, but the actual communion consummated and realized in one's own living being is the one factual Real. Whilst fulfill*ing*, argument and difference are absent. They arise afterwards only, when describing or remembering the dead past, the fulfil*ment*.

The Buddha declared, 'I lay down simply *dukkha* (suffering, or the ill-state) and the stopping of *dukkha*'[16]. Of the Four Noble Truths, the first states that birth or re-birth (*jāti*), ageing and dying (*jarā-maraṇa*), sorrow, lamentation, pain, grief, despair, association with the unloved, separation from the loved, not to get what one wants, in short the five aggregates (that is the five constituents, according to Buddhist analysis, which make up the existential person observed and named 'a man') are, one and all, *dukkha*.

Reading the above, I the ordinary man naturally interpret birth as 'my birth', the event which took place when my mother successfully propelled me out of her own body, and rebirth as 'myself' being born again some time after the death of my present body. This 'myself' is thought of as the Atman or the true being or the soul or whatever we like to call it, and is regarded as immortal. Buddhist analysis presents a different picture of man.[17] But both Buddhist and Hindu popular belief uphold the idea of a succession of incarnations on earth culminating in the attainment of perfection or liberation.

Such is the common belief in re-incarnation in various parts of the world. Buddhaghosa, who flourished about the ninth century after the Buddha[18] and whose Visuddhimagga, 'the principal non-canonical authority of the Theravāda (which) forms the hub of a complete and coherent method of exegesis',[19] says this:[20] 'When he (a man) is confused about death, instead of taking death thus, "Death in every case is a break-up of aggregates", he figures that it is a (lasting) being that dies, that it is a (lasting) being's transmigration to another incarnation, and so on. When he is confused about reappearance, instead of taking rebirth thus, "Birth in every case is a manifestation of aggregates", he figures that it is a lasting being's manifestation in a new body. When he is confused about the round of rebirths, instead of taking the round

[16] M., I.140.
[17] See below, p. 158.
[18] i.e. during the 5th century A.D.
[19] Visuddhimagga (The Path of Purification), tr. by Bhikkhu Ñāṇamoli, p. 9.
[20] Ibid., p. 625 f.

Note: Regarding the ethical problem arising out of no-self and no re-birth (reincarnationally) see E. J. Thomas *Perfection of Wisdom*, p. 67 ff.

of rebirths as pictured thus, "The endless chain of aggregates, of elements, of bases too, that carries on unbrokenly, is what is called "the round of births", he figures that it is a lasting being that goes from this world to another world, that comes from another world to this world.'

Clearly, then, the reincarnational form, namely a permanent being or entity that ensouls and inhabits a succession of bodily lives, is a false picture of the true meaning of rebirth. Buddhaghosa says (as in the above quotation) that rebirth (or birth) is a manifestation of aggregates. Nārada Thera in his translation of the Abhidhammattha Sangaha says: '*Jāti* (birth or rebirth), strictly speaking, is the arising of the aggregates'.[21]

What are these aggregates? The Buddha taught that the observable human being was a bundle of aggregates (*khandhas*): *rūpa*, shape, form or appearance; materiality or body; *vedanā*, feeling, sensation; *saññā*, perceptions, cognitions (the remembered and also the forgotten); *sankhārā*, the mental concomitants, or adjuncts which come, or tend to come, into consciousness at the uprising of any cognition (*citta*), as well as others dissociated from consciousness; and *viññāṇa*, consciousness.

The Buddha affirmed that each of these aggregates, as well as their combination, that is, the existential man who is the observable phenomenon, is impermanent, devoid of any permanent essence or entity (a 'self' or 'soul' or fragment of ultimate reality, *atta*), and that each one is itself *dukkha* and a source of *dukkha*. The becoming-process, *saṃsāra,* is a continuous uprising and deceasing, birth and death, re-birth and re-death, of impermanent aggregates only. There is no permanent re-incarnating entity, no changeless identifiable transmigrant.

Thus *jāti*, in the statement, '*jāti* is *dukkha*', is not *my* birth. It is the arising of the existential man, a seemingly fixed, coherent pattern but which actually consists of impermanent, continuously changing aggregates. These aggregates are not *my* property. The onlooker addresses this pattern of aggregates as 'you'; the living pattern regards and talks of itself as 'I'. The Buddha himself used the words 'you' and 'I', but only because, as he explained, they were convenient colloquialisms, they were current speech. In actual fact there is no permanent 'I' or 'you'. The usual expression of self-consciousness, namely the 'I-am-I' conception, so tenaciously held and so strongly felt, is a misrepresentation of the facts. When a man says 'I decided to do this', the decision

[21] *A Manual of Abhidhamma*, Pali Text, Translation and Explanatory Notes by Nārada Thera, Vol. 2, p. 83.

was, in actual fact, the resultant of egoism, ambitions, skills, desires, circumstances, available resources, thought, memory, and several other factors, conscious and unconscious, known and unforeseen, all reacting together. No permanent I-entity was in charge. The emergence of the decision was a dependent origination, a conditioned genesis.

And this enables us to see that wherever there is a *jāti*, there is a conditioned state. Every birth is the birth of a finite, limited creature or thing, unfree. In fact *jāti* and the conditioned or unfree state are inseparable. *Jāti* is *dukkha*, said the Buddha, and *dukkha* is explained[22] as being compounded of *du* (bad) and *kham* (the 'void'; more in the sense of a [contemptible] emptiness than in the profound, paradoxical sense of the Void which is the creative Plenum).

Emerging out of the unborn and undying Unconditioned, there is manifest the birth of the conditioned. Let there be a constriction or disturbance in the Infinite, and that disturbance is manifest as the finite. The conditioned finite is the excrescence of the unconditioned Infinite, and as such, whatever be the ephemeral impression it makes as it hastens ineluctably towards its disintegration and death, it is an expression of *dukkha*. It is *dukkha* in this transcendental sense which is the Buddha's profounder concern. His direct answer to all *dukkha* is Nirvana. His direct answer is not merely to produce another *Jāti* in the shape of a welfare state for society, or in the shape of a healthy, educated, adequately self-expressed good citizen as popularly conceived at present. Nirvana, the direct answer, means the extinction of ignorance (*avidyā*) and craving (*taṇhā*) and evil. It transcends man's incomplete answer of the welfare state or of personal gain in all aspects of his life. Worldly man's answers all lie in the deadly grip of insatiable desire; they all burn in the fires of delusion, hate and greed; they are all generators of conflict and misery. A true answer comes only from a source which is transcendent to the problem. It is not a mere opposite to the problematical state, for that would be only another conditioned state. It is somewhat akin to harmony in music. Two or more different melodies are played or sung together. When two or more different notes are sounded together we hear chords. Some chords are concordant, others are discordant. The discords are resolved, by making the melodies move in an appropriate way, into concords. The overall effect of single sounds and silences, of discords and concords as the melodies move, is harmony. There is no mere acceptance and rejection of pleasant or disagreeable sounds. There is creation which is harmony. The

[22] Vism., Ñāṇamoli p. 563.

transcendental answer is a complete re-solution into perfect harmony, not just a solution. The former is timeless and unconditional, the latter is temporal.

Here let us consider two sayings of the Buddha when he was staying near Sarnath in Anāthapiṇḍika's pleasance, discoursing on *dhamma* that was centred on Nirvana. First: '*Bhikkhus*, there exists that condition wherein is neither earth nor water nor fire nor air; wherein is neither the sphere of infinite space nor of infinite consciousness nor of nothingness nor of neither-perception-nor-non-perception; where there is neither this world nor a world beyond nor both together nor moon and sun. Thence, *bhikkhus,* I declare is no coming to birth; thither is no going;[23] therein is no duration; thence is no falling; there is no arising. It is not something fixed, it moves not on, it is not based on anything. That indeed is the end of *dukkha*.'[24] And the second: '*Bhikkhus,* there is a not-born, a not-become, a not-made, a not-compounded. *Bhikkhus*, if that not-born, not-become, not-made, not-compounded were not, there would be apparent no escape from this here that is born, become, made, compounded. But since, *bhikkhus,* there is the not-born . . . not-compounded, therefore the escape (liberation) from this here that is born . . . compounded is apparent.'[25] These sayings are unequivocal affirmations of Transcendence.

We must see clearly that the end of *dukkha*, namely the timeless and unconditioned (the not-born), is not the mere opposite of the temporal and conditioned. The latter is in the sphere of duality, of birth-death, of finite elements coming together and falling apart; it is in the state of conflict, of *dukkha*, which is suffering or the ill-state; it is the not-transcendent. To transcend does not mean to be the opposite of the ill, the conditioned, but to be other than it without being separate from it. Otherwise, the so-called transcendent is but another finite, which would necessarily be something that comes to birth and dies, which is in conflict, which extends the continuity of *dukkha*. The transcendent holds the not-transcendent within itself. The not-transcendent displays all that we, existential mortals, can perceive and feel: coming, going, arising, falling, growing, developing, in short the entire becoming process, the restless ocean of *saṃsāra* which spells *dukkha*. This self-same *saṃsāra*, when rest-ful, when in its Sabbath, is the transmuted here-

[23] cf. Varāha Up., 3.5: 'To an exalted yogin there is neither birth nor death, nor going (to other spheres) nor returning (to earth); there is no stain or purity or knowledge, but everything shines as absolute consciousness.'

[24] Udāna, 8.1.

[25] Udāna, 8.3.

now which is no shadow-making obstruction but is wholly transparent to the transcendent. It is fully subsumed in the transcendent.

The conditioned is, as it were, the manifestation of the disturbance of the unconditioned. It is as if the vibrating of primordial energy in motionless space is the universe. No vibrating, and there is only the No-thing. No not-transcendent, and there is only the transcendent. But the vibrating is dependent upon the No-thing, the not-transcendent upon the transcendent, whereas the transcendent, the No-thing, the infinite, is not dependent upon the not-transcendent, upon the thing or the conditioned finite. Thus the Infinite is not the opposite of anything. Its absolute is-ness transcends – by a transcendence which wholly contains – all the conflict, the evil, the *dukkha* of all that we, as we are, perceive and feel.

If we do not understand this we fall into the error of striving for a desire-projected, finite goal, mistakenly named nirvana, an opposite of *dukkha*. We present to ourselves another picture of perfection put together by our ignorant, impure mind in the service of our pleasure-drive. It is because we are caught up in this error that we hold on to the re-incarnational misinterpretation of rebirth or *jāti*. Further, we restrict the meaning of *dukkha* to pain only. Pleasure, too, is characteristic of the conditioned state exactly as pain is. Pleasure runs its cycle, ages, breaks up and dies. In the first Noble Truth, *jarā* (ageing and breaking up) and *maraṇa* (dying) are expressly stressed, as much as is *jāti*, as constituting *dukkha*. Thus freedom from the conditioned state means freedom from both pleasure and pain. Since every situation, event, experience or state consists of both pleasurable and painful elements, both pleasure and pain are unavoidable in the process of daily life. The pleasure-pain mechanism is in fact indispensable for the healthy subsistence of the body. So the freedom from the unavoidably felt pleasure and pain can only mean freedom from attachment to pleasure and aversion from pain; from the conflict, the illusions, and all the evils that arise out of and flourish upon attachment and aversion. The freedom, in fact, is the freedom of mind (*ceto-vimutti*), a word constantly used by the Buddha.

Clearly then the teaching about *dukkha* is basically concerned with the mind, the receptive-responsive sensitivity of the living organism. If this sensitivity were absent there would be no pleasure-pain, no attachment-aversion; and our ordinary life as *human* beings would be impossible. Because we do have this sensitivity, because we are conditioned beings, and because we are ignorant, *dukkha*, both in its restricted, petty sense of personal misery and ill, also in its universal sense, is our real problem. Thus: no mind, no *dukkha*. Because there is mind, *dukkha* is experienced, and can be perceived, understood and transcended. This transcending is *not* an escaping from *dukkha*, but a ceasing to be a producer and maintainer of *dukkha*.

One other significant pointer to the profound sense and the transcendental context in which the Buddha considers *dukkha* must be understood. This is seen in that autobiographical discourse, the Ariyapariyesana Sutta, No. 26 in the Majjhima Nikāya: 'So I, *bhikkhus* . . . seeking the unborn, the uttermost security from the bonds, *nibbāna*, won the unborn, the uttermost security from the bonds, *nibbāna* . . . seeking the unageing . . . undecaying . . . undying . . . unsorrowing . . . the stainless . . . I won the unageing, undecaying, undying, unsorrowing, stainless, the uttermost security from the bonds, *nibbāna*. Knowledge and vision arose in me: unshakable is freedom for me, this is the last *jāti*, there is not now again-becoming.' (M., 1.167)

What is the unborn, unageing, undecaying, undying, sorrowless, stainless? Obviously not anything bodily. Is it mental, psychical? Equally not, for feelings, thoughts, moods and states of mind, all apprehensions and cognitions and all that is named by the mind or held in consciousness, and consciousness itself as it functions in us as existential beings, are all conditioned, temporal expressions. Not body, not mind, is the unborn, undying, the transcendental Real or *nibbāna*.

The Unborn was sung by the Ṛg-vedic poet-seers.[26] The Upaniṣadic teachers realized it as Brahman, and to them it was, 'That from which speech and mind return, not having found'.[27] How then did they realize it at all since any and every instrument of knowledge, any ways to the transcendent or techniques of realization are themselves conditioned means and states and not the Unconditioned? Here we come to that which bears the name of Atman.

What did these teachers declare? 'That Atman is not this; it is not that; it is unseizable for it cannot be seized; it is indestructible for it cannot be destroyed. It is unattached for it does not attach itself. It is unbound. It does not tremble. It is not injured.'[28] Clearly Atman is not the conditioned. It is transcendent, for it is unattached and it does not attach itself. It does not tremble – that is, it does not move, thrill,

[26] AV., 9.5.20; 10.7.31; 10.8.41. RV., 1.67.3; 1.164.6; 8.41.10; 10.82.6. As the One, or that One thing, or One Supreme Being or Spirit: 10.82.2; 10.129.2. (As *Aja ekapād*: 10.65.13; 6.50.14; AV., 13.1.6; 19.11.3.)

[27] Taitt. Up., 2.4,9. Tejobindu, 1.20; 3.8,38. Sāṇḍilya, 2.

[28] Bṛh. Up., 4.4.22; 4.5.15.

vibrate, or act in our conditional sense of these words. Here there is no fear; the Atman needs no protection, for it cannot be attacked or injured.

'Verily,' says Yājñavalkya, 'that great unborn Atman, undecaying, undying, immortal, fearless, is Brahman. Verily Brahman is fearless. He who knows this becomes the fearless Brahman.'[29] 'That is the Atman, free from evil, ageless, deathless, sorrowless, hungerless, thirstless, whose desire is the Real, whose conception is the Real. He should be searched out, Him one should desire to understand.'[30]

In the third chapter of the Tejobindu Upaniṣad, cast in the form of the Divine Dialogue, Śiva tells his son, Kārttikeya the Kumāra: 'Being purely of the nature of Brahman, I am the eternal Atmā . . . I am the primeval consciousness alone, the partless and non-dual essence, beyond the reach of speech and mind . . . I am of the nature of the all-void . . . and ever of the nature of the unborn . . . I am the unconditioned, the permanent and the unborn.' And in chapter six of the same Upaniṣad, Ṛbhu teaches his disciple Nidāgha: 'I am the supreme Atman . . . the birthless and deathless Brahman . . . the unconditioned, the stainless.'

The question, how did these teachers realize the Unconditioned Transcendent and then affirm it, may now be considered. The Adhyātma Upaniṣad says: 'That is called *samādhi* in which the attention, rising above (that is, become free of) the conception of the contemplator and the contemplation, merges gradually into the state of the contemplated, like a light undisturbed by the wind. Even the mental states are not known (at the time when one is in the embrace of Atman). They are only inferred from the recollection which takes place after *samādhi*. Through this *samādhi* . . . pure *dharma* is developed. Knowers of yoga call this *samādhi dharma-megha* (Truth cloud; or cloud of unknowing) . . . then, that in which speech was hidden till now, appears no longer so and shines as Truth.'

In *samādhi*, attentiveness has become free of all separate self-consciousness. Differentiation between cognizing subject and cognized object has ceased. The living psycho-physical organism of the yogi in *samādhi* is there, unquestionably a distinct, finite entity. But he is no longer 'awake' and 'knowing', in the conditioned state and in the finite sense. Subsumed wholly in the Unconditioned Atman, 'he' is neither conscious nor unconscious, neither personal nor impersonal (and

[29] Bṛh. Up., 4.4.25.
[30] Chānd. Up., 8.7.1,3.

certainly not de-personalized!). We could use the term superconscious. But perhaps it would help us to understand more clearly what happens if we were to use terms such as trans-personal and trans-conscious in order to suggest that the transcending leads to being wholly other than the self-conscious person without being separate from the person, and to the integration of personal and impersonal, which is a profounder dimension of Being than either personal or impersonal.

Is not this *samādhi* the meaning of 'winning' the unborn, the unageing, the undying, the unsorrowing, the unstained? Is the Atman of the Upaniṣads, in truth, any different from the unborn Unconditioned, the end of ill, the uttermost security from the bonds, *nibbāna*, which the Buddha sought and found?

Now the Buddha gave a categorical answer to the question, 'What is the cause of *dukkha*?' His practical, and at the same time transcendental answer was *taṇhā* – that is, craving, or, in its special form, the fever of longing.

As a prelude to the consideration of *taṇhā*, let us see the significance of the transcendental answer to the experienced fact of *dukkha*, the ill-state. It is not an alleviation of evil, or a prevention, a counterpoise, a consolation, a repairing or in short anything that the mind of man as he is can think of or do. It is not a mere rejection or resigned acceptance or compromise or relentless onslaught upon and destruction of evil as the objective fact. *It is a transmutation of one's own mind.* The transmuted mind is marked by its natural, effortless negation of all worldliness. The liberated intelligence – that is the power to see the truth with unerring insight and freedom from inner conflict, from the burden of mere beliefs, assumptions, preconceptions, prejudice and bias, in short, from any conditioned state – and the heart of love wherein greed, hate and delusion are extinguished, all characterize the transmuted mind. It is the whole and free mind, peaceful and wise. We conditioned mortals, suffering endless conflict in our impure, unredeemed state, are in no position to attempt a critical examination of such a mind, the mind of any Perfected Holy One. We are wholly free however, to enquire, to learn, to understand and to realize truth.

The fact that the answer of the Holy Ones is the transcendental answer is in itself strong evidence that *all* this, that is, all worldliness, the 'world of the flesh and the devil', is evil, the ill-state. We as we are cannot deal with evil and the reason is simple: I as I am, am the producer of evil! I as I am must undergo transformation. But no transformation is possible as thought out or projected by my mind, for my ill-mind cannot generate the pure. I must remain intensely mindful as the Buddha taught, passively watchful, as Krishnamurti says, alert in every fibre of my whole being, and *allow* the transformation to come about. This is the key, in brief, to the transmuting of the ill-mind. The actual transmutation which is the culmination of the process, long or short as it may be, takes place in a flash. It is peculiarly like the 50-million degree temperature for 1-millionth of a second which transmutes one chemical element into another. The Ṛg-veda symbolized this white-heat state by the god Agni; Zarathuśtra by the Holy Fire, the Fire which was the Son of Ahurā-Mazdā. This is the Fire referred to when it is said that the Christ will baptize with Fire.

The serious, religious-minded person is likely to see – the others refuse to see – that all worldliness is the ill-state. If he does really see and not merely deduce logically or believe blindly that all worldliness is evil, he will also see that the world – the world as nature's fact – is good, in a sense similar to that in which it is said in the first chapter of Genesis, 'And God saw it was good'. It is this which makes it possible to live in the world and disengage ourselves from the ill-state of being *of* the world.

At the centre of worldliness lies *taṇhā*, the craving for things and experiences: the pleasures of the senses; the ambition to become wealthy, powerful, great or learned, or to achieve any goal whether secular or spiritual. This craving is responsible for *dukkha*.

Now this *dukkha* includes an element, sorrow (*śoka*), which is *dukkha*'s cure. This sorrow is the passion. It is another pointer to the fact that the Great Teachers were concerned essentially with evil and suffering in the profoundest sense, and to which the only answer could be the transcendental answer.

To see this, consider first the opening of the seventh chapter of the Chāndogya Upaniṣad. The sage Nārada approaches Sanatkumāra and says, 'Teach me, Venerable Sir'. Sanatkumāra says, 'Tell me what you already know. Then I will teach you what is beyond'. Nārada retails all his skills and his knowledge of the Scriptures, and ends as follows: 'Such an one am I, Venerable Sir, knowing the sacred sayings but not knowing the Atman. It has been heard by me from those who are like you, Sir, that he who knows the Atman crosses over sorrow (*śoka*). Such a sorrowing one am I, Sir. Do you, Sir, cause me to cross over to the other side of sorrow.' The intellectually rich sage, Nārada, was one who had not realized Atman, though he knew its verbal meaning. This was his divine passion, his sorrow. The Muṇḍaka

Upaniṣad says (3.2.9): 'He verily who knows the supreme Brahman becomes that very Brahman . . . He crosses over sorrow (*śoka*). He crosses over sin. Liberated from the knots of the heart he becomes immortal.' The realization of the Transcendent is the answer, then, to *śoka*. In the Ariyapariyesana Sutta (M., 1.173) when the Buddha says 'Seeking the un-sorrowing . . . I won the un-sorrowing', the word he uses, significantly, is *a-soka*.

The *paṭicca-samuppāda* is the Buddha's exposition of the arising and the ceasing of ill, *dukkha*. Its basic principle is simple: this not being, that becomes not; by the ceasing of this, that ceases to be. *Paṭicca-samuppāda* means dependent origination, or conditioned genesis. 'Depending upon ignorance (*avijjā*) are the predisposed activities of mind, speech and action (*sankhārā*). Depending upon these tendencies is discriminative consciousness (*viññāṇa*). Depending upon consciousness is name and shape (*nāma-rūpa*).' *Nāma-rūpa* is also understood as body-mind or the psycho-physical or individual organism. And in this strain the cycle runs on through the six sense-fields (*saḷāyatana*), contact (*phassa*), feeling or sensation (*vedanā*), craving (*taṇhā*), grasping (*upādāna*), becoming (*bhava*), birth or the arising of aggregates (*jāti*), decay and death (*jarā-maraṇa*), sorrow (*śoka*), lamentation, pain, grief and despair. Such is the uprising of this entire mass of ill.

'But from the utter fading away and ceasing of ignorance (comes) the ceasing of activities . . . ageing, dying, sorrow, grief, lamentation and despair. Such is the ceasing of this entire mass of ill.'

In which way can this 'utter fading away and ceasing' process work in me, the existential being? Ignorance having faded away, the volitional activities, *sankhārā*, cease to be; consciousness having faded away, *nāma-rūpa*, that is name-form, or body-mind, ceases to be. But if consciousness and body-mind, the whole of me the existential being, has utterly faded away and ceased to be, the rest of the *paṭicca-samuppāda* is cut off. There is no arriving at craving, birth, death. The problem of *dukkha*, the treading of the Middle Way, the realizing of *nibbāna* is smashed up.

Obviously, then, *nāma-rūpa* cannot refer to me the whole existential being. I the psycho-physical organism, continually changing, must continue alive.

Let us recall what was said above (pp. 161 f.): the teaching about *dukkha,* in the context of the existential being, is basically concerned with the mind: no mind, no *dukkha*. The *paṭicca-samuppāda* exposes the rationale of *dukkha.* Thereby it lays bare the mechanism of the ill-mind. Thus it immediately becomes clear that *nāma-rūpa* refers to the shape of the thought or emotion, to the 'thought-form', which is the *rūpa*, and its verbal designation,[31] its *nāma*, by which we recognize that *rūpa*. The consciousness of, and the actual content, shape and name of a thought, a feeling, a mood, a state of mind, can undergo change, can in fact utterly fade away and cease to be without me the person being extinguished. If it is insisted that *nāma-rūpa* is to be taken in the literal sense of the living person, then on the night of the Enlightenment, Siddhattha Gotama, the living *nāma-rūpa*, should have utterly faded away and ceased to be, as the inevitable consequence of the extinction of ignorance (*avijjā*) and of the activities (*sankhārā*) in which case it is unlikely that for twenty-five centuries at least people would be trying to understand a *paṭicca-samuppāda*!

We must briefly look into the actual working of the *paṭicca-samuppāda* in daily living. I the person have to use my senses and mind throughout the day. There is an object, here is my eye. If the light from the object passes through my eye and I am conscious of the object, there is contact, *phassa*; or we may say an impression has been made. If there is pure, unreactive observation only, that could be the end of the story. If after such contact I have a feeling, *vedanā*, of pleasure or pain, I could still note dispassionately the objective fact that there was a feeling of pleasure or pain, and the story would end there. This, however, happens rarely. Owing to my ignorance and to my predilections or tendencies, my store of likes and dislikes from infancy onwards, I feel repulsion towards any painful impression. All that emerges thereafter – annoyance, anger, conflict, anxiety, loss, pain, etc. – is *dukkha*. If I feel attraction towards the pleasant impression, my attachment to pleasure grows and impels me to repeat it. Thus there arises craving, *taṇhā*, which in contexts like sex or wealth or power can rage like a deadly fever. From there to the end of the cycle of *dukkha* is obvious.

The factual starting point is the use of my senses, and it is impossible to live at all without using the senses. The troublemaker after the operation of the senses is the arising of attachment or aversion, the excited desire. This happens inevitably because of my ignorance, my predilections, in short, because of my past conditioning. One root source of my *dukkha*, the negative or passive one of ignorance, I cannot be free of at the beginning. I can read the Scriptures, or I can be told that

[31] As also its informing principle or vitalizing energy.

ignorance consists in not knowing the Four Noble Truths: all this is *dukkha*, suffering; there is a cause of *dukkha*; *dukkha* can be completely ended; there is a Way – the Noble Eightfold Way – for the extinction of suffering. Intellectual acceptance of those verbal statements is not actual enlightenment, not the extinction of ignorance.

The other root, positive and active, namely craving, *taṇhā*, is the one I have to deal with. Enlightenment, or ignorance extinguished, is the transcendent state of fully awakened awareness. For me, at this moment, that is still hidden. But I in this very moment am well aware of my craving, even if at first I cannot see it in its totality. By constant mindfulness there comes freedom from craving. Thereupon the rest of the cycle up to death never arises in my mind. In other words, there is the extinction of *dukkha*.

Says the worldly man: 'I am not interested in this enlightenment, this airy-fairy flight into transcendence. Is not ordinary, normal life good enough? Of course there are difficulties, pains, sorrows. But I can take them in my stride, which in fact I do, more or less. And especially nowadays, at least in welfare states, life is quite good, with its pleasures and opportunities, its comfort and security. I have my own simple religious life – I worship God, I help my neighbour in a sensible way, I do not harm anybody.' Such is the attitude of many people. They will progress no further than lightly wearing the cloak of religion. Then there are those who, driven by difficulty or fear or some such cause, flee to religion for consolation, for the assuagement of pain. If religion acts upon them anaesthetically, they might as well have not been touched by religious feelings and doctrines, for they will spend their days with blinkered eyes. And, too, there is that little multitude which is engaged in professional practice under the banner of religion.

Yet there is no insuperable obstacle to prevent anyone soever from realizing the religious life at its very heart, if one all-powerful element is present – transcendental sorrow. *This* sorrow was in Nārada, in Siddhattha Gotama, in Jesus (in whose life-and-death story it finds poignantly dramatic expression) and indeed in all who realize the transcendent.

The *paṭicca-samuppāda* is presented throughout as the closed circle of mournful mortality. It is the way of ill which makes this world a vale of tears, lorded over by the Prince of Darkness. There is one solitary exception to this presentation. It occurs in the Saṃyutta Nikāya.[32] After tracing the factors in the usual way from ignorance up to *jāti*,

[32] S., 2.30 f.

the conditioned state, the next item is not the usual *jarā-maraṇa*, ageing and dying. It proceeds, instead, as follows: 'Becoming is causally associated with grasping, birth (*jāti*) with becoming, sorrow (*dukkha*) with birth, faith with sorrow, joy with faith, rapture with joy, serenity with rapture, happiness with serenity, concentration with happiness, the knowledge and vision into things as they really are with concentration, disenchantment with the knowledge and vision into things as they really are, passionlessness (*virāga*) with disenchantment, liberation with passionlessness, knowledge about extinction (of intoxicants, *āsavas*) with liberation.'

What is this sorrow which is usually associated with *jāti*? It is not only the personal misery associated with the pains and frustrations and anxieties experienced in the conditioned state, trapped in the cage of evil. It is also the transcendental sorrow that one is not in perfect communion; that the unborn, unageing, undying, unsorrowing and unstained, which is the uttermost security from the bonds, *nibbāna*, is still distant, still unrealized, not only by oneself, but also by mankind. It is *this* which makes a Siddhattha leave home, undergo asceticism close to death till the Transcendent be found. If this burning passion does not pierce through one's heart, no freedom from self-ness, no communion with the Transcendent can be realized, and one stagnates in the ranks of the religious dilettanti.

This sensitivity, experienced as anguish at this stage, never deadens. It grows in intensity as it flowers into divine compassion. But this means that *dukkha* as the world-woe has entered into and suffused one's whole being. There is complete personal involvement, in the form of active compassion, with the whole of *saṃsāra*, the becoming process. Reject any part of it, refuse to respond to each and every moment as it flows past, and one is again a producer and maintainer of evil. This personal involvement is an involvement free of all self-ness. Hence one drinks of the poisoned cup of the world's evil and, unstained, transmutes it.

This transcendental sorrow is the wound of love. Cherish it and tend it, for this wound allows the river of Life Abundant to flow out of it, the river of *mahā-karuṇā*, the Great Compassion. It releases understanding by the heart, and one knows that oneself is ignorant. It silences the chatter born of ego-centred craving. There arises faith, the faith which is the assurance that in the silence is contained healing love and enlightening truth. When the mind is empty, 'in its natural state', as Tibetan Buddhism puts it, the creative action of the transcendent nothing proceeds unhindered. This gives rise to joy, rapture, serenity and the other factors culminating in liberation and knowledge about the extinction of the *āsavas*.

The word *āsava* means an exudation, or outflow, as from a sore or from a tree which has been slashed. It also means the intoxicating extract of a tree or flower. Psychologically, the word stands for ideas which muddle the mind so that it cannot rise to higher things. The four *āsavas* are those of sense-pleasure, the lust for becoming this or that according to one's ambitions, speculative views and ignorance. The extinction of the *āsavas* means that the mind is free of craving, void of fantasy and of delusion. This is the empty mind, the silent mind. Cleansed of awareness in worldly terms, free of ill (*dukkha*), there is present pure awareness of the actual 'IS' here and now. This is transcendental awareness. It does not overflow, spill over, into the forms of worldliness. *Dukkha* is extinct. And yet, the liberated one holds the world's *dukkha* in his heart.

Whereas the first and second truths – *dukkha* and *taṇhā* – lie in the worldly context, presenting the greatest of all problems, *viz.* man's salvation, the third truth – the extinction of *dukkha* – clearly lies in the transcendental context. This throws a searchlight on the fourth truth: the Way leading to the extinction of ill. It lies, too, and can only lies, in the transcendental context. The third and fourth truths therefore are transcendental truths. The nature of the Way to the extinction of *dukkha* cannot lie in the realm of *dukkha* for then the way would be characterized by all that marks *dukkha*. But the Way is the negation, the resolution, of *dukkha*. Each of its eight constituents[33] is prefixed by *sammā*, which means right or perfect. In this context, the word 'right' is too feeble: 'perfect' is true to the quality or nature of the Way. For the perfect Way resolves absolutely the conflict of the duals which characterize the whole realm of *dukkha* – the realm in your mind or my mind – and it negates everything including the highest values and noblest living that emerge out of the mind in the state of *dukkha*, that is, out of the impure mind.

This Way, the *Majjhima-Paṭipadā*, is the way of the Empty Silent Mind. It is the Way of the NO-THING, or the Nothing Between, the Way of the Void. This is the Stainless meaning of the Middle Way: that Middle which is the Unconditioned, the Transcendent which is unconstrained by space, time, matter, form, cause or anything whatsoever that the mind of man as such can ever seize or know. But that 'Middle', the non-measurable, is the fount of Action which is Beneficence – so

[33] Views, aspirations, speech, action, mode of living, effort, mindfulness and communion.

Nirvana is spoken of as non-finitely blissful. To our discriminative consciousness, that invisible Action and Beneficence are as Non-Action, for our discriminative consciousness, *viññāṇa*, can perceive only separative and disturbing activity, activity which generates fresh conflict. It cannot perceive that Action which is perfect equilibrium. So, Buddhist teaching, with that superb psychological wisdom which characterizes it, never attempts any positive verbal formulation of the Transcendent, but confines itself to negating the not-transcendent. For example, Perfect Vision is not declared by Sāriputta to be such and such a view or vision, but is declared to be the clear perception that all-this (that is the experienced existential world of birth, ageing and dying) is *dukkha*, the not-well, *anattā*, the not-unborn and not un-dying.[34]

The *paṭicca-samuppāda* presents the rationale or mechanism of *dukkha*, of the mortal, the dual, the conflicting. The *Majjhima Paṭipadā* is the Way of Transcendence. Perfect understanding, aspiration, speech, action, living, effort, mindfulness and communion *is* the Transcendent, the Perfect. The indispensable preliminary ground for this Holy Living is the *sīlas*, the moralities, presented with typical psychological wisdom in negative form as not hurting, not stealing, no sense-indulgence, no wrong speech, etc.

The Middle Way is usually understood to mean the avoidance of the extreme of self-tormenting asceticism on the one hand and self-indulging sensuality on the other. But look clearsightedly into the true nature of the Middle Way, above all tread it, and it will be luminously realized that the Perfect Way, in meaning, implication and factual living, utterly transcends all our worldly meanings, implications and practical expressions of asceticism and sensuality. Contemplate that statement by the Buddha in the Prajñāpāramitā:[35] 'Just the path is enlightenment, just enlightenment is the path', and it will be clear that the *Majjhima Paṭipadā* is the Way of Transcendence, a wholly other-worldly Way, but *in* the world. And this is the supreme meaning of asceticism and the ascetic life. The true recluse is the one who is in complete relationship with everyone and everything and simultaneously is The Alone. His very life is the luminous, austere Middle Way, the most powerful evidence that the absence of Perfect Communion is the supreme evil.

* * *

[34] M. I. 48,49,54.
[35] *Selected Sayings from the Perfection of Wisdom*, E. Conze, p. 115.

The Purāṇas present the deep teachings of the Hindus in mythological form. In the Bhāgvata Purāṇa[36] it is related that the Earth, oppressed by hosts of demons (*daityas*) born as proud kings, sought Brahma. The Father-God, accompanied by other gods, by Earth and cow with tearful face, piteously lowing, and poured out her plaint to Brahmā (God the Father) as her refuge. She appeared in the form of the Lord Śiva, the third Person of the Hindu Trinity, proceeded to the shore of the ocean of milk, the abode of the Lord Viṣṇu. Brahmā first prayed to Viṣṇu in terms of the Puruṣa Sūkta.[37] Entering into a superconscious state in which he heard a voice in the sky, Brahmā said to the gods: 'Hear from me, O gods, the word of the Supreme Person (Viṣṇu), and then act accordingly at once: let there be no delay. The affliction of Mother Earth had already been known by the Supreme Person. (Therefore) let yourselves be born among the Yadus (the kingly race from which Kṛṣṇa was born) in part manifestation (and continue there) until the Supreme Lord walks on earth, reducing the burden of Mother Earth through His own Envoy in the shape of Time. The Lord Viṣṇu himself will be manifested in the house of Vasudeva; let celestial women (also therefore) be born for His pleasure. With intent to do what pleases Śrī Hari the thousand-headed self-shining Lord Ananta (the serpent-god Śeṣa), a part manifestation of Lord Vasudeva, will precede Him (as His elder brother). Commanded by the Lord, the Divine Māyā of Lord Viṣṇu by whom the universe stands bewitched, will also be born in part manifestation for the purpose of doing his work.'

The answer to the cry of Mother Earth is the birth of Kṛṣṇa, the Lord Himself incarnate. It is the transcendent answer.

The teachings of Śrī Kṛṣṇa are contained in the Bhagavad Gītā. The warrior, Arjuna, is overcome with the consciousness of committing a great sin in endeavouring to kill others from greed of the pleasures of kingship.[38] In terms of worldly ethic Arjuna and his four brothers are entering upon a righteous war against their cousins who treacherously and unjustly deprived them of their kingdom. Yet when Arjuna faces the fact of the actual situation he is conscious of greed of the pleasures of kingship in his own soul, of the sin of killing, and of all the evils that will inevitably follow the carnage of war. Here is the problem of the evil in the psyche.

Kṛṣṇa gives Arjuna the transcendent answer: by yoga realize Brahman; by devotion to Me, know Me in essence and enter into THAT (the

[36] Bhāg. Purāṇa, 10.1.15-25.
[37] RV., 10.90.
[38] B.G., 1.45.

Supreme) by My grace; renouncing everything come unsorrowing to Me alone as the haven, for I will liberate you from all sins.[39] In the course of his teaching he speaks of insight into the pain and evil of birth, death, old age and sickness,[40] and of liberation from birth, death, old age and sorrow (*dukkha*).[41] Throughout the discourses he points out the root ills in the psyche – desire, greed, passion, anger, fear, ignorance, delusion; he shows Arjuna the path of purification from these ills; and he names the virtues which mark him whose soul is pure.

This riddance of evil in the psyche is also taught in the Upaniṣads and in yoga as the indispensable preliminary to liberation from that most radical evil, the absence of perfect communion. To effect this they laid down the disciplines known as *yama* and *niyama*,[42] together with meditation. The key to the discipline is well expressed in the verse: 'When all the desires that dwell in the heart are cast away, then does the mortal become immortal, then he enjoys Brahman of his own accord.'[43] Desires that dwell in the heart (mind) arise out of the experience of pleasurable and painful sensations. Life inevitably presents us with pleasurable as well as painful experiences, out of which grow mental attachment to the pleasurable and aversion to the painful. We desire the repetition of the pleasurable and the avoidance of the painful. The right operation of the pleasure-pain mechanism is necessary for the well-being of the body. It is also important for the well-being of the psyche, but with a difference: when the mind becomes the thrall of desire, the psyche is diseased, it is evil; and, lusting stupidly for pleasure, it makes the body, too, diseased and vile.

The slave of sensuous desire lives sub-humanly, with mind confused and full of delusions and illusions. When freed from such slavery, the human being can realize the Transcendent, if his whole desire impels him towards communion. *This* desire is utterly unlike the 'desires that dwell in the mind'. It must be clearly understood that desire-energy cannot be extirpated and only the ignorant person or the deliberate evil-doer would attempt it, and of course fail. Desire-energy is the psychical expression of the functioning of the electro-chemical energy of the body. The right expression of desire depends upon the clear seeing of the facts of the immediate situation as a whole, that is, the within as well as the without, oneself and the environment. The supremely

[39] B.G., 18th Discourse.
[40] B.G., 13.8.
[41] B.G., 14.20.
[42] See above, p. 40, and below, pp. 256 ff.
[43] Bṛh. Up., 4.4.7; Kaṭha Up., 6.14.

right desire is the desire, which is the perfect passion, for the realization of Brahman-Atman.

Yājñavalkya says to Kahola Kauśītakeya: 'The Atman is that which transcends hunger and thirst, sorrow and delusion, old age and death. Those Brahmans who have known that Atman, who have overcome the desire for sons, the desire for wealth, the desire for worlds, live the life of mendicants. For desire for sons is the desire for wealth, and desire for wealth is the desire for worlds, for both these are but desires.'[44] Yājñavalkya ends his exposition of the Atman to Kahola, as also to Uśasta Cakrāyana and to Uddālaka Āruṇi, with the affirmation, 'aught else than Him (the Atman) is wretched'.[45]

* * *

The Great Teachers clearly understood the facts of evil and suffering. They showed, each in his own manner, the way of release from the ill-state. They had true insight. So they presented no Utopia, no fool's paradise. Moral purity and mental sanity were keynotes in their teaching.

Whoso cared, could cease to do evil. Those who did, left the unimpeachable testimony of simple, holy lives. But the evil and suffering in the world through the ages prove how few were those who really cared.

And today . . .?

* * *

THE JUDEO-CHRISTIAN APPROACH

The One Total Reality, the absolute all, contains you and me and everything. Here and now, I the ordinary man am conscious of this Reality in the worldly mode, the mode of isolative self-consciousness and of multiplicity. Confined to ambivalence, I experience Reality as the conflict or alternation of good and evil, joy and sorrow, vice and virtue, in short, of all the duals.

Like all living creatures, I undergo change. If that change is such that religiousness within me comes to full fruition, the consciousness of Reality in the worldly mode undergoes radical transformation. Transcendence realizes itself through the psycho-physical existent that bears my name. Then there is beatific awareness of existence in the mode of

[44] Bṛh. Up., 3.5.
[45] Bṛh. Up., 3.5; 3.4.2; 3.7.23.

immortality, most intensely so in supreme communion, the I AM state.[46] There is no isolative self-consciousness in the midst of the factual multiplicity, no confinement to ambivalence and hence no conflict of the duals psychologically. Life is wholly VIRTUOUS[47] – a sharp contrast to the life confined to consciousness in the worldly mode.

There are not two (or more) different worlds, a material world on the one hand and a spiritual on the other. It is my mode of awareness of the one Reality which undergoes various changes right up to the full transformation possible for me. In each of these changed modes of awareness I see the One Reality in a different way. Instead of recognizing and admitting that it is I who see the One Reality in a different way according to my different mode of awareness – worldly or inspired or enlightened – I assert, mistakenly, that there are different worlds: material, mental, spiritual, demonic and so on. In the transcendent or immortal mode of awareness the One Total Reality is experienced in its unbroken holiness.

The emergence of the intensely sensitive, living awareness of Transcendence is the creative source of all the scriptures. The Holy Ones of very ancient times transmitted the esoteric wisdom orally – the original Qabalah and the Veda for instance. In later millennia some of this sacred knowledge was committed to writing. All these scriptures are concerned with the nature and action of Transcendence in mankind and its self-realization through individual men. They tell the story of the stirring into life of man's dormant sense of Transcendence and of its unfolding and fruitive transformation into intensest awareness in full communion. Realized Transcendence can never be literally formulated in thought and speech. It may be named – God, YHWH, Ain Soph, Brahman, Atman, Super-Essential Reality and so on – provided we remember that the Name is an indefinable sound representing real transcendent energy. The state of realized Transcendence, which is the factual condition of Revelation, cannot be transmitted, for it is the flight of the 'alone to the Alone' in the words of Plotinus; or in the words of the Buddha, the *sammā sambodhi*, the perfect total awakening which is a self-awakening, the lone-awakening; it is the *asamprajñāta samādhi* of the Hindu.

What can be transmitted, in the early stages, are the teachings which can help the aspirant to grow towards realization. At an advanced stage the transmission of an influence which acts as a fecundating energy on the mind of the disciple (the 'son' of the prophet or guru)

[46] See above p. 67.
[47] See below, chapter 17.

who proves his worthiness to receive it from the Holy One can be effected. The disciple is tried to the limits of his power. This is 'Temptation'. It is a trial not only of moral and/or intellectual strength but also of spiritual power: that is, of undergoing a transformation of the inner depths of consciousness itself – and this is not directly perceived and remains unknown to me in my ordinary consciousness in my worldly state – without any shattering effect on my morality and my intellectual functions. For it must be remembered that such transformation of the inner depths of consciousness manifests as a sweeping away of the old order so that the New Man may emerge. The emergence of the New Man is a *transformation of consciousness* and does not consist in modifying my old ideas or burdening myself with a different set of beliefs. The sweeping away of the old order can be a purifying and regenerating tide or an evil-producing explosion. The first Adam (me myself in the sinful state of duality and worldliness) failed the test. The second Adam (me myself in the sinless state of transcendent awareness) succeeded, and hence redeemed man (*adam*).

When Elijah was 'taken up to heaven',[48] his 'mantle' fell from him and was taken up by Elisha. This mantle is divine glory – *Shehinah* – radiant power, a transcendent energy. Its falling and its being taken up by Elisha expresses poetically the transmission of this transcendent energy to Elisha who, previously, on Elijah's saying, 'Ask what I shall do for thee, before I be taken away from thee', had answered, 'I pray thee, let a double portion[49] of thy spirit be upon me'. Elisha was able to receive Elijah's transmission and respond to it – he 'saw' Elijah being taken up to heaven. The meaning is that Elisha was enabled to enter the same or a similar state of profound realization of Transcendence as did Elijah. This is a great example of spiritual induction. The biblical narrative is a symbolic picture of what takes place in the psyche and in the innermost depths of mind, as Teacher and disciple sit together in *silent* meditation and realize the wordless Truth, free of thought-forms, in pure communion.[50]

* * *

[48] 2 Kings, 2.1-14.

[49] A Jewish father's bequest to his eldest son was a 'double portion', that is, twice as much to him as to each of the other sons. In the religious context the disciple nearest to the Teacher in spiritual realization was designated the eldest son.

[50] Many such examples are scattered through the scriptures. For example: The Father-and-Son Ceremony, or The Transmission, in the Kauṣītaki Up., 2.15 and in Bṛh. Up., 1.5.17: the incident when the Buddha holds up a flower and Kaśyapa

An old tradition has it that there are certain keys to unlock the esoteric Wisdom of the Holy Ones. Hints and clues are given, usually in veiled form, in the written scriptures. It is useful to consider a few essential points regarding these keys, bearing in mind that the original teachings were given orally by those who probably lived in the lands stretching from the Fertile Crescent and the shores of the Caspian to the Himalayas, thousands of years ago.

Their basic principle was that all that exists composes a universe which is a whole consisting of co-related parts. Numbers, letters, colours, sounds, shapes, patterns, elements (earth, water, etc.), configurations (of the stars for example), ideas and concepts, events and actions, states of mind and modes of awareness, and all energies, physical or mental, are all correlates. The material and spiritual, the mortal and immortal, bore a relationship to each other expressed in such phrases as: 'the microcosm (man) is the reflection of the macrocosm', and 'as above, so below', phrases which it is easy to misunderstand or apply incorrectly in particular contexts.

A correlative pattern can give information about its correlates. For instance, a pattern of behaviour can tell me if someone likes me or dislikes me; a pattern of gestures can warn me of danger ahead or assure me it is safe to go on. More complex correlates are patterns of letters and numbers. For instance, $s=\frac{1}{2}gt^2$, or $e=mc^2$; this is *abracadabra* to the uninitiated, but lucidly meaningful to the knowing one. The above examples are straightforward; they can be understood by most people. But the systems of correlates concerning religious teachings and practices are so worded that they often baffle rather than clarify.

The esoteric wisdom concerning God, man and the cosmos had its codes in ancient India, Iran and the Fertile Crescent. Letters and numbers, for instance, were correlated to metaphysical concepts. Colours, sounds, the elements and the signs of the zodiac were correlated to the Sephiroth, to the angelic and demonic orders, to modes of awareness, to mental states and to the nature and functioning of various energies, psychical and spiritual.

Religious rituals, specially designed for the initiated, and the several systems of yoga, were of great importance in the living of the religious life. But when the Chaldeans descended to ill practices and magic, Abram, who was afterwards called Abraham, took the sacred know-

---

smiles. When he who has realized holiness and has developed the necessary power to do so, lays his hands in the act of consecration on the recipient's head, there is a real transmission of energy.

ledge of the Qabalah westwards towards Canaan in order to preserve the Revelation in its pristine purity. The Revelation is hidden in the Qabalah which is the main root of the tree of Judeo-Christian religious teaching. And the root of a tree is within the earth, invisible to the eye of flesh.

It is easy to give names to some of these keys, such as music, mathematics, astronomy, gymnastics, alchemy, yoga, philosophy. But words like music or astronomy can be misleading rather than illuminating. Today, music does not usually mean ritualistic intoning or *mantras*, or the use of gongs or drums for producing psychical effects or a religious atmosphere; and astronomy does not mean, for the scientific astronomer, the use of the symbolism of the zodiac (astrology). However, even as extra-sensory perception is being investigated today, scientifically and psychologically, so too the old keys to wisdom need an open-minded enquiry, free of both credulity and incredulity. Such an enquiry lies outside the scope of this book, but a few relevant points need mention.

In the I AM state there is Awareness-Being as unitary wholeness. I the individual person am the nexus, in and through which the One Total Reality realizes Itself. There is no otherness present, no differentiation. This state is 'alive'; active but unstirring; without movement. When disturbing movement starts up in this rhythmic vibrant poise, the emergence out of the I AM state and the change back to ordinary sense-mind consciousness sets in. Thereupon the proliferation of the single Awareness of the unitary wholeness of the One Total Reality into the separative consciousness of its many aspects takes place, and the previously undifferentiated Totality which was realized as a unitary whole is then cognized and presented in two main aspects: as the innumerable differentiated particulars, measurable, finite and mortal, of our everyday sense experience and cognition; and as a transcendent unit, immeasurable, non-finite and immortal.

This transcendent unit has been presented by all the great religions in their own way: as the one and only God; as trinities which are triune unities; as many gods constituting a single whole (sometimes completely including all finite, differentiated particulars).[51]

Of these presentations one of the most remarkable is the theosophic doctrine of the Zohar.[52] In this doctrine the term *Sephira* (plural *Sephir-*

[51] See RV., 1.164.46, and the presentation of Brahman and Atman in the Upaniṣads.

[52] See *Major Trends in Jewish Mysticism*, C. G. Scholem, p. 205 ff. and *The Zohar*, trans. Sperling and Simon, 5 vols.

oth) plays an important part. Its original meaning was number, which changed in time to signify the emergence of divine powers and emanations. God in himself is hidden, the dark Unknown. This inmost Being of God, regarded as devoid of qualities and attributes, is called by the Zohar and the Qabalists, *Ain-Soph*, the Infinite. When God relinquishes his state of rest and turns to creation, the first pulse transforms *Ain-Soph*, the fullness, into the mystical no-thingness, whence all the other stages of God's Self-revelation in the ten *Sephiroth* emanate. The emanation of the *Sephiroth* is seen as a process which takes place *in* God and which at the same time enables man to perceive God. The ten *Sephiroth* constitute the mystical Tree of God, each *Sephira* representing a branch whose common root is *Ain-Soph*, the hidden Root of all roots and also the sap of the Tree.

The ten *Sephiroth* are:

1. *Kether Elyon,*	the 'supreme crown' of God;
2. *Ḥokmah,*	the 'wisdom' or primordial idea of God;
3. *Binah,*	the 'intelligence' of God;
4. *Ḥesed,*	the 'love' or mercy of God;
5. *Gevurah* or *Din,*	the 'power' of God, chiefly manifested as the power of stern judgment and punishment;
6. *Raḥamim,*	the 'compassion' of God, to which falls the task of mediating between the two preceding *Sephiroth*; the name *Tiphereth* 'beauty' is also used:
7. *Netzaḥ,*	the 'lasting endurance' of God;
8. *Hod,*	the 'majesty' of God;
9. *Yesod,*	the 'basis' or 'foundation' of all active forces in God;
10. *Malkuth,*	the 'kingdom' of God, described in the Zohar as *Keneseth Israel*, the mystical archetype of Israel's community, or as the *Sheḥinah*.

The *Sephiroth* may be represented as a tree or visualized as a man – Adam Qadmon the primordial man.

The system of the Qabalah has correspondences with other systems, such as Vedic and other pantheons, the *devic* psycho-spiritual cosmos of Buddhism, the Ameshā-Spentās and Ahurā-Mazdā of Zarathuśtrianism and so on. There are, necessarily, differences between them. What needs to be noted here is that all these presentations of Transcendence in human language are symbolic. They purport to express or reveal the 'above' in the statement 'As above, so below'. Do they in actual fact? Our word mercy, for instance, is meaningful for us in our worldly

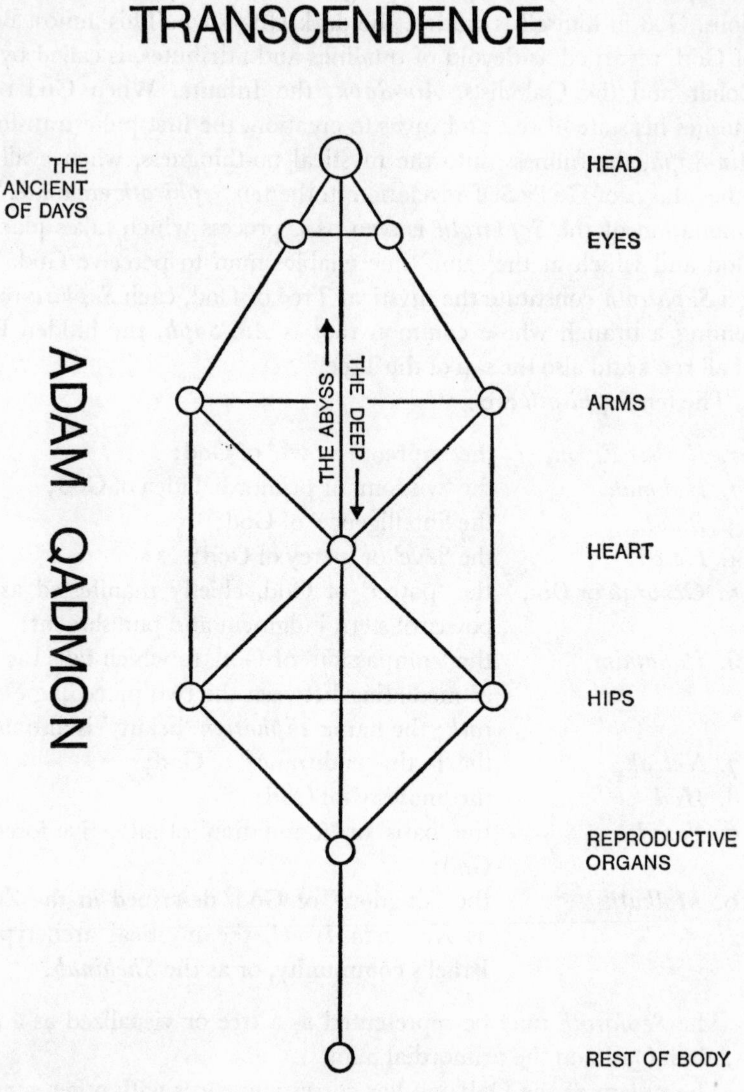
TRANSCENDENCE
THE ANCIENT OF DAYS
ADAM QADMON
HEAD
EYES
ARMS
THE ABYSS
THE DEEP
HEART
HIPS
REPRODUCTIVE ORGANS
REST OF BODY

THE SUPREME CROWN

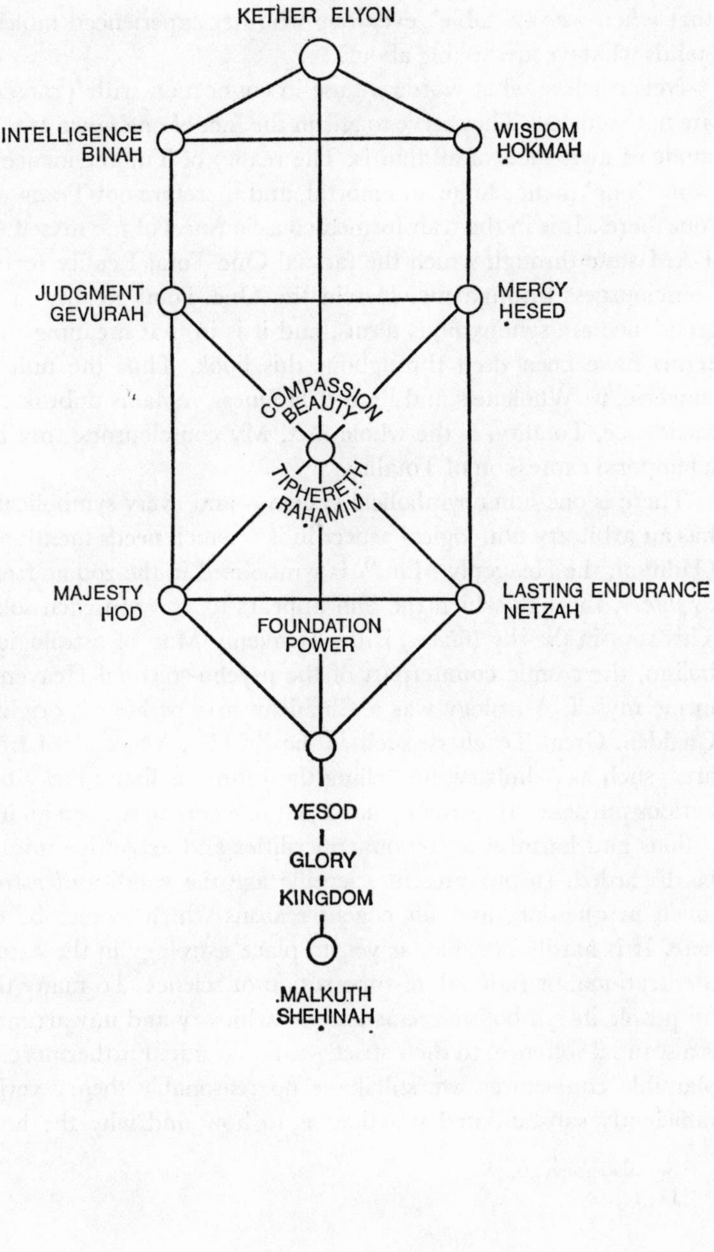
KETHER ELYON
INTELLIGENCE
BINAH
WISDOM
HOKMAH
JUDGMENT
GEVURAH
MERCY
HESED
COMPASSION
BEAUTY
TIPHERETH
RAHAMIM
MAJESTY
HOD
LASTING ENDURANCE
NETZAH
FOUNDATION
POWER
YESOD
GLORY
KINGDOM
MALKUTH
SHEHINAH

non-transcendent context. And it is what *we* feel and experience as mercy which we postulate (in apotheosis) for the transcendent. In actual fact we read into 'the above' only what we know here 'below'. Thus all our expositions of Transcendence are only ways of talking about it, and not the actual fact or the 'Truth' of Transcendence, in the sense that when we say 'table', everyone who has experienced tables understands what we are talking about.

Nevertheless, what words we use in connection with Transcendence are not valueless. They serve to affirm the fact of one's own transformed mode of awareness of all that is. The reality of Transcendence is not a 'something' (hence finite and mortal, and therefore not Transcendence) 'out there'. It is in the transformed consciousness of me myself. It is the I AM state through which the factual One Total Reality realizes self-consciousness through me. Herein the One Total Reality and Transcendence are synonymous terms, and it is in that meaning that these terms have been used throughout this book. Thus the unity of the universe, its Wholeness and Perfect Holiness, remains unbroken. Transcendence, Totality, is the whole fact. My consciousness, my being, is a temporal expression of Totality.

There is one other symbolical system – and every symbolical system has an arbitrary non-logical aspect in it – which needs mention. Adam Qadmon, the Heavenly Man,[53] is symbolized in the zodiac from Aries to Pisces, through which the Sun appears to move in each solar year. This MAN-in-the-sky (*ākāśa*) is the Heavenly Man of astrological symbolism, the cosmic counterpart of the psycho-spiritual Heavenly Man in me myself. Astrology was a Chaldean art; perhaps it originated in Chaldea. Great Teachers, such as the Buddha,[54] kept aloof from 'low arts', such as palmistry, foretelling the future or fixing lucky times for various purposes. If astrology has a genuine core to it, then all its superstitious and harmful accretions, puerilities and exploitive misuse must be discarded. In our present scientific age the validity of astrology is much in question, and for cogent reasons which cannot be detailed here. It is hardly possible, as yet, to place astrology in the category of the irrational or rational, of superstition or science. To many thoughtful people its symbolism seems unduly arbitrary and unwarrantable; it is a scandal (offence) to their strictly rational side. Furthermore, despite plausible conjectures, we still have no reasonable theory verified by sufficiently substantiated practice, as to how and why the horoscope

[53] See also above, p. 78.
[54] D., 1.9.10.

could be a pointer to our nature and our life. But if in our own day matters psychological – extra-sensory perception, etc. – have at last entered into the sanctum of scientific investigation, astrology, which is a-rational, like Life itself, and not wholly irrational, might in time be amenable to scientific investigation, once we are fortunate enough to come across some genuine, significant clues, together with evidence that cannot be ignored.

It is not reasonable to reject astrology out of hand. The subject needs a very different approach from that of the ignorant or of the blindly prejudiced either against it or in favour of it. A few points for consideration, points which are not familiar to most people, may be suggested here.

The horoscope is a symbolic pattern (a *maṇḍala*) of my whole being, of my environment and my relationships and interactions with this environment. It is a cipher which, if correctly read, reveals the play of both transcendent and physical energies in me. Fundamentally, it indicates the inmost modes of awareness (not merely the changing states of mind), the profound states of consciousness which could be entered in deep meditation or in contemplative prayer, specifically distinguishing me, the particular person, and it reveals the main modes, such as Love or Power or Wisdom or Beauty, in which Transcendence could manifest itself through me. For example: Transcendence manifested as Purity (*ashā*) through Zarathuśtra, Wisdom through Gotama, Love through Jesus. This is the spiritual aspect of astrology, little known, if at all, to the practicers of the art.

It is better not to regard the signs of the zodiac, astrologically speaking, as being identical with the astronomer's constellations of the same name, physically speaking. Astrology may be regarded as a psycho-spiritual counterpart or correspondent of astronomy; and whilst astronomy, which provides us with scientific knowledge of the stars as objective realities, is completely independent of astrology, as indeed it should be as a science, astrology is dependent upon astronomy for constructing its physical cipher, the horoscope (even though the mathematics and positions of the planets in the signs do not exactly correspond with the astronomer's calculations!).

The astronomer's constellations are congeries of scientifically measurable 'physical' (a better word in this context than 'material') energies and radiations. Some day we may gather some knowledge regarding the part they play, if any, in building or protecting or maintaining our own living bodies. The astrologer's 'signs', which are 'associated' with the constellations, are *symbols* of archetypal psycho-spiritual energies. We have no knowledge – no publicly available knowledge – of the rationale of how these energies function, how they are related to physical energies, and how or why the astrological signs are 'associated' with the astronomical constellations. It is a mistake to talk in terms of Mars or Jupiter, or Cancer or Libra 'producing' such and such effects or of 'being the cause responsible' for what we are and what happens to us. A barometer neither produces nor is responsible for the changing pressures of the atmosphere and the consequent weather conditions – it simply indicates, by means of pointer readings. But whereas with a barometer we do know the rationale of its working, with astrology we are – somewhat at sea! It is a fact, however, that if one is open-minded and dispassionate, and patiently keeps a record of careful observations of states of mind, health, events, aesthetic, intellectual and spiritual changes and growth, relationships, attitudes and actions with respect to people, the environment and historical movements in one's own lifetime, and also records the astrological configurations prevailing at those times *without looking up beforehand in the ephemeris what they are going to be*, – if we do this honestly with the intensity of the scientist over a long period, a good forty or more years, we will find a pattern emerging out of it and we can say that there is a degree of correlation between oneself the living individual and the changing configurations as the planets move through the astrological signs.

But even if physical scientific investigation successfully brings astrology into an acceptable place within the ambit of science (as it has, for instance, with psychology and extra-sensory perception in this century), a suggestion may be made in all kindliness: wholly eschew astrology as popularly practised by the ignorant and by exploiters the world over. If one comes across the true astrologer, well and good. But then, have I, the ordinary man, sufficient depth of perception to recognize a true astrologer? And how difficult to find one such person! For the genuine astrologer, a master of his art, is himself an enlightened and holy man – and it is as easy to find such a man as to meet the Unicorn!

The most important indication by the horoscope, as mentioned above, is concerned with the transcendent sphere. One other point needs mention here. The horoscope gives a penetrating insight into my own nature (basic character) and my own potentialities as a psychophysical being. It shows me my weaknesses and the difficulties and trials I am likely to meet; and it can warn me of positive dangers, which I need not rush into out of foolhardiness. The science of the symbolism of the zodiac is a key to self-knowledge. When rightly used, the unfolding of the pattern of one's destiny finds less obstruction.

* * *

It is a remarkable feature of the scriptures that one may approach them in different ways, such as the mystical or psychological or metaphysical, all of which are valid and will move one to realization. Remarkable also is the fact that although each one of us can see and appreciate the several ways, one can realize the truth only in one's own distinctive way. The affirmation by another person of his vision of truth may stimulate and inspire, but the actual seeing has to be one's own.

Ain-Soph, the infinite, primordial Creative Energy, by self-limitation, becomes the finite manifest: the contained and the container; cosmos, being, existence. There is no beginning or end to it. To us it may seem as a sequence of events or be realized as the pulsation of eternity, according to our prevailing state of consciousness.

Creative Energy, and existence-being as it manifests, de-manifests, manifests, de-manifests, endlessly, is the cosmic drama: a game, in which Creative Energy, the unknown and unknowable, repeatedly is the 'winner'. The phrase, 'thy will', belongs to it. The phrase, 'my desire', belongs to me as a finite existent. To the Immortal, the former; to the mortal, the latter. The former is represented by the Hebrew letter *aleph* and by the number 1, the finite existent by the letter *yod* and by the number 10.

The book of Genesis, written in the Hebrew tongue, is an account of this cosmic drama which is the game of life. If I read it as literature, I read it merely as an aesthete, and there is no vision which glimpses the mystery. I must know something of the code. The letters of the Hebrew alphabet are *proper names* for different states of cosmic energy.[55] Hebrew, having no numerals, expresses numbers by the letters of the alphabet, each letter corresponding to a number. Each letter and number[56] has a meaning in relation to cosmic energy. Most of the letters, such as *aleph* or *beth* or *gimel* or *daleth* or *yod*, are themselves words consisting of other letters, and hence numbers. It can be seen then, that even a single sentence in Genesis, indeed in the Old

[55] Carlo Suarès, *The Cipher of Genesis*.

[56] This type of secret code was also used in India. Thus in the Chāndogya Upaniṣad, 7.1.2, the word *rāśim* should not be translated as mathematics but as the secret science (*gupta vidyā*) of numbers. Simple mathematics in the ordinary sense was also known; but in the above context, mathematics is a misleading term. This science of numbers was also used by the Egyptians, the Pythagoreans and others.

Testament, involves a wealth and depth of meaning beyond imagining. Truth is not only stranger than fiction; it is beyond all plumbing.

Since the word of the Bible, according to the above approach, is a revelation of the play of creative energy, and since God as Creator also means creative energy, it is not so absurd to say that scripture is the word of God. It is worth noting that about the 4th century B.C., the Indian grammarian Pāṇini refers to *sphoṭāyana*, and the theory of *sphoṭa*, essence of sound revealed by letter, word or sentence. This sound-essence, 'produces the cognition of the thing; it is said to be eternal, and self-existent, bearing a permanent relation to the thing signified by it. Letters, words and sentences manifest, but do not produce, the eternal meanings'.[57] Later thinkers of the Nyāya and Vaiśeṣika philosophies regarded the supreme Īśvara (God) as the eternal author of the Vedas. We can understand, therefore, the grounds on which some of the zealous of any faith claim that their scripture cannot be translated into other languages without mutilation. Translation merely changes the garb of seminal ideas – and sometimes it can do this sensitively. But the living truth-energy which is the divine Word, about which even the ideas and certainly human speech are only wrappings and not the actual power, cannot be transmitted by skill in linguistic equations.

The name Elohim represents the whole process by which the creative Life/other-Life principle (*aleph* (1), timeless and immeasurable) is projected through its archetypal containers into physical existence as objects and living creatures (*yod* (10), the manifestation of *aleph* in temporal continuity). Its activity is confined to the repetitive production of prototypes: as said in verses 12 and 25 of the first chapter of Genesis, 'And the earth brought forth grass, and herb yielding seed after his kind, and the tree yielding fruit, whose seed was in itself, after his kind . . . the beast of the earth after his kind, and cattle after their kind, and every thing that creepeth upon the earth after his kind.'

Yet from Elohim *also* proceeds man, *adam*, a pattern of life which is not a fixed prototype. He can introduce indetermination : unpredictability, uncertainty, and a greater degree of probability rather than exactitude. Thus, up to a point, he can alter the character of nature's mechanical, repetitive process. Man is not to remain merely procreative. In him is the potentiality to be creative in a very profound sense – the THINKER.[58]

Man can be sensitive to the rhythm of the Universe. In him every

[57] Radhakrishnan, *Indian Philosophy*, vol. 2, p. 106, Revised Second Edition.
[58] See above, pp. 78, 83, 133.

possibility lies hidden; and it is his special calling to let his possibilities emerge and fructify. He is the 'image' of Elohim, male and female; and it is in his female[59] side that the creative Life/other-Life can be active, through his own intelligent perception and with his deliberate co-operation, and bring him to fulfilment.

YHWH is not an anthropomorphous deity. The name represents an immanence. The name *adam* signifies Aleph, the creative pulsation, inside the blood (*dam*). There are two vitalities in us which we can regard as the existent organism and the immanence, the finite and the transcendent, the container and the contained, and so on. The name YHWH expresses an existence fulfilled by the two lives of body and psyche mutually fecundating[60] each other. This can happen only in man, not in any of the fixed species. Thereby YHWH the immanence is alive in us and is actualized through us. Thus is witnessed the emergence of the New Man, the redeemed or sinless Adam, in whom YHWH is fully and perfectly incarnate. Then the name YHWH signifies realized Transcendence.

Elohim and YHWH are not two separate entities. They are a not-two. The different names are useful aids to us for understanding the One Whole Reality as manifesting in us and through us. My own being is the Elohimic process of the contained and the container, and the Yahwic immanence moving towards its culmination as realized Transcendence. The Elohimic-Yahwic unity is in me; using me, burning me up, light enlightening the uncomprehending dark, by which the divine purpose or 'Thy Will' is fulfilled.

Elohim unfolds the universal process in which is the inherent order of things, the Law. YHWH presents the challenge to me to wrestle with Elohim, and prove strong enough, worthy enough, to be a conscious active participator with the Elohimic process and thus introduce a necessary new element in it: namely, to become free of the compulsion to remain bound within the narrow limits imposed by a fixity of type – termite or whale or bird or beast or creeping thing on earth, and always of earth, the earth which is the primordial, producing female.

Prior to becoming the whole, pure individual, I cannot, because of my imperfections, respond rightly to the Yahwic challenge without breaking the Elohimic Law. If I merely abide by the Law, assuming that I could do so, necessary developments – the awakening of my

[59] cf. the role of the electrons, particles of *negative* electricity, in determining the properties and chemical activities of the atoms of any element.

[60] cf. the Upaniṣadic teaching above, p. 85.

within-ness, self-responsibility, free action by self-motivation, perceiving and co-operating with the Elohimic process with clear knowledge of the fixation-destruction and anabolism-katabolism of *man's* life-process – cannot take place. To precipitate the crisis which will set going all this development I myself have to 'deviate from the Law', or else I will be stuck in angelic fixity, in compelled rightness, devoid of all options.

So I *have* to 'pluck the fruit', or like Prometheus 'steal the heavenly fire', and work out the primary consequences in terms of sin, suffering, evil, death. But I pluck the fruit through the heavenly female in me as the instrumental motivator, acting contrarily to that lulling siren the primordial earth-female of my bodily existence.

The earth-female spells bondage to desire, and to the finite and familiar forms of enjoyment and security which desire produces. The heavenly female spells the vision of truth which continuously keeps me free from being caught and held captive in the net of fixed forms, and thus keeps the way open for ever-creative life. When desire is understood and transcended, the heavenly female, holding the secret of creative power and creation, acts freely, and *Ḥokmah*, by virtue of inspiring presence, free of concupiscence, fecundates *Binah* : one meaning of the marriage made in heaven. This conjugative union is the origin of Love as a transcendent fact and value.[61] The influence (action) of *Ḥokmah* and *Binah*, eternal and timeless in its own divine sphere, is perpetual in time for me on earth. I, here, whilst ignorant and desire-driven, prevent its operation through me. Enlightened and sinless, this Grace functions unhindered in and through me. If it were not so, this could never have been revealed to mankind.

I, Adam, am the main trunk in the Tree of Life on earth, symbolized in my erect bodily position and in my root, the brain, pointing to the zenith and not to the centre of the earth, as with trees; and as long as the mind aspires and the spirit reaches out to the heavens, I am unlike all other species which are restricted lateral branches of the Tree of Life whereas I, man, ever grow upwards. For I am composed of two dualities: a male-female as *this* the psycho-physical existent, the man of earth, as well as *that*, the male-female who is the Heavenly Man, Adam Qadmon.[62]

[61] cf. the union of Śiva and Śakti of the Yogi; and the timeless conjugation of the Sovereign Lord and Sovereign Lady of the Bṛhadāraṇyaka Upaniṣad, 1.4.4. (see also above p. 85 f.)

[62] See also above, p. 78.

Living Nature (the Elohimic process) brought forth man the psycho-physical existent as the most remarkable animal on earth. I the animal have my limitations, like other animals – my intimate touch with creatureliness, and my rootedness in earth. But in the animal me is a potentiality, a germ, which is MAN, which is capable *in mind and consciousness*, of conceiving, comprehending and realizing the unlimited – as indeed I, MAN, have done today, unlike me the ancient primate, the million-year old primordial ancestor. My personal responsibility, the responsibility of every member of the human race through the ages, is to stir into active life, nurture, tend and bring to fruition, this germ, this Yahwic Immanence. Nature, in its aspect of externality to me cannot do this if I choose to remain uninterested, ignorant and incapable: in other words, ir-religious and spiritually clumsy. When I cease to obstruct – 'dis-obey' – the Yahwic Immanence, then my cooperation with the Elohimic process establishes the harmony in action of Nature external to me with Nature internal to me – that is, as me the existent animal and me the Heavenly MAN. This is the meaning of YHWH-Elohim, redeemed (fulfilled) MAN, Adam Qadmon. The two dualities, the earthly *adam* and the heavenly *adam* are one Adam Qadmon. Conflicting dualities are resolved into the One Whole, the Holy One that is.

How can such assertions be made? When I am absorbed into the supreme communion, the I AM state prevails. That which is realized in that state, on my returning to the state of ordinary sense-mind functioning, is formulated as the ten *Sephiroth*, the divine emanations out of, and yet wholly within, *Ain-Soph* the Infinite, the Incomprehensible, the mystical Nothing. In this Sephirothic Being, the names YHWH, Elohim, Adonai, El Shaddai and so on, have their place in a transcendent unity. All this is an expression by men – by you, by me – in Hebrew Qabalistic terms of what happens to men through whom Transcendence realizes itself.

In that condition of transcendent realization, awareness is unitary. It is non-discriminative, non-isolative, non-descript. Before the capacity to enter into that state reaches fruition in me, I am only discriminatively and isolatively conscious of myself in relation to all that I label the not-self. I am conscious of myself as made up of separate parts – body and mind; matter and spirit; skin, bones, organs, and so on – and of the not-self as a collection of countless particulars, as entities separate from each other which may or may not be inter-related. Prior even to the state in which there is the functioning of discriminative consciousness – of I the subject sensing, cognizing and experiencing you or it the object –

I was neither isolatively conscious, nor was I self-conscious in the everyday sense of the term; I functioned 'naturally', I knew 'un-knowingly'. This was my primordial Edenic condition.

I would have remained helplessly imprisoned in this stupor of bliss (a miserable bliss) if not for the Yahwic Immanence throwing the challenge to me to wake up. It threw the challenge both ways – the one through the 'serpent', the Life-Force in the psycho-physical state, which is one manifestation of YHWH, acting from 'below' upwards, and the other through *Ashah* the Woman, the heavenly female in me, the Life-Force in the psycho-spiritual state, also a manifestation of YHWH, acting from 'above' downwards.

I plucked the fruit of the Tree of Life – and that fruit is the consciousness which is pure Awareness – a fruit which is 'forbidden', except to Elohim or YHWH or to 'one of us'. Eden is my own living psycho-physical existent being, and the Tree is my own brain and nerves and spine, brought into being and maintained by the Elohimic process, holding in itself all the possibilities characterizing the Yahwic Immanence and awaiting my personal vision and activity from within for its emergence and fruition. I may do this, without sin and sorrow if I am pure and possess the skill. But in my primordial Edenic state I have purity only as one who is devoid of the urge and power to be impure, that is, I have an unenlightened, impotent purity; and of skill, that is, insight and mental power, I have none at all.

The heavenly female, the Woman, *Ashah*, is the daughter of the cosmic fire, *Ash*.[63] Her influence, drawing out my aspiration towards Transcendence, is irresistible. So, unfit though I am, I 'eat of the fruit' held out to me. That is, I experience states of consciousness, either unsought or through deliberate effort, which makes me aware of the Yahwic Immanence within me and to the reality of Transcendence. But this awakening is unclear. Not only is it confused or dim, but is also attended with doubt and fear. Thus I become an imperfect 'one of Them (the Holy Ones)'. The fruit of the Tree of Life has not enabled me to soar into the state of pure Awareness of Transcendent Reality *in which I can constantly abide* – which would mean the fully and perfectly realized Adam Qadmon. It has only enabled me to scar the Tree of Life and realize only discriminative consciousness – which means the state of non-wholeness, or un-holiness. Now I am conscious, and function, in terms of the earthly female's strong tendency to stay

[63] cf. the Zarathuśtrian *āthro ahurahe mazdāo puthro*, Fire the son, or purifying agent, of Ahurā-Mazdā.

put and not change what appears to be an agreeable, pleasurable, desirable and 'secure' (bound or conditioned) state, in conflict with the activity of the transcendent Creative Power which wants to sweep away outworn forms, go beyond what has already been achieved in expression, and release greater beauty and more abundant life. The former, *tov* (translated as 'good') is in conflict with the latter, *raa* (translated as 'evil'). Both words, 'good' and 'evil', are misleading.

By scarring the Tree of Life, I have converted it into the Tree of discriminative choice, choice in favour of pleasure, fixation and stagnation, against displeasure, growth and fruitive creation. Furthermore, I have established the conflict of the duals, attachment and aversion, in my psycho-physical being and life. And yet, this very misfortune is the way of Life, of Transcendence!

There is no disobedience[64] to a divine command involved in all this. Indeed the 'serpent' is no other than the embodiment of the creative Life-power of Transcendence. The Adam-and-Eve story is not an event in time and place concerning two particular individuals. It is one of the profoundest myths teaching us what happened and keeps on happening to us, to you and to me, throughout our lives; to us living now; to all members of the human species who have lived on the earth and who will live.

It was a blessing that I was shaken out of my 'secure', stagnant Edenic happiness. In fact this very Eden (my existent being) holds within itself all the potentiality of YHWH which would shake me out of a lotus-eating existence, save me from degenerating into a mere lateral branch of the Tree of Life, and compel (whenever necessary) and preserve me, MAN, as the main branch growing ever upwards. This upward growth means constant change, which means, to my discriminative consciousness, the 'death' of what is present to give place to the new. 'And YHWH-Elohim (Lord God) commanded the man (*adam*), saying, Of every tree of the garden' – the sensory life of the body – 'thou mayest freely eat: But of the tree of good (*tov*) and evil (*raa*)' – the Tree in the middle of the garden, the Tree of Life, the spine and brain or *the tree of consciousness* – 'thou shalt not eat of it: for in the day[65] thou eatest thereof thou shalt surely die'.[66] Assuredly I die. *Not bodily,* but to each and every state of conditioned descriminatory consciousness, to

[64] In the sense of wilful, evil-intentioned contrariness.

[65] Day – light, knowledge, conscious mind. Night – the dark, state of unknowing, unconscious mind.

[66] Gen., 2.16,17.

each incomplete, lesser realization until the light of Transcendence shines in fulness.

Being impure and imperfect I do not see the links between the successive states of consciousness as they move through time, even though YHWH-Elohim tries to wake me up by the reproachful 'Where art thou?'.[67] Nor do I see them in their relationship to, and thrown up against the background of, my total life-process. Furthermore, the successive states are sullied by my defilements. I am a prisoner harshly harried along by desire, wrapped up in the black fog of ignorance, torn by the unresolved conflict of the 'this-or-that' of discriminative consciousness, of choice which is lustful, fearful, grasping, violent, stupid.

Thus I am caught in the evil of my own making, in the anguish of the excommunicated state, the absence of that I AM state which is the timeless communion of Transcendence realizing itself eternally through me.

* * *

Have not I, mankind, poignantly sung of this sorrow through the throats of the prophets?

* * *

Let us approach the understanding of the above in another way.

When the Elohimic process and the Yahwic Immanence function together in balance, I, the main trunk in the Tree of Life, grow healthily. In my ignorant and imperfect state the earthly female in me craves for the unchanging continuity of what is pleasant and secure. But Life brooks no stagnation. The serpent, who is the creative fire,[68] from Earth to Heaven, stirs the heavenly female in me to pluck the fruit of the Tree of Life. Because of the resistance of the earthly female to psychological change and the urge of the heavenly Female for spiritual growth, the conflict between the two converts the Tree of Life into the Tree of 'good and evil', of *tov* and *raa*. Indeed the two trees are one and the same Tree.

Tov, translated as 'good', is the no-change, stagnating condition, whilst *raa*, translated as 'evil', is the energy which disrupts obstructive fossilization and frees me, again and again, into more developed states – subtler sensitivity, deeper insight, finer responsivity. Because of the dis-

[67] Gen., 3.9.
[68] *kuṇḍalinī.*

ruption produced when there is conflict between *tov* and *raa* it is said that 'in the day thou eatest thereof thou shalt surely die'. Indeed I die to each state of bondage; and *this* death is attended with the pain and suffering born of my ignorance. But when I understand the nature of the trend of the Life-process and do not cling, psychologically, to any fixation, there is no resistance offered to the Yahwic Immanence. Then change takes place without violent disruption; there is right transformation at the critical moment; there is no 'sin' or 'evil'; and YHWH and Elohim function as the harmony of YHWH-Elohim in and through me. This dying to the old is attended with the wonder and joy of new birth.

This change at the critical moment, a climactic moment, is usually quite sudden. It may even appear catastrophic. If the psyche, the earthly female, is dutiful, obedient to the behest of Life, cooperative with the heavenly Female who holds the secret of creative action at her own transcendent level in response to the upsurge of the Yahwic Immanence, I am transformed into the total Life-process. I know *tov* and *raa* as the gods know the Tree of Life.

To live in sweet obedience to the behest of Life! In loving service of the Lady of Heaven through whom the sovereign will of Heaven's Lord finds expression! Breath of Salvation!

Who – what – is the redeeming power?

* * *

Have not the prophets promised peace and perfection when the sinless, suffering servant of the Supreme comes as the Messiah?

* * *

As said earlier,[69] I am composed of two dualities, the heavenly androgyne and the earthly androgyne. *Ashah*, the heavenly Female, holds the secret of creation, which is ever new, never repetitive. She sees that the tree in the midst of the garden is 'good for food' (spiritual sustenance), 'pleasant to the eyes' (for it gives the vision of Transcendence), 'a tree to be desired to make one wise'. The serpent gives the assurance that 'Elohim doth know that in the day ye eat thereof, then your eyes shall be opened and ye shall be as gods knowing *tov* and *raa*'. The knowledge of *tov* and *raa* (mistranslated as good and evil) is the knowledge of creation-transformation/re-creation-transformation . . . The

[69] See above, p. 188.

transformation necessitates preliminary dissolution, and the subsequent re-creation is always a new creation. So *Ashah* partakes of the fruit and also gives it to me, Adam. She is in the enlightened state, for as *Binah* (the Mother) she is creatively inspired by *Ḥokmah* (the Father), the Power that fecundates by presence only, beyond all sensuousness, free of concupiscence, that is, of binding desire.

If I, Adam, here and now, could partake of the fruit in the right way, I would undergo transubstantiation and my entire being would be made holy, perfect, creative. But I the earthly Adam, made of the dust of the ground, am an imperfect androgyne – as if in a daze, unperceptive, somewhat under the thumb of the earthly female in me, subject to the mortal psyche which craves for established comfort and the security of the already known. Therefore, although I receive the fruit of the Tree of Life from *Ashah*, I absorb (eat) it through the earthly female and thus fall short of communion with Life in its Transcendence. I reach out to it through my sensorial-intellectual apparatus, that is through sense and discursive mind only, and develop no further than introducing duality and its attendant conflicts – 'thorns and thistles'.

When I eat the fruit given me by *Ashah*, the feminine moiety of the heavenly androgyne, the effect on me the earthly androgyne – I and my wife Eve (not *Ashah*), my male body and female *anima* (and in the case of a woman, her female body and male *animus*) – is intoxicating. I the earthly androgyne am confused and fearful when the awareness of YHWH makes its first powerful impact. Elohim makes me in the first instance as the heavenly androgyne. YHWH-Elohim brings me, involutionarily, into more concrete existence as a living soul, *nephesh*,[70] and lays down the injunction regarding the fruit. As the heavenly androgyne I am universal; as the living soul, I am one out of the many finite expressions of the one universal; on eating the fruit, discriminative consciousness (the intellectual faculty) emerges. Between that which is spoken of in verse 6 and verse 7 of the third chapter of Genesis, a great change occurs. That which spells suffering, evil, sin and birth-death on the one hand, and the growth of isolative ego-consciousness which is to flower out ultimately into pure individuality on the other hand, comes into being.

[70] *Nephesh*. The vital principle, the lowest of the three grades of the soul. *Ruaḥ*. (literally, the spirit). The intellectual faculty, the middle of the three grades of the soul. *Neshamah*. The moral consciousness or the highest of the three grades of the soul.

We can also approach the understanding of Genesis in terms of the symbolism of the zodiac. This interpretation will differ in some ways from that revealed by using the letter-number code.

Aries represents primordial creative power or energy, which, by self-resistance, sets up its container, Taurus, itself becoming the contained. Gemini, the twins, represents the divine androgyne. Cancer, the waters of Life, is the unconscious, the deep, the womb out of which will come the manifestations of organic life and of consciousness, culminating in Leo which represents man. In man is the promise: the incarnation, that is the cosmic fire incarnate (and this is the fire that is 'stolen from heaven' in the first instance); and individuality. Virgo is the feminine counterpart of the male Leo; and it is the sign of the Virgin which is associated with that part of the body enclosed by the lower ribs.[71]

The ancient teaching first presented only ten signs. Virgo was Virgo-Scorpio, the Woman and the Snake constituting an androgyne. The Snake inspired the Woman to eat the fruit of the Tree of Life. Owing to the imperfections of me the earthly Adam, matters went awry. The dynamism of Scorpio, which works for the sweeping aside of the old, however agreeable the established may be, in order to prevent fixation and prepare the way for the new, proved too strong. Scorpio represents the power of interacting duals, positive and negative, male and female, a power that is overwhelming at times. Thus Eden was swept away. The enmity decreed henceforth (till Redemption comes) between the Woman and the Snake made the ancients separate Virgo and Scorpio, and introduce Libra, the Scales or Balance, in between, representing harmony, love, justice. Compassion mediates between all-forgiving mercy and stern judgment or punishment. This is *Tiphereth*. It is the Son of the Father. Libra is associated with Hermes and with Enoch. It is of Enoch that it is said in Genesis 5.24: 'And Enoch walked with God: and he was not: for God took him.' The name Enoch means *tuition*, *teacher*.

A combination of adverse influences thus put the two androgynes, the heavenly and the earthly, out of rhythm with each other. The shortcomings of the earthly androgyne keep me imperfect, un-whole. So I remain merely procreative, that is, repetitive, subject to birth-death instead of pulsating creatively as Life/other-Life. The disharmony between the heavenly androgyne in me and the earthy androgyne, because of the incapacity of the earthly to soar up to the heavenly, and

[71] In Gen., 2.21,22, it is said that YHWH-Elohim made Woman out of one of the ribs of Adam.

hence the 'fall', is the meaning of man 'disobeying'[72] God's command.

Man the infant, naturally stumbling, calls forth mercy and loving-kindness *Ḥesed*. When man, knowing the law, deliberately does wrong, he calls down upon himself stern judgment and punishment, *Gevurah*. Punishment does not heal. It frightens; it hurts; and it engenders revenge or hate. (Occasionally, it equilibrates. Rarely, it awakens a man, healthily, to the right and the good.) Men and women being what they are, the force of *Gevurah* let loose in the world is very great. This is the force of evil. It breaks out from the organism which is Life like a disease of mankind. It is a wound and an anguish in God's own being. It is mainly of the nature of anger, of wrath, of explosive violence.

I, man, am the indispensable medium through whom the healing can come. God, foregoing freedom, produced me. I, relinquishing all selfness by realizing the climactic point of right self restraint, rejoin God, and there is perfect freedom.

* * *

Ḥesed and *Gevurah* both have to operate, mediated by *Raḥamim*, compassion, the sixth *Sephira* which is also called *Tiphereth*. The Lord neither condones my wrongdoing nor fails judgment. He makes his covenant with me again and again. Who is this 'He', the Lord? He is no external despot. The Lord is the inconceivable infinite Unknown, my ultimate nature, my essential religious being or mind of religiousness embodied in me and the source of the transcendent moral imperative within me. The covenant is made by the Lord, the Lordliness within me, with the man, the manliness that is me. The Lord makes the covenant with me in the first instance. Suffering is the inevitable consequence for both when the covenant is broken; moreover, I the earthly Adam, am in the pain and darkness of the ill-state; even overswept sometimes by evil – hell! But the Lord, wise and compassionate, tempering hot justice with the rain of his mercy, is ever ready to save. Taking the initiative, he makes a new covenant with me. And he does this again and again, transcendentally faithful unto me of the dust till I return unto dust.

But the Lord never panders unto me, which means he is never on my side whensoever and wheresoever I obstruct the Yahwic Immanence in me. The Lord influences me to grow into the full-fledged

[72] Disobedience, from *dis, ob* and *audire*, means literally not giving ear to, or not listening to.

'Israelite', that is, he who rules with God.[73] The total concern of the Lordliness in me is the Complete transformation of me as I am, faulty and erring, into Adam Qadmon, MAN the living Word of the living God. Through *Ashah* comes the inspiration, until out of her as the archetype I abstract *Hheva* (Eve) as the earthly correspondent.[74] In my single being, when the female component in me (Eve) is in harmony with the male in me, I am in that healthy state in which the Lord can salve me. It is never I who can 'work out my salvation'. It is Transcendence that manifests salvation through an unresisting me. Unresisting, I am not against the Lord. I am obedient, listening to the divine Voice and living by it.

There is no option for me, a man, for me, mankind, but to grow into that state which spells right relationship with the Lord. Other than that, there is but evil and suffering. The Prophets of the world, those living bridges between man and God, are the voices of God giving erring man renewed energy for his true fulfilment. As long as I fail to answer the divine call, the Prophets, too, know sorrow.

Consider the words of the prophet Jeremiah, deeply afflicted by the sufferings of Judah and the plight of Jerusalem. 'The Lord hath afflicted her for the multitude of her transgressions', he declares. (The Lamentations of Jeremiah, 1.5) Identifying himself with Judah, he says, 'Is it nothing to you, all ye that pass by? Behold, and see if there be any sorrow like unto my sorrow, which is done unto me, wherewith the Lord had afflicted me in his fierce anger.' (Lam., 1.12) But, 'The Lord is righteous; for I have rebelled against his commandment . . . I have grievously rebelled.' (Lam., 1.18,20) How significant that Jeremiah should confess he had grievously rebelled, he the man to whom the Transcendent granted communion, the one to whom came the word of the Lord, saying, 'Before I formed thee in the belly I knew thee; and before thou camest out of the womb I sanctified thee, and I ordained thee a prophet unto the nations'![75] A man may be a saint or a prophet, *in* himself, yet no man is, *by* himself. He is a living part of his family, his community, his world in fact, and as such is a participant in the total life. He breathes the same air as his neighbours breathe. The 'others' may have sinned, but 'he' as a living part of 'others' is also under the shadow of that sin. A saint or a prophet sees this, thereby

[73] See also above, p. 70.

[74] The rôle and influence of woman as mother and as wife is of paramount value and importance for mankind if and when she successfully represents her divine archetype.

[75] Jer., 1.5.

opening the door for the redemptive restoration of communion with the Lord. Sin brings catastrophe in its trail, hurtful to body and soul. Failure to see sin as sin prolongs and aggravates the damage to the soul and breeds more sin. See the sin, understand it fully, and the Lord within is then free to heal and save. Fail to understand it, and the wages of sin – 'death' – cannot be averted.

Jeremiah understands sin – sin which is the rebellion against the Lord, underlying the wrongdoing of one or more members of the Tribe of Judah. Seeing the evil in the heart, and also seeing the radical evil of being out of communion with the Lord, he is afflicted in spirit: 'Behold, O Lord; for I am in distress: my bowels are troubled; mine heart is turned within me; for I have grievously rebelled; abroad the sword bereaveth, at home there is as death.' (Lam., 1.20) He then speaks of his 'enemies' and expresses a wish: 'They have heard that I sigh: there is none to comfort me: all mine enemies have heard of my trouble; they are glad that thou hast done it; thou wilt bring the day that thou hast appointed, and they shall be like unto me. Let all their wickedness come before thee; and do unto them as thou hast done unto me for all my transgressions: for my sighs are many and my heart is faint.' (Lam. 1.21,22)

This wish shows Jeremiah's compassion for his enemies. If their wickedness does not come up before the Lord within, and if, thereon, the Lord does not do unto them as he has done unto Jeremiah, their salvation is far from them. If the stimulus of spiritual distress is slight, a man will fight against it and his blind ego[76] may score a victory. But when his distress is at white heat, he truly sees his personal inadequacy. So he becomes quiet, wholly. Thereupon the Lord, unhindered by man, heals and comforts. And the nature of this healing and comforting is unlike anything a man can imagine.

Jeremiah says something quite extraordinary: 'Thou wilt bring the day that thou hast appointed, and they shall be like unto me.' So in fact, this deepest reality within our own selves, 'the Lord', plays the master-rôle in bringing about salvation. The Lord within 'brings the day he has appointed'. Nothing can come to perfect fruition except in the ripeness of circumstance. Man's divine fulfilment needs the ripeness of the divine circumstance. And this is open only to the divine vision.

'The Lord hath done that which he hath devised.' (Lam., 2.17) And what did he do unto the people and unto the Prophet? The third chapter reveals the action of the Lord in the soul of the Prophet.

[76] Again and again the Lord says to the Israelites, 'Ye are a stiff-necked people'.

'I am the man that hath seen affliction by the rod of his wrath. He hath led me, and brought me into darkness, but not into light. Surely against me is he turned; he turneth his hand against me all the day. He hath hedged me about, that I cannot get out . . . made my paths crooked . . . When I cry and shout, he shutteth out my prayer . . . He was unto me as a bear lying in wait, and as a lion in secret places . . . made me desolate . . . filled me with bitterness . . . And thou hast removed my soul far off from peace: I forget prosperity.'

Indeed, the Lord does not do things by halves! Jeremiah goes on:

'And I said, My strength and my hope is perished from the Lord . . . My soul is humbled in me. This I recall to my mind, therefore have I hope. It is of the Lord's mercies that we are not consumed, because his compassions fail not . . . For the Lord will not cast off for ever: But though he cause grief, yet will he have compassion according to the multitude of his mercies.'

Hear now the Voice of Isaiah:

'Comfort ye, comfort ye my people, saith your God. Speak ye comfortably to Jerusalem, and cry unto her, that her warfare is accomplished, that her iniquity is pardoned: for she hath received of the Lord's hand double for all her sins. The voice of him that crieth in the wilderness, Prepare ye the way of the Lord, make straight in the desert a highway for our God. Every valley shall be exalted, and every mountain and hill shall be made low: and the crooked shall be made straight, and the rough places plain: And the glory of the Lord shall be revealed, and all flesh shall see it together: for the mouth of the Lord hath spoken it.
Behold, the Lord God will come with strong hand, and his arm shall rule for him: behold, his reward is with him, and his work before him. He shall feed his flock like a shepherd: he shall gather the lambs with his arm, and carry them in his bosom, and shall gently lead those that are with young.
Hast thou not known? hast thou not heard, that the everlasting God, the Lord, the Creator of the ends of the earth, fainteth not, neither is weary? there is no searching for his understanding. He giveth power to the faint; and to them that have no might he increaseth strength.' 40.1-5; 10,11; 28,29.

'The Lord himself shall give you a sign; Behold, a virgin shall conceive, and bear a son, and shall call his name Immanuel.'

7.14.

'For unto us a child is born, unto us a son is given: and the government shall be upon his shoulder: and his name shall be called Wonderful, Counsellor, The Mighty God, The everlasting Father, The Prince of Peace. Of the increase of his government and peace there shall be no end, upon the throne of David, and upon his Kingdom, to order it, and to establish it with judgment and with justice from henceforth even for ever. The zeal of the Lord of hosts will perform this.' 9.6,7.

'And there shall come forth a rod out of the stem of Jesse, and a Branch shall grow out of his roots: and the spirit of the Lord shall rest upon him, the spirit of wisdom and understanding, the spirit of counsel and might, the spirit of knowledge and of the fear of the Lord; And shall make him of quick understanding in the fear of the Lord: and he shall not judge after the sight of his eyes, neither reprove after the hearing of his ears: But with righteousness shall he judge the poor, and reprove with equity for the meek of the earth, and he shall smite the earth with the rod of his mouth, and with the breath of his lips shall he slay the wicked. And righteousness shall be the girdle of his loins, and faithfulness the girdle of his reins. The wolf also shall dwell with the lamb, and the leopard shall lie down with the kid; and the calf and the young lion and the fatling together; and a little child shall lead them. And the cow and the bear shall feed; their young ones shall lie down together: and the lion shall eat straw like the ox. And the sucking child shall play on the hole of the asp, and the weaned child shall put his hand on the cockatrice's den. They shall not hurt nor destroy in all my holy mountain: for the earth shall be full of the knowledge of the Lord, as the waters cover the sea. And in that day there shall be a root of Jesse, which shall stand for an ensign of the people; to it shall the Gentiles seek: and his rest shall be glorious.' 11.1-10.

* * *

How does a man living in the everyday world view the coming of the Messiah?

Concretely. The Hindu sees the Kalki *avatāra* come riding on a white horse; the Soul of Creation (*geush urvā* in Zarathuśtra's *ahuna-*

vaiti gāthā) expects an all-powerful leader of might and valour; the Jew looks to a scion of the royal house of David and his strong hand.

That vision represents the tragic delusion that Power will forcibly establish the Kingdom. The public sees with a material eye; the eye of the spirit is not open. A Messiah cannot be any other than one who is in communion. Such a being is never a temporal overlord who establishes the spiritual kingdom by might. Power and glory belong to God who is Lord. Man is the servant. Service is perfect through humility. It is not self-assertive. Service is obedience, and obedience is unafraid and unservile when the servant gives his whole heart and mind to his Lord. The good servant is he who loves and understands, for only he can rightly wield the power entrusted to him by his Lord.

The Messiah appears on earth as a man. He serves MAN, whereby God is fulfilled. Several Messiahs have appeared – Enoch, Abraham (who went out of the land of the Kasdeems who had descended into magic), Moses, Elijah, Elisha, Jesus, to cite a few – and will continue to appear. Rare is the man who can recognize the Presence who is the Holy One lit up by Transcendence, the reclaimer of the lost sheep, the quickener of the lifeless to Life, the re-joiner of man with God through his own selfless Self. Such is the man who sees how impossible it is for the Messiah to brandish steel, or to touch or be touched by gold.

The power which the Messiah wields is the power of the sixth *Sephira, Tiphereth* : the Sacrificed God, the Son : the Christ-consciousness : the Beauty beyond all the beauty of manifestation and measure. The Christ-consciousness deeply hidden within each man is the redeeming power. When it blossoms into full fruition, my restoration to whole relationship with God is not simply a re-establishment of unknowing communion or a re-acquisition of an 'Edenic' happiness. It is the beatitude of perfect communion of him who is the embodiment of sacrificial love, of divine compassion and wisdom.

When I scar the Tree of Life, the Face of the Ancient of Days becomes grave and the light of that countenance grows dim to my sight, for my act is an act of usurpation. I bring division into the unity of Adam Qadmon : and this is sin. I fall from the unselfed state of the total, still, contemplation of God, of God-Alone, Only-God, to the state of the Adam of earth entranced by something particular at the cost of the whole Holiness; and then I am merely the man who is made of the dust of the ground and who as such must return to dust.

Within me, none the less, is the sacrificing God, the Alone-begotten Son. It rests with me to let the Christ-consciousness within take charge of me. This is 'to confess Christ'.

Confessing Christ, waking up to *Tiphereth,* my will gives place to Thy Will. I learn not to obstruct Grace. Also, I learn to 'obey the commandments'; that is, not to break the Law, the Elohimic process *as it functions in him 'who walks with God',*[77] thus enabling the Yahwic Immanence to come to transcendent realization. Then the covenant with the Lord can never be broken.

Tiphereth is the domain of the Son of God. It lies on the 'Middle Pillar' of the Temple ('Know ye not ye are the Temple of God, and that the Spirit of God dwelleth in you?' – 1 Cor., 3.16).

Let us consider some aspects of the traditional symbolic teaching regarding the conception and birth of John the Baptist and of Jesus the Christ.

The angel of the Annunciation is Gabriel, chief of the angelic guards at the eastern gate of Paradise. The name means 'God is mighty'. He symbolizes the strength and power of God, the Messiah with the strong arm. Not for anyone to gainsay the force of the divine decree. The first Annunciation[78] is to Zacharias the old man that his old wife Elizabeth[79] who, like her husband, lived a pure, devoted life, always praying in the Temple, would conceive and bear a child. This Annunciation takes place at about the autumnal equinox when the sun is moving out of the sign of Virgo into Libra. Elizabeth conceives; a pure Conception, because Zacharias and Elizabeth both live pure lives and because it is divinely ordained. John,[80] who was born at about the summer solstice when the sun is moving out of Gemini into Cancer, became John the Baptist, the Voice in the wilderness preparing the way for the Lord.

In the sixth month after the first Annunciation, Gabriel is sent by God to Elizabeth's cousin Mary, a virgin espoused to Joseph, and the second Annunciation is made that Mary the virgin will conceive of the Holy Ghost and bring forth a son whose name shall be Jesus, who shall be great, who shall be called the Son of the Highest, to whom shall be given the throne of his father David, who shall reign over the house of Jacob for ever and of whose kingdom there shall be no end.

This Immaculate Conception takes place at about the time of the spring equinox when the sun moves out of the sign of Pisces into Aries.

[77] As did Enoch, and who 'was not, for God took him'; as did Noah, who 'found grace in the eyes of the Lord' and was saved in the ark from destruction by the flood.

[78] Luke, Chapter 1.

[79] The name means 'God is swearer', signifying perhaps God as the maker of covenants on oath.

[80] The name, Johanan, means 'the gift of God'.

Jesus was born on Christmas day, the name-day of the birth of Christ,[81] at about the time of the winter solstice when the sun moves out of Sagittarius into Capricorn. Pisces represents commingling, the dissolution of the established or the fixed, the universal love that unites all life, the self-sacrifice and death that is the portal to the resurrection which is new creation as represented by Aries. Sagittarius represents revelation, the sun of knowledge shining in the unclouded heavens, and the ideal of truth and right or righteousness. Capricorn represents authority (the serene face of age and wisdom of The Ancient of Days); it represents resources and organization.

In the context of the Heart of Religion – the context of Transcendence – how may we approach some understanding of Immaculate Conception? As said above (page 175) the scriptures tell us what happens to you yourself or me myself in the inner depths of mind and consciousness as we live the religious life. When a creative upsurge from within, from the profound Unknown, springs out spontaneously and irresistibly and then gathers itself into its own withinness, it makes its own container for itself, which is now the contained. This is Conception – something quite different from our usual worldly dictionary meaning of the word. One 'knows' this meaning when it actually happens to oneself. It happens to the pure one, to the soul made virgin. The upsurging creative impulse is a pure passion, motiveless, devoid of selfness. The Immaculate or Divine Conception is the Logos, the Word that is Light, the 'Thought'-Power (Archetypal) in the Divine Mind. He that is born, Jesus, is YHSHWH, the containment of YHWH.

To me myself can come the Gift of God, 'John', if I live the pure life. This gift is the arising in me of the sense of Transcendence; thence, the vision of Transcendence. From the arising of the sense of Transcendence to the actual Vision is the preparing of the way. When the mind is utterly pure, innocent (non-harming), virgin, past all petitioning to God or craving for the Transcendent, the creative upsurge and the sinking into its own withinness can take place, giving rise to its container, 'Mary'. (The name Myriam means,[82] from its root *mareh*, image, appearance, vision, mirror; and *iam* refers to the sea or to still water acting as a mirror. Mary the mother of Jesus regresses into the past[83] –

[81] cf. the Buddhist writings which say Siddhattha Gotama was born on the full moon day of Wesak – the (first) full moon in May – and that the Enlightenment also takes place at the Wesak full moon.

[82] Suarès, *The Cipher of Genesis*, p. 213.

[83] cf. the death of the lady Mahā-māyā (=the great illusion) the mother of the Buddha, seven days after giving birth to him.

Jesus refutes her now and again). Mary represents the psyche, which, fecundated by the flood of Divine Energy at the ripe moment of the divine circumstance, enfleshes the Word that is Light. And the Son of God is manifest through oneself. The living YHSHWH is here on earth.

* * *

Jesus knew sorrow.[84] The Son of God lamented[85]:

> 'O Jerusalem, Jerusalem, which killest the prophets, and stonest them that are sent to thee; how often would I have gathered thy children together, as a hen doth gather her brood under her wings, and ye would not! Behold, your house is left unto you desolate: and verily I say unto you, Ye shall not see me, until the time come when ye shall say, Blessed is he that cometh in the name of the Lord.'

Jesus knew the pain of Gethsemane[86]:

> 'Then cometh Jesus with them unto a place called Gethsemane, and saith unto the disciples, Sit ye here, while I go and pray yonder. And he took with him Peter and the two sons of Zebedee, and began to be sorrowful and very heavy. Then saith he unto them, My soul is exceeding sorrowful, even unto death; tarry ye here, and watch with me. And he went a little farther, and fell on his face, and prayed, saying, O my Father, if it be possible, let this cup pass from me: nevertheless not as I will, but as thou wilt. And he cometh unto the disciples, and findeth them asleep, and saith unto Peter, What, could ye not watch with me one hour? Watch and pray, that ye enter not into temptation: the spirit indeed is willing, but the flesh is weak. He went away again the second time, and prayed, saying, O my Father, if this cup may not pass away from me, except I drink it, thy will be done. And he came and found them asleep again; for their eyes were heavy. And he left them, and went away again, and prayed the third time, saying the same words. Then cometh he to his disciples, and saith unto them, Sleep on now, and take your rest: behold, the hour is at hand, and the Son of man is delivered into the hands of sinners. Rise, let us be going, he is at hand that doth deliver me.'

[84] See above, p. 113.
[85] Luke, 13.34,35.
[86] Matthew, 26.36-46.

Thereafter came the last darkness which precedes the eternal light: *'Eloi, Eloi, lama sabachthani*[87] – my God, my God, why hast thou forsaken me?'

When I am pure and live religiously, devoted to Thy Will and free of all personal desire, *nephesh* and *ruaḥ* are void of selfness. They become transparent; a unity, and unified with *neshamah* to which I am now intensely sensitive. This is a state of communion, a constant tranquility in which there is a peaceful interchange between Thou and I. This unified pure mind has an identity of its own, functioning through the living existent person. It is Eloi, Infinite God in finite man. There is, here, the consciousness of self-identity still present.

The cross is with me and I am the cross from the start, with the descent of *Aleph* into matter. The immured Life/other-Life pulse is 'dead' to spirit. Bodily existence (biological life) is the 'grave' of the spirit (transcendent Life). 'He came down to earth from Heaven.' The descent into existence (matter) is the plunge into death – inanimity – a wishing to be bound by the death which spells the unawakenedness to Transcendence. This is a state of pain, of evil, of ceaseless and largely fruitless travail. If in this state of death, there is a stir of Life to break through the imprisoning shell of blind and deaf worldliness, then the true human can come alive. Redemption can begin with purification, vision and communion (in deep prayer or meditation), and this very bodily existence can be sacrificed – MADE SACRED – and used as a 'ransom' for the Spirit immured in all beings, in all manifestation.

This flowers in the Death which is the transmuter, the agent that brings to perfection and consummation – the meaning of 'It is finished'. (John, 19.30.)

I must never deny, reject, run away from, or attempt to destroy the cross – that would be sinful. And foolish – for bodily existence is the only means for the realization of Transcendence, for the perfect fulfilment of God's Will. I start as the opaque dumb cross. My life is a senseless oscillation in worldly duality – a sort of Gadarene swine way of life:

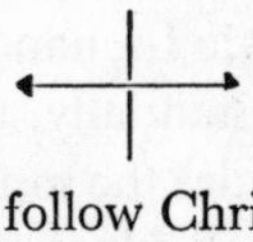

I pick up the whole cross and follow Christ. Thereupon I cease to oscillate stupidly with the world-direction. Also, I do not oppose the world ('Resist not evil' – Matt., 5.39). What I do is to make the ascent, to

[87] Mark, 15.34.

move upwards towards the pure Light, thus converting this cross of evil, of Spirit buried in the dark unconscious of matter into the Cross of Christ:

I myself, clearsighted, AM the Christian Cross. 'I' am bound, crucified, on this Cross, until all its 'matter' is transmuted into Light. Then the body is no longer vile, and existence is the Face of Beauty of the Ancient of Days. Crucifixion is the ceaseless Dying which is Eternal Life. Shrink from this Crucifixion, and I remain fixed in my swine state and my viper state.

Thus I, man, become the living evidence of the fact that Man is the main trunk of the Tree of Life, growing ever upwards. In living thus, the 'world' is always against me ('He that is not with me is against me' – Matt., 12.30); hence the stream of tribulations marking the life that is good.[88]

On the Cross, there comes the point when I am lifted up into pure *neshamah* – and *neshamah* is the deepest power of insight in me, a spark of the Divine Intelligence, *Binah*, which leads to the secrets of God and the universe. Crucifixion, whether it be in the mind only or actually of the body, is agony. The problem is the maintenance of the purity of *nephesh-ruaḥ*; which means that the psyche does not react in terms of violence or any form of evil. The words of Jesus,[89] 'Father forgive them; for they know not what they do', perfectly express this purity of mind.

Even as the descent or 'fall' into existence is a dying of non-finite immortal spirit into finite mortal matter, so too the return home is a dying of mortality into immortality. To lead up to this death, Jesus gives the sop which he has dipped to Judas. Jesus, of his own action, cannot compass this death – he openly challenged other Rabbis, violated the Sabbath, and so on, all in vain. Jesus had come to fulfil the will of the Father, namely that God become fully manifest, glorified, through him, or that the Yahwic Immanence come to complete realization. The right agent, circumstantially, to bring about this death was not Jesus but Judas. Giving Judas the sop was an act by which a powerful transmission of energy took place so that Judas could fulfil the

[88] cf. 'The path of a Buddha is filled with unutterable woe.'

[89] Luke, 23.34.

divine mission ('inscrutable are the ways of Providence') entrusted to him by Jesus, who in turn received his mandate from God. Satan is the name for this form of energy which led to ultimate consummation – 'It is finished'. This energy operates by dis-integrating the form, which really means restoring it to infinity.

Judas is the son of Doom – the doom which is the last pain-sorrow-evil which transforms itself into God as it expends its 'satanic' energy in a final manifestation before its release into the infinity of the silent Unknown. Simultaneously, it enables the sinless Holy One to be an undying influence for Good, for Life in its transcendence. This Judas-Jesus or Satan-God interplay has to be understood and fulfilled in each one of us, whether it be enacted in its Christian or any other formulation.

And here we come again to the cry of the soul: *'Eloi, Eloi, lama sabachthani'*. *Neshamah* is not 'my' essence or property. If it were, it would be finite and mortal and the scythe of the Lord of death would cut it down. The pure unity of *nephesh-ruaḥ-neshamah* is to be taken up into Godhead, into the silence of eternity, into the Infinity where there is no identifiability in our human sense. In short the sense of self as a separate identity vanishes. No longer Thou *and* I. Only Thou, the ALONE. The unified *nephesh-ruaḥ-neshamah*, the Eloi in Jesus, is lost to consciousness in that crossing of the abyss. There is only the divine dark, the absolute Awareness-Being which is the One Total Reality. 'The Father is in me and I am in the Father' remains the factual reality in its own transcendent realm – but I, the separately self-conscious I, can never know it, although I *am* it.

The experiencing of the disappearance of 'Eloi' in me is the moment of truth – fearful, awesome. It is the experiencing of the fullness, the wonder and the beauty of Death whilst alive. Felt first as a forsaking, it is realized in truth as the glorifying of God through 'me', and of me in God. This 'forsaking' is the final transformation, the deification. In Awareness-Being, matter is spirit, body is mind, man is God and God is MAN unblemished by man.

Jesus made manifest the Supreme Beatitude in terms of the Transcendent Passion.

* * *

What, proud Intellect, didst hope to find in these pages? Argument? Analysis? Explanation? A solution of the problem of Evil?

Witless Intellect! No man can spin a web of knowledge to tie up Suffering! When the light of Understanding shines, the gloom of the knowledge of good and evil ceases to darken the mind.

Impotent Intellect! Thou canst no more conquer Evil than thou canst wrest the Truth or annihilate Life.

Be patient, O Intellect! Casting away fear and lust, cherish the wound of Love. It will hurt! It will hurt till thou art born anew, blessed with the knowledge of the Immortals that Evil is the mortal name for self-ness, that self and not-self are the arch-conspirators who use the unbreakable thread of desire to weave the net of Suffering.

Thou wilt be born anew for Love shows the way of purity, Love is VIRTUE, Love is Holy Communion.

CHAPTER SEVENTEEN
VIRTUE : MIND : PSYCHE : KARMA

WALKING in the way of purity and living in communion is a reversal of the ordinary condition of worldliness. I cease to be of the world. But I am always *in* the world : even in cloister or cave. I may try to escape by avoiding people and discarding things. Yet how shall I run away from myself, the miniature of all the world? So I see that communion must include relationship with the world. Never *incommunicado*, I am glad; for now I can suffer and love and therefore do right.

The reversal of the condition of worldliness is seen in that change of heart, that clarity of mind and that simplicity and purity of daily life which express the transformation of one's mode of awareness of all existence. Instead of the worldly mind there is now the religious mind in action.

This is VIRTUE.

* * *

The religious mind in action is the expression through me the finite mortal of Mind-only, the infinite unknown energy spoken of as All-Father Mind in the Hermetic writings,[1] as *vohu-mano,* the Good Mind, in the Avestā, as Mind-only in Buddhism, as *Ḥokmah-Binah* in Jewish mysticism, as *cidātma* in the Upaniṣads. It is Power of a nature beyond my ability to control or to know, apart from the fact that it deals unto me and can function through me if I am pure.

Formless and dimensionless, immeasurable and inexhaustible, this Mind-Power formulates itself, and the Void-Plenitude displays part of its Plenitude[2] as the multitudinous, measurable forms and forces that I experience as the universe. The One becomes the Many. The human psycho-physical organism is one out of these many, an individualized form manifesting the creative activity of archetypal Mind-Power. In the holy state, it is the perfect expression of the Divine VIRTUE.

This Mind-Power or Divine VIRTUE, bodied as me the temporal existent, is the soul-strength, or fundamental original VIRTUE of me, the VIRTUE that is not my acquisition or property. It cannot be sought or

[1] See G. R. S. Mead, *Thrice-Greatest Hermes*, Vol. 2, pp. 3 ff.

[2] cf. B. G., 10.42: 'With a single fraction of myself I pervade and support this universe.'

cultivated by me the finite being; but I can cease to obstruct it and thus let it freely express its unimaginable wonder.

It is amoral, transcending the ambivalence of the conceived and the conventionally accepted good-and-evil of everyday dualistic living. It characterizes that pure, choiceless Awareness which is free of the partiality and conflict that mark discriminative consciousness. It is the VIRTUE of the unselfed. In its VIRTUOUSNESS is subsumed all the virtuousness expressed in the ambivalent living of the self-oriented. No real virtue, however, be it of the sphere of worldly duality or of unitary wholeness, is virtueless.

This VIRTUE is the spiritual health and life of me. *Haurvatāt* (spiritual health) is of the very Being of Ahurā-Mazdā (God) and is always associated with *ameretāt* (immortality). This VIRTUE is comfort, the strength that is infinite resilience. It is God's gift – which means God's giving of God-self – to me, to you, to all. Not only do the heavens declare the glory of God; Mother Earth does likewise. And I the child of Earth can also do likewise and sing praise as the unburdened Father showers blessings charged with divine VIRTUE – unburdened, because of *my* becoming clean, empty, transparent, unresisting. So my eye sees eternal light, and my heart lies in blissful rest in the all-containing Heart.

I cannot, I must not, pray for the granting of the divine gift, for it *is* me. Transcendence made me that way – and you, too – and also the animals and trees, the mountains and rocks, and the winds and waves. And also the silent infinitude. One difference between them and us: we can say, 'Nay'! We can be wayward! We can becloud VIRTUE! That is why we weep as none other weeps.

This VIRTUE is Life's intelligence in me. It can bring to fruition the general purpose of me as man as well as the special use of me as an individual distinct from all other men, provided I do not sully its workings. It flows through my very brain and spine. Let me be wide-awake and clearsighted, for it is of the nature of Elohim, the eternal Who and the eternal What in creative interplay. And if I the mortal existent breathe in harmony with that Life-Rhythm, the fruit of the action of this VIRTUE is wholly true and good and beautiful. It is not I the temporal shade who am, or will become, good. It is this VIRTUE that is the Good: 'Why callest thou me good? None is good, save one, even God', said Jesus the sinless.[3]

Life's intelligence comes to full flower through me as unerring

[3] Luke, 18.19.

insight, the eye of wisdom (*prajñā*) which sees only by virtue of the embrace of love (*karuṇā*). These, the inseparable twins, are the mark in me to show that mankind has realized manhood through the person (*puruṣa*) in whom all evil-mindedness has been burnt out. These, two faces of VIRTUE, fair and incomparable, in their harmony show the final accomplishment of the task of Elohim, the making of each male-female human being. For every one of us is both male and female, disjoined in his or her fallen sub-human state. Made whole by VIRTUE, the divine hermaphrodite is perfectly imaged as a living reflection in the male-female being restored to pristine holiness: a One Man, a One Alone, a unitary that is not-two. It is VIRTUE that absolves and resolves my sinful state, the male in me in disharmony with the female in me. Then, the marriage made in heaven, interrupted temporally, resumes its timeless conjugation which is the natural state of Elohim, of Śiva-Śakti; the state which is Wisdom-Love perpetually expressing the Buddha-nature in me; the state which is the Christ-consciousness in me; the state which is the bliss (*ānanda*) of VIRTUE.

This VIRTUE is Beauty, a power of genius which crowns the Lord in majesty and shapes the loveliness of all the world. It endows me with a sense which through Earth's beauty thrills in silent wonder to this Beauty that is the soul of all the beauty of the Earth. Then, I see the invisible and hear the wordless. So when I look at Earth, all Heaven stands revealed; and when I listen to the Silence of Heaven, the roar of the world is music.

This VIRTUE is Love. Never interfering, Love's virtue absorbs all, be it fair, be it vile, and lets it transform itself into the Beauty which is VIRTUE. Love never struggles, never imposes. Non-opposition is invincible; non-manipulation allows Life in freedom, the ease which is happiness. Divine VIRTUE!

* * *

Archetypal Mind is creative Power which is constant creation, Action in eternity which is the whole meaning of Life. Creation, a living pulsation of creative Power, a rhythm of Life/other-Life, is the primordial and supreme meaning of the word *karma*.[4] As divine creative Action, karma is free of consequence. In Transcendence there is no causation, no cause-effect sequence, for eternity is not subject to the constraints of time though it is carried on the wings of time.

[4] From √ *kṛi* = to do, to make. 'These worlds would fall into ruin if I did not perform action,' says Kṛṣṇa. B.G., 3.24.

Transcendence which is Awareness-Being is spaceless-timeless eternity. Space we do not cognize; but we can measure distance between finite objects which, we declare, exist in space. Discriminatively conscious only in terms of limitation, our experience of finitude or atomicity is necessary in order that we may postulate the undifferentiated field, space. Time we do not experience; but we perceive change, as the movement of objects through space and as the process of origination, growth, decline and death, and cyclic phenomena such as the seasons. Thus we derive our concept and frame our measure of chronological time.

In addition, there is psychological time. According to our feelings and states of mind – joyous, anxious, bored, fearful and so on – we are conscious of chronological time (of which the factual measure is exact and precise) in qualitative terms such as too short or too long, too slow or too swift, miserable or happy, gay or good or dull or difficult and so on. When we ourselves are in true harmony, poised, in communion, unselfed, then psychological time is in perfect rhythm with chronological time. In the holy state of realized Awareness-Being, space is at-oned with time, and space-time is subsumed in the transcendence of eternity. 'Immortality and also death, being and non-being am I, O Arjuna', says Kṛṣṇa.[5] Such is the operation of karma as divine creative Action.

This karma knows no duality, no conflict, no mortality. It displays no finitude, for it is immeasurable. I can never be discriminatively conscious of this. Yet I can affirm it, because it is free to BE through me when 'I' am absent from myself.

This action is divine VIRTUE, absolute, the source of the moral imperative in me the existential being in the world of the relative. In my mortal, unawakened condition, subject to time, I cognize karma as a cause-effect sequence. When fully awakened, my karma is VIRTUE, free of the bonds of cause-effect; and the moral imperative is the temporal expression of the absoluteness of the Law (*dharma*)[6] of the Spirit. Pure Mind 'knows' the Law, for the Law not only characterizes but also constitutes Mind-Power which is VIRTUE. For the Spirit, knowing is being, and the being is creative Action.

In Heavenly Man (*puruṣa*) VIRTUE is unhindered, for the constant creative interaction of male-female, positive-negative, is free of the conflict of opposing duals. If I am blessed with the Third Eye with

[5] B.G., 9.19.
[6] $\sqrt{}$*dhṛi* = to uphold.

which to see its unitary Action, I speak of it with earthly tongue as the activity of transcendent love and wisdom and all the other spiritual values – transcendent, because they are unconditioned and unconditional, free of all ambivalence. But if I am not so blessed, that VIRTUE is obscure to me and is obscured in me. In my darkness there is only the futility of battle, the battle in the ambivalent field of virtue against vice. This bitter worldly virtue always contains the seed of vice, and this miserable vice always swings towards the lap of virtue. Both virtue and vice await the redemptive power of divine VIRTUE.

* * *

Karma as divine creative Action being free of cause-effect sequence and of space-time limitation, there is no problem of the 'working out' of such karma. But in the context of duality or multiplicity, that is, in the space-time world of appearances, the world of the becoming-process, there is the incessant working out of karma, that is, there is a constant play of energies and objects and creatures in action, continuously producing change and themselves undergoing change. For us mortals, the psyche, that is, that which each man commonly calls 'my mind' or 'my soul', plays a major role in the working out of karma.

Mind-only, the immeasurable energy which I cannot deal with but which deals unto me, meets Body (Matter, the measurable energy which I can deal with and control), and in living creatures there is manifest what we call psyche. We cannot isolate or examine the psyche as we can a bodily organ such as the liver or the thyroid gland. In our experience of ourself or any human being, we are aware of what we call thoughts and feelings, intellectual and emotional states and processes, distinctive non-physical characteristics and abilities, and so on. It is with reference to all these in each person that it is convenient to use the single terms psyche or mind or soul. Again, if I say 'my collarbone', the possessive pronoun has sufficiently substantial meaning and identity as its basis (namely, the bone) to warrant its use. But when I say 'my out-breath', it is usually impossible a few seconds later to identify the gaseous molecules that made up what I conveniently called 'my out-breath', and entirely impossible to claim proprietary rights over them. Still less identifiable and possessively appropriable are thoughts or feelings. And yet mind or psyche is very real to us, for we know only too well the dominating influence of our desires and beliefs and thoughts over our behaviour, and their energy drive in our actions.

Furthermore, we also experience what we call the psychical atmosphere – as in a concert hall, at a wedding or a funeral, in the midst of national jubilation or of mob frenzy, or, very simply, the 'atmosphere' produced by the mood of the person in whose company we are.

Conveniently, psyche may be spoken of in relation to Mind-only as a differentiated finite object is to undifferentiated space, a universal field. Actually, we observe only a ceaseless flux of mental processes.

The psyche is distinctive of each person, displaying his particular characteristics. In that sense it is *his* psyche, whereas Pure Mind is nondescript and universal. Like space, it is there, unspoilable, eternal. Thus the *dharma* in the supreme sense operates in me through the psyche whenever my heart is open to it; and each time this happens, the Law of the Spirit is upheld ($\sqrt{}$*dhṛi*) as an absolute morality, that is, as transcendent Love-Goodness.

Living plants and creatures are organizations of cells. The living cell is able to learn. When it responds to the stimuli it receives, it can even display choice.[7] In this ability to learn and in this functioning of the receptive-responsive sensitivity characterizing living organisms,[8] we witness, perhaps, some of the earliest manifestations of mentality. It is concerned, basically with self-preservation, the response being one of attraction and attachment to a pleasurable stimulus and of aversion from a painful one. In highly organized creatures such as ourselves, this attraction-repulsion, this attachment to and seeking of pleasure and this aversion from and avoidance of pain, exercises a most powerful influence on our life, physically and psychically. Our ordinary daily existence is tightly enclosed in the mortal, dualistic round of pleasure-pain, joy-sorrow. Our calm or balance is but a see-saw equilibrium, precarious, and not a dynamic poise in freedom; our true well-being, short-lived. The psyche is the prisoner of attachment-aversion, of the relative, of the conditioned state (*jāti*).

Each person is a manifestation of mentality-materiality.[9] In the body are things of wonder – the brain and nervous system, heart and blood and ductless glands, genes and hormones and seed of new men and women, and many a marvel besides – and these are the physical root of psyche. The psyche of each man is a finite expression of Mind-only, his mental face and limbs so to say, even as the body is of matter. Matter and Mind, as universal undifferentiated 'fields', are pure Mind and

[7] See *Man on His Nature*, chapter 9, by Sir Charles Sherrington.
[8] See above, pp. 41, 54.
[9] *Nāma-rūpa*.

Matter. Not so, psyche and body, mutable panorama in time and space of two which strayed away from but constantly surge towards their unity. This panorama is the changelessness of change. Sphinx-like is the question posed : will you suffer from virtue-vice, or be delivered by VIRTUE ? Psyche-body in suffering, in the sick state, is ugly and weak. The female who longs to be lovely, the male who strives to be strong, is in truth yearning for VIRTUE which is Beauty, for VIRTUE which is creative Action, pure karma. Psyche, blemished, is the estranged daughter of Mind the Father-God. Unblemished, she is the ever-virgin bride of the Lord of Creation.

By virtue of my psyche and body, and of the nature of the functioning of the whole psycho-physical organism, I am self-conscious, isolatively; and I also have the potentiality to cross over, in awareness, the gulf of separateness from the One Total Reality and realize full communion unself-consciously. Through psyche, I the single and lonely part am wedded into the all-inclusive whole.

I the living existent am rightly described as a psycho-physical organism. Likewise, the animal. But the human psyche is distinguishable from the animal psyche, for I can deliberate Transcendence and my communion differs from that of the donkey listening to the stars. I can make smooth passage between time and timeless, Grace permitting. The donkey lives enfolded in the rhythm of Life, unconsciously, Grace never forbidding.

The psyche of me is not immortal. When the organism that bears my name dies, psycho-physicality completely disintegrates and undergoes dispersion into unidentifiability so utter, that the innumerable atoms and energies and activities and processes formerly associated with the cognizable, distinctive and coherent though changing pattern that was me, can no longer be found and labelled with my name. There is no more a 'me', the existential being, to whom anything can be rendered or from whom anything can be extracted. Only the One Total Reality remains the One Total Reality, unannihilated.

There is no absolute purpose of my existence for me. But Totality displays purposiveness through the temporal me in relation to mankind. In the psyche there works the measureless Power of Mind, of VIRTUE or Love. Psyche is usually unawake to her divine Lord, this creative Power which is Eros (*kāma*), imbedded in her. In and through the mortal psyche resides and acts the immortal infinite. Psyche knows this unconsciously, unanalytically. Time and again psyche trembles in ecstasy and responds to the transcendent love-power of her Lord. Then we witness in ways little or great those lightning flashes of Transcendence which live like the stars, self-shining lights, revelation. When psyche is wholly pure, VIRTUE itself, she lives in the felicity of timeless union with her Lord. The divine nuptials of Eros and Psyche are realized. But now they are not-two, for Psyche in such union with Eros cannot continue to exist as a mortal entity in the framework of duality. For the rest of one's days she has become the pure chalice, the Holy Grail, of Eternal Life, her VIRTUE undistinguishable from divine VIRTUE. She has grown into the soul of the world. And because the Holy One's sensitivity has become all-embracing, he sees and understands the minds and hearts of all men even without their speaking to him. This is the omniscience ascribed to the Perfected Holy Ones.

When you are such, you are the transparent nexus for the free inflow and outflow of Transcendence. Thus is purpose fulfilled through the temporal existence of you or me. Remember, there is nothing whatever of reward or gain for a 'you' or a 'me' in perpetuity. Only if this selflessness and understanding are perfectly realized can the immortal infinite release true fulfilment, the only worthy fulfilment, in and through us who are mortal and finite. Organism perishes, that is, limited being *consummates* in unconditioned non-being, in order that Spirit may triumph. But – there is quenchless brighter light in the world because the absence of 'me' has been realized.

And in terms of present humanity in relation to a new kind of being whose emergence lies in the lap of the future, one may venture to imagine a purposiveness related to the above at work. This, if unthwarted, may lead to a greater and greater refinement and intensification of the receptive-responsive sensitivity; to ways of growth, unforeseeable at present, of mind's power to penetrate and understand nature and things and beings; and, as its climax, to a mutation of mind and body on account of which a far more complex, advanced and wonderful creation than man, the present existing species, may emerge in the world.

* * *

Whereas universal Mind-only knows the *dharma* non-discriminatively, my mind knows it discriminatively. If my mind were to know it as Mind-only knows it, my mind would itself be the Law, it would itself be Creative Action in Eternity, immeasurable and formless. This is not the case. My mortal psyche can only know the Law of the Spirit in its several forms such as transcendent Love and Goodness and

Beauty, when her heart,[10] that secret cave[11] which is my inmost sensitive point of infinity is touched by Pure Mind and I am quickened to divine VIRTUE.

In connection with this we may note that the symbolism of *haṭha-yoga* presents a series of *cakras*,[12] i.e. wheels or centres of psychical energy (not to be confused with energy as understood by science), located spatially from the base of the spine to the brain. The seventh, or Crown Centre, associated with the brain, and known as the *sahasrāra cakra* or the thousand-petalled lotus, represents the infinite variety and sum-total of all that is represented by all the *cakras*. It is regarded as something belonging to a higher order altogether, transcendent in nature, for it is the home of the Third Person of the Hindu Trinity, Śiva Sadāśiva, that is, Śiva the ever-suspicious. This Centre, associated with the brain, may be associated with 'the heart, the secret cave which is the inmost sensitive point of infinity', mentioned in the previous paragraph. Clearly, these are associations, and not identifications, for the brain is a physical thing which can be handled, whilst the psyche is not. Buddhist yoga tends to regard the sixth centre, *ājñā*, representing insight into Truth or Transcendence, as non-separate from the Crown Centre, merging the sixth and seventh into a single centre, a not-two. This may be a more helpful symbolism, for it represents an intimate relationship between mortal man and immortal Being. In the symbolism of the Qabalah, *Ain-soph*, the Crown on or above the head, *Ḥokmah*, Wisdom, associated with the right eye, and *Binah*, Intelligence, with the left eye, bear resemblance to the Hindu-Buddhist symbolism.

Transcendence itself thus resides in me, the mortal existent. Mysteriously it presides in absolute power over my whole life. Transcendence is in total freedom. I too am in freedom in innermost being; as the finite existent, I am hedged in by conditions. If this were not so there would be no stimulus by the friction of the becoming process and by the sting of bondage to awaken me to the fullness of Transcendence. I would remain for all my life in that little round of *saṁsāra* confined to food, sex and the market place, veneered with a touch of culture. This confinement is my usual ordinary worldly state. It is my inheritance from nature, for this psycho-physical organism which is 'me' evolved out of some primitive creature in the dim and hoary past. The body, an integration of countless living cells, carries in itself the natural

10 *hṛidaya* in Vedic literature; the 'heart' in mystical writings.
11 *guha*.
12 See Lama Govinda's *Foundations of Tibetan Mysticism*, p. 140 ff.

heritage of that evolution – the instincts and conditioned reflexes of the forest animal, the dweller in the jungle constrained by the law of the jungle. Innate in me, therefore, there is fear, anger, greed, aggressiveness, and so on; and the overriding natural urges for protectiveness for the brood, tenderness for the progeny, self-preservation, and the perpetuation of the species.

That is only a part of my conditioning, for my primordial ancestor changed with the march of life through thousands of generations. Structure and function have undergone remarkable development in which increasingly erect posture, stereoscopic vision and more sensitive hearing, the development of the hand with an opposable thumb into a skilful, delicate instrument, the lengthening of the period of pregnancy of women from about two hundred and twenty to two hundred and eighty days, and the much longer time span of helpless infancy of the human baby as compared with other animals, the differentiation of labour between the sexes, and the phenomenal growth of the brain and of the speech faculty and communication through language, have all played rôles of major importance. Heredity and environment interacted. So I, the psycho-physical organism of today far outdistance my ancestor.

This is not all. Throughout the vast cultural epochs the world over, the generations bequeathed monumental achievements; knowledge, skills and tools; and control over the energies of nature and the resources of the earth. They established ways of life, norms of behaviour, codes of law and systems of belief; and some beings soared to the higher heights and plunged into the deeper depths of intellectual, aesthetic and spiritual exploration and realization. What an inheritance! And how very different is my psyche and my mental life from that of my primordial ancestor!

Yet all this cultural heritage of which we are so proud has been associated with and all too often been obtained at the price of untold suffering and inhumanity. Through the ages, ignorance, stupidity, greed, violence, power-lust and self-indulgence have lacerated the lives of countless millions. These talons of evil have pierced deep into the psyche, so the mind of man is sorely ill, caught in the net of sorrow. A cankerous shadow has formed itself inside him, and whilst he remains impure and ignorant it lives parasitically upon his life-energy. No VIRTUE.

For all that the past has handed on to me, and for all that my present upbringing and education have done for me, I am in contradiction and conflict. Something did not go right during the cultural and evolutionary process as I outdistanced my ancestor. There was an accumulation of knowledge and skills, but no commensurate growth of wisdom and love. So in the fields where I could exert deliberate choice, and in situations where I was constrained by circumstance, it was usually a low animal cunning, animated by the craving for pleasure, which operated in service of the isolated self. Only rarely did pure intelligence and large humanity find free expression through me. This happened only when I was unself-conscious. In the dualistic, worldly state, I was, and always am, not VIRTUOUS. Whence this ill-state, this sorrow, this unvirtuousness?

* * *

In the process of development from my primordial ancestor to me today I became increasingly conscious of self as separate from others. For me the ordinary man the word 'I' has an intimacy and vividness denied to the word 'you'. The self is 'I'. All others are addressed as 'you', and all of them, several thousand millions of them, form only a fragment of the total not-self. Yet for me the self is the one, whereas the not-self is merely the other one. This is the basic duality. And in me, the potency of the conceit[13] of the self quite outweighs that of the not-self. This dualism and conceit at the very centre of my mode of awareness of all existence is the root of conflict, of selfness and of evil.

The brain and nerves and sense organs, in short all the apparatus of my receptive-responsive sensitivity, have limited scope and efficiency. I can hear tones when the sound waves consist of vibrations varying from about 20 to 4,750 per second; beyond that they become shrill, and between about 12,000 to 41,000 as an upper limit they become inaudible. I am sensitive to light waves varying in length from about 3.9 to 7.6 ten-thousandths of a millimetre, and so I see the different colours of the spectrum from violet to red according to their varying wave-lengths. Waves varying between 3.9 and 1.0 ten-thousandths of a millimetre, the ultra-violet range, are invisible to me but are manifested by their photographic and other chemical action. Those exceeding 7.6 ten-thousandths in length are also invisible to me but are detected by their heat effects. My organs of sight and hearing, in fact all my sense organs, are like small apertures admitting only a fraction of the frequency range of electro-magnetic and sound waves. Strangely enough, even this little is too much for normal living. The brain and nervous system

[13] conceit = fanciful notion.

eliminate a good deal, by a system of filtering and classifying devices, as irrelevant 'buzz', and the relevant information is processed into manageable shape before it is presented to consciousness.

My senses, therefore, convey the world to me not as a whole but as a collection of finite, separate phenomena, objects and creatures. I am conscious of only a few of their inter-relationships, and of mine with them. Thus I am mainly, if not solely, aware of the world in terms of finitude and separateness. It is true that I can hold the thought of the unitary wholeness of the one total reality: but holding a belief or a thought (which is only a string of words) is not a live realization, not a creatively functioning awareness. If, however, I do sensitively awake to the wholeness of the world I am aware not only of the particulars as separate objects but also of the relationships between them, and between them and myself. Thus, contradiction or conflict within me is eliminated or at least minimized.

As I grow out of childhood into adulthood I become increasingly conscious of myself as an 'I-am-I' different from any and every 'you-are-you'. Thus I, the seeing subject, see and deal with you, the observed object, as a being quite separate from me. In my daily life, my consciousness functions essentially as a discriminative consciousness: I am vividly concious of my separate egohood, of my 'I-am-I'-ness.

But I rarely ask what is this 'I', and what exactly do I mean when I affirm that 'I am I', or that 'my innermost being is the real me or the true self'. From childhood I am conditioned to use the word I, or the word 'myself', when referring to the living organism that bears my name. In practical everyday life such use is sensible and not misleading. Other people, traditional doctrines and beliefs, my own feelings, my fear of losing my self or my unwillingness to be deprived of my separate individuality or ego, condition me still further. So I think of, believe in and passionately cling to, an intellectual abstraction, namely, an arbitrarily postulated immortal soul or spark of God which is the I, a separate eternal entity which survives bodily death.

As long at this concept and belief that a finite but eternal entity is the real I is obstinately upheld by me, it exercises a dominant influence for ill over my whole life and environment. For this delusive I-concept is the root of self-orientedness, of distorted relationships, of conflict and of sorrow. It is a misperception, fraught with tragic consequence, of the nature of the temporal phenomenon which is me the living existent. It binds me securely to duality, to the ambivalence of virtue-vice. Hence NO VIRTUE.

Thus I am afflicted by isolative self-consciousness, by separative object-consciousness. Self and not-self are not complementary polarities for me; they are conflicting contraries, sometimes irreconcilably hostile. Perforce, I have been stopped short of clarity of perception, short of mature understanding. As long as I am bogged down in this mire of separate selfness, the state of sin, inevitably there is misdoing and misery. It should be clearly understood that there is nothing wrong with pure self-consciousness. Indeed, it is indispensable for everyday living without coming to harm, especially bodily. And indeed the actual trend of development from childhood to adulthood – let us say, generally, till the early thirties or so – is towards the release and harmonious expression of the fullness of conscious egohood, and only thereafter towards emergence into the freedom of true individuality, of egoless unself-conscious being. It is when self-consciousness is poisoned by isolativeness and separativeness that evil invades and tyrannizes over the psyche. Then my life is devoid of VIRTUE. Hence, I as I am, one ordinary man amongst similar ordinary men peopling the world, find that I am rampantly egoistic, far distant yet from being the realized human, the *puruṣa* or Person.[14]

How has the trend been thwarted? How have I strayed from the Way during my aeonian journey from my tree and cave-dwelling ancestor to me today? What has locked me in this dungeon of isolative self-consciousness?

* * *

The living cell accepts a comfortable pleasant stimulus but recoils from a painful one. In me, a complex organism, the efficient functioning of this pleasure-pain mechanism is indispensable for bodily well-being and survival. My psychical response to the pleasant is expressed by 'I like', and to the unpleasant by 'I dislike'. But I do not use the nervous-cerebral pleasure-pain mechanism simply as a skilled worker uses a good tool; and my 'I like/I dislike' is not purely a discriminatory mental activity, measuring the experiencing of physical pleasure or pain. I do not remain poised, detached and free, for in my psyche there grows attachment to pleasure and aversion for pain. So I want to repeat old pleasures and seek out new ones, to avoid the disagreeable and to get rid of or destroy what I dislike or fear. Thus arise craving and violence.

[14] See above, pp. 82 ff.

Rooted in the indispensable pleasure-pain mechanism of the body, craving and violence hold the soul in bondage, for any activity proceeding from craving (including the lust for God or Nirvana, Goodness or Wisdom) is self-indulgence, which is always at the expense of the not-self, the other one. It is in fact a violation of both self and not-self. Craving, whether gratified or frustrated, is associated with violence and always gives rise to violence, and any activity born of violence is against Life and denies fulfilment.

Captive of craving and violence I am an exile from Heaven. For by taking sides with pleasure against the undesired – and *every* particular desire is a divisive force – the mind is not whole. Hence I cannot perceive or understand in its wholeness the present reality as it actually is, and act skilfully in harmony with Life. It then becomes easy for me the human animal to de-grade to subhuman brutishness in everyday life. Seduced by my bodily pleasure-pain mechanism and enticed psychologically into taking sides with what I like against what I dislike, I become preoccupied with the pursuit of pleasure. This, an almost whole-time preoccupation, effectually obstructs the proper function of the mind, namely to feel and to see with clarity the truth of things. With the mind ill and inefficient, I misperceive and misunderstand nearly everything.

My socio-cultural heritage, the bequest of men afflicted in like manner, so conditions me from infancy, that the mind is not free to grow into Truth by discovering it for myself, happily and fearlessly. From birth I am made to accept, by threat or by cajolery, beliefs and ideas, patterns of behaviour and norms of life. I become a bundle of biases and prejudices. I am prone to make assumptions and form preconceptions for which there is no warrant in Truth. Thus I cannot help but perpetuate my inward state of contradiction and conflict within my own psyche and also between me and the world.

The norms of society are not wholly wrong or evil. There is always room and need, however, for change, change which is not whimsical or regressive but is in line with the developmental trend. It is because I am compelled to conform mechanically that the seeds of conflict within myself and of violence against society are sown. Of necessity, many of the norms and much of the morality of society justifiably demand, in the context of reciprocity and interdependence, the non-expression of some natural urges and impulses, ambitions and pleasure-drives. So the shape of my life's activities displays 'virtue' or 'vice' as defined by society, and my psyche is the battleground of the virtue-vice conflict. But the ethic and values of society are necessarily confined to ambivalence. Society has to live in terms of conditioned reciprocity. It cannot live in terms of unconditioned Transcendence, for only individuals can attempt to live – and how few succeed! – by a transcendental ethic, by an absolute unitary good which transcends a relative, ambivalent good and evil.

It is impossible for the moral code of any society to be free of evil. The long line of generations which formulated the moralities and set the standards for action and behaviour for any community, based them upon the isolated self, a self as large as the collective self, i.e. the whole community, or as small as the single individual. Unavoidably, the forces of greed, delusion, violence, conceit, ambition, vanity and egoism adversely affect all the sensible and beneficial elements in any laid-down moral code. No blame or praise attaches to anyone on this account. Man changes and grows experientially, and also experimentally by trial and error. No blueprint of what he is intended to be was ever presented to him. He is discovering for himself the nature of his destiny. He did not spring into existence as a fully fledged perfected creation, like the goddess Athene did out of the brain of Zeus. Our psychical life today and our intellect and imagination have far outstripped anything realized by our primordial ancestor simply because of this long process of growth, which, however, is still far from its culmination and which, like most growth, involves 'growing-pains'.

The majority of human beings experience the urge to rebel, and actually do rebel, against irksome rules or restrictive authority imposed from without. I as an individual may be stirred to rebel for various reasons: an innate urge and longing for a particular fulfilment; reaction against social injustice; a passion to advance my society and country; to alleviate human suffering; to promote a worthy cause; or to serve God.

Sometimes, it is my own vision of a superior ethic which compels me to oppose and try to change the accepted moral code.

I attempt this in the name of a larger whole, mankind or God, with whom I identify myself and for whose sake I am prepared to sacrifice myself. I fail to see that such identification and self-abnegation is actually self expansion and glorification. I am still isolatively self-conscious. I am trying to impose a betterment – let us assume it is a betterment – on society by reacting against the imposition of society's lesser good upon me. But this is still conflict, not true transformation. I am still trapped in ambivalence, for I am merely hopping out of the trouble of virtue/vice into the turmoil of greater-virtue/lesser-virtue. As long as there is comparison and measurement there is but wearisome toil and bondage, not VIRTUE.

It is not my vision of betterment or urge for fruition which is at fault. It is my way of action which is mistaken. My rebellion is a violence upon both self and society. Karma which consists of violent action inevitably breeds further violence, unvirtuous action which is binding karma. No liberation.

* * *

What keeps me imprisoned in this ambivalent sphere of conflicting duals, in contradiction and conflict within myself and with the world? The answer is my own state of ignorance, *avidyā*. We must be perfectly clear as to the meaning of ignorance in this context.

It does not mean that I do not know history or science or art, or that my mind is not stocked with information of one sort or another. It does not mean that I am altogether ignorant of myself, of the ways of my heart and mind.

It does mean that I am isolatively self-conscious, separatively object-conscious, so that I am not in that state of attentiveness in which there is perfect communion between me the observer and you the observed, a state in which the observer and the observed are one *in awarness*. The state of *avidyā* in the religious sense is the excommunicated state, the state of denial of divine VIRTUE. Because it has no reference to either the possession or the lack of discursive knowledge, it cannot be dispelled by the mere acquisition of ideas, beliefs, doctrines and dogmas, or by logical reasoning from intellectual premises, or by evanescent psychical or mystical experiences. All these, by themselves, are impotent to release me into the state of *vidyā*, the state of enlightenment which is the state of unself-conscious communion in which Transcendence or the One Total Reality has realized its own Being through a wholly transparent and unresisting 'me'. But when such unself-conscious communion is realized, I am 'converted'. The total *metanoia* has taken place. I am the purified, holy one, the *puruṣa* or the Person. It is the absence of the divine VIRTUE, of *vidyā*, which holds me prisoner in the ambivalent sphere of the conflicting duals, the sphere of self-enclosed and self-oriented discriminative consciousness, *viññāṇa*.

The evidence for this, to cite only one example, is that I am conscious of bodies but am unaware of universal space in itself, *ākāśa*. I am conscious of thoughts but am unaware of Mind-only. Consider one consequence of this. Since I am conscious almost exclusively in terms of finitude and of ephemeral appearances called bodies and thoughts, I tend to regard 'my soul' as a finite entity, and to postulate, out of my ignorance, egoism, fear and wishful thinking, that it is immortal – as if anything that is a finite entity can possibly be immortal! A postulated soul-entity perpetuates my separative selfness.

If I stop short at the stage of egohood, however well realized, I remain bound within the limitations of discriminative consciousness. My world is then just a world of multiplicity, of differentiated particulars. If and when I transcend analytical discriminative consciousness (*viññāṇa*) and realize pure Awareness-Being,[15] then there is the One Total Reality. Confinement to discriminative consciousness spells conflict in the ill-state of duality or multiplicity. Yet it is this very suffering which is the stimulus for outgrowing the limitations of discriminative consciousness and allowing the unhindered emergence of transcendent Awareness-Being. VIRTUE that is Action in eternity, or Karma in its transcendent creativity, is the real power that moves me non-compulsively to this fruition, whereas the intellectual perception through the force of logic – that stripping the ego of its separative egoism is indispensable for the emergence of Transcendence – is only the first step.

Discriminative consciousness is indispensable for physical living or else the body cannot survive. But where the vision and understanding of life in its wholeness and the realization of Transcendence and living here-now by a transcendental ethic is concerned, it is an obstacle, because it exercises preferential choice which, inescapably, is a divider of the whole. My preferential choice in favour of pleasure and gratification against pain and frustration lies at the root of the un-ease of the mind. When there is a deeper social or ethical or spiritual stirring within me I try, of my own accord, to suppress or extirpate vices and cultivate virtues. But as long as I am discriminatively conscious in this dualistic way I perpetuate the virtue-vice conflict and remain confined within ambivalence. No VIRTUE.

From the active functioning of each of the duals, virtue or vice, proceeds the next conditioned state, pleasant or painful, good or bad. It is this aspect of the action process, the karmic process, which has been popularly presented as reward-retribution, credit-debt. It is this very partial and inadequate, and in some ways misleading presentation

[15] Atman or Brahman of the Upaniṣads: *viññāṇaṃ anidassanaṃ anantaṃ* of the Buddha.

which has bedevilled any enlightened understanding of karma and, in relation to it, ethical living in the deep and practical religious sense.

Summing up the main factors making for unvirtuousness, sorrow and the ill-state, we see that:

> Consciousness predominantly functions discriminatively. The sense of self, 'I-am-I', is very intense and is strictly limited to each single person, whereas the awareness of the vast not-self is relatively dim. Self/not-self is the basic duality.
>
> Because of insufficient perception of inter-relationships between self and not-self, self-consciousness is isolative and object-consciousness is separative. There is nothing wrong with self-consciousness – it is, in fact, necessary for daily living. It is the isolativeness and separativeness which produce conflict and suffering.
>
> The pleasure-pain mechanism of the body has its psychological counterpart in like-dislike. We side with what we like against what we dislike. Craving and violence arise. Preoccupation with pleasure obstructs intelligence. So we fail to see any situation in its wholeness and any fact as it actually is.
>
> Reaction against socio-cultural conditioning and against being forced to conform to the established traditional way of life produces conflict.
>
> Being confined to discriminative consciousness prevents liberation out of the unenlightened state, the state which is devoid of VIRTUE.

* * *

Broadly, the forces at work in the psyche are:

(1) All that has been derived hereditarily in the course of evolution from man's primordial ancestor.

(2) The socio-cultural heritage: that is, the way of life and social morality (customary action); the conditioning by upbringing and education, environment and circumstance, and by history and tradition.

(3) Rebellion against (2) because there are drives born of one's own ideas or vision for promoting the good of society or for opposing or extirpating its ills; or because there may be the violent passion born of frustration or other causes to destroy what is actually present.

(4) The power of Transcendence – VIRTUE – which remains a mystery until Grace awakens the Third Eye in the dedicated one who is pure in heart and mind.

Lying within the sphere of duality and coming within the prospect of discriminative consciousness, the forces in the first two groups give rise to confusion and conflict. They obscure the light of Transcendence. Yet these very forces – turbulent waves of the longing mind lashing the beaches of eternity – are the goads which turn my heart to the Unknown. I must understand this fully, or else I repeatedly err by blindly rejecting pain and feverishly grasping at pleasure, thus perpetuating my ill-state.

These forces in the psyche resist Transcendence, unknowingly. Transcendence, however, does not resist them. Transcendence is still, silent, poised. Its action in eternity is infinitely effective – and all is made holy. Transcendence purifies and transmutes all my unvirtuousness into VIRTUE – and I am redeemed. I who am in bondage – and I alone – can let it do so by ceasing to resist it.

The law of the jungle as well as the law of the spirit – using the words jungle and spirit without any implication of either condemnation or approval – operate through the forces in groups 1, 2, and 3. The law of the jungle is concerned with the preservation of self and the species. I the animal am occupied with drawing from the world, the not-self, all that makes for the survival of me the separate self. The law of the spirit is concerned with enabling me the isolated ego to become wholly related to the Total Reality. Having realized limited individuality (in-divisibility) within the confines of egohood, I have to grow into true individuality, the indivisibility of all the world, *in actual awareness*. Thus I the spiritual individual, the religious being, am concerned with letting the temporal me become fully integrated into the Total Being. In this, instead of my drawing from the world to me, I am taken in by Transcendence. I am freed from the shackles of discriminative consciousness into pure Awareness, I am liberated out of isolated egohood into pure Being. The finite I-am-I sense is no more.

Through me there proceeds the development of mind. The nature and extent of this development outstandingly distinguishes me from any non-human creature. This mind (or spirit) finds its supreme fulfilment as Pure Mind, in which there is no trace of evil-mindedness. The law of this development and fruition, unlike the jungle law of the animal, is not concerned with the preservation of the separate self (for that is seen to by the animal in me), and it is not rooted in selfness. It is concerned with the liberation from selfness and reaches out into the divine immensity of unselfness; it is concerned with my disimprisonment out of separative self-consciousness into the freedom of whole awareness in which the conflict of self/not-self has ceased, and sin and the ill-state are no more.

When the law of the spirit operates unhindered, an absolute morality is at work, witnessed as transcendent love and goodness and in short as a transcendent ethic in action. This is VIRTUE. As long as I am worldly-minded, and hence impure and unenlightened, still subhuman, my psyche is a battleground of seemingly opposing laws – that of the jungle and that of the spirit. In this state of disorder I live by a relative good-and-evil morality. But when I am pure and see Truth, the apparent opposition between the two laws vanishes, and the two laws become the one law of pure human living. The animal and the divine in me have integrated into the true human, man the living reflection of God, the man who is the *avatāra*.

In terms of the *cakra* symbolism of *haṭha*-yoga, the first three centres of energy are concerned with our worldly life as animals belonging to the species *homo*. They are *mūlādhāra* at the base of the spine, *svādhiṣṭhāna* at the genitals and *maṇipūra* at the navel. They represent, respectively, the storehouse of psycho-physical energy, sexual potency (which, in action, is the most intense assertion of separate selfness), and the forces of physical and psychical transformation. In other words, they represent the obtaining of food and sex, or the commerce of daily life; the digestion of food and the use of materials and exchange of goods and services (physical transformation); and the experiencing (enjoyment) of the worldly life and the conversion of this experience into knowledge, thoughts and ideas (psychical transformation). Buddhist yoga tends to combine *mūlādhāra* and *svādhiṣṭhāna* into a single root-centre – a view which helps us to be more keenly aware of the psycho-physical and not exclusively physical nature of the organism.

The centre at the heart, *anāhata*, represents my human-ness. I see that I am not merely an animal, that I am capable of self-cognition, that others of my species are beings like myself and that we are all interrelated and constitute one mankind. I begin to understand *human* nature and perceive the trend of its development. The sense of humanity, characterized among other things by love and understanding, is now lively and active. Significantly it is spontaneously expressed in the language I use when I say, 'I take you to my heart'. I do not say, 'I take you to my head'!

The centre at the throat, *viśuddhi*, represents speech. As long as I am confined to worldliness, the meaningful and effective part of my speech expresses and conveys only the finite and the mortal. Even though I may use the words infinity and immortality, they lack operative energy, creative power. My thinking is only discursive thinking – a string of words, silent chatter in the brain, or a silent succession of sounds or tunes, of visual or other sense images, all of which are recognized by me by their names or their verbal descriptions. Thus my daily life-experience involves constant speech which, in my confinement to relativity and ambivalence, represents only the finite and mortal.

When aspiration leads to vision and love bursts through the shackles of attachment-aversion, and purity and peace prevail, then auspicious Transcendence, Śiva in his abode of *ājñā-sahasrāra* is met by Śakti, the creative energy which lies dormant (coiled up like a serpent) in *mūlādhāra*. And there is blissful unity. Now the heart centre, *anāhata,* represents the true human, *puruṣa*, the divine Person. Now the throat centre, *viśuddhi*, represents the divine communication which is prophecy, that is, the speech which quickens the listener to an awareness of the supreme potentiality within him, namely, the full flowering of religiousness, the realization of Truth.

Mūlādhāra – Earth – and *sahasrāra* – Heaven – represent the inexhaustible wells of the divine Bounty and Grace.

The nature of the full fruition of human-ness in which Transcendence inheres is beyond imagination and defeats comprehension. What does not defeat comprehension is that despite outward appearances, organism and MIND are in fact not inimical to each other. The very cells of the body display remarkable characteristics, which make for preservation and healthy growth. The self-healing tendency, which constantly makes for organic wholeness, is perpetually complemented by Pure Mind, the energy of Transcendence which is itself perfect Holiness, divine VIRTUE. Most pertinently then, I ask, 'If that is so why am I imperfect, confused, stupid, in conflict and misery?' Some of the main factors responsible for my unvirtuousness and sorrow and ill-state have been presented and summarized above.[16] Furthermore, it must be borne in mind that life constantly presents challenges, which are indispensable stimuli to make us observe, experiment and understand. Without all this there can be no true growth, no fruitive change. Thus the very ambivalence and conflict inevitably associated with our discriminative consciousness and dualistic (divisive, 'sinful') functioning is part of the Book of Life which we have to learn to read aright. When the light of

[16] See p. 226 f.

understanding glows bright, we are healed and happy. And we gratefully bless the Wisdom-gone-beyond which bore sorrow in company with us with infinite patience until we fulfilled our divine destiny – MAN the creative THINKER, the perfected Holy One, VIRTUOUS.

When we see this, we see that Nature serves God as the Female serves the Male, and that Nature is the co-equal cooperator with God as the Mother with the Father. Thus we see that the divine Hermaphrodite's Life-process is the timeless conjugation which is creative Action, transcendent karma wherein is no evil but only the absolute a-causal good, VIRTUE.

* * *

The psycho-physical organism is the containment of all the karmic energies. All that I am, measurably and beyond measure, is karma, the whole of karma (universal karma), active and alive, manifest to limited human vision as 'me'. We humans are not conscious cosmically. Normally, we are conscious as separate selves. So we are ignorant (insensitive and unaware) of the Total Reality or universal wholeness which is the actual Fact, the Truth. Were there no 'you', no 'world', no Total Reality, could there possibly be a 'me'? Could it possibly subsist for even an infinitesimal moment? Bearing this in mind as vividly as possible, we may use the limiting words you and your, me and I and mine, and I can go on to say my karma is me, I am my karma, one single life-movement, not two separates. Karma means activity. And activity is energy, one universal reality ex-pressing and re-absorbing countless finite particulars, as if it were playing a cosmic game of hide-and-seek.

This organism which is the temporal me, is the karmic containment known by my name. Containment means the inseparability of container and contained. The living being – me – is not comparable, say, to a statue contained in a leather case perfectly fitting the outline of the statue. The statue can be taken out of the leather case and it still is the whole statue, and the leather case is still the whole leather case. Container and contained are separable; they are possessed of two different identities and functions. As regards me the living being, this living being is contained in myself – I am self-contained. When there is perfect self-containment there is pure continence, that is, there is no energy squandered or ill-expressed.

It may be said that I am contained in space like an object in a box. But space, like Transcendence is all-permeating. The existent me localized somewhere in space at any particular time has not displaced any space. When I move away, no displaced space rushes in to fill up a vacancy brought about by my movement. There is no such thing as vacant space. Space is a plenitude which appears as an emptiness to us ordinary mortals. Space sub-tends (up-holds) me and I am sub-stanced (ex-pressed) out of space. Thus there is the containment of me in space. The containment of Viṣṇu in Kṛṣṇa, of YHWH in YHSHWH (Jesus), meant the manifestation of God in Man. The containment of the *dharma-dhātu* in Siddhattha Gotama meant the manifestation of *sambodhi* (supreme enlightenment) through *satta* (the existent being). These containments were the embodiments of transcendent karma, Action in Eternity; and hence were divine VIRTUE.

Like the winds which freely blow through space, all the world flows into me whether I like it or not. I cannot shut my castle gates against its entry, for the whole psycho-physical organism subsists by virtue of ceaseless interaction with the world. I cannot bar out of my psyche anything which I call vicious or evil, for the very fact that I am conscious of it as evil and wish or strive to be rid of it means that it has made an impression on my psyche, whether or not it has established firm lodgement in my being. So, too, what I call good or virtuous, touches my being, unavoidably.

Again, just as the 'outer' world flows into me, my 'inner' world of thought, feeling, desire, etc., flows within me, interacts with all that comes into me, and flows out of me into the world. The environment and I are in ceaseless play. The name of this play is karma. As said above, the psycho-physical organism is the containment of all the inflowing and outflowing energies and their interaction. My karma is this phenomenon of an active process which both myself and others are aware of as the life of the body and psyche. Living is a process of constant and ineluctable change. Every single stimulus or influence or energy that enters me from without or arises within or goes out of me produces a result. It itself becomes, or transforms into, that result. In other words the cause *grows* into the effect. Living-process, movement, action and change – these are inseparables.

Because this is the very nature of everything that exists, including that which has been regarded as inanimate or inert, I see quite clearly that my karma is inescapable. It is impossible to dodge, outwit or disregard it. Every single energy is active, every 'cause' is ceaselessly becoming the 'effect', and every effect from moment to moment is the cause of the new effect, whether I am conscious of it or not, whether I deal with it or try to ignore it. I the living existent *am* this process – a constant change, nothing immutable.

My karma consists of every single thought, feeling, urge, desire, word, action; of the effect of my whole environment – parents, family, home, school, office, climate, people, government, law, society, way of life, history past and present; of the effect of my whole heritage – bodily, socio-culturally, psychologically, intellectually, ethically and spiritually. I cannot deny or arbitrarily reject any of it for all of it actually constitutes me in some degree and manner or other, and is constantly operative. My personal involvement with all the world is total in actual fact.

The world karma, that is, the entire becoming process, functions in its wholeness in the immediate NOW. There is no 'past' karma working out NOW, no present karma waiting (postponed) to be worked out in the future. The immediate NOW is the actual fully worked-out condition *bred* by the immediately past different total condition, and in its turn it breeds the very next fully worked-out condition. The creation/re-creation, or Life/other-Life process of the universe is incredibly rapid. My intellect reels and my senses are quite incapable of registering or grasping it. My awareness, even when awakened to its most intense sensitivity cannot take it in but stays still in silent awe before such marvel and mystery. Since my perceptions are so lamed by my slow wit, the time-lag makes me talk of karma as past or present or future karma.

Despite my slowness or mental inertia, I begin to sense the urgency in life from the moment I catch the first gleam of the truth. I see that the working of the karmic forces is displayed as the pattern of my life in relationship with all the world as it emerges from moment to moment. I am responsible for it. But I am not solely responsible, for I am inextricably interwoven with all the world. My neighbour and I do in fact keep each other – and my neighbour is every creature and every thing next to me and around me, and the world and I are jointly responsible for everything that happens to me and to you and to the world. We all suffer for 'each one's sins'; we all enjoy the fruits of 'each one's goodness'. This does not mean that the patterns of our lives display a dull sameness. On the contrary, there is an extraordinarily rich variety in the shape of our individual lives because we are so different from each other – there is no one else in the world quite like any one of us.

The body exercises a considerable influence in shaping the pattern of my life. The genetic structure and hormones are powerful determinants physically and psychically, indicating my development potential and the likely lines and fields of such development possible for me. The body is my most deterministic karma. Am I born with a robust or sickly constitution; energetic and well-co-ordinated, clumsy or asthenic? Am I cheerful and outgoing or morose and withdrawn? Have I a good brain, well oxygenated in my pre-natal days, or not? In short, is my body an asset or a liability?

But for me the human creature, the psyche is of special significance. It is the living link between the transient and the Transcendent. Rooted in the known and conditioned natural body, it flowers in Mind-only, the unknown and unconditioned. The psyche is the crucible of transformation on account of which all relative virtue and vice are redeemed and transmuted into divine VIRTUE, the transcendent karma or Action of Pure Mind and Body in union. And thus – though it is born in 'sin', is in the ill-state, and is subject to death – bliss and VIRTUE can be realized through it, and through it alone, in deathlessness.

In order to walk out of the prison of duality and to be free of the miserable conflict of the ambivalent state, it is essential to see all the forces constituting the psyche, or, to see my karma. In my worldly state, the psyche is in grievous disarray. A tumultuous confusion! A seething cauldron! See: animal urges, passions, lusts, angers, fears, aggressions, vanities, ambitions, greeds, envies, hates, jealousies – beliefs, ideas, convictions, fixations, prejudices, assumptions, biases, preconceptions, stupidities, delusions – neuroses, psychoses, madness – emotional and intellectual explosions of violence, destruction, gloom, misery, megalomania, paranoia – kindness, magnanimity, aspiration, compassion, self-sacrifice, nobility, wisdom – indeed the recital seems endless. Let there be no delusion that my psyche in the worldly state, or the psyche of the man of the world described as honourable and pure by ambivalent worldly standards, is veritably an Augean stable whose cleansing needs the labour of a Hēraklēs, a man-god. Worse still, should such cleansing appear to be effected by a herculean effort, I cannot rest on my laurels, for all the world flows into me and before long I have to act again. In fact, purificatory action has to be as continuous as life itself. A daunting prospect! One sees, then, why India has always called him who dedicated himself to it the hero, and him who realized pure-mindedness the victorious one.

It is with respect to the whole of psycho-physicality and with respect to the living-process of the individual as well as of the world, that the Buddha said in his Fire-Sermon at Gayā Head:[17] 'Everything is burning . . . burning with the fire of passion . . . of hatred . . . of stupidity'.

[17] Mahāvagga, 1.21. 2-4.

This burning – smoky, sulphurous, suffocating – is the hell-fire of the ill-state, of sorrow, strife, and sin. Emerging out of this in him who cares, and makes true sacrifice, the burning of selfness is the healing light of the world.

With growing understanding of the fact that my karma is inescapable, I see that I cannot refuse to deal with it on any grounds whatsoever. I certainly cannot eject any influence out of my psyche in the same way that I can throw away a rotten apple. All these living karmic influences *constitute* me; they are not like external objects disposable according to my fancy or need. Hence I *have* to shoulder my responsibility to deal with my karma. I have to be alert to the fact that I am a continuously changing product of conditioning, a conditioning which goes on constantly whether I am conscious of it or not, whether I accept it or resist it; and also to the fact that the conditioning is effected by forces which themselves are changing. Thus at any moment of my existence I am the resultant of all the forces at play – physical, psychical, spiritual, internal and external – in this space-time phenomenon, this self-containment which is me. The whole of the living-process is indeed very complex.

Some of the main karmic elements which make for bondage and the ill-state may be presented summarily as follows:

IF . . .

I enjoy a pleasure through food, sex, art, nature's beauty, possessions, authority, power, personal skills and endowments, physical or aesthetic or intellectual, social graces, 'doing good', 'removing evil', 'achieving success', and so on,

OR give pleasure to others through the above,

AND harbour it in my memory, desire it again, have nostalgic feelings, use it as a criterion or standard for present action or observation, AND regret that the pleasurable experience is no longer present, that such and such elements were missing or left uncompleted, OR feel morally reprehensible for 'sins of omission or commission' in connection with it OR suffer from fears or fantasies or dreams about it

AND be attached in any way whatsoever to that pleasure,

I am in bondage. Attachment spells further grasping at pleasure, which only spells more bondage.

IF . . .

I experience displeasure in any way or am frustrated, deprived or compelled by circumstance, or by other persons, or by my own conscience, or by fear of the consequences,

AND harbour bitter memories, feelings of hatred, vengeance, malice and so on, or I indulge in fantasies,

OR if I have wronged others or done foolish evil things, made regrettable mistakes or taken irretrievable steps,

AND wallow in self-pity, vain remorse and so on,

I am the bond slave of my aversion.

Attachment and aversion each prevent clearsightedness and understanding quite effectively. Any refusal, conscious or unconscious, to deal with karma means no 'release' from suffering, *dukkha.*

Even if I have 'forgotten' any pleasure or pain or experience, its impress exercises a binding karmic force in the unconscious depths until it is fully worked out, that is, transmuted. Meanwhile, the character of that impress continues to affect me in the same qualitative way (it 'breeds' after its own kind), for 'good or evil' as long as I am confined to a relative ethic, consciously and/or unconsciously. I remain in bondage. Oriented to a self-centre, functioning dualistically, I continue to obstruct Transcendence, as if I were an opaque block or a 'piece of death'.

The Upaniṣads call these karmic energies which are unresolved mental impressions, the *vāsanās* (see for instance the Muktikopaniṣad). The Buddha calls them substrates for giving rise to other conditioned states of bondage.

A few illustrative concrete situations may be helpful:

IF . . .

I, as a barrister, successfully procure the discharge of the wrong-doer or the conviction of an innocent,

OR I, otherwise, wield authority or power and cause suffering to anyone,

OR go on strike and thereby harm others, especially those who have done me no wrong but depend, sometimes for their very lives, on my service (e.g. if I am a fireman, ambulance driver or lifeboatman, or if I control the supply of electricity for an emergency operation), . . . then my psyche is laden with karmic forces for bondage and sorrow.

IF . . .

I transgress the moral codes of the society in which I was born and bred,

OR disregard or repudiate or inadequately fulfil any vows, responsibilities, promises or agreements in any sphere of life,

OR if I, born and bred a European and Christian, later on exercise a preferential choice and take to another, say an Asian, way of life, and to another religion, my ingrained Christian and European conditioning will continue to have its say and I shall find myself in bondage until I have fully understood the karmic forces and released harmony in my being.

IF . . .

I reject various aspects of my social, cultural, and especially my religious conditioning, because I see that the ways of life to which I conformed are harmful or foolish or hypocritical, because I see better, more humane refined and skilful ways, because I see that the beliefs I held have no warrant in Truth and the rituals I performed are but superstitious mummery or a travesty of VIRTUE . . .

I shall have to suffer on account of such rejection. What I am rejecting has roots in my psyche, strong or weak according to the extent of my conditioning. My new outlook, even if truer or more advanced, clashes with the conditioning I am rejecting and this conflict brings pain.

IF . . .

for pleasure, or for livelihood, or to satisfy my lust for power and possessions, I destroy or cause hurt to living creatures, or am associated in any way with such destruction or hurt – as a hunter, a butcher, a trapper, a pedlar in drugs or intoxicants, a prostitute or pimp, a gambler, a robber, a murderer, an armaments maker or dealer, a spy, a nefarious diplomat (not to be confused with the real ambassador of peace and goodwill), a government official or business magnate who exploits the weak and ignorant and poor or destroys the small trader, a liar and seducer through advertisements, electioneering, appealing to man's base nature (his lusts and greeds, his vanities and egoism in any and every shape, however subtle), a producer of systems of thought or clichés such as 'the end justifies the means' or 'enlightened self-interest' or 'we are the master-race', etc., etc.,[18] then my body and soul is ravaged with hell-fire. Rich man, powerful man, if your wealth and power are born of godly grace and purity within you, you are a trustee for Heaven's benediction on earth. Are you? Answer your own conscience. Or are you the supporter of the expensive lawyer, doctor, insurance agent, lewd entertainer, quack, and fellow thief and exploiter and oppressor?

* * *

[18] It will be said that if all this were eschewed by mankind, hundreds of trades and professions would close down. Unquestionably so. But if you had the sanity and decency to try it – and the manliness – see the difference made to your own well-being and happiness, let alone your neighbour's.

What is there in me that is the arbiter of karma? Unerringly moral? The power that underlies the working out of my karma and the world-karma? It is the power of Transcendence, the energy of VIRTUE itself, expressed in those forms which we name divine or absolute Love and Wisdom and Goodness and Beauty and Truth. It is quite different from my relative and conditional morality, characterised by the conflict of dualistic values (love-hate, truth-falsehood, etc.), by self-orientation, by confused groping (because of my ignorance – my state of *avidyā*) to discover what is true morality. This VIRTUE, symbolized in the Ṛg-veda by Varuṇa the 'moral governor of the universe' and also by Yama (the 'first' mortal who found his way to immortality and was granted lordship over the highest of the three heavens) who is the Lord of Death the Consummator and Perfector, of Death the other-Life, and also is death the punisher, the deliverer of 'the wages of sin' – this VIRTUE, embodied in my own being, knows with the knowing that transcends all the limitations of logical discourse and of dualistic and conditioned discriminative consciousness, everything that flows into and out of me the temporal existent, everything that I think, feel, speak and do, everything that I am as I change from moment to moment through the inexorable movement and pressure of the universal becoming-process.

This VIRTUE does NOT decree reward-punishment to me – it transcends relativity. Its omnipotent power works non-compulsively. It works fruitively whereby my dualistic consciousness (*viññāṇa*) is transformed into pure Awareness-Being (*ātman*, or *viññāṇaṃ anidassanaṃ anantaṃ*) in relation to which I can never again use the qualifying words 'my' or 'mine'. This VIRTUE (Śiva residing in *sahasrāra*), simply by its very presence, is the non-determining and non-conditioning but liberating influence because of which the whole karmic process keeps going ceaselessly, myself being slightly conscious and perceptive of it and largely unconscious but also in a mysterious way (which heals the psyche like sleep restores the body) perceptive of it. I the temporal mortal, functioning ambivalently and being conscious in relativistic terms, perforce *interpret* the process as reward-punishment, retribution-fulfilment, good-evil, heaven-hell, both here and hereafter, etc. Seeing karma only in these terms is like seeing a distorted image in a dust-covered mirror and mistaking it for the exact reality.

Mind-only, this energy which is VIRTUE, is not concerned with my pleasure-pain, my happiness-misery. It is 'concerned' with the transcending of relativistic values so that it, non-finite im-mortal VIRTUE, functions freely through me the finite mortal. Purified, pacified, I the mortal see and am the realized bliss (*ānanda*) and the eternal Beauty (*kalyāṇa*) of Transcendence. It is 'concerned' with the burning out of evil-mindedness in me the sub-human and my release into the full true human, the Son of Man, *manuṣyaputra*, who is verily the Son of God, *brahmaputra*.

If the lightning touch of Transcendence produces a radical turning about (a conversion) in the deepest seat of consciousness, then a white-hot flame of purification is lit in the whole psyche. It burns the dross of worldliness – duality, ambivalence, self-orientedness, greed, hate, delusion, violence, fear – and transmutes that very dross into VIRTUE. Nothing – no energy, physical or psychical or spiritual – is, or can be, annihilated. Its mode of expression is transformed.

But in this transformation process, I suffer, not only on my own account but on account of all the world, since the world and I ceaselessly flow into and out of each other. Vicariousness is a fact of life which is constantly operative. There is no 'justice' in this in the petty worldly sense. There is only divine redemption. Jesus the Sinless suffered, and suffers, on the cross. The path of the Buddha, the Holy enlightened one who realized Nirvana's ineffable bliss, is always filled with unutterable woe. Such is the fact which I must understand, and to which I cannot refuse to respond except at dire peril to myself. When Transcendence touches me, the mortal, I have to bear responsibility as the full human, as the man-God.

* * *

In order to deal intelligently with my karma, I must first see that it is futile to plead youth, ignorance or misfortune; that it is petulant to say I did not choose my parents or race or any of my conditioning; that it is egregious folly to curse the devil or bemoan fate or fulminate against God; that it is inept to say I could not foresee how situations would develop. Above all, it is a useless waste of energy to ask where is the justice and what is the purpose of it all. Any answer is at best an inadequate answer. The fact is that the world and I are totally involved with each other, that the situation is what it is and I am what I am from moment to moment, and that everything is constantly changing. My business is to see the whole situation as it actually is and respond to it to the best of my ability.

* * *

Attachment and aversion together with craving and violence make for the unvirtuousness of all my sense-functioning and my daily living process. Lacking true understanding because of worldliness, ignorance and the ambivalence which binds me to a self-centre, my urge to live the religious life is misapplied in taking sides with virtue against vice. I cannot deliberately build a house of virtue. The virtue which is thought out or deliberately engineered by me the imperfect, unvirtuous one, always has at its heart the gnawing canker of vice.

Whatsoever is thought out is a mechanical put-together, not THOUGHT, the spontaneously creative Mind-Power. As such it inevitably falls apart. It lies at the mercy of time and circumstance and under the doom of death. Once and for all I must see the uselessness of attempting to cultivate the thought-out or defined virtue and of fighting against its opposite dual, vice. The duals are deathless twins as long as I am bewitched by quality, confined to discriminative consciousness and exercising preferential choice. Thus there is no release from conflict and evil, no VIRTUE.

I must see clearly that I do not have to come to terms with my 'shadow' – an uneasy truce between God and the Devil in me, fraught with anxiety and erupting repeatedly into open conflict. When the self-centre dissolves, the shadow vanishes, together with the god-devil or the good-evil duality functioning actively as the virtue-vice conflict.

I have to *let* Transcendence work freely through me. Like all true healing of bruised life, the resolution into harmony comes out of a transcendent depth. Only a temporary alleviation of a symptom can be effected by any means belonging to the plane or at the level of the disease. The way of battle – the imposition of *my* will – is the way of evil. Anything forcibly imposed is merely a reshuffle of the old ill, not a transformation into the true. Pure Life is the transforming power, unknown and mysterious. When I am still and silent, I am unobstructive. Fully attentive, I am skilfully co-operative. Then Life's transmutative magic works unhindered and heals the soul. Psyche is with Eros, and Transcendence smiles benediction on the whole of the world that flows into me and soothes the world's heart-ache. Separate self-centre dissolved, 'my' psyche is the soul of the world, is VIRTUE.

The Buddha said: 'The cessation of all grasping (including grasping at virtue as conceived or defined by mortals) is Nirvana.' Jesus said: 'Resist not evil.'

So the secret of the Way which spells the reversal of all worldliness and the release of the religious mind into action is simple, though arduous: neither grasp nor resist. This does not mean that I stay supine. In fact I use all my energy continently. Then only can that instrument of salvation with which all men are potentially endowed, perfect attentiveness, be used for that spiritual alchemy by which the right working out of all karma, the purification and healing of the psyche, and the transformation of dualistic discriminative consciousness into unitary pure Awareness can take place. This purification and transformation are Life's action in me: they cannot be desirously engineered by me. The labour is mine. Transcendence reaps the whole fruit. Therein I die divinely and live eternally.

Dying divinely! When I truly SEE that I am self-oriented, that I relate everything to a self-centre and try to humiliate Life by subjugating it to a finite, mythical 'I-am-I' wrenched out of the one Total Reality, then at last my illusion of the separativeness of self and not-self vanishes like mist dispelled by the risen sun. My relative virtue-vice morality disappears. Seeing also, that since there is no separate immortal self-entity there is no reincarnation of this falsely postulated self, or of my neighbour, and seeing that karma functions here-now, I SEE that I cannot 'make amends', 'put it right', 'pay my debt' or 'receive what is owed me', 'be wise, pure, whole', tomorrow or even next hour. HERE-NOW, and imperatively HERE-NOW must I live, awake to Transcendence or else I am in perdition. HERE-NOW must I be wise, pure, whole.

So I must die completely to all conditioning, to memory, to the acquired, to the known, to duality, to selfness – to death. This is dying divinely.

To live fully in the present, awake to Transcendence, it is necessary to see beyond a shadow of doubt that the only way to live humanly is by a transcendental and not by a relative ethic. I must see that no problem confronting me or society can ever be solved, no ill-state of mind or body can ever be healed, no relationships can ever be made right by means which are tainted with my greed, ambition, egoism, violence, fear and so on. Evil in oneself, crime in society, violence and wars the world over can never be repressed or exterminated. I have to live – we all have to live – by absolute values: Love, Purity, Goodness, and so on. If I ever react with anger or fear, greed or violence, to any person or situation, I only worsen the evil. The moment I generate an evil thought or feeling, speak untruthful, malicious, dirty, hurtful words, or perform evil actions, knowingly or unknowingly, the karmic energy of that feeling and thought, word and deed, immediately begins to produce effects within my own being. It is well known that anxiety, depression, fear, anger, love and other feelings produce various secretions, and likewise that desire and thought are associated with electrical and chemical processes in the body. The nature of the effects which I experience depends upon the nature of the karmic forces I generate.

Furthermore, my thought and feeling, word and deed, injects karmic forces into the psychical atmosphere, and I, in turn, am enveloped and influenced by it. Do I inject destructive or constructive influences? Conducive to ill or to welfare? The pollution of the air we breathe is harmful to everyone present in that area, be he sinner or saint, be he one who is or is not responsible for the fouling of the air; and sometimes, as with radioactive fall-out, a very wide area can be afflicted. But with the psychical atmosphere, since thought and feeling have much less 'inertia' than the gases of the air we breathe, this affliction is usually very widespread; occasionally, world-wide. Consider the storms of violent feelings, of greed for possession or pleasure, of fear and of destructive thinking generated the world over by the news one hears every day, or by the propaganda with which whole nations are stupidly and cruelly pounded! If one is sensitive to it, how significant become the words in Genesis (6.5): 'And the Lord (YHWH) saw that the wickedness of man (*adam*) was great in the earth and that every imagination of the thoughts of his heart was only evil continually'.

Is it so surprising, then, that mass exterminations by brutal conquerors or paranoid megalomaniacs or religious fanatics have disgraced human history? In all these holocausts, in all revenge, murder and violence, the accumulated power of evil in the psychical atmosphere is indiscriminately let loose upon anyone and everyone caught in it. It is impossible to apportion guilt or innocence either to the evil-doer or to the sufferer. Every one in the world contributes to this evil with the endless thousands of evil thoughts and feelings and words and actions generated by him throughout his lifetime.

Even if I were sinless, it is impossible for me to sever all relationships with the world psyche. Bodily, I can remain separate, even very secluded. Psychically, your psyche and my psyche, the world psyche and our 'own' psyches, interpenetrate and interact ceaselessly. There are no ivory towers for souls. Thus even a sinless one suffers, perforce, on account of the evil in the world psyche. So it behoves me never to seek justice for myself, but to see clearly that there is no option to the imperative necessity to live by absolute morality, by VIRTUE, every moment of my life, whatever the situation. Such is religious living in practice.

But being what I am at the moment, I have not the ability to live VIRTUOUSLY. I cannot compel myself by an act of will to do so – compulsion is violence, not VIRTUE. I cannot wave a wand and be winged with divine VIRTUE – this is to attempt an egocentric equalising with God.

I must see that VIRTUE can never be acquired, achieved, possessed and worn or displayed as a spiritual adornment by me. There is no 'me', no selfness, where there is VIRTUE. As and when I am truly alive to this fact, the sense of Transcendence becomes active within the psyche and then I can *let* Transcendence work. Now I am in a clear-seeing state and I see what is actually present in me from moment to moment – fear, anger, stupidity, generosity, kindness, or whatever it is. Above all, I see that all this, 'good' and 'bad' alike, proceeds from or is oriented to the self-centre. Only when I see this with clarity, only when I am intensely aware that I am obstructing Transcendence, the obstructiveness – 'my will' and all self-orientedness – vanishes.

Then there is no 'taking sides'. There is full understanding. Attention is whole, awareness is pure and choiceless, and therefore psychological time is in rhythm with chronological time. The burning of 'me', a psycho-spiritual metabolism, a constant baptism by fire, is a smokeless flame that warms the chilled heart and lights the way of Action in Eternity – transcendent karma. Living eternally! Living by transcendent Love – *the* ointment to heal the world-woe – VIRTUOUSLY – is living eternally!

Then see the river of tears that flows from the eye! Feel the pain born of my ill, your ill, the world's ill!

See, too, the fountains of Compassion, and hear the springs of Wisdom! Listen to the Song of Life!

And behold the Plenitude that fills the Void with Silent Eternity! Why be in sorrow when Bliss throbs through all? Let the whole heart be VIRTUE, and sorrow will be a spent dream and the body's ache leave no scar.

Behold Beauty – your own Beauty! For the beauty of the morning star that holds the lone sky in solitary splendour, the loveliness of the rose and the sweetness of the song of the bird in ecstasy, is YOU YOURSELF, the face of Eternal Beauty not to be seen in a mirror, the face that is everywhere, shining, smiling, sustaining, serene.

* * *

And all that is for you, and for me, freely given. And how wonderful is the skill in giving! Given through the cracks and rents of my soul, be I 'virtuous' or be I 'vicious'! The Holy of Holies washes me clean and makes me hale. So I see that by intense white-hot attentiveness to *any* 'virtue' – that lesser worth, dogged by vice, confined within the sphere of ambivalence – a transformation of the nature of the psychical energy which manifested itself as that virtue takes place. It is as if obscuring fog disappeared and there is clear space. What is realized fully by such attentiveness to any one 'virtue' is realized for the whole psyche. Then Mind-only functions freely through the empty (unobstructive) and transparent psyche. Its creative action is VIRTUE and whatsoever happens through me the living existent is VIRTUOUS. The isolated 'I-am-I' has dissolved. The one and only I AM is present. Transcendence realizes itself. Deification and Reification, Spirit and Matter, Thought (creative Power) and Thing are an unsullied Identity.

Precisely the same happens by total, intense, white-hot attentiveness to 'vice'! Behold here the mystery of Grace, the beauty of transcendent karma.

'Vice' and 'virtue' are relative descriptions of the differing manifestations of the one psychical energy in bondage. In freedom, that energy is divine VIRTUE. When the psyche is no longer caged in ambivalence, the golden-winged Heavenly Bird[19] soars in unrestricted freedom, immortal. The eternal spirit, pure Awareness-Being, is at Home in its own infinitude.

Here on earth, here in the body, the garden of Eden, there lives the one in whom there is no selfness, one who is devoid of isolative self-consciousness, one who, divested of all egoism has grown to perfect egohood, laid it on the altar of Supreme Being, and conjoined with the Transcendent is the true individual, the one without darkness in himself, the living link between the eternal light and the perpetual dark, the restored Whole.

He is the one who walks in the way of purity, who lives in communion, in whom is the complete reversal, by transmutation, of the condition of worldliness. In him is the religious mind in Action, transcendent karma, a-causal, free.

He is VIRTUE.

* * *

Child of the immortal Light,
have you treasured each tear
like a pearl in your heart?

[19] RV., 1.164.46.

The voice of One that loves
  calls incessantly,
Come home, beloved,
  come home by the road
    of VIRTUE.
There is no other Way.

Let the natural springs of your heart
  move your feet, unbleeding,
    on the Road of many names –
Love and Beauty and Wisdom and Peace.
  And Joy.

As you walk you will see
  the Goodness of God
    fill all the world.

Such is the Way
  of VIRTUE.

PART FOUR
THE HOLY LIFE

CHAPTER EIGHTEEN
THE HOLY LIFE

LET the call be answered. Let me go home by the road of VIRTUE. Let us all go home together – and yet each one must walk alone on his own road which is in and through his own being.

The road of VIRTUE is the universal road, the spacious pathway which is itself enlightenment. The Buddha tells Subhuti: 'Just the path is enlightenment, just enlightenment is the path.'[1] The Ṛṣi Sunaḥsepa, son of Ajīgarta, sings[2] thus of the Lord of VIRTUE:

> King Varuṇa hath made a spacious pathway, a pathway for the Sun wherein to travel. Where no way was he made him set his footstep and warned afar whate'er afflicts the spirit.

This spacious pathway is the pathway of immortal gods. It is our pathway when we are in the pure state free of selfness, the unself-conscious state in which Transcendence throbs here-now, the state of wholeness in which the Person (*puruṣa*) is holy in his very body, the state of *vidyā* in which all the senses are living cords of communion.

I move on that spacious pathway only in and through my own being. But first I have to enter and to be my own true being. And here, strait is the gate of entry and narrow the way into the depths, dark with duality's dolour and swarming with the stains and seductions of sin infected sense.

How shall I be my own true being? How else but by knowing myself! How else but by using my senses rightly, by being awake and attentive to what is actually present within me from moment to moment instead of looking for a preconceived – always misconceived – 'true self'!

Thus may I know and be myself, move on the spacious pathway and go to the eternal home. No, I can never *go* home. I can only *be* at home in the cosmos which is the existential me, and also this the universe. And be free, a man.

* * *

[1] E. Conze, *Selected Sayings from the Perfection of Wisdom*, p. 115.
[2] RV., 1.24.8.

Wholeness is One. The One in wholeness is the harmony of the Many. When I am in the pure state, still and silent, I am fully sensitive to the harmony of the Many; this harmony is the one-ness of the One. To live the holy life means, therefore, that my life as it moves through conditions of dissonance and assonance circumstantially, is a Song of Life. As long as I remain the bond slave of worldliness, it is cacophony. To transform it into a song, only one step is needed, namely, to step out into the Void – the Unknown. It is a stepping into Pure Mind, the Mind of God.

What does this mean in earthly fact? It means that I am constantly ceasing to grasp at and to cling to the known. For the known is finite and restrictive, and as long as I cling to it or put my faith in it, the immeasurable Truth cannot fill me with its Light. I discover that I must not cling to any formal expression claiming to be Truth: certainly I must never search for such expression. Forms or expressions inevitably emerge. Any and every form expresses the living Truth only if I let it freely have its temporal life, that is, let it change or grow *and pass away*. If I dispense with form finding, and therefore also with fault finding with the old form, and let my senses and attention be unconditionally awake, without interference from concepts, memories and experiences – all of which belong to the static known – then I *am* the Truth. For in such awakenedness and unconditionality there is freedom from 'my' will or desire or thought. Then I do not obtrude on the world which is the perpetual flow of expressions, nor do I obstruct Transcendence, the Unknown which is the timeless Real.

To step into the Void is thus to step into the death of the known, which means into the other-Life of the known, each moment of my daily life. It is *this* death which spells Resurrection. Out of limited being into infinite non-being. 'I am life immortal and also death; being and non-being am I', said Kṛṣṇa.[3] And also,[4] 'All consuming Death am I and the source of all things to come'. Death and Resurrection is here-now, on and in earth. Earth, the existential me, opens up – every grave opens if I do not cling to it – and delivers up the dead – the known – transmuted, into renewed life. In perfect communion, when earth opens up, a Son of God, a liberated Holy One, joins the hosts of Light. Death and Resurrection, a constant pulsation, means the real fullness of Human Life : the meaning of Phoenix.

When the final death of me the psycho-physical existent is at hand, may I be perfectly ready to die. Let me not die till I have truly learned

[3] B.G., 9.19.
[4] B.G., 10.34.

to cease to cling to any and every form in which Life clothes itself, including the form of bodily death, or to any and every contingent appearance of the Absolute. If I do die 'unready', non-being will have to constrict itself and ex-press another being – ignorant, in the ill-state, the victim of craving. Even during my bodily lifetime I go through a million deaths, unready, and thus there are a million demons hidden inside me awaiting redemption.

When I step into the Void I know the 'Fear of the Lord'.[5] And again, when I am ready to die.

The Holy Life is one whole living-process. It cannot be separated from ordinary daily life, for it is precisely my entire daily life of thought and feeling and speech and action which has to be healed of its illness and restored to its holy state, which in truth is its natural and rightful state. The age-old separation between worldly and religious, profane and sacred, with the implication that one of the duals has to be discarded or overcome in order that the other may be preferentially sought or achieved, has been a root mistake which has been so productive of evil and of so much unnecessary sorrow. Unfortunately, the recorded teachings do state that we should discard or fight against and destroy evil. Such stating was due to the shortness of knowledge and the imprecision of language in the past, when transformation in the sense of transmutation, and live integration instead of mechanical synthesis, were not understood so clearly as they are now. Moreover, consider: where will you throw out the discarded? Nothing can be thrown out of the cosmos! It can only be transformed. And what do I fight against and destroy when I battle with evil? Only myself – for *I am* the evil! Facing my soul and seeing its ill condition, the war game against it would prove an operation fatal to me! There is no need for such folly, for Life which is VIRTUE is sweet.

* * *

At the heart of all teaching by the Holy Ones regarding the religious life, there is a perfect psychology which is the fruit of clear insight into the soul in the ill state, as well as of faultless understanding of the purified psyche which is virtue itself.

It is said[6] that the Buddha spent seven days looking at the spot on which he sat at the foot of the tree of enlightenment. This tree is seen

[5] See above, p. 138 ff.

[6] See Jātaka, Vol. 1. p. 75 ff. based on Buddhavaṁsa Commentary pp. 8, 9, 289, 290. See also Ananda Coomaraswamy's *Buddha and the Gospel of Buddhism*, p. 36.

only by the purified one. It matures and bears fruit in the 'earth' which is the psycho-physical organism of a realized Human Being, *puruṣa*. The brain and the Crown Centre (*sahasrāra cakra*) where Mind-only confluences Body, is the root of this tree, the sacred *aśvattha* tree. It grows downwards. The root is heliotropic not earthbound. Its psychical rootlets go up into the infinite void, *ākāśa*. The benediction of Heaven (the water of Varuṇa, the rain of Parjanya, the power of Indra, the light of Sūrya, the warmth of Agni and all that the gods have to bestow) is the perpetual *manna* nourishing this root and tree, through which the transcendent influence of Mind-only permeates all Earth, the mother of each one of us who dwells in earth.

In the state of perfect communion (*sammā samādhi*), Power (*śakti*) is one with Transcendence (Śiva). What the Buddha 'looks at for seven days' is not a location on the planet Earth but at the 'spot', the *bindu*, which is now the undefiled, incorruptible psyche through which Transcendence can function freely. Such is the Mind of the Lord of Wisdom and Compassion, the Mind wherein is no separation of conscious and unconscious, the entirely whole or Holy Mind, the psyche which is VIRTUE itself. Such a psyche is unknown to the orthodox worldly psychologist. It is known by those who have realized Holiness. The enlightened one 'looks', by entering into communion, *samādhi,* and not by the analytic and discursive process of discriminative consciousness, at this psyche become VIRTUE itself, and 'knows' the Truth, the Truth which is Mind-only, or the Father, or Nirvana (*saṁsāra* transmuted), or realized Atman and on account of which the Holy One says *aham brahma'smi*, or I and the Father are one, or in the words of al-Hallāj, *ana'l haqq*, or of Eckhart:[7] 'For man is truly God and God is truly man.'

When he who is free of all stain and who is capable of unerring insight looks into the psyche of any mortal he sees the truth of the state of that man. The worldly man or psychologist perceives with the eye of one who is himself caught in the ill-state of unwholeness, the eye of one who sets his sights on the worldly values of society which are the begetters of confusion and conflict and misery; but the Holy One sees with the eye made single, the eye of the selfless and the undeluded one whose sights are set on that VIRTUE whence flows the real good and fulfilment of man here and now, and not in the mythical hereafter, earthly or heavenly. The Teacher is a doctor who can truly heal by

[7] Meister Eckhart: *Sermons and Collations*, LXXV (No. 4, Hindrances). Franz Pfeiffer's Collection, translated by C. de B. Evans, p. 194.

awakening the sufferer who has patience and faith to the truth about himself. So the 'blind' opens his eyes, the 'lame' stands on his feet, the indolent becomes diligent and the sleeper awakes.

The Holy Ones fully understood the ambivalence of virtue-vice through their own experience. The realization of divine VIRTUE in their own persons was also theirs. So they were master psychologists, and they were rich beyond measure in the wisdom concerning the way of life which transformed the ill psyche into Pure Mind. Such a way of life, spontaneous and distinctive of each single person, and hence not a mechanical routine which only fixates a state of bondage, is the meaning of living religiously, of 'treading the Path'.

It is supremely significant, therefore, that the living of the VIRTUOUS life of which they themselves were exemplars held a place of prime importance in all their teaching. The ethical precepts or commandments which they laid down are the indispensable foundation of religious living.

One outstanding characteristic shines in their ethical teaching. The starkly simple words in which it is presented have full meaning and application in the relative context of duality and also in the transcendent context of unitary wholeness. Unlike business or social morality, which derives from selfness and is concerned essentially with gain for one-self, religious ethic originates from VIRTUE, from the transcendent Law of the Spirit. This religious ethic releases me from the conflict of virtue-vice, takes me out of the fearful and confused state of mind into fearlessness and clarity, and in the VIRTUOUS state finds natural expression as transcendent values in everyday living.

* * *

Although the Holy Ones propounded no system of philosophy, there is an implied metaphysic subtly interwoven with their transcendental ethic. This metaphysic is the philosophy of the Fact which is the transcendent Real. The Fact, in the words of the Upaniṣads, is 'THAT, from which speech and mind return, not having attained'.[8] The Fact cannot be conceived by thought or formulated by speech. If the ethic is fulfilled, and the holy life is lived, it is realized in the Silence.

Before realization man philosophizes about the Fact. This is man's

[8] Tait, 2.4; Śāṇḍilya. 2; Tejobindu. 1.20; 3.8,38. See also above, p. 79 f.

Fiction, a mortal phantom springing out of duality's illusion-producing power – *māyā*. The philosopher and Holy One are rarely the same person. Not every philosopher lives by a transcendental ethic. The Holy One does, and the power of the philosophy of the Fact operating within him enables him to present the living of the holy life in an illuminating and efficient way suitable to each man's needs and present condition.

The Fact which is the transcendent Real is the Truth which is a pathless land. As said above[9] there is no way to Transcendence. Nevertheless, Truth being paradoxical, it can also be unequivocally affirmed that the Path for me the living existent is whatsoever Life presents to me here and now. It is the one and only Path, Life in its wholeness, the mortal becoming-process and Transcendence. It is the Path for me, just as whatever Life presents to you is the Path for you. It is as large as Life the Totality, it is as homely and well-fitting as the fraction of mother earth upon which one stands. I have to take only one step, as said earlier, on this divinely accommodating Path, the step into the Unknown Eternal which is Transcendence. If I am aflame with that passion of Love, the *tad-vanam* of the Upaniṣads, which lights my being out of all selfness, which burns and transmutes the whole of mortal me, dross and metal alike, into the pure gold of divine VIRTUE, I am cradled by the power of my faith in the security which is the uttermost security from all bonds.

The path *has* to be the Unknown, for Life is the Unknown. Life breaks through all fixed moulds returning them to the dust. Traditional teachings setting forth the path are only signposts pointing to the Living Path. The mechanical observance of a routine supposedly leading to a preconceived goal dismisses the whole procedure from the sphere of creative living in the eternal NOW. It spells bondage to time-enfolded karma which is anything but the freedom of Action in Eternity.

The Path or the discipline of the Holy Life is not a vale of tears or a pit of fear like the old fashioned school or prison. There is no blueprint of the Path, for spiritual growth is nothing engineered or planned out by thought, by the known which is the dead past. It is like the growth of a flower. It is not 'my' growth, for it is the bud of Transcendence blossoming out in MAN-FORM, *puruṣa-vidhah*;[10] and the unfolding of the flower of humanity is as spontaneous and beautiful as a golden sunrise after a cloud-filled night. Hence the Holy One is not a type, like a soldier or a civil servant, and an assembly of the Holy Ones[11] does

[9] p. 138 ff.
[10] See above, p. 78.
[11] Excluding all professional, exploitive, self-appointed 'holy ones', 'Masters', etc.

not look like a crowd of crocodiles basking in the sun, nor like a flock of sheep, nor like members of certain committees concerned with high finance or power politics. The Holy One is unobtrusive wheresoever he is, not a blot on the landscape. This very unobtrusiveness catches the eye of him who has eyes to see. If I can see the VIRTUE in nature, in creature and creation, I can also see the holiness of the Holy One.

The discipline of the Holy Life is a Living-process, an organic activity of growing of the within and the without in harmony. It is marked by unselfness, by naturalness or physicalness which means action which is VIRTUE. In this action is also in-action.[12]

The discipline of the Holy Life is a learning by the play-way. I learn to play the game of Life, in a non-worldly way. In any worldly game, if you make the first move and I refuse to make my move in response, the game vanishes. But in the context of the religious life in which the players are Transcendence and I (and Transcendence wholly subsumes me), I always make the *first* move, in time, as my *response* – paradoxical! – to the non-compulsive yet pressing invitation, in eternity, by Transcendence to play this game.

But there is a mystery about this game. There are, and also there are not, TWO playing it. I make the first move by stepping into the Unknown. But Transcendence just looks on, wrapped in the silent folds of eternity. Instead, I myself make the response-move for Transcendence! How is this so? It is so because in my first move is the power of the Law (karma) in ceaseless operation which brings about the response-move, myself being used as the instrument of performance. And it is the only right move in answer to my first move. Transcendence never takes sides, never opposes, always lets be the Life-process.

This is one of the deep lessons I learn in living the religious life – to live by letting live.

See this game in another light. I woo the beloved with a wooing so true, that the wooed one, who wants to be wooed in this way and who does not want to be made to say nay, says yea, because *I* have elicited, lovingly elicited, the inevitable yea.

* * *

The WAY is one only, in so far as it is through and in oneself. It is one, even as mankind is one, or hunger or thirst is one. But even as the one mankind is composed of several distinctive types of men, such as

[12] 'He who seeth inaction in action, and action in inaction, he is wise among men, well poised in all his actions'. B.G., 4.18.

the scientific or artistic, the one WAY is presented in several distinctive ways in the great religions and in the religious and moral philosophies of the world. To cite a few examples, religious living can be viewed as

> threefold: as in the Zarathuštrian Good Thought, Good Word, Good Deed; or as in the Purgation, Illumination, Union of the Christian religieux; or as in the Buddhist Morality (*sīla*), Meditation (*samādhi*), Insight (*paññā*).
>
> fivefold: as in the Awakening or Conversion, Self-knowledge or Purgation, Illumination, Surrender or the Dark Night, and Union of the Christian mystic, culminating in the active Unitive Life, in deification.
>
> sevenfold: as in the Sufi journey through 'Seven Valleys' in 'Attar's poem *The Colloquy of the Birds*, namely the Valleys of the Quest, Love, Knowledge, Detachment, Unity, Amazement, Total Unselfing.
>
> eightfold: as in the Buddha's Noble Eightfold Path; or as in the eight-limbed Yoga.

It is important to note that in the modern world there is an increasing number of people who do not nominally subscribe to any religion but whose lives exemplify religious living.

Fundamentally, the living of the religious life consists in living in constant communion with the One Total Reality. How? By complete unselfconscious attentiveness from moment to moment to the whole situation in the immediate here-now. This is the whole of the discipline of the Holy Life. It must be clearly understood that discipline means learning – a live function of a living being and not an automatic conformity to a time-tabled routine. The Buddha gives the key to this in *sammā sati*, perfect mindfulness, the seventh item in the Eightfold Way; Jesus says, 'Watch';[13] Krishnamurti emphasizes 'total attentiveness'; yoga teaches *dhyāna*, attention.

This perfect mindfulness is the practical expression of the stepping into the Unknown, the Void, the one and only step which is an eternal dance of the spirit whose variations are all the 'other' steps. The central features constituting this attentiveness are purification, meditation (or deep prayer) and unconditioned freedom of mind. They are not separate aspects. In togetherness they constitute one whole religious living

[13] Matt., 25.13; Mark, 13.37.

which spells the reversal of all worldliness whilst living in the world. Religious discipline is no escape, least of all an escape into pleasant comfort. Indeed, any attempt to escape from what is actually present here and now is irreligious, for it is an attempt to escape from Truth.

Religious living, or the Way, may therefore be seen essentially as

> twofold : Purification and Meditation.
> or as
> unitary : Constant Communion.

CHAPTER NINETEEN
MORALITY : RELIGIOUS OBSERVANCES : THE DISCIPLINE OF THE BODY

THE word yoga ($\sqrt{}$ *yuj* = to yoke or to join together) is best understood as the restoration into full relationship with the Total Reality, with Transcendence. It is my reinstatement into the state of grace, the absolution from my graceless state. Rejoined to the Whole, I am liberated from isolative self-consciousness.

The sage Śāṇḍilya asks his Teacher to explain the various parts of yoga, and Atharvan the Holy One answers :[1]

> The eight limbs of yoga are morality, *yama*; religious observances, *niyama*; posture, *āsana*; control of Life-energy,[2] *prāṇāyāma*; withdrawal of the senses from worldly objects, *pratyāhāra*; collectedness of mind, *dhāraṇā*; meditation, *dhyāna*; absorption or mental union of the meditator with the meditated, *samādhi*.

Yoga is the way of Power involving the right use of one's whole psycho-physical energy. Power is invariably and inevitably misused unless there is the harmony of love and wisdom, and above all, the indispensable foundation of morality. Morality means customary action. Right conduct in thought, feeling, speech and deed is the customary action characterizing the Holy Life. The Śāṇḍilya Upaniṣad presents morality as harmlessness, truth, non-covetousness, continence, kindliness (or ruth), equanimity, patient endurance, steadiness (or firmness) of mind in gain and loss, abstemiousness (especially with food and drink), cleanliness of body and mind.

Atharvan teaches that each of these ten constituents of morality must be observed in mind, speech and body. In the Sermon on the Mount, Jesus says :[3]

> Ye have heard that it was said to them of old time, Thou shalt not kill; and whosoever shall kill shall be in danger of the judgment : But I say unto you, That whosoever is angry with his brother without a cause shall be in danger of the judgment; and whosoever shall

[1] Śāṇḍilya Up., 1.1-3.
[2] Usually spoken of as breath-control.
[3] Matt., 5.21,22,27,28.

> say to his brother, *Raca*,[4] shall be in danger of the council; but whosoever shall say, Thou fool[5], shall be in danger of the hell[6] of fire ... Ye have heard that it was said by them of old time, Thou shalt not commit adultery: But I say unto you, that whosoever looketh on a woman to lust after her hath committed adultery with her already in his heart.

Jesus accepts the Mosaic Ten Commandments as presented in Exodus (20.3-17) and Deuteronomy (5.7-21); and also the Commandment in Deuteronomy (6.5), 'And thou shalt love the Lord thy God with all thine heart, and with all thy soul, and with all thy might', and in Leviticus (19.18), 'thou shalt love thy neighbour as thyself'. In relation to some of these commandments he makes explicit the importance of observing them in thought and speech as well as in deed.

So also, in accordance with some of the daily penitential prayers from the later Avestā such as the *Ahuramazda Khodāe* and the *Sarosh Bāj*, the devout Zarathuśtrian prays:

> From all my sins do I repent and turn back. From every evil thought, evil word and evil deed, which in this world I may have conceived of, uttered or committed, which from me has come forth, or originated through me; of all such sins of mind and speech and deed, pertaining to my body or soul, pertaining to this world or the spiritual world,
> O Lord! with sincere contrition I repent, making the three-fold affirmation (of good thought, good word, good deed).

And in the *Jasa-me Avangh-he Mazda*, he affirms:

> I extol thoughts conceived purely, words spoken cleanly, deeds done skilfully.
> I extol the holy Mazdayasni religion which (exhorts us) to avert strife, cast aside instruments of war, put away selfish interests and live the holy life.

Some of the virtues[7] are right reason (or the wisdom which discriminates), temperance, modesty, honesty, gratitude and hope: the vices are concupiscence, despair, deceitfulness, arrogance and acquisitiveness, of

[4] An expression of contempt.
[5] Or *Moreh*, a Hebrew expression of condemnation.
[6] *Gk*. Gehenna of fire.
[7] Denkart (ed. Madan) 266. 1 ff. Quoted from *The Dawn and Twilight of Zoroastrianism*, by R. C. Zaehner, p. 276.

which the first is the worst. In Zarathuśtrian teaching body and soul are intimately interlinked. Material and spiritual well-being are of a piece; and bodily sickness indicates an ill-state of the soul. By clear vision man gains insight into spiritual verity. There is clear vision when one's mind is united with the Good Mind (*Vohu Mano*), and by eliminating, like a champion victorious in battle, vices such as concupiscence, envy, heresy and vengefulness.[8]

The form in which Buddhist morality is presented is known as the *sīlas*. A *sīla* may be understood as a working rule or direction, conducive to skilled action or right conduct. It is of the nature of an advice or a recommendation. The five basic *sīlas* are couched in these terms: I undertake the rule of training to refrain from harming, stealing, sensual indulgence, wrong speech, and liquors engendering slothfulness. Each rule is undertaken freely and self-responsibly by oneself, and is not imposed by external authority. The consequence of succeeding or failing in carrying out the undertaking is not a reward or punishment; it is the natural working out of the psychical and physical energies generated. The paramount importance of the mental aspect of morality is often expounded by the Buddha, as for instance in his discourse with Upāli.[9]

Śrī Kṛṣṇa says:[10]

> 'He who restrains his organs of action but continues in his mind to brood over the objects of sense,[11] this deluded one is said to be a man of wrong conduct.'

whereas[12]

> 'He whose undertakings are free from desire and expectations (of advantage), whose actions are burned up in the fire of wisdom, him the wise call a sage.'

It is significant that the great teachers have emphasized the observance of morality in thought and speech and action. When such threefold morality characterizes the daily life, there is no contradiction between the inward thought and feeling, which is private, and the public outward speech and action; no conflict within the psyche between an

[8] Ibid. (footnote 7) p. 273.
[9] M., I.376-378.
[10] B.G., 3.6.
[11] The meaning in this context is that he indulges in sensual pleasures in imagination.
[12] B.G., 4.19.

'I wish to . . .' and an 'I am forbidden, or I ought not, to . . .'; no fragmentation of the wholeness of one's living-process. The threefold morality lays the foundation for living as an integrated human being.

The task is no light one. Consider the commandment, 'Thou shalt not kill'. Most of us do not intentionally kill other human beings. But what do we do in war? Or when we drive a car carelessly, or under the influence of drink? Or to be rid of the consequences of self-indulgence? Or drive another person to suicide? How far do we contribute, directly or indirectly, towards killing living creatures by being inventors or manufacturers of lethal instruments? By being hunters or butchers or by being involved in trades involving the killing of living creatures? How many of us kill off in our thoughts and wishes the aged relative whose presence alive prevents a legacy coming to us, or gratifying a passion near to our hearts? Or whose senile, decrepit state has become a heavy burden or a disagreeable nuisance to us? How often do we venomously spit out the words, 'I wish he were dead'?

Consider the precept or undertaking to refrain from harming by act or speech or thought any living creature. This has a far more extensive sphere of daily application than the specialised and dreadfully dramatic form of harming, namely killing. How often, each day, do we harm, not only others but also ourselves, by act or speech or thought?

True morality is the living expression of VIRTUE. For morality to be the threefold morality, our right conduct is our customary behaviour which has grown free of the conflict and confusion of the ambivalent state and has become natural to us, second nature as it were. The Holy Ones spared no pains in pointing out, unequivocally, the perfect meaning and expression of the values which distinguish the human from the sub-human.

Jesus says:[13]

> 'Ye have heard that it hath been said, Thou shalt love thy neighbour and hate thine enemy.
> 'But I say unto you, Love your enemies, bless them that curse you, do good to them that hate you, and pray for them that despitefully use you, and persecute you.'

And on behalf of those who crucified him, he prays:[14]

> 'Father, forgive them; for they know not what they do.'

[13] Matt., 5.43,44.
[14] Luke, 23.34.

And after the last supper, before he went forth with his disciples over the brook of Cedron :[15]

> 'This is my commandment, that ye love one another, as I have loved you.
> Greater love hath no man than this, that a man lay down his life for his friends.'

Speaking of the friend who is the same in happiness and adversity and is sound of heart, the Buddha says :[16]

> 'He lays down even his life for your sake.'

In the *Parable of the Saw*[17] the Buddha instructs his monks that howsoever others act or speak to them or of them, gently or violently, they should train themselves thus :

> 'Neither will our minds become perverted nor will we utter an evil speech, but kindly and compassionate will we dwell, with a mind of friendliness, void of hatred; and we will dwell having suffused that person with a mind of friendliness, and beginning with him, we will dwell having suffused the whole world with a mind (of friendliness) like the whole of space – far-reaching, widespread, immeasurable, without enmity, without malevolence.'

A few moments later he says :

> '*Bhikkhus*, even if low-down thieves were to carve you limb from limb with a double-handled saw, yet even then whoever (monk or nun) sets his mind at enmity, he (or she) for this reason, is not a doer of my teaching. Herein, *bhikkhus*, you should train yourselves thus : "Neither will our minds become perverted . . . (as above) . . . without enmity, without malevolence".'

What begins as simple morality is allowed and helped, by whosoever cares, to flower into VIRTUE, the transcendental ethic by which the true human lives.

* * *

The leg of morality (*yama*) has religious observances (*niyama*) as the other leg to enable one to walk rightly on life's way. Atharvan teaches[18] that there are ten observances :

[15] John, 15.12,13.
[16] D., 3.187.
[17] M., 1.128,129.
[18] Śāṇḍilya Up., 1.15-25.

Austerity in bodily life; *contentment* with what comes to us naturally and easily (for daily living); *confidence* in scriptural statements as to what is religious or irreligious; *charity,* or giving food and wealth, lawfully earned, to those in need or deserving help; *worship* of God (or the gods or tutelary deities) with a happy mind; serious *study* of the deep teachings of scripture; *shame* felt in contravening social standards and religious rules : *faith* in the paths laid down in the scriptures for living religiously; *reciting,* aloud or mentally only, words or phrases which have a beneficial, spiritual effect; constancy in the *observance of the injunctions and prohibitions* laid down in the scriptures.

Religious obervances such as the above are systematically prescribed, with appropriate differences and variations, in the disciplines of all the religions. They are, to use a Christian phrase, the external instruments of grace, and together with morality, constitute the ethical and practical discipline preliminary to the more intensive living of the religious life.

When I worship or pray, let me do so to God, never to 'my' God. His is the earth and the heavens and all therein. He is in you and in me. And when I die there is but He, not 'more' not 'less', the Fullness from whence I appeared and which remains the changeless equal Fullness with either my appearing or disappearing. So to the whole of mortal me He is absolute, immortal, ungraspable and unpossessable. Let me never be guilty of saying 'my' God. Likewise, never may I say 'my' Atman. He is the pulse of Life/other-Life in which I am an infinitesimal flash. By never clinging to 'my' life out of fearless trust in Life, 'my' death spells release into the infinite other-Life. Is not this the true 'security', the uttermost security from all bonds? He, eternal God, is the immortality of mortal me! God be praised, God be worshipped with my praying which is the total self-giving and the wholly unresisting unselfness which lets the Divine Life vibrate freely through me.

Let my prayer and worship be pure transparency. If I be seen or heard by Thee, I have stood in the way, to my hurt, and 'minished the light. Let me do the suffering – else I am Thy suffering. And that is sin, whose lust-conceived child of darkness is death.

But I, frail web spun on the loom of time, do suffer the pain and ill-fortune of I-hood. And cry. A whimper, cacophanous, for I said 'my' God : a fond youth begging for easement of pain, a pain of ignorance, loneliness and innocence of wrong, deep in the night when the moon was full in a cloudless tropical sky. Ever-present Mercy healed the pain. But I-hood remained, giving birth in ill season to new pain, to other prayer, till Grace triumphed. I relinquished I-hood, with grace. Thus prayer is the transparent state of communion where division is no more, an enlightenment not weighed down by an enlightened one. God is Light. God is Love wherein the hatefulness of otherness is not. And God is worship : not a mere object of worship but the reality of the immeasurable Worth.

* * *

To this is the going – to the trackless and the untraceable, the Unknown and Unknowable – by the frail web spun on the loom of time. No web is there at journey's end, for it is transmuted into the timeless Nothing whose Being is immeasurable Life, without beginning or ending, birth or death. If it is not transmuted it smashes into cosmic dust, also untraceable. And the smashing is God's suffering, for there has to be stepping down into another web on time's loom and the Immeasurable Holy suffers the constraints of mortal finitude.

Let me then be constantly in the state of true prayer, the prayer devoid of 'I'-hood, of me and mine, the prayer where the storm of words is no more. How does that state supervene? That state cannot be sought. Woe betides him who makes a picture in his mind – a false idol – of the unimaginable state and pursues it. So I start from here, just as I am, here and now. Have I not been conditioned from childhood to 'say my prayers', to *my* God who is the God of the 'true faith', and whose nature is such and such? If, and because, I care with passion for Truth and am unafflicted by mere intellectual curiosity, do I not suffer the pain of conflict and disillusionment as I see the falsity in all this conditioning? Have I not witnessed my own self-centred greedy, blindly assured of salvation and smugly self-righteous participation in worship, private and public, and have not I heard the clangour of words of scriptures gabbled at speed by priest and participants alike in Zarathuśtrian fire-temple and Christian Church, in Hindu and Buddhist temple and in odd circles with their own quaint (though harmless) ceremonies, for many years? Seeing and hearing, with compassion and with an open mind, I learn to remain quiet, unselfconscious, and the beatific state of true prayer supervenes, by grace.

If I have a genuine passion to pray, then let me say the words of the chosen prayer softly, sweetly and slowly; preferably very slowly. For then I can allow my whole heart to flow reverently and gracefully into my living act of praying, and my whole mind can be awake to the true significance of the words, and my whole being can be sensitive to the spiritual power released by the act of prayer. Try it out with the *asato mā sad gamaya* (from the unreal lead me to the real) in the Bṛhadāraṇyaka Upaniṣad, the paternoster (Our father which art in heaven) as taught by Jesus, the *hṛidaya sūtra* (the 'heart discourse') of the Buddhist *prajñāpāramitā,* the *ashem vohu*[19] of the Zarathuśtrians; or with any prayer which wells out of your heart and impassions your whole being.

Take, for example, the paternoster. When the need or urge arises, spontaneously say the words very softly and feelingly. Repeat the prayer a few times, quite silently if preferred. Several minutes may pass by in this way. Let mind and body be at peace, not expecting or desiring results. Prayer for gain is not prayer. Let attention dwell on, and in, the prayer, which is then an affirmation, with transcendent power, of Truth.

If the occasion be such, a sense of communion will supervene. Instead of a few minutes, the prayer may take an hour, or even much longer, to live through once only. If I can give myself wholly to it, a rich transformation of my being takes place. 'Our father'. Whose father? Mine to start with. Soon I am sensitively aware he is also your father. You and I are now becoming close knit – my friend's father – my enemy's father – father of us all – OUR father! Let the whole being stay still, suffused by this intensely living awareness – *not* a mere thought (an inanimate string of words) – of this factual unity, this simple, real love which is realizable in contemplative prayer, in deep meditation.[20] And in this state of realization (= making real) when the father is in me and I am in the father, the psyche is cleansed of its poisons of anger and hate and fear and envy and jealousy and proud self-esteem and the mind is at peace, and I see the truth of my human nature and am freed in some measure or other of my isolative self-consciousness. If such purification does not take place there has been no realization but only discursive musing. All this issues out of just the first word of the prayer. But do I come to a stop there? No. The father is the father of all living creatures. And so it is that 'not a sparrow falleth to the ground but my father in heaven knoweth it'. Still more. The father is the father of the whole world, and the entire universe throbs with his life-energy. How tremendous is this mystery! It takes me right beyond that which I in my ignorance used to call the living world, separating it from 'dead matter'.

[19] *Ashā* (the equivalent of *Ṛta* in the Ṛg-veda) stands for the eternal order, the Law inherent in the workings of the cosmos. In Zarathuśtrian teaching it represents Righteousness, Truth, Holiness, Purity. *Ashem vohu vahistem asti* = *Ashā* is the supreme good.

[20] As in the Buddhist *brahmavihāras,* the divine residences or states of union with Brahmā.

There is no 'dead' matter. There is only Life, infinite Livingness. And God is the 'father' of it.

Where am I now? Still here. I do not have to go 'there' to meet the Omnipresence. And having communed with 'our', I then commune with 'father'. But let no more words be written. Whoso cares must himself commune. Let not imagination run riot; nor let the brilliancy of intellect disgorge a tumultuous, muddy stream of discursive thought and futile words. Let me beware – and again beware – of destructive illusions and delusions: that I entered into such and such profound states of consciousness (like that which St. Paul did enter, as and when he writes in his Second Epistle to the Corinthians, 12.2-4, that he was 'caught up to the third heaven . . . to paradise, and heard unspeakable words, which it is not lawful for a man to utter')[21]; or that I am of the Elect, the Chosen Few, the Saved; or that God spoke to me and entrusted me with the mission to save the heathen – the heathen may be nearer God than I in my conceit; or flaunt the statement 'I am God' or countenance a mass of unbalanced followers to publicize it for me – for that is the procedure of the rogue and exploiter. When 'I am God' is simple fact, it is the unspeakable Truth. If and when there has been an entry into deep modes of awareness, I remain silent about it, for the state of communion is not an 'achievement' by an isolated self-conscious 'me'.

Let the heart open out freely to the Supreme. But be adult and do not pester God. When the heart opens freely it is God which goes to God and God who comes into his own within me. This is what I 'conceive' and 'bear' in the womb of my soul (*Hiraṇyagarbha*), even as a mother conceives and bears divinity embodied, by the act of Love's divine communion. Thus my soul immaculately conceives the Alone Begotten of God. Let not true prayer, *samādhi,* holy worship, ever be underestimated.

Heartfelt prayer and the flame of pure aspiration in silent passionate worship release powerful psychical energies. The *feeling* of and for God[22] stirs the psyche into action. If the mind is pure – quiet, empty of desire, free of self-orientation and of the dark shadow of separative otherness – that action is beneficial. It 'turns on the switch' and sets flowing the currents of archetypal energies represented by the Name, God or Buddha or Christ or Raphael or Varuṇa or whatever be the Name invoked.

[21] See above, p. 19.

[22] or Transcendence or Supreme Power or The Holy; or the Great Teachers, or the Holy Ones or *devas* or angels or any archetypal ideas or forces.

Consider this passage from the Zarathuśtrian *Ahuramazda Yast*, in which, Zarathuśtra having besecched Ahurā Mazdā, '... do thou clearly reveal unto me these Names, and that which among Thy Names is the mightiest, holiest, fairest and the most effective, which is the most victorious (against evil) and the most healing ...', receives this answer from Ahurā Mazdā:

> 'My name is: I WHO AM, O holy Zarathuśtra: second, The Gatherer; third, the All-Pervading; fourth, perfect righteousness ... Knowledge ... Wisdom ... Prosperity ... the Lord of Life. I bear the name Mazda ... Creator ... Nourisher ...' (*The list is long*).

The names of God represent actual spiritual potencies, archetypal energies. If I am devotedly attentive as I pray, without my intellect disturbing the living psychical process of communion with the dictionary meanings of righteousness, prosperity, etc., something quite remarkable happens. These potencies are activated and realized in my own psyche. Scripture teaches us what we ourselves are growing into – God-nature.

There are dangers, even serious dangers. Deep prayer (or serious meditation) energizes the whole psyche. The energizing of the whole mind – the so-called unconscious as well as the conscious – means that all my qualities, 'good' and 'bad' alike, are intensified. For instance, I come out of the sanctum, be it church or temple or my private shrine room in my house, uplifted and angelic. I stand in the bus queue with peace and love in my heart and a seraphic countenance. A burly rough man jumps the queue knocking an old lady's handbag out of her hand. Where is my peace and love and angelic state? In a flash I am seething, red-eyed, two-horned, fork-tailed, cloven-hoofed! And this happens all the more fiercely when I have stepped out of the temple of God than out of the office.

It is a mistake to seek ways and means to protect myself against such outbursts, or the possibility of their arising. To 'protect against' means I am caught in the trap of conflict within myself. This situation will be considered later on in connection with mindfulness and meditation. Suffice it to emphasize again the indispensability of the basis of morality. If the mind is pure, there is no soil available for psychical evil to take root. Then it is possible for the constant state of true prayer to supervene.

* * *

When fate does not grant proximity to the Holy One, who is the father, where is the mother, spiritually mature, who can help the child to grow in spirit? Who will feed the hunger and quench the thirst for that mysterious *something,* unknown but intensely felt? The child's quest for the Source of Being – how impossible to answer! The child meets his own aloneness. But he cannot cognise its true nature. The words spoken by parent, teacher or priest veil the silent truth of God. On the throne of the Transcendent sits an idol. And the child worships it and prays to it because his loved ones, his trusted ones, do it.

Yet some of the words – love, goodness, wisdom and happiness – are treasured in the heart. And immortality is a sound with strange overtones: assuring; terrifying; irresistible. Can I, can you, even though a child, ignore it? The baying of the hound of heaven sounds both distant and close. The menace of its muffled thunder! The soft music of its resonance inside one's being! Respond to it even once in your life, and there can never again be a turning away. I run away from Transcendence! Oppose it! The jaws of the hound hold me for ever, like a priceless treasure which will be laid at the feet of the eternal blessed. Perfect fidelity.

That is how it was; that is how it is; and will be.

'Queer!' exclaims the worldling. Even so: for it weaves the weft of suffering; but also, of an invisible beauty.

Above the din of the world is heard a whispering: 'It is right. Keep going without flagging. You are my substance. I am the Immortal'.

And the event is on God's side and wholly in God.

* * *

Prior to the event I am unwise. So I study the scriptures enthusiastically. Or rather, I devour the books to gorge my intellectual pleasure lust, to satisfy my spiritual greed. With my head packed tight with concepts and creeds, I think I am learned.[23] I am puffed up with the conceit that I know the truth and that whoso disagrees with my firm beliefs is wrong.

Life compels me to challenge the validity of this knowledge. Decades pass in the distressful discovery of the invalidity of so many concepts and beliefs. On ceasing to cling to concepts I see that they are useful and necessary in every limited context, finite and mortal, but have no place where Transcendence is concerned. Hence all acquired knowledge

[23] Like Śvetaketu the son of Āruṇi, Chānd. Up., 6.1.2.

filling the mind with thought forms is worldly; it is relative truth. Empty the mind of thought forms. Thereupon this transparent mind, unconditioned and pure, is its own light. The words and concepts and dogmas of scripture no longer obstruct the living energy of Transcendence from operating freely, and I see that spiritual 'knowledge' and spiritual 'action' are an identity.

Hearing or reading, reflection and meditation, *śravaṇa, manana* and *nididhyāsana*, have already been considered.[24] Religious knowledge in the wordly sense, acquired by the study of scriptural texts, is the usual preliminary step taken by those who mean to live the holy life. This study conditions the mind, which then tends to set up a resistance, a friction, to prevent the creation of the new, or the emergence of the Unknown into manifestation. *This very friction, however, is necessary for the generation of the new.* When the worldly mode of religious study is transformed into the study of the Book of Life, unconditioned freedom of mind is realized.

In practice, therefore, as with worship and prayer, so too with the study of the scriptures. Let the turmoil of thoughts and of feelings calm down. Read a short section, more than once if necessary. Now let the mind dwell quietly upon a sentence, or a phrase, or even a single word. Attention must not be concentrated with effort. The mind which is compelled is an inefficient or dull mind; it distorts. When there is effortless attentiveness, the mind is sensitive, poised and perceptive; it understands. Whilst the deep sensitivity of the mind remains unobstructed, the words of scripture speak to me – speak the truth.

The Truth of religion is a wordless essence. Its realization is changeless. But its formulation in thought and speech, for the purpose of communication, is conditioned by the climate of thought of the prevailing culture. From age to age and region to region, the formulations differ. If I see through the words to the essence, to the living meaning which is an energy actually influencing my whole life of thought and speech and action, then that truth is realized by me and through me. Until I see through the words to the essence, they stand between me and the truth. They are a challenge to me to grow into my real manhood – to be the man in whom evil-mindedness is burnt out. They are a menace – my 'temptation', my trial. Because I, mankind, do not come through this ordeal unscathed, evil is continuously done in the name of religion. The study of the truths of religion can be carried out only in the religious way, based upon the actual living of the religious life. Otherwise,

[24] See above, Chapter Four.

religion remains a powerfully divisive force preventing me from loving my neighbour as myself and from giving my whole being to Truth.

Mention was made earlier[25] of some 'subjects' comprising the keys to unlock the secrets of the esoteric wisdom. In the Chāndogya Upaniṣad[26] Nārada enumerates the subjects and skills he has mastered. Included in these are:

> All the Vedas; Legend and Ancient Lore; the knowledge of the nature and functions of gods and demons, and of the 'serpent clan'; the serpent science; the science of language, of letters and numbers, of the constellations (astronomy and astrology) and of power; and the knowledge of Brahman.

The 'serpent' plays an important part in scripture: for instance, in the garden of Eden; and in the encounter between Aaron and Pharaoh's magicians. Well-known is the serpent-power of *kuṇḍalinī* yoga.[27] At the base of the spine, life-force or libido or psychical energy, more or less dormant, is pictured as coiled up like a serpent. It is in action in moments of profound perception, inspiration, exaltation, passion, creation by genius, in procreation and so on. This use is spasmodic, not under one's conscious control. It is wasted by mere sensuous and physical indulgence, especially sexual indulgence which is the enemy of healthy – and sacramental[28] – sexual expression.

The word 'serpent' is also used to signify the knowledgeable and skilful ritualist, psychic or spiritual healer, 'magician', and the one who can utilize the serpent-power, *kuṇḍalinī,* in the living body. The trained yogi rouses this energy and raises it through its various centres (*cakras*)[29] in the spine. Each of the *cakras* is associated with various letters of the Sanskrit alphabet. The full fledged yogi knows how these letters or phrases such as *Om maṇi padme hūṃ* or *Om namo Nārāyaṇāya*, or whole hymns, should be intoned or sung, accompanied by the appropriate postures and gestures and breathing. Also, there are favourable and unfavourable 'configurations of the stars' for the yogic practice, and

[25] See above p. 177 ff.

[26] Loc. cit. 7.1.2,3.

[27] See also above, pp. 217, 228 f.

[28] Let not the term 'sacramental' be desecrated by using it as the excuse for any perverted or cranky rite or behaviour.

[29] See below, p. 364 ff. See also *Foundations of Tibetan Mysticism*, by Lama Govinda, p. 137 ff. for a detailed exposition from the Buddhist approach. *The Serpent Power*, by Arthur Avalon, offers an exhaustive treatment from the Hindu approach.

hence 'auspicious times' are chosen. A sensitive, balanced person, feels and can respond to the psycho-mental 'atmosphere' present under different prevailing configurations.

He who knows the science of the zodiac understands the nature and action of archetypal Mind-energies represented by the names of the planets and constellations. This is a science for understanding the workings of cosmic and psychical energies in our own selves. Fortune-telling and the forecasts fed out to the populace have no relationship to the religious life.

As in the case of the Qabalah, numbers[30] are used as symbols for metaphysical concepts embodying the nature, function and various modes of action of the one cosmic energy. Both the Qabalah (and the word literally means 'tradition', the tradition of things divine) and the original Veda recognize that the Ultimate Reality is the Unknown and remains unknowable, the ever concealed Mystery. To live religiously means to let that Mystery, the omnipresent Unknown, act directly upon and through us. So the study of the 'sciences' of numbers, letters, language (meaning words or sounds used as *mantras,* that is, producing psychical effects), constellations, gods and demons (anabolic and katabolic energies), is intended to free the disciple from all that hinders religious living.

The question arises, naturally and sensibly, 'Must I study all these subjects mentioned above in order to live religiously?' There is no 'must' about it – even including the study of existing scriptures! But if I am spontaneously and strongly drawn to music or philosophy or public health or space-travel or any other subject, I will naturally devote time and energy to its study. If my vital interest is the religions of the world, I will study the scriptures and whatever else helps me to understand them. If my all absorbing concern is to live the religious life, to be as no-thing myself and so to be the transparent focus for the inflow and outflow of Transcendence, to live constantly in the state of communion, then naturally I pay complete attention to everyone and everything with my whole being. *This* attentiveness is study in its transcendental reality, whole and holy. The totality of my life-process is my study. Arduous, but free of the inward conflict ensuing upon compulsion. Such study is identical with meditation.

* * *

[30] To cite one example out of many, consider RV., 1.164.

Today, the study of Science is of prime importance.

If I am a scientist I closely scrutinize the world in which I live. I see cosmos and chaos; matter; forms of energy such as heat and light; living things; the phenomena of nature, of life and of mind. I see ceaseless activity, pattern making and pattern breaking, and continuous change. I believe I can discern laws of nature operating under given conditions, but should the conditions change, these laws have to be modified.

This world thus observed by me, I call reality. In my young years I regard the description of the scientific investigation of any part of it as truth. I begin to doubt if it is the truth when further research exposes inaccuracies in the observations made and inadequacies in the explanations given and the 'laws' laid down. With the continuous elimination of error, and if I grow to ripeness in understanding, I reach the stage where I am constantly enquiring 'What is the truth, what is reality?' I become keenly aware that my own subjectiveness and the quality of my own mind are involved with truth or reality in the deep or ultimate sense. Complete objectivity is not possible. I in my entirety am an infinitesimal and conditioned fragment of the total reality. The objective observation of reality is therefore an observation of this immeasurable immensity which is total reality by a tiny and conditioned portion of that very reality.

I discover on my maturing that that which in my early days I called truth was only my mental construct of the strike of the omniform – the appearance which is the universe – on my senses. All knowledge in my state of ordinary worldly consciousness is in fact my mental construct of the impact of reality on me. It is my 'known'; but it is only an image, of which the substance is the ever-receding mystery which I name ultimate reality or truth. And yet, this fragment which is the known is true – mortally – within the framework of my ordinary discriminative consciousness, for it dies in giving birth to a more accurate mental construct of reality.

If I am a scientist worthy of my calling, the discipline of the scientific method helps me to see my own conditioning and shortcomings. I awaken to the limitations of discriminative consciousness and I see that reality or truth in its very own nature, its absoluteness, can never be known through sense-functioning, mental constructs, speech patterns, logical intellectual activity, or in any other finite way. Nevertheless, I see that I *am* the reality, and reality *is* me. But I can never produce a mental construct which can contain or convey this transcendent fact.

The process of the Total Reality is beauty. If I am a dedicated scientist, I am the instrument of revelation of the wondrous craft of Transcendence.

* * *

The discipline of science (and in this very day and age we must join modern mathematics with modern theoretical and experimental science) helps me to learn the art of dispassionate observation; to learn to be free of wishful thinking; to structure my calculations and scientific conceptions quite logically, following the truth with complete integrity wheresoever it may lead; to cleanse and strip bare my imaginative power to the limit and then let it make its creative leap to the truth of the actuality with unobstructed insight. It educates me to attend with an open mind. It is a powerful dispeller of illusion, of unwarrantable assumptions, of prejudices and preconceptions. Science and mathematics are austere, ascetic disciplines for they train me to discard everything which is unessential. Since the presence of the unessential or the untrue hinders that discovery which is the object of research, finding out the unessential or untrue is the constant counterpart of discovering the true. Furthermore, if I can rise to the pinnacle of being a true scientist, I will have discovered that intellectual integrity goes hand in hand with moral purity. Otherwise the mind is fragmentary; it has blind spots and often it only grazes the truth tangentially.

What a wonderful, what a religious discipline, is science and mathematics. Today science has shown me that all that it has discovered is only an approximate knowing, and that in fact I cannot even reach, leave alone touch or overstep the frontiers of knowledge. And when I confidently predict such and such consequences and results on the basis of scientific, experimentally verified knowledge, I am not affirming absolute certainties but only suggesting probabilities, of greater or lesser degree of accuracy as the case may be. Absolute certainty is inelastic, whereas the universe does display resiliency. Seeing this clearly, I the scientist am free of the conflict of conceit and diffidence. Thereafter may come a happy day when the objective search for truth and the subjective realization of truth have become one whole activity, when the scientist and the seer are the self-same person in whom the scientific and prophetic functions are in harmony.

Let there be no delusion here. The unwary may say, 'Yes, science will at last prove what religion has always affirmed". Decidedly not, for the two contexts are different. Not that the One Total Reality has two different contexts. It is I, scientist in the state of worldly consciousness investigating Reality, who constitute the one context; and it is I myself in the state of communion, in that Awareness-Being in and through which Reality functions unobstructedly, who constitute the other context. Thus it is I who *cognize* Reality in one way as the scientist, and *experience* Reality in a very different way as the one in communion. The root source of the difference lies in the different modes of awareness of Reality, namely the worldly mode and the transcendent mode; and in each mode the state and the type of activity of the mind is different.

This could be more easily understood with the aid of diagrams.

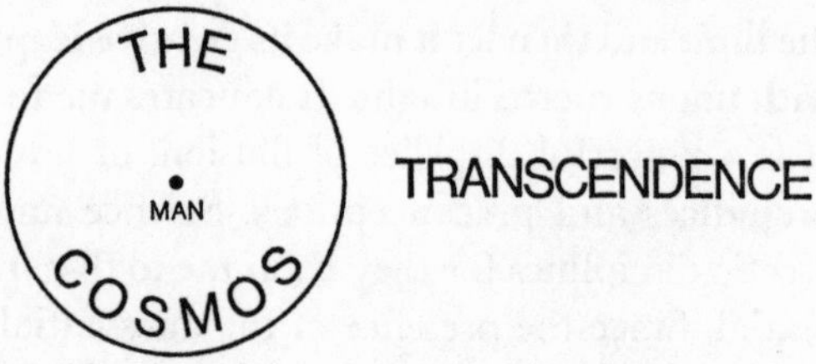

FIG 1 FIG 2 FIG 3

Figure 1, a blank space on the paper, indicates the Unknown: in the words of the Upaniṣads, THAT from which speech and mind return not having attained. The dot in the centre of Figure 2 represents me the ordinary man in the everyday world, or me the scientist, observing and studying the cosmos. Figure 3 represents me wholly subsumed in Transcendence in the experiencing of supreme communion. There is no mark in this figure to represent me as a separate entity, a finite subject.

If the differences between the mental states and activities characterizing the scientist of Figure 2 and the seer of Figure 3 are set down in tabular form, the contrast between them may be seen at a glance.

Figure 2	*Figure* 3
The scientist observing the cosmos.	The seer in communion.
Conscious of Reality as the world of separate particulars: isolatively self-conscious and separatively object-conscious.	There is Awareness-Being, and the One Total Reality is the all-pervasive Fact.
Awake to particulars only.	Awake to Totality.
Subject-object separation.	Not-twoness: *unio mystica*: *cit*, pure attentiveness only.
Separate senses functioning: stream of percepts: concepts and fixed ideas fill and condition the mind.	Senses pacified: freedom from conceptual conditioning: unified mind, the *ekāgra* state.

Figure 2	*Figure 3*
Speech-thought active : mental constructs made.	Speech-thought silenced; beyond sensation : no mental constructs.
Mental activity analytic-synthetic: descriptive in terms of sensation, distinguishing characteristics, and categories such as time, space, substance, causality, etc.	Integral : non-descript : not limited by categories : non-finite : timeless and spaceless : immeasurable : signless (no characteristics).
Acquisition of knowledge about the finite mortal world, and accepted as real.	Realization by Total Reality of itself as immortal, as Transcendence, through the finite living man in the state of communion.
Man can control and utilize different forms of energy and bend matter to his will.	In supreme communion man does not bend anything to his will. Transcendent Power deals unto him.
Man remains in discord within himself and with the world. This is the challenge of life, indispensable for worldly progress as well as for awakening spiritually to Transcendence.	The man is in perfect harmony within himself, and within Total Reality. Archetypal forces, uncognized by discriminative consciousness, work through the unresisting mind which is pure and transparent.

Language is the means of expression and communication for the findings of science and also for religious affirmations. But the language of science is at variance with the language of religion giving rise to fiercely debated and distressing questions. Which is true, science or religion? Does science invalidate religious affirmation? Or is science, which had moved to the extreme of materialism by the end of the nineteenth century, now veering round towards a position in support of religion? Or are science and religion doomed to remain mutually exclusive spheres? Can I, the man in the world today, hear a resolution of the discord between the findings of science and the affirmations of religion?

Any language we use is a system of symbolical sounds representing daily life and experience – objects, events, persons, actions, qualities, processes, relationships, sensations, percepts, concepts, feelings, thoughts, ideas, inspirations and so on – within the ambit of our discriminative consciousness of Reality through sense-functioning and mental activity. This same language is used for the findings of science; and hence we understand what we are talking about and we can use our scientific knowledge to produce precise practical results.

Now look at the right hand column in the above table. We see that for the realization by Transcendence of itself through us – and this supreme communion is the very Heart of Religion – sense functioning is pacified, speech-thought is silenced and the mind is emptied of all its constructs. Obviously, no language has place or function here. Our state is that of Awareness-Being, the I AM, in which the One Total Reality is the all-pervasive fact – non-finite, undifferentiated, unconditioned. Obviously there can be no finite tool or method whatsoever, leave alone language, to express and convey this undeniable experiencing of the One Total Reality.

And yet, I who legitimately and truthfully use everyday language for scientific findings, do use this very language for affirming the experiencing of Reality transcendentally as the seer in communion! And this in spite of the fact that although the language of the Heart of Religion may be mystical, poetic, suggestive, inspiring, uplifting, unworldly, alogical, heart-warming and healing, moving the deepmost core of our being, arousing our noblest feelings and impelling us to our finest endeavours, it can also be and often is imprecise, obfuscating, beyond normal comprehension and misleading. In stark contrast, the language of science is exact, terse, factual, comprehensible by any scientifically minded person, composed of statements whose accuracy can be tested out experimentally, and reliable for the purpose of practical application and obtaining the predicted calculated result. Furthermore, it can satisfy us aesthetically when it has literary merit, stir our sense of wonder and awe at the marvel and majesty of Reality, and move us to reverence and even to worship.

How then does it transpire that I the seer do use language, an efficient means of communication in the sphere of the finite, measurable and describable, as a means of communication of the infinite, immeasurable and unimaginable?

The seer does not stay permanently in the still silence. By far the greater part of his life, especially if he lives in a social milieu, is spent in the ordinary state of sense and mind activity and the full use of his discriminative consciousness. When he returns to this state on emerging out of supreme communion, and if he stays quiet for the requisite period of time, the impress on the mind and the psycho-physical organism by the experiencing of Reality in the transcendental mode gives rise to mental forms, not sharply defined, as if they were a shadowy moving picture of that transcendent Reality, and these inevitably become clothed in words – although the proper context of words is the finite and mortal. These words, however, are the prophetic speech uttered by the seer to the serious minded enquiring disciple whose deepest concern is Transcendence.

Again, there is no option for you and me but to use the language of mortality, inefficient though it be, for communicating the Immortal. If and when we are so developed that mind directly communicates with mind, the necessity for language, or for any other means for communicating, will have vanished. Two minds in union are just one mind.

Perhaps it is now clear how the language of science is of necessity at variance with the language of the Heart of Religion. Understanding this, each man can answer for himself the perplexing questions arising out of the variance, helped by a little further consideration. The least misleading statements regarding Transcendence are those which negate the finite and conditioned. There is the 'not this, not that', *neti*, *neti*, of Yājñavalkya; the Unborn, Undecaying, Undying, or the Not-become, Not-made, Not-compounded of the Buddha. There is the *Ain Soph*, the Unknown, the Incomprehensible of the Qabalah. In a different genre, there are the parables of Jesus about the kingdom of God (or heaven). And then there are those words of which no picture in the mind can be made: Absolute, Infinite, Eternal; Nirvana, Mukti; Transcendence, Truth, Reality, the One. And those which spring to life in the heart and set it aflame with Love: Ahurā Mazdā, Yahweh, God, Allah, Brahman, Atman, Creator Spirit, Father, Kṛṣṇa, and so on. And all these are the Words or Names which occupy the vital centre in all religions, the seat of the Holy; Names which sum up the transcendent realization in supreme communion in a single sound which bursts through the barriers of the conditioned into the freedom of the Unconditioned.

Let us use one more diagram, placing man, who is both scientist and seer, in the middle. The figure overleaf shows that the scientific description is a presentation of Reality apprehended in its concrete form; the religious, in its most subtle. The scientific approach is exterior, through the knowledge of things; the religious is interior, through being (*in awareness*) the No-thing, or in other words, through the total mergence with the everything and the complete vanishing of isolative self-consciousness.

Each Testament of Reality, the scientific and the religious, is wholly valid for its own mode of approach and of awareness. The two find their source of unity in the living man himself when he has grown to perfect humanhood. Till then it is he himself who sunders that latent unity by his ignorance of the fact that the seemingly unbridgeable chasm between his own two modes of awareness and of verbal formulation of the one Reality can be crossed by him; and further, that his physical, mental and spiritual natures, disjointed though they are in his worldly ('fallen') condition, are integrated into a spiritual organic whole by living the religious life in its fulness.

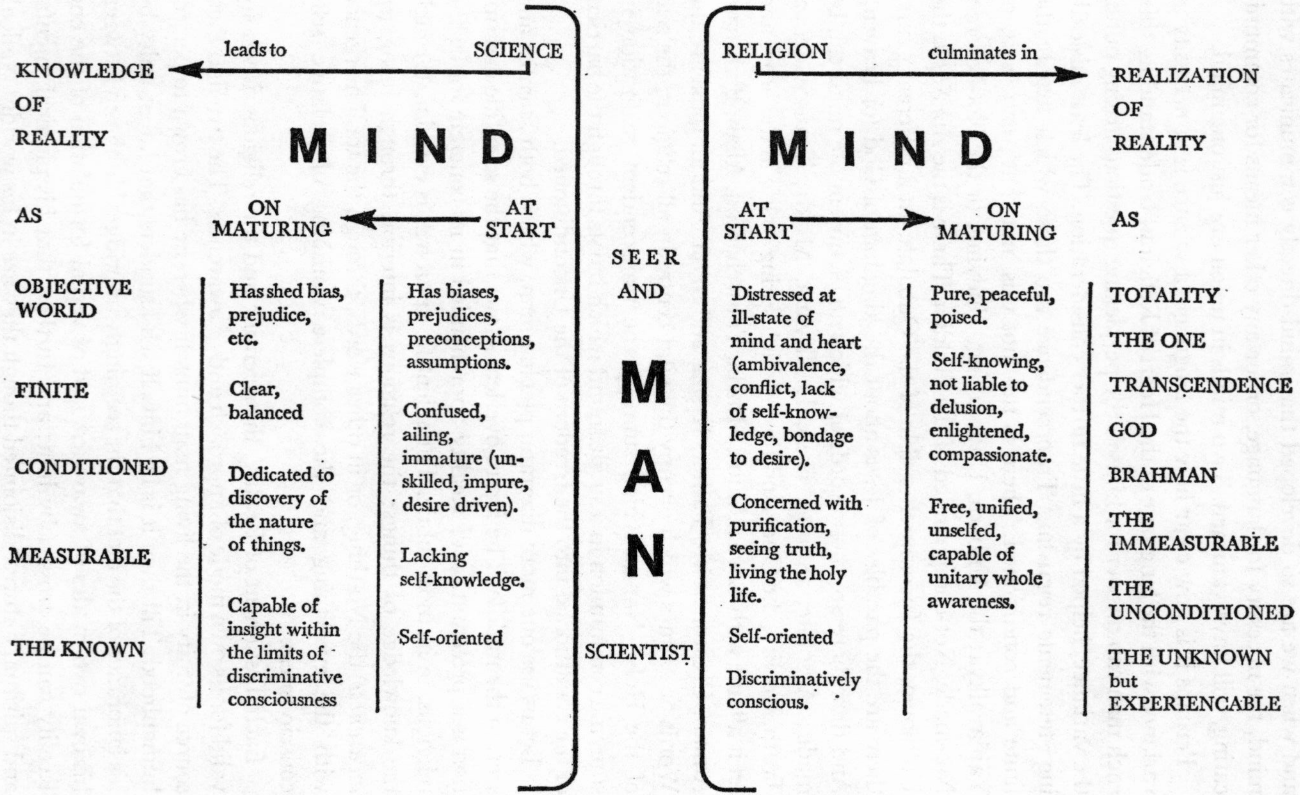

KNOWLEDGE OF REALITY
leads to
SCIENCE
MIND
AS
ON MATURING
AT START
OBJECTIVE WORLD
FINITE
CONDITIONED
MEASURABLE
THE KNOWN
Has shed bias, prejudice, etc.
Clear, balanced
Dedicated to discovery of the nature of things.
Capable of insight within the limits of discriminative consciousness
Has biases, prejudices, preconceptions, assumptions.
Confused, ailing, immature (unskilled, impure, desire driven).
Lacking self-knowledge.
Self-oriented
SEER
AND
MAN
SCIENTIST
RELIGION
culminates in
REALIZATION OF REALITY
MIND
AT START
ON MATURING
AS
Distressed at ill-state of mind and heart (ambivalence, conflict, lack of self-knowledge, bondage to desire).
Concerned with purification, seeing truth, living the holy life.
Self-oriented
Discriminatively conscious.
Pure, peaceful, poised.
Self-knowing, not liable to delusion, enlightened, compassionate.
Free, unified, unselfed, capable of unitary whole awareness.
TOTALITY
THE ONE
TRANSCENDENCE
GOD
BRAHMAN
THE IMMEASURABLE
THE UNCONDITIONED
THE UNKNOWN but EXPERIENCABLE

When a man awakens and restores himself to Reality he has fulfilled his destiny. And then the Holy One remains in unbroken communion in all situations and in all his actions, a living revelation of the spirit of God.

* * *

How grave is the responsibility and how difficult is the task of the theologian! The greater part of that which is called religious knowledge is a collection of ideas, beliefs, stories and so on. There is, also, a vast collection of tomes on religious topics and polemics, exegeses and apologetics and ponderous commentaries, some so anfractuous that the mind is lost in the labyrinth fabricated by those who are loaded with learning. Straw bread and ash cakes! It is instructive to note that St. Thomas Aquinas, a great theologian, when occupied with the third and most important part of his monumental *Summa Theologica*, received in ecstasy such a revelation of divine truth that he was convinced that all he had written was useless and referred to it as rubbish.[31] The *Summa* was left incomplete. St. Thomas Aquinas observed thereafter the angelic silence – which indeed is theo-logy.

Theo-logy, truly, is the inspiring word of the Holy One, the prophetic speech which must be lived, not merely read or argued. It is the voice from within, the voice of the 'Master' heard in silence at *ājñā*. It is the love-music of truth sounding in the pure heart: the song of Orpheus or the flute of Kṛṣṇa. It is the word of the Doctor who heals.

Paradox! I understand this prophetic speech only when I am beyond the need of reading the word of scripture. I am beyond, when the lips of the heart are unsealed and I listen to the speech no mortal tongue ever utters. Then the words of the scriptures come alive. I understand.

In the thunder of heaven and the roar of the storm I hear the Veda. I see it writ in the leaf of the tree and the flower of the field. The spring song of the bird and the light on the firefly's wing are a Bible for me. The clean strength of that youth and the modest charm of that maid are my Avestā. For now I am reading the Book of Life. Theo-logy.

What made me read awry, yesterday? Only the dust in my eyes, gathered whilst I did not rightly understand the nature of things and this bubble the self. Pursuing reflections rippling along time's trail, reflections of the Imageless in the mirror of space, I took them for truth. Grace blessed me with poverty and sorrow. Mine eyes were washed of dust.

[31] Jacques Maritain, *St. Thomas Aquinas, Angel of the Schools*, p. 51.

Let him who would be a theologian bear on his heart the signature of Inward Love shining with Transcendent Light.

* * *

What passes muster as religious knowledge, the turn out of intellectual spinning machines, lies within the confines of discriminative consciousness and is composed of the mental constructs of conditioned minds. He alone who has been lighted by the torch of Transcendence may attempt to be a theologian. The pure, the capable, the free from any and every vested interest, the one whose vision is stainless and who has been through the baptism by fire, he is the one who may assay the task, if such be his destiny. And he will know when he has reached the point of silence.

For him who attempts to write about the deeps of religion, science is a powerful aid, for the scientific discipline helps in curing the mind of intellectual cobweb-spinning, of using misleading analogies and of false reasoning.

Science, however, has unfortunately become a god today for many. A modern idol! Applied science, technology, holds the human race in thrall to the machine. Drugs, chemicals and various inventions destroy man and nature alike and fill the plundered Earth with pollution. Mankind, perhaps all life on the globe, is in danger of extermination by man. No animal has shown such ingratitude to Life. Vast hordes senselessly look to technology to solve human problems and produce human fulfilment.

Science has opened up many beneficent possibilities and put undreamed of power into our hands. But we have shamefully betrayed our trust by criminal misuse of power, due to our lamentable shortness of understanding, compassion and self-restraint, and because of our abject slavery to greed, fear, power-lust and licentious self-indulgence. Inevitable catastrophe has castigated us again and again but we remain unchastened, and point a finger of blame always at the other person instead of to our own hearts burning with the poisonous passion for wealth and power and pleasure.

Technology is merely a tool, a lifeless mechanism. If – and only if – it is operated by a clean hand, a wise mind and a pure heart, will it serve us for our lasting good instead of crushing us relentlessly under its juggernaut wheels.

We are the children of God and Nature. Mother Nature is the living milieu which cradles us. We must live ecologically. This is scientific living, in which our dominion over Nature finds expression in protecting and nourishing the earth and all its creatures and its plants, its soil and its waters which are the foundations of healthy, happy living biologically. To achieve this and prove that we have good sense, we must cease to be brutal sub-humans and live as pure mature humans. And for this our sights must be set on Transcendence.

* * *

ASANAS AND PRANAYAMA

In recent decades meditation and yoga, and various religious practices of which the majority are anything but religious, have spread over many parts of the world. Yoga is in fashion. For most of its practitioners it means a system of exercises in physical postures and breathing. Far more important aspects such as the pure ethical life in thought and speech and action, the discipline of the mind, meditation and communion, are barely considered, or else altogether ignored. The common appeal to greed and vanity and egoism – get fit; acquire a lovely figure; enjoy the pleasures of life even more; achieve success and triumph over your competitor – meets with an eager response from the multitude, so that a rapidly expanding field of exploitation has opened up, financially and psychologically.

The spirit can never be bought and sold. The self-centred acquisitive approach to the postural and breathing practices, the *āsanas* and *prāṇāyāma*, leads me to the ill-state, although the practice improves health and makes me fit and vigorous in body. But what do I – or you – usually do with a fit body if the soul is still sick? Do I not misuse it, out of folly, egoistic conceit, lust for pleasure or the passion to dominate or succeed? And if I look within and scrutinize my motives for wanting to be healthy and strong, do I not find that they are self-centred and worldly? Only when a flash of truth penetrates the darkness of my soul, I begin to pay attention to being fit in order that Life's purposes may come to fruition or that Transcendence may function freely through the body.

Because my sights are set upon self indulgence or aggrandisement, I squander my energy unwisely and am reduced to illness. Then I hope to restore myself to physical fitness by yoga. But if I remain the slave of self-centred drives I am still a miserable producer of ill.

Any discipline energizes the whole being, good and bad aspects alike.[32] The genuine yogi and the sensible well-instructed learner know this.

[32] See also above, pp. 256, 265.

Hence, they see the indispensability of the foundation of righteous daily living, and the importance of being well aware of the true purpose of the discipline of the body.

The religious life is the life in full relationship with Transcendence, unblemished by any stain, in which I am in the state of constant meditation, of timeless communion. Whoso is serious about his religious discipline knows too well the intrusiveness of the body upon the mind. The body is rarely at ease, calm and poised. There is muscular strain, nervous tension, itching, rumbling, involuntary jerking, unnecessary movement of limbs and jaws and head and eyes, in short everything that indicates the absence of the state of natural repose. Perhaps the greatest drawback is the absence of a gentle rhythm in the breathing. Thus the body sounds many a discordant note, interfering with meditation.

Clearly, then, the right kind of physical discipline is one conducive to calm and poise, and to a rhythmic functioning of the whole organism. Obviously it is not calculated to produce the fitness of the boxer or rugby player or the breaker of athletic records. The practice of the yogic postures (or any similar practice) makes for a remarkable degree of suppleness, great nervous energy which is easily conserved, unusual endurance coupled with bodily ease and mental calm, and healthy functioning of all the bodily organs. Some ill-states, not needing surgery or unavoidable medication, may disappear after practising the postures and simple rhythmic breathing. These, and perhaps other benefits, may or may not accrue. In no case should I seek them. If they appear, let me be thankful and content. If they do not, let me be equally thankful and content: for that is yoga, namely, to be contented and peaceful in all situations.

The purpose of the yogic postures and breathing, or of any bodily discipline for the sake of the religious life, should now be clear. It is to train the body in such a manner that it will not obtrude itself upon meditation (even if it lasts for as long as seven nights and days) and distract attention; and that it will be a pure, calm, highly sensitive and eminently fit organism full of nervous energy and stamina for living as a religious being. The spiritual life is arduous and exacting, and calls for a rich fund of the finest and most refined bodily resources, even as a great musician needs a superb instrument to make the music which is a revelation of the beauty of Transcendence.

* * *

In Plato's *Symposium*, Alcibiades recounts the natural temperance, self-restraint, courage and wisdom of Socrates; his extraordinary power of sustaining fatigue, of going without food and his faculty of endurance of frost and ice in cold weather. He then describes how Socrates was thinking one summer morning while he was on the expedition to Potidaea about something which he could not resolve. Socrates stood there all through the day and the night until the following morning; and with the return of light he offered up a prayer to the sun, and went his way.

Socrates stands fixedly for a whole day and night calmly meditating. A century earlier, the Buddha tells[33] some disciples of Nāthaputta :

> 'I, reverend Jains, am able, without moving my body, without uttering a word, to stay (in meditation) experiencing nothing but happiness[34] for two nights and days, for three, four, five, six for seven nights and days.'

Ellina von Crevelsheim fell into an ecstasy lasting five days, in which 'pure truth' was revealed to her and she was lifted up to an immediate experience of the Absolute.[35]

In his discourse on Mindfulness of Body, the Buddha tells[36] his disciples that there are ten advantages to be expected from this discipline, of which the third is as follows :

> 'He is one who bears cold, heat, hunger, thirst, the touch of gadfly, mosquito, wind and sun, creeping things, ways of speech that are irksome, unwelcome; he is of a character to bear bodily feelings which, arising, are painful, acute, sharp, shooting, disagreeable, miserable, deadly.'

Śrī Kṛṣṇa says[37] that the disciplined one is equable in cold and heat, pleasure and pain, and whether honoured or insulted.

The discipline which enables the body to remain impassible needs to be intelligent. Those who, like the Buddha[38] or Henry Suso[39] practised extreme austerities, put them aside in due time. From very early times there is sensible and scientific instruction regarding food and drink. Śrī Kṛṣṇa says :[40]

[33] M., 1.94.
[34] The happiness of attaining the fruits (of the Way).
[35] Jundt, *Les Amis de Dieu*, p. 39; Rufus Jones, *Studies in Mystical Religion*, p. 271.
[36] M., 3.97.
[37] B.G., 6.7.
[38] M., 1.242-249.
[39] Suso, *Leben*, Chapter 17.
[40] B.G., 6.16; 17.8.

'Yoga is not for him who eats too much, nor who abstains to excess, nor who is too much addicted to sleep, nor even to wakefulness. Men who are pure like food which is pure: which gives health, mental power, strength and long life; which has taste, is soothing and nourishing, and which gladdens the heart of man.'

The Yogatattva Upanisad states:[41]

'Eating light meals is the most important discipline (bodily).'

The Buddha says:[42]

'Be moderate in eating . . . eat, not for fun or pleasure or adornment or beautifying, but just enough for maintaining this body and keeping it going, for keeping it from harm, for furthering the Brahma-faring (the holy life).'

And the *Memories* of Hegesippus,[43] which he wrote about A.D. 70 at a very advanced age says this about James the brother of Jesus:

'James, the brother of our Lord, has been called the Just, from the days of our Lord to our own. From his mother's womb he was dedicated to God . . . He drank no wine or other fermented beverage; he ate nothing living (meat) . . . and he alone was allowed to enter the Holy of Holies (of the Jerusalem Temple) where, prostrate or kneeling, he prayed that the sins of Israel might be forgiven . . . He was called *oblias*, which means (in Hebrew) the bulwark, the wall, because all believed that only his prayers, the prayers of a saint, could save the people from the wrath of God.'

Must I abstain from meat and wine to live the religious life? The simple fact is that I cannot eat flesh food unless I myself kill a creature or am an accessory before and after the killing, unless I eat the flesh of an animal which has died a natural death. If I am sensitive to the fact that each creature loves its own life (perhaps more than I do mine) and often looks to me for protection and love, I find it difficult, impossible, to participate in senseless and brutal murder. As for wine – any intoxicant, narcotic, etc. – must I be so foolish as to desensitize myself, deplete nervous energy and lay myself open to inebriation?

A word about fasting. The continued forcible deprivation of food, as

[41] Op. cit. 27.

[42] M., 1.273; 2.138.

[43] Eusebius, H. E., 2.23.3-19. Preuschen, 72; 159. Hennecke, 1.103 f. Quoted from D. Merezhkovsky, *Jesus the Unknown*, p. 220-221.

by famine, war and so on, is starvation. No good. Fasting is a judicious *willing* abstention from food for a sensible period – say one to three days or so, as suitable to your own constitution. Very beneficial, usually. A convenient practical procedure is to carry out a thirty-six hour fast: no food after a light supper on, say, a Friday until a light breakfast on Sunday morning. No smoking. Use good sense.

The Aristotelian doctrine of the Mean[44] – the balance point between excess and defect – may be useful and good for the man of the world, in the context of duality and reciprocity. But the religious man sets his sights on Transcendence. He is concerned with outgrowing the conflicting state of the virtue-vice duality so that VIRTUE may function freely through him. In all religious discipline it is each man's own responsibility to live in accord with what he himself clearly sees is true.

Whilst the main purpose of the yogic discipline of postures and breathing is to be free of interference by the body during meditation there is much deeper purpose, associated with the deeper meanings[45] of the words *āsana* and *prāṇāyāma*. It is that the body shall be a fit instrument for the reception and transmission of the energies of Transcendence associated with the states of Awareness-Being realized in the different intensities of communion, *samādhi*.

For this, the finest discipline is required. And here it is necessary to understand that discipline means learning by growing happily and healthily. Gruesome austerity or self-inflicted pain is masochism, a perverted form of self-indulgence through experiencing intense sensations, a manifestation of a sick soul, a means for winning the worthless respect and adulation of a stupid multitude.

Right austerity, a complete contrast to the gruesome austerity of the misguided of East and West alike through the centuries, means abstention from self-indulgence, violence and ego-assertion masquerading all too often as self-expression, and any and every form of evil. Right austerity is not an incontinent continence, a consequence of a hate reaction against past misery or of a lust for superiority over others. Right austerity is present when I see the truth for myself and act spontaneously in accord with the vision, and not out of mere conformity with the imposed word, of which I have not clearly understood the spirit. An ignorant, foolish man slavishly 'doing the right thing' in the absence of clear perception, not only remains ignorant and foolish but also suffers from the conceit that he is good, 'doing the right thing'. Right austerity demands

[44] Aristotle, *Ethics*, Bk.2, Chapter 5.
[45] See above, p. 48.

ceaseless attentiveness on my part, clear seeing and right doing which are the mental and physical aspects of learning by growing, and the constant natural discarding of unessentials, unessential because I have outgrown them.

The Buddha declares:[46]

> 'The person who is neither a self-tormentor, not intent on the practice of self-torment, nor a tormentor of others, not intent on the practice of tormenting others, he, neither a self-tormentor nor a tormentor of others, is here-now allayed, quenched, become cool, an experiencer of bliss that lives with self Brahman-become.'

This is a weighty declaration; a careful study of the whole discourse would amply repay the serious student.

* * *

How easily I say '*my body*'! Some scriptures tell me it is vile, a thing of sin and corruption, of bondage and temptation and misery, doomed to die. Quite true. Those same scriptures also tell me of my great good fortune in obtaining human birth for it is only through the human state that the realization of Transcendence is possible, that the body is a temple of the Holy Ghost[47] (the third member of the Christian Trinity), of Śiva[48] (the third member of the Hindu Trinity). Also quite true.

'*My* body' is a statement of fiction, of empirical convenience. I have no exclusive proprietorship over the body. My breath comes in and goes out speedily; food and drink likewise, more slowly; the cells of the body undergo constant change. What shall I hold and say, 'this is mine, or me'? This body, a living pattern apparent to sense perception, is entirely dependent for its existence upon you and everything that is 'not this body'. Self exists by virtue of not-self. Not for a moment could there be my body or self if it were not for you and the world-body, the not-self.

Let me understand this with all my heart. Free of the illusions born of isolative self-consciousness, the delusion generating words – I, you, mine, yours – may all be used less misleadingly, and less violently and uncompassionately, when we converse together.

Freed of the ownership of this body, I do not misuse it or torment it. Nor can I harm your body or any body in the world. To hurt myself is to hurt you: to hurt you is to hurt myself. For now I see that there is only one body in fact – the BODY which is the manifested totality, all

[46] M., 1.348,349.
[47] I Cor., 6.19.
[48] Maitreya & Skanda Upanisads.

nature, the physical world. Physical, from φύσις (nature), means natural. All manifestation, whether I name it material or mental for practical convenience, is nature. And Nature is the Body of God. You and I could never sense and worship God or Transcendence were there not the BODY, the TEMPLE.

Thus, body includes life, mind, consciousness, in short everything that I can talk about, anything of which I can make a mental construct. And by the same token, mind, spirit, life and other such words are seen as including everything else, for without the everything else, no one thing is manifest. The one-ness of the Total Reality is irrefragable.

Now I can reverence and love life. 'With my body I thee worship'. And the Supreme Mystery, God the Unknown Transcendence, I can love, honour and obey. To Caesar I can freely give my penny. Afore God I can stand in loving awe and pray that he take me wholly. And God adores the sweet undeniable prayer and takes himself unto Himself. This is Death the other-Life for me whilst living in the mortal body, now the Temple sanctified by the Ever-Auspicious Eternal Holy.

Such is the supreme meaning of the yoga of bodily discipline, which must proceed together with meditation. Such is the state of chastity.

When the dust of desire blinds my eye or the wind of passion scatters my good sense, 'be still!' I say to the body, 'be still!' And the stillness of the body releases healing silence in the mind. Peace reigns: and the face of the Immortal smiles again. The yogi, the mystic, the religieux – they are the rapturous variety of the One – know this. And are happy.

Happiness is the crown of BODY. Transcend all the folly and pursuit of sensational excitement and fevered pleasure, and health, wholeness, and the holiness of creative action in its most concrete form will be the Happiness of bodily existence, beyond conceiving and seeking but which lies at the heart of bodily being. This is the purity of body which complements the pure ethic of the heart, the religious morality.

* * *

Let me awaken, then, to the wholeness of being. To neglect the body is to confound the mind. To despise the body is to condemn the spirit. To deny the spirit is to insult the body. Not to be sane in mind is to destroy the body. Therefore I take good care of the body, not out of vanity, not for the gratification of ambition or pleasure lust. Right food, drink, work, play and rest; cleanliness, fresh air and sunshine; peace and beauty of environment, and good relationships with those around one – these are the main factors constituting proper care of the body.

All talk, such as 'I am not my body but an immortal soul', or 'I am neither body nor mind but the Atman', is nonsense talk – spirituous fumes of the confused mind. There is no mental construct, no conception or verbal formulation which can contain the answer to 'Who am I?', for the answer is beyond measure and form. Rest content that even as eternity rides on the wings of time, immortality lives through the flesh and blood of mortality.

The body of flesh and blood is, as it were, a *maṇḍala* or horoscope, that is, a pattern or code, of the whole being. Being alive, the pattern changes constantly. To read this changing code correctly is no easy task. The saying that appearances are deceptive is well known. But is it true? Perhaps it is nearer the truth to say that if *I* was clear-sighted and not liable to delusion I would see the whole person as he really is when I look at his body, an ever changing appearance accurately expressing the ever transforming reality.

The psycho-physical organism, a miniature cosmos, is an immense power-house embodying in itself many forms of energy. It is roughly estimated that an average-sized body is composed of 10^{28} atoms, which represents a sizeable amount of measurable energy, scientifically speaking. There is also the aspect of immeasurable energy, that is, Mind energy[49] symbolized as gods. And here it may be fruitful to ponder over some verses from the Atharva-veda. In the eighth hymn of Book Eleven the question is asked, who made the various parts of man's body and brought them together? The answer is that different gods (*devas*) made the different parts, and thereafter entered them. Verse 18 says:

> 'Gods made the mortal their abode and entered and possessed the man.'

Then sleep, sin, old age, prosperity, knowledge, ignorance, in short everything constituting man entered into the body. So did all the great Gods, and verse 32 affirms:

> 'Therefore whoever knoweth man regardeth him as Brahman's self:
> For all the Deities abide in him as cattle in their pen.'

The body is in fact Transcendence embodied. All bodies are different from each other in some respect or other: there is no limit to the variety displayed by Life. Whilst today we seek to understand these differences in body, mental ability and character through scientific investigation

[49] See also above, pp. 85 ff., 96 ff., 209, 211 ff.

the main practical concern of the religious man is simply this: How shall I live my daily life with respect to the body? Shall I tread the path of Pallas Athene, goddess of wisdom, or drink of the cup of Circe the sorceress alluring me to destruction? The path of Athene is the path of hygiene, temperance, prudence and chastity; of discipline and skill in action (physical and mental); of virtue. The drugged draught of Circe means the disregard of natural law (regarding clean, healthy living), self-indulgence and of cunning in order to escape the consequences of vice and wrong ways; the use of pills and palliatives, stimulants, intoxicants and drugs; cheap artifice instead of fine craftsmanship. The goddess leads to human fruition. The enchantress turns her victims into swine.

Mine is the burden of choice. With the first flash of realization that the body is Transcendence Incarnate, I stand at the cross-roads, and ponder the sphinx-like question which arises: What does this Incarnation mean to me? If I fail to answer rightly, I am rent.

The timeless beyond ex-presses me through star-encircled solitudes to incarnate here and answer now. The beyond, the solitude, the incarnation and the answer are the transcendent here-now, the measureless point which is the Temple, the BODY.

Look at this BODY with the Third Eye – this is your vision in communion, *samādhi*. You will see the *dharmakāya*, the body of Law, of eternal Order.

Experience this BODY through purified and perfected senses, free of all grasping – this is your *pratyāhāra*.[50] You will enjoy the *sambhogakāya*, the body of Bliss.

Invoke this BODY to work upon and by means of your body – this is the work of the Saviour, the Teacher, the instrument of salvation transforming the world. You will make manifest the *nirmāṇakāya*, the body of Transformation.

* * *

Science has investigated the workings of the 'pleasure areas' in the brain[51] and the need for pleasure in order to be healthy.

There are at least two kinds of pleasure. One is the sensational and lustful, rooted in greed, confined to the wild urges of the body, leading to frenzied excitement. Various cults indulge in practices which produce religious frenzy – a misuse of the word 'religious'. Has anyone seen

[50] See above p. 256.

[51] Dr. H. J. Campbell, *The Pleasure Areas*.

a Buddha or a Christ working himself up to a frenzy? It is enthusiasm, not frenzy, which is present in him who is sane and capable. So the religious man eschews all diabolical pleasure.

The other is the birthright of the human, the crown of physical existence. It is the concrete expression of that subtle happiness of the *sambhogakāya* in which there is no disease, evil, sorrow, fear or binding consequence. Where the mind is pure, the psyche free of ambivalence and conflict, and the body clean-living, all the senses function at their highest intensity and refinement.[52] When you are sensitised to this degree and remain poised as you observe intently, what you see or hear, touch or taste or smell, gives you happiness quite beyond that which you as an ordinary mortal experience. Not only what you see or hear, but also what you feel and perceive mentally. And in the exercise of artistic gifts and bodily skills and prowess, or in scientific or any creative activity, this happiness pervades your being and is one of the most powerful influences for good health.

If I am truly and actively religious I cannot prevent this tide of happiness suffusing and saturating, as it were, the whole body. For Life is generous from day to day with all the loveliness it pours into me through my senses; and also with all the love-evoking pain and sorrow and the terror of terrible doings and shattering catastrophes in the world, which produce an awful, mysterious and humbling happiness if I give my heart to it all, selflessly. The sorrow that is unconditionally absorbed by the whole of my being is transmuted into that strange bliss which is like the sheer dark of clear night which wipes out the separation between my eyes and the brilliance of the stars.

Certainly, this happiness is health-giving pleasure for the human being, whereas the pleasures which, alas, too many deluded mortals pursue bestially are the surest guarantee of misery.

The whole of the religious discipline of the body is a happy discipline. Where there is true happiness there is goodness: where there is real goodness there is happiness. They are inseparable.

[52] This is one meaning of the term 'subtle senses' used in the Sāṃkhya philosophy and other religious texts. The ignorant and greedy may induce a similar state by drugs, etc. – the Circean path leading to a swinish end – but the person being devoid of purity and refinement, illusory and destructive phantasms and hallucinations are his net gain.

CHAPTER TWENTY
MINDFULNESS

THE dictionary meanings of meditation confine it to the thinking process. Hence when I am meditating I am talking silently, sometimes holding an idea or a state of mind with concentrated attention in order to extract and absorb its full significance. My mode of awareness is that of discriminative consciousness; my concepts, acquired knowledge, convictions and mental conditioning are all at play. Such is the nature of meditation in the worldly sense.

In the religious sense, meditation is much more deep and inclusive. It involves the disciplining and right use of the senses and the body; moral and intellectual purification; release from the ill-effects of the conditioning by our natural as well as by our socio-cultural heritage[1]; the proper use of speech and thought; the nurturing of our power to see truth and our power to love. In its intensest state, meditation spells the emergence out of discriminative consciousness through the pacification of sense activity and the silence of thought and speech, culminating in the immergence into Awareness-Being, into THAT the One Total Reality.

In its perfection, meditation means being in the state of constant communion. It means living the stainless holy life, the unitive life of the sinless one, of the *mahātmā* (the Great Soul), *mahātmā* in truth and not by self-arrogation or by popular proclamation. Can 'I' find a *mahātmā*? Never. Only a *mahātmā* recognises a *mahātmā*, on the instant. And he who is a *mahātmā* never goes out to find a *mahātmā*.

The Great Soul is he who can truthfully declare, in the words of Śiva to Kumāra the Kārttikeya, 'I am the I that has given up I'[2]. He is the perfect meditator even as Śiva the blissful is ever in meditation.

* * *

Mindfulness characterizes all forms of meditation short of the supreme communion. A continuous discipline irrespective of time and circumstance, it is the constant ground-state of all meditation or deep contemplative prayer. In the supreme communion, and in the living of the unitive life, the Holy Life which is now second nature, all distinctions

[1] See also above p. 217 ff.

[2] Tejobindu Up., 3.3.

between mindfulness and the immergence into Transcendence vanish. The mindfulness itself has become transcendent.

Right mindfulness, *sammā sati*, is the lynch-pin of the endeavour to live religiously.

The Buddha declares[3] that mindfulness is the one way to release oneself from sorrow, to set oneself on the right road (the Eightfold Path) and realize Nirvana. Jesus says,[4] 'Watch and pray that ye enter not into temptation'. Krishnamurti strongly emphasizes intense, choiceless awareness or complete attentiveness. In various religious disciplines mindfulness holds a key position.

If the mind develops healthily, its receptivity and responsivity operate efficiently and intelligence functions freely. But this cannot be realized as long as I am the victim of the conflict and confusion caused by the law of the body driving me one way and the law of the spirit pulling me the other way, thus making the psyche sick. Mindfulness is the medicine.

From the very beginning, stimuli make impressions on the brain by way of the sense organs and the nervous system. The successive sense stimuli impinge upon and sometimes hold attention. These percepts are the immediate, living experiencing of the world. Those around, speaking aloud, tell me the names of persons and objects, and teach me the words which stand for actions, qualities, relationships, feelings and so on. The specific impressions received through the different senses can be coordinated and expressed as a coherent whole experience by means of language, and in time I can communicate with others through my growing faculty of speech, one of the most remarkable (and perhaps the most misused) of all the faculties distinguishing the human race.

Whilst the act of perceiving is the immediate, living experiencing, the concept is a mental and verbal construct abstracted out of many percepts. We know what we are perceiving by referring it to our mental card-index; that is, concepts enable us to recognize percepts. Furthermore, concepts structure the succession of percepts, without which structuring a mere succession of percepts could not be properly understood and dealt with. When concepts go beyond serving simply as tools for recognition, they can come to life, so to say, in their own inner mental realm of abstract thinking, as in philosophy and mathematics.

Speech holds a dominant position in our daily lives. But the words of any language, with extremely few exceptions such as absolute or infinite or God, represent only that which is finite and particular, which

[3] D., 2.290; M., 1. 55,56.

[4] Matt., 26.41; Mark, 14.38.

comes into being and perishes. All concepts are dressed in specific word patterns. By speech, therefore, which enjoys such lordship in the whole realm of discursive thinking and discriminative consciousness, we are held in bondage to the limited and the finite and we suffer the sorrows of mortality and of separation from the supreme whole. Moreover, unskilled or misused speech presents a false picture of the fact, and begets misleading concepts. It is a seductive conditioner. It is a gift too destructive in the mouths of the unwise or ill-willed. Mindfulness, which makes me clearly aware of my bondage and of my evil, is my instrument of release.

Just as the earth is touched by anything that falls upon it, so is the mind by the stimuli that meet it. Not every stimulus but only the relevant information processed into manageable shape is presented to consciousness. True mindfulness is a right receiving and bearing in mind, and a right responding by both mind and body. Since right receiving, bearing and responding involves keen attention, it is of the greatest importance to understand the meaning of attention in the context of the discipline of religious living and the realization of Transcendence.

A concept is not fluid like the stream of passing percepts out of which it is abstracted. It is fixed or rigid to some degree or other, just as a physical tool has to be solid or else you cannot handle it. It is a composite mental image of the actual thing or person observed or event experienced. It measures, confines, fixates. All our beliefs and convictions, our opinions, ideas and knowledge, our inclinations, plans, desires, aspirations and so on exist in the form of conceptual images. As long as we are immature, these images inhibit the free functioning of intelligence. When mature, intelligence is awake and the full-statured human is a true manifestation of Archetypal Man, the *puruṣa vidhaḥ* or the man-in-the-image-of-God.

Till then, all that we know is our mental constructs, that is, the descriptive verbal patterns or images of any thing or person or process. So, when I meet you – and you and I have known each other for the last fifty years – do I meet you the person as you really are or am I greeting the image of you which I have formed in my mind? Again, with respect to myself, I have no true self-knowledge but am acquainted only with an image that I mistakenly regard as my very self. Hence when we meet, there are two images which are chattering away, but hardly any true conversation between you and me as we actually are. Under these conditions, you and I are not really paying attention, however vehemently we might like to deny the fact.

When I ask, 'How are you', you reply, 'I'm fine!' These are conventional noises. Conditioned to behave automatically in that manner, we are not in live communication. So there is no true perceiving here-now of how you really are. Two concepts, verbalised as 'how are you?' and 'I'm fine', have interfered with the immediate living experience of actual perceiving, and inhibited or even totally denied a true communing by peremptorily dismissing the living percept. We are deprived of the joy of meeting. There is boredom. Our fifty-year old images of each other are barriers between us and a burden to us both. Whenever recognizing damps down immediate and live perceiving, there is no real attention.

Again, what do I do while you are talking to me? My brain is ceaselessly chattering back at you – agreeing, disagreeing, liking, disliking, etc. – as I hear your words and interpret them in terms of *my* concepts, outlooks, convictions, values, and in short in terms of all my conditioning. Thus, I am not listening to *you*. Pure attention is absent.

So, too, I am constantly reacting to what I hear or see around me, with pleasure or displeasure, praise or blame, instead of looking intently, free of bias and prejudice. I am not attentive.

When my attention is caught up by anything to which I am naturally inclined, or which fascinates me or compulsively holds my interest, I am not attentive. The mind is not free, for it is taken over and absorbed (gobbled up) or held captive (like a child by a toy) by something outside, which maintains its dominating otherness against me and prevents true attention.

When I deliberately shut out the world, or forcibly drag my mind back to the original subject when it wanders away, or strive to enter within to pray to God, or strain to become united with my God, or enter with effort into deep states of consciousness or enjoy sublime ecstasies by any means, fair or foul (such as drugs or self-hypnotizing sounds, or exalted concepts presented by theologian or poet or teacher), I merely delude myself that this is pure attention.

There is pure attentiveness only when I am fully awake in the religious sense, that is, in the absence of all self-consciousness. In my ordinary worldly state, to attend means to attend to something *other* than myself. But can I be in the state of attentiveness with no separate object, no other, to attend to? Or be wholly observant with nothing other to observe? Ordinarily, I cannot. There is, however, that state in which all the limitations of discriminative consciousness, isolativeness and separativeness, are transcended. And there, in perfect stillness and silence of the mind, there is perfect attentiveness.

In this attentiveness, there is Pure Awareness *which is identical with* Being, devoid of any excision caused by the consciousness of otherness. This is the only knowing-the-thing-in-itself.

Certain words – Being, Awareness, Bliss, *sat-cit-ānanda* – have been used in connection with Brahman by the Holy Ones of the Upaniṣads. Brahman is the Absolute, the One Total Reality, Transcendence. Feel the transcendent import of the word *cit*. Usually translated as consciousness, its deep connotation here is attentiveness – an attentiveness which none with burdened mind can understand. For what can be the meaning of attentiveness in the context of the One Totality? Can the One attend *to* the One in which there is no other to attend to?[5] If we are graced by a flash of this, we may see the difference between attention in the worldly sense, and attention in the supremely religious sense where it is identical with the state of perfect communion.

* * *

As a man in the worldly state, not capable of being attentive in the religious sense, I have no option but to start from where I am, namely, here-now. Nothing is more here-now than myself. So my discipline begins with the exercise of mindfulness with respect to body, feelings, thoughts and mental states. Since I am perforce involved with the world, my mindfulness is not confined exclusively to myself but takes in all that part of the environment with which I interact.

Mindfulness trains me to observe all that is actually present physically and mentally and thus develop and rightly use – never repress or inhibit – every sense faculty.

I observe all bodily conduct, paying attention to the *fact* that I am sitting, standing, lying down to rest or sleep, walking, driving a car, writing, cooking, dining, scrubbing the floor, bathing, obeying the calls of nature, turning the handle of the machine in the factory, digging coal – in short I pay full attention to every bodily action throughout the whole day.

If I am attentive to the fact, I become aware of *how* the body is working : sitting quietly at ease or tensely or fidgeting : lying down restfully or tossing and turning; driving the car like a road-hog or a dangerous demon, or like a skilled and considerate citizen; eating moderately and peacefully, or wolfing the food; doing my daily professional work honestly, happily, efficiently, and whole-heartedly giving all the best of myself, or excitedly, messily, riddled with anxiety, resentfully, always

[5] Consider also Matthew 10.29 and Luke 12.6.

growling for more pay and giving bad service, surreptitious and guilty of truancy; standing or walking, or getting on or off a vehicle gracefully and unobtrusively or rudely, obstructively and injuring others; talking too loudly or softly or inarticulately, unnecessarily, irrelevantly and interruptively, or courteously, listening to the other, never invalidating him as a person, as my fellow-human; breathing rhythmically or jerkily – and so on with respect to every action. And also with respect to one other physical action which makes or mars millions of lives: am I approaching and engaging in marital congress like a husband who is the artist of love or like a brutal beast; am I to my husband as a responsive wife, as the Sovereign Lady is to the Sovereign Lord,[6] or am I gracelessly ungiving or ruthlessly demanding. And remember that the whole of married life and love is a sexual congress – physical, emotional, intellectual, aesthetic and spiritual.

This discipline which marks the early stages of awakening to the knowledge of the ways of the self and its environment opens up the deeper aspects of mindfulness, which concern the sense-activities, the relationship of the moralities or commandments to the whole of life, feelings, thoughts, perceptions, mental states, the fantasy life and the dream life, the activating of quiescent sensitivities of the mind, and the experiencing of reality in the state of perfect clarity. Furthermore, the problem of right receptivity, freedom from helpless and uncontrollable reactivity, and of right responsivity begins to be understood.

As said above, the concept inhibits the fulness of the percept or even dismisses it, and diminishes the intensity of the immediate experiencing. So when I see a tree on my usual round in the park I say to myself or to my friend, 'That is the old oak.' No. Not the 'old' oak, for the old oak is my concept, a fossil of the dead past. I am seeing that tree *now*, in the living present, and if I am looking with full attention, my concept would simply tell me it is an oak tree and would not harshly dismiss or distort the immediate perceiving. Then I am truly seeing the tree; the tree and I are in living relationship; there is love, beauty and the vision of reality present; and my sense of sight is a thrilling cord of communion and not a binding chain of attachment or aversion.

(Is this how I look at wife or husband, employer or employee, friend or stranger or indeed any and every human being?)

Such is the nature of pure mindfulness, the right receiving and bearing in mind, and right responding by my whole being. I am not lost in some fantastic transport, but am wholly matter of fact and see the tree

[6] See above pp. 85 f., 188, 230.

as it really is *now* both with respect to its general appearance and also its details. My observation is scientific – accurate, dispassionate, free of illusions. Above all, it is free of any interference by my conditioning or imposition of myself on the tree or on the act of seeing. This means that I see what there is to see and not what I wish to see; and that my brain is not chattering back at the tree rending the music of nature by my cacophany. The tree and I are verily looking at each other so harmlessly, so purely, and unpossessively, that we are validating each other's existence divinely.

Thus, my sense of sight is used sensitively and sensibly and not senselessly. This is one meaning of the term 'good sense', used in this book. Happy the man who understands this basic spring of the religious life and human flowering : never take leave of good sense.

Consider calmly what difference it would make to human relationships and well-being if we all exercised good sense, unconditionally.

True mindfulness never precludes critical observation, critical in the sense of being meticulously accurate : that tree is so many years old; it is healthy, well tended by the gardener. And right judgment is also present : some people have bruised the trunk carving their initials upon it. The judgment is purely a dispassionate statement of fact, free of any hate or contempt for those who bruised the tree. Should there be evidence of ill-treatment of the tree, I observe it and state that steps need to be taken for the protection of the tree. And if I am in a position to do so without fuss, without hurting others, without bubbling over with self-righteous indignation, I take those steps quietly and unobtrusively, finish the whole business neatly, and immediately turn with full attention to the very next matter in hand.

Sense functioning gives rise to likes and dislikes, to attachments and aversions,[7] which are active and powerful conditioning factors from early days, long before the serious living of the religious life moves me to be mindful; the discipline of mindfulness rouses every sense faculty into full activity; and as observation becomes keener I become more intensely aware of my psychical reactions to what I observe. All this gives rise to moral and intellectual travail.

The trouble does not lie either with any sense organ in itself or with that which is apprehended, namely the object, in itself. Neither sense organ nor object in itself is a fetter; pure mindfulness produces no disturbance. It is the desire-reaction which is the disturbance and is the

[7] See also above p. 221 f.

fetter. In the *Saṃyutta Nikāya*,[8] Citta the housefather puts it thus to a group of elder monks discussing this question :

> 'Suppose, my lords, a black steer and a white steer are yoked together by one rope or one yoke. Now he who should say that the black steer is the fetter to the white one, or the white one to the black one, would he in so saying be saying rightly?'
>
> 'Not so, housefather. The black steer is not a fetter to the white one, nor is the white one a fetter to the black one. But the fact of their being yoked by one rope or yoke, that is the fetter.'
>
> 'Well, my lords, just so the eye is not a fetter of objects, nor objects a fetter to the eye . . . the ear to sounds . . . the nose to scents . . . the mind to mind-states. But the desire and lust that arise owing to the pair of them, that is the fetter.'

* * *

It is extremely difficult at first to let mindfulness be pure – bare observation with full attention, *and nothing else*. See a fine car and up rises the desire to possess it; an attractive member of the opposite sex, and the passion for gratification; a pain in body or mind, and the impatient and anxious urge to be rid of it : the stimuli and the reactions are innumerable. Moral conflict is stirred up : I ought/I ought not. As I see in myself envy, jealousy, self-pity, fear and the whole host of human qualities, good and bad alike, I feel depressed, somewhat crushed in spirit. By and by the discipline becomes more irksome, disheartening and psychologically disturbing. It entails the loss of pleasure, beliefs, the security of mediocrity, old convictions regarding the true and the good, and of the old settled way of life. The temptation arises : had I not better conform to the well-worn ruts?

Tribulation is the test. Do I care – really care – for Truth? For Transcendence? Now, if I stay alone with my problem, I can do right. But if I run to another for comfort or advice, then whatever steps I take afterwards, or do not take, will not be pure action. Paradoxically, this does not preclude right enquiry, including discussing with others. For if I observe this tribulation and how it leads me on to further investigation, and if I am attentive to what is presented in the course of consideration with others, I am being eminently mindful, because mindfulness is a living function of a living being, not to be stifled by the nutcracker

[8] Loc. cit. 4.282.

action of a mechanically operating imposition/prohibition. A mechanical vehicle has roads and the laws of the road laid down for it, whereas for any living being, the way opens up in the actual living process from moment to moment, provided he is wide-awake and not automatically conforming.

Mindfulness acquaints me with myself. Great courage and perseverance is needed. The self-revelation invariably shocks, producing both emotional and intellectual distress. When courage fails, energy flags, the enormity of the task is overwhelming, and depression and fear engulf me, let me not cry for help, seek consolation or delve into a book of wisdom. Keep quiet; or else I surely get hurt. Look. Under the compassionate gaze of the sleepless immortal eyes, the confusion in the mind and the turmoil in the heart come to rest.

I may say, 'But I can't look!' I answer unto myself, 'Stay still *and do not struggle*, and you *will* be able to look'. When caught in a monsoon downpour with no shelter available, I just get wet – and keep cool! Soon, I enjoy the downpour, and smile if I neither resist the rain nor wallow in the mud.

And *that* is the secret of mindfulness: neither resist nor indulge; for if I do, I remain the slave of aversion or attachment, of violence or craving. My business is to see and understand so truly and completely that there is nothing left over by way of unresolved psychical discords or not fully worked out mental impressions, the *vāsanās*. Thus the mind is free of the burden of any karmic debt. These *vāsanās* are the seeds of 'rebirth' *in my mind* whilst I am alive, not reincarnationally in another body, for further bondage to ill-states.

The Buddha's phrase, 'the peril of the senses', stresses an ever present and very real peril in every context of human life, material or psychological, personal or communal. The peril consists in the arising of desire with its accompanying lust, frustration, violence, dejection, anxiety, fear, delusion and bondage. Mindfulness appears at first to enhance the peril. But this is the very sign of its efficacy. If I am blind to a peril it is impossible even to begin to take right action. Therefore, to see the fact as it actually is, is an essential step. The senses can be, and are, the instruments by which we all make hell for ourselves through unintelligent indulgence instead of true happiness through right use.

I must see clearly the manner in which I am mindful. When I look into it, I see that it is self-conscious and self-oriented. I practise because *I* want to be free of suffering, become purified, achieve saintship, develop latent powers, realize peace, happiness and nirvana, be God's servant and establish the city of God on earth, all of which contradicts in present fact the delusive rational argument that I am doing so in order that I can help my fellow-men in the future. If my beloved and I are shipwrecked and drowning can I swim to safety first and return in the future in a beautiful ship to welcome the beloved on board?

Self-serving mindfulness takes the form of *I* see this, *I* feel that, *I* am angry, *I* am doing right, and so on. The first release from self-conscious self-centredness occurs when the observation changes into the form of '*this* is violence or envy or ambition or suffering'. Whereas previously the reaction to a self-centred observation was 'I must get rid of it or fight against it', this impersonal objective perception makes me sensitive to the fact that envy or ambition are world forces moving all mankind to evil and sorrow, and that suffering is a universal phenomenon. As my mindfulness becomes purer, my perceptions as to the sources and the growth and spread of evil in the world become keener. Since evil doing and suffering are world wide I become intensely aware of the fact that each and every one of us is a generator of evil and that the healing of souls cannot be effected by vengefully punishing particular evil doers or by any form of violence; and that I the individual cannot exert, and that it would be futile and harmful to try to exert, any compulsion upon any evil doer, myself included.

What happens then? I see that I must be endlessly patient and forebearing with myself and with everyone. I must suffer with the world's suffering. And as I see that, compassion and understanding of a nature transcending all duality and free of the conflict inherent in ambivalence is immaculately conceived in the soul and grows into a divine power for healing and beneficence.

Mindfulness must be free of the attitude of being on guard, which inhibits observation. If mindfulness is not wholly open-minded and fully receptive, devoid of inward resistance which defeats the learning process, there is no clarity in the mind. The efficacy of mindfulness depends on being aware choicelessly, that is, without taking sides for or against that which is observed.

This choiceless awareness means that all observation must be free of praise or censure. Praise, when I see something in myself which I approve of, leads to pride and complacency. The approval means that I am in bondage to my mental construct of the good. Censure gives rise to a guilt complex, which leads to neurosis and to violence upon myself and upon others. What punishment is subconsciously decreed and inflicted upon oneself is executed more harshly upon others.

The bestowal of praise or censure implies that I have criteria or standards of judgment. So the arising of approval or dispraise presents the opportunity to search out and scrutinize these standards. Thus I discover how I am conditioned, and the various influences – people, events, cultural background, my own nature and urges – which made for such conditioning. And as these come to light fresh reactions spring up in the mind, such as resentment against people, conditions, fate, and surging anger or seething hate impelling me to vengeful violence. (Recall, here, that the discipline of the religious life rouses up and energizes everything in onself, good and bad alike).

In this situation of peril, peril of emotions and thoughts begotten by peril of sense functioning, let me not flinch. I must stay with it, calmly, not opposing it, not indulging in the folly of trying to overcome evil. I must look at it steadily, steadfastly. Never run away or try to push aside the devil; and the stronger the devil the better is the good that emerges. For the devil is me. His strength is a reliable index of my power for good. I look at him, only look, free of any desire whatsoever, free of fear and of hate. He is me. By seeing him as he actually is quite clearly, I see the selfness of the self that is me and bears the name by which I am recognized in the world but not truly known except by the clean-hearted ones.

This steadfast looking is cool, even coldly intellectual, analytical to the minutest detail. It will tell me all about my devilishness. But it will not, by itself, release understanding, compassion, wisdom, without which there is no flowering of the religiousness within my being, nor the transformation of me the sub-human into the mature, true human.

My looking must not continue to hold the object of critical examination at a distance. The cold glare of glazed eyes does not heal. Rather, it rubs salt into the wound. Having seen the devil I must take him to my heart. This means that side by side with cold, analytical perception at a distance, there must be warm, intimate embracing, intensely, sensitively, of this devil-me. Remaining vulnerable, offering no resistance, I let the psyche *absorb* him fully as he enters into my being. If I merely accept or reject him, there is impotent spinelessness or hate on my part and I remain split, unhealed. But if I let the absorption by the psyche happen without engineering it, myself remaining choiceless and intensely attentive, there is no self-conscious centre, a *separate* observer who is glaring at the devil.

In this unselfed state, I realize that the psyche is neither hurt nor pleased, but is possessed of an incredible absorptive power for all that comes to it through pure and intimate personal involvement. In the state of selfness, there is a degeneration of mind if the psyche is hurt (*or pleased*) too much. In the unselfed state, however painful or destructive the situation may be, the psyche cannot be killed whilst the organism is still alive.[9]

When unselfconscious attentiveness is maintained at white heat then the conjoined activity of the cool intellectual perception and the warm feeling absorption releases me from the ill-state. Many earnest practitioners experience disappointment, even bitterness against this discipline of the religious life, because after many years of the practice of mindfulness they are still confused, groping, miserable or lost. Perhaps they have missed out in their practice this indispensable feeling aspect.

The warm, intimate, intensely sensitive feeling-observation transcends all sentimentality and shoots like the fiery arrow of Eros, divine Love, (not of Apollo which gives death) into the heart of the devil-me, converting this devil into the pure human. The fire of this fiery arrow is the Fire of VIRTUE, transcendent Love. It transmutes cold intellectual perception of myself into Understanding. Where Love and Vision are wedded, there indeed is Understanding, the Understanding which is compassionate Wisdom and wise Compassion in free action.

Such is the deep meaning and power of understanding in the religious consciousness. It is not obtained by mere logic; it is not merely an intuitional feeling or a sixth sense. Evil minded men too can exercise remorseless logic; and have intuitions and intellectual comprehension. But understanding in the religious sense transcends intellectual comprehension. It belongs to the mind in the undefiled state. It is unerring insight or direct perception, which is the meaning of *buddhi*. 'Give me understanding and I shall keep thy law; yea I shall observe it with my whole heart.'[10] Whenever there is the operation of *buddhi*, intellectual comprehension is undefiled and at its clearest.

* * *

Thus I see the nature of mindfulness. I see why it is the lynch pin of the religious life; and I see the rationale of its working and how I may apply it in practice. Beyond all doubt, it has to be a lifelong activity, like breathing. It has to be free of all self-serving goals, including liberation or serving God or any purpose that can be trapped in the cage of conceptions formed by my imperfect mind. When I am wholly selfless in

[9] This is one meaning of the miracle of conferring invulnerability on Prince Asphandiar by Zarathuštra and on Achilles by Thetis.

[10] Psalms, 119, 34.

my approach, mindfulness is an efficient power of this unselfed or egoless being which makes manifest the reality of liberation or the kingdom of heaven or nirvana through this very self. And this manifestation is beyond the power of the unmindful mind to imagine or preconceive.

Where there is mindfulness there is an end to wishing that the immediate situation, which is the present actual fact, were otherwise. All such wishing is rooted in isolative selfconsciousness. The separate self is the centre to which it is related. Hence it involves the pursuit and gratification of sense pleasures. This includes the pleasures of the discursive mind, for discursive mind (in both its logical and aesthetic aspects) synthesizes sense impressions, mainly by means of the faculty of speech, broadly classifies them as pleasant or painful, and chooses the pursuit of the pleasant. Skilful dispassionate scrutiny will reveal this to be true in every instance of wishing that which is actually present to be other than it is. Desire is blind and fevered, dealing wounds.

If I am a faithful disciple, my task is to learn a lesson out of each and every passing situation and not try to change it according to my desire. It is I who have to change rightly and grow in understanding, which can be done only by learning fully from what is actually present. Every situation changes, if through no other influence than my desireless attentiveness. On my part there must be perfect mindfulness, eternal vigilance. This it is which pacifies all sense functioning, brings relief from the fever of desire and the wild pursuit of pleasure, and allows the mind to come to maturity so that Life's purpose to release true humans on this globe may come to fruition. Only by transcending pleasure by right mindfulness is the mind freed into the healthy state of serene happiness.

Attention links up the person and the environment. When bodily awake, self is in relationship with not-self. When awake *and mindful*, I am in right relationship with the world around, which foreshadows the full and perfect awakening in the religious sense. In my worldly state, characterised by discriminative consciousness, I am aware of both self and not-self only as a set of mental constructs which is *my* collection of mental photographs of reality, and hence inevitably illusory in some degree or other – *māyā*.

My mindfulness is therefore not merely an observing and identifying of externals, such as chair, man, sunshine, riot and so on, and of internal psychological states or processes such as elated, fearful, absorbed, outgoing, inspired and so on. It is being as widely awake as possible, without praise or censure, to the entire consciousness process, the rushing stream of consciousness in its wholeness. This is the meaning of the words of Jesus, 'Watch and pray'. In its preliminary stage I do so lest I 'enter (enticed by the senses and desire) into temptation'. In its culmination, Transcendence flows through me freely; the Father and the Christ-consciousness make their abode in me the egoless being.

Discriminative consciousness, *viññāṇa*, the surface layer of the ocean of Awareness-Being which is perpetually poised creative action, is in endless commotion. It cannot pick and choose what it will be conscious of, except by an act of will. Not by will as a repressive power, giving rise to conflict, but by mindfulness the pacifying power one may say, 'Peace, be still', and the storm subsides. Thereupon wide-awake dispassionate observation flowers into understanding. The *sammā sati* frees me from the clutches of the basic duality of self/not-self and from attachment and aversion. I understand the *māyā*vic nature of the becoming-process. So I can be *in* it, not detached from but non-attached to it; and also, I can be not *of* it. Such is VIRTUOUS living. Herein all the five senses and, as India has always put it, discursive mind (the silent talker) which is the sixth sense, are the cords of communion and no longer seductive sirens dragging me down into worldliness. Unless the senses function freely and purely, self remains isolated from not-self, which is not exactly the whole and holy state.

When the senses do function as the cords of communion, I am in that state in which revelation can take place. Barefoot betimes on the little lawn on a dew-glittering morn stood one who silently greeted a blade of grass. The whole lawn lit with love. And that little blade slanting under his tread laughed when it rose again to its height, and whispered the secret of omnipotence.

Words cannot tell that living secret. But it was somewhat this wise: infinite resilience – Love that the redeemed know – the comfort of the Holy Spirit – omnipotence. And: the psyche that is vulnerable and wholly unresisting can never be killed as long as one is awake to the here-now, the birthless-deathless moment of eternity, the omnipotent Life/other-Life.

Mindfulness which glows with the intensity necessary for revelation means that there is no intrusion by memories or images to disturb the effortless silence of the mind. There is no uprising of any desire or thoughts or feelings common to the ambivalent state. The mind is void of all ill – a meaning of the empty mind. In this state I can look, listen, touch and use all my senses without being sullied by memories, images or any conditioning. Then, every time I see, hear, touch, there is Love, Truth, Wisdom, Goodness and Bliss, transcendentally. In that is the actual experiencing of The Holy. And I understand that The Holy is not a separate speciality characterized by the limited meaning of the human word holiness, but that it is the Whole Reality, the mysterious and inconceivable Unknown.

* * *

In being awake to the entire consciousness process it is essential to watch the psychical reactions to all the stimuli which affect me. The external stimuli reach me through the senses; the internal arise out of memories, fantasies, the listless wandering of the mind, the apparently causeless uprising of moods, urges, whims, impulses, emotions, the compulsive repetition of words or ideas or tunes, deliberate planning or thinking about any problem or procedure or theme, my repressions, *vāsanās* (unworked out mental impressions), susceptibility to the psychic atmosphere, and my own bodily state which has no small influence upon my mental processes. The external and internal stimuli are not unrelated. They constitute one whole process.

I observe the sources of stimulus: sights, sounds – objects, persons, events, news – prevailing conditions such as the weather, state of health, nature's cataclysms or beneficence, state of war or peace, of affluence or deprivation – accidents and changes of fortune that befall me or others – the actions, thoughts, attitudes and behaviour of all people such as politicians, business men, unions, councils, committees wielding authority, neighbours, members of my family including myself, and of all with whom I am personally in touch or who affect society – new inventions, fashions in dress, manners, speech and thought (climate of thought as it is called), new ideas and scientific discoveries – changes in social and business morality, in relationships between groups of people such as employers and employees, teachers and pupils, administrators or government or law and the people of the land.

I observe further sources of stimulus: my own thoughts, feelings, speech, actions, desires, fantasies; ubiquitous sorrow, injustice, evil, lack of skill in living, absence of vision, inhumanity; art, philosophy, religion, nature; philanthropy, self-sacrifice, goodness, love and beauty.

In fact the whole of everyday life offers countless stimuli for mindful observation.

The observation of the stimulus produces, at first, an immediate reaction. It may be one of attraction or repulsion, pleasure or pain, joy or grief, praise or censure, attachment or aversion. I note whether it is rooted in, or associated with the uprising within me of greed and lust for possessions, power or pleasure; or of hate, ill-will, anger, envy or jealousy; of fear, anxiety, confusion, delusions or illusions; of vanity, pride, conceit, megalomania, ambition and egoism. Or the reaction may be evoked out of pity, concern for another's difficulties, clear perception of facts such as the injustice of conditions or the stupidity of procedures. Such observation discloses my inner nature and tells me a good deal about my conditioning.

Apart from the immediate reactions there are delayed reactions – delayed shock at news, or through accidents or grievous sorrow, is a well-known phenomenon – all of which I must observe.

There are certain states which call for mindfulness to the utmost degree. First, the pleasant states. If the external circumstance is favourable and I am in a highly sensitive condition, I am lifted up into a sublime mood or I experience an exalted state. The influence which stirs such responsivity may be nature – daffodils sunflooded in spring, or a bright crescent moon with Venus and Jupiter above her in a clear western sky when twilight has just shaded into cool darkness; or it may be the beauty of art; or an insight; or a meaningful gesture; or my little child climbs on to my lap and rests its head on my heart in utter trust, and I savour the divinity of parenthood and am filled with a boundless – and yet apprehensive – courage to carry my responsibility. Then again there are moods of deep content, suffused with ease, which almost make me imagine I am enlightened, or in the *unio mystica*, or that I am a chosen one on whom lies the benediction of God.

I have to be extremely alert now. Unseducable and incorruptible. All particular states, however, sublime or inspiring, arise and pass away. However exquisite the flowers it bears, the rosebush in the garden of the soul has its thorns – illusions, self-gratulation, pride, disparateness[11] from my neighbour.

Of the unpleasant states, greedy and violent states, depression, anxiety and fear are perhaps the most frequent and widespread afflictions; time and again they are contributory causes or exacerbating sources of bodily disorders, nervous and functional. An outstanding generator today of unpleasant states is 'the pressure of modern life' – its ever increasing speed and noise; its compulsive, ugly and stupid demands upon whole communities; its apparently indestructible network of conscienceless, brutal and criminal exploitation of all men and its devilish use of cowardly murder or kidnapping or torture or lunatic destruction –

[11] A tearing out of a living organism; a diduction.

indeed it seems as if the hellish brood of Satan, in battalions, has successfully obsessed hordes of sub-humans in every continent.

My first reaction to an unpleasant or evil state is to get rid of it. I try to forget or to ignore, to suppress or to run away from it. In desperation, I may try to destroy the cause of it. These are futile ways, because violence or hate can never be cured by violence or hate. I have instead to be fully observant, dispassionate, sensitively absorbing it in my psyche and allowing my own psychical ill to become transformed into compassion and understanding. Such mindfulness calls for every skilled resource, *upāya*, and every ethical and spiritual energy, *viriya*, in my being. The painful and horrible is the heaven-sent opportunity for exercising mindfulness and developing its therapeutic power to the highest possible degree.

Therefore I must not be primarily concerned with getting rid of the unpleasant or the evil state, be it moral or intellectual, or a physical illness. I must be as wholly attentive to it as possible and learn all that it can teach me: such is the discipleship. As I learn, the ill within me is cleansed and transcended. The mind is healed. Thereafter, I never react helplessly like an automaton to any stimulus, nor am I overcome by any mood. Instead, I respond rightly to the situation.

The neutral state is one of indifference; or it is brought about by my deliberate refusal to observe; or it is due to my incapacity to pay attention because of tiredness. If I am truly mindful of tiredness I will act sensibly at once – take a rest, or go to sleep. If I am mindful of my deliberate refusal to observe I shall make valuable discoveries about my repressed fears or resentments; my prejudices, complexes, egoism or self-conceit; my conditioning and the mistakes made in my upbringing and education. The positive refusal to observe is usually a rigid and obstinate rejection out of hand of that which needs calm consideration. At times it is associated with indifference.

This indifference is all too often mistaken for mental poise. I pride myself that I am 'above such petty or contemptible matters'. The truth is different. For when I am in true mental poise I am intensely sensitive to the whole of the prevailing situation without being perturbed or swayed by it, and then only can I deal with it rightly. Truly poised, I am never above or below any matter or person, for now I am in right relationship with the whole situation. This is the right kind of neutral state, free of preferential choice and the conflict of ambivalence.

*　　*　　*

Wanting to be rid of that which is unpleasant, troublesome or acutely painful is a natural reaction. But as long as its source lies within me, it is folly to be rid of it before I learn what it has to teach me. Suppose I fall ill. The immediate practical and sensible step is to call in the doctor. Whilst I am undergoing the treatment I must be as mindful as possible. What had I done or left undone which contributed to this illness? In what manner am I reacting to the discomfort I feel? To the pain I endure? What are the thoughts and feelings that arise and pass through my mind? How does my mode of awareness in illness contrast with my everyday ordinary mode? Does the illness awaken compassion for others who suffer? Do I grow in understanding or do I remain cemented in my harsh 'Serve me right (or, at another's illness, serve that other man right) for being so foolish as to go against nature's laws'? If I have a modicum of wisdom in the religious sense I examine most searchingly: Am I clinging to life? Or am I precipitating death? The former is rooted in greed; the latter in hate against self as well as against others, for self murder is an inverted form of vengeance wreaked upon those who have hurt me. Both clinging to life and precipitating death are plagued with ignorance and fear.

Let me be mindful, then. If I do well, I am cleansed in body and soul. And if Life which holds the play of birth-death in its measureless compass smiles upon me, I am granted the vision and experience, if only for a single moment of embodied eternity, of the reality hidden in the word immortality. Healed, verily healed, of illness in body and soul there dawns calm certainty that this is not an illusion but the simple truth.

Similarly, with respect to the pleasant and the neutral, and to the entire consciousness process.

* * *

Many a voice will be raised in tumult: this is starry-eyed idealism: unrealistic: egocentrically concerned with personal salvation: a product of ignorance of the stark realities and terrible problems, political, economic, social, national and international, concerning war and peace, law and order and our very survival on the face of the earth.

Let there be peace. In the peaceful state, let us consider together.

Our condition is the result of the interaction between the environment and ourselves. The environment consists of the natural environment on the one hand and the way of life and the institutions we have established through the centuries on the other. The natural environment – soil, climate, geography, natural resources and so on – is a fairly stable factor over a long time span; it changes slowly, except when there is the catastrophic activity of nature, such as earthquake or volcanic eruption.

We the people adapt ourselves to this natural environment and also adapt it to us in order to live, not only for the sake of sheer survival but also for the sake of enjoying a satisfying life. Thus have arisen the different cultures and institutions of people inhabiting different lands; and the interaction between the different nations has brought the world situation into being.

Of these three factors – the natural environment, culture and institutions, and ourselves – we have least power over nature. We cannot change the geography of the land. We can affect the climate to some extent, by afforestation or denudation of woodlands or by pollution, and we have some power over the soil.

We have much more power to change our institutions and our way of life by our will, perception, skill, industry, invention, science and our ideas and ideals. The rate of change needs intelligent control, or else there is violent disruption and rapidly growing misery and confusion.

What of ourselves? We are the most flexible factor of the three.

Although we cannot change the natural environment very much, we have remarkable power to adapt ourselves to it even where it is very unfavourable to us. Of much greater consequence is the fact that we can adapt it to suit us. How have we done this through the centuries? Much more important, how do we do it today? Do we utilize it intelligently? Serve it lovingly with gratitude and reverence? Have a sense of reciprocal relationship and mutual interdependence with it? Are we ecology-minded?

Or are we still stupid, barbarous exploiters of the environment? Can any man in his senses deny we are sub-human exploiters? How comes it that we are such, not only in relation to the environment but also amongst ourselves in relation to each other? It is impossible to disregard the fact that the history of man, seen in terms of truly human and not sub-human values, is predominantly a sorry tale, and the history he is making today is an accelerating movement towards degradation and possible destruction.

Consider these statements made in ancient days:

St. Paul's Second Epistle to Timothy, Chapter 3.

1. This know also, that in the last days perilous times shall come.

2. For men shall be lovers of their own selves, covetous, boasters, proud, blasphemers, disobedient to parents, unthankful, unholy,

3. Without natural affection, trucebreakers, false accusers, incontinent, fierce, despisers of those that are good,

4. Traitors, heady, high-minded, lovers of pleasures more than lovers of God;

5. Having a form of godliness, but denying the power thereof; from such turn away.

6. For of this sort are they which creep into houses and lead captive silly women laden with sins, led away with divers lusts,

7. Ever learning, and never able to come to the knowledge of the truth.

8. Now as Jannes and Jambres withstood Moses, so do these also resist the truth, men of corrupt minds, reprobate concerning the faith.

12. Yea, and all that will live godly in Christ Jesus shall suffer persecution.

13. But evil men and seducers shall wax worse and worse, deceiving, and being deceived.

The Viṣṇu Purāṇa Part 4, Section 24, (abridged)

These rulers will be of churlish spirit, violent temper, addicted to falsehood and wickedness. They will destroy women and children and seize the property of their subjects. The people will be of a similar nature.

Virtue will decrease daily until the whole world be depraved. Wealth will be the test of virtue, passion the only tie of marriage, falsehood the means of success, women the objects of sensual gratification, mutual consent will be marriage. In the end, most of humanity will be annihilated.

Part 6, Section 1, (abridged)

In the Kali age (*of dissolution*), laws regulating conduct will be flouted . . . property will make men proud . . . spouses will desert each other . . . wealth will be spent on ostentatious dwellings . . .

The minds of men will be wholly occupied with making money, even dishonestly, and squandering it on the gratification of selfish desires. People will consider themselves as good as any of the best . . . they will suffer through fear, scarcity and other afflictions . . .

Women will follow their own inclinations and be given to pleasure-seeking . . . be selfish, slovenly, scolds, liars, indecent and immoral, attaching themselves to dissolute men . . .

Abandoning agriculture, people will gain a livelihood by servitude or the mechanical arts.

There spoke the voices of truth. Such we are today, and in some respects even worse. Society is rotting, the world over – and the word society means each and every one of us individually. There are some pure humans; but it would take no long time to count them. Each and every person, nevertheless, has the potentiality of divinity within him. All societies therefore have the possibility of being social in truth and not pretence.

What, then, is required in *practical* terms? First, each person must understand clearly that our institutions and way of life, and all our polity, economy, social organization and in short our total everyday life and all that happens to individuals and nations is the result of the interaction between what he is in himself and the whole environment. Next, he must be well aware that he has hardly any power to alter the natural environment, and only a little power and skill to change for the better the cultural and institutional environment. And last but most important of all, each and every person must see for himself (and not because he is told by another) that the factor which he has most power to change is himself. If I change, you too change, however imperceptibly. If you and I change, our world changes inevitably, even though the change is not immediately obvious to either of us. This is the deep meaning of social service. It is the meaning of Faith which is selfless and therefore creative practical action, not impotent fancy or blind belief.

Let us see with the clarity of the clean heart some plain facts connected with the points in the previous paragraph.

Man will constantly reap misery as long as he in his impure and incapable state blindly worships wealth and power. Thereby he remains the self-centred slave of his greed, violence, fear, delusions and ignorance. Slave that he is, he has lust not love, cunning not wisdom, and he bends his energies to the pursuit of false wealth and evil power. Money buys him pleasure, status symbols and the gratification of desire and vanity. It provides him with security, fraught consciously or unconsciously with anxiety. It enables him to flirt with a 'higher standard of living', which in fact is all too often more wasteful of time, energy, virtue and money itself, which arouses the envy and violence of the equally foolish have-nots and is doomed to frustration in the long run. Power enables him to impose his will and dominate others, which satisfies his blood-lust and egoism. Ambition, the sin by which the angels fell, is impossible to fulfil without antagonism and violence. Devoid of a true social sense – because he is devoid of selfless love and of the unconceited wisdom which knows that the 'I' does not know, which cannot produce a panacea, nor have the capacity or the aggressive right to 'save' others – he holds others in bondage, especially in the name of socialism (!) be it of the national or communal or any other brand by which he deceives and ensnares the multitude. He, in fact, is the one who produces and maintains with cruel brutality the inhuman authoritarianisms of the world. All power corrupts. All power is invariably and inevitably misused somehow or other, except where there is the harmony of Love and Wisdom operating through skilled action and in the absence of any self-consciousness that *I* am wielding authority.

Just as the individual's outlook and activity is geared to pleasure and success, the polity and economy of nations is geared to power and finance.[12] Wealth and power have been acquired through the ages by conquest, domination, oppression, plunder, robbery, inhumanity. History books have glorified tyrants and tycoons and glamourized successful pirates and plunderers. Education attempts to prepare youth for earning a living. Because of the influence of various destructive forces, it is unable to awaken the intelligence which can perceive the meaning and significance of human life, or to foster the ability to live honourably by the light of pure vision. Too many, therefore, in the developed and advanced countries, so called, never earn their living. They believe that the world owes them a living. Shameless, vulgar and insolent, they demand, and extract, the bounty of the state. They shirk, not work; strike, not come to a just and sensible agreement with those who see problems from a different angle. The jungle obeys its own laws. But man . . .? In the underdeveloped countries, millions suffer and die of disease and starvation and natural disasters.

Every society perishes where there is lawlessness and lack of vision. Let it be understood without equivocation that governments, systems and ways of life are the inevitable resultant of what we ourselves are, interacting with the environment. The latter we cannot change much, whereas the former is what we can tackle, and must tackle immediately and always. Every change of system or of anything external to us while we ourselves remain what we are, is like exchanging one disease for another. If a change of system could have assured our fulfilment as humans, in the real, factual meaning of the word human, it is unbelievable that in thousands of years we have never discovered even one system which preserves us free from avoidable evil and unnecessary misery, and leads us to fulfilment.

[12] This is evidenced by 'the end justifies the means' 'enlightened self-interest', 'the balance of power', 'spheres of influence', and other such phrases expressing man's ignorance and evil.

Thus the healing of this world-wide ill and disorder lies in changing ourselves. It is my own – and your own – greed, fear, violence, ambition, vanity, egoism, stupidity, delusion and self-indulgence which are the most powerful forces for our own ills and the world's ills.

Man will always have economic disasters whilst there is greed in me; constant wars and strikes and violence whilst there is ambition, egoism, fear and hate in me; endless muddle and confusion and wasteful futility whilst there is stupidity, delusion and neglect of duty in me. Have no illusions that man will ever have peace, well-being and fulfilment unless he purifies himself, grows to maturity of mind, abjures the pursuit of wealth and power, and freeing himself from selfness in all its forms serves Life's purpose of bringing to full fruition the religiousness within him which preeminently distinguishes him as a human being from all other creatures.

It is only a religious mind, free of vested interests, desire and prejudice, disciplined to see the fact as it is in actuality, which can be a truly practical mind.

* * *

Mindfulness is the most powerful means for purification and for growing to maturity of mind. Through right mindfulness I learn how to renounce and relinquish everything: the whole psycho-physical organism, the burden of psycho-mental lumber and all self-ness. Without the supreme relinquishment of self, which is the meaning of crossing the abyss, the crucifixion, the cessation (in Buddhism), the *asaṃprajñāta samādhi* of yoga, there is no mutation of mind or transformation of discriminative consciousness into Pure Awareness, no supreme communion, no reality to the words 'It is finished', no ascension and resurrection.

Right relinquishment comes through freedom from grasping. Whatever one desires to grasp is intimately bound up with illusory mental constructs of the desired object – as when a man marries because he is in love with his images of the other person and of love and marriage. In the clarity of perfect mindfulness, seeing the true nature of a thing dissolves any false image of it. Then one is in right relationship with it and the desire to grasp it vanishes. This is right relinquishment, free of heavy-hearted conflict. At root, all renunciation is mental, a natural consequence of the understanding of reality. He who has truly renounced and relinquished, acts purely as a trustee of whatsoever is at hand, be it a penny or a fortune, a child or a nation. Wisdom guides him and compassion animates him. He is the Grail of Transcendence.

* * *

In the process of self-observation, I the person, functioning as the onlooker, am the observer, and I the self-same person as the object of observation, am the observed, as if I see the image of myself in the mirror of cognition by means of the light of clearly conscious attention. This seems tantamount to saying, at least as far as the psychological component of self-observation is concerned, that the observer is the observed. When I am clearly aware of my psychological process I say that I 'see' my mental state as it changes from moment to moment. The continuously changing mind is both the seeing eye and the seen object. The paying of attention, in order to see, is the constant factor in self-observation, except that the intensity of attentiveness changes according to my state of freshness or tiredness.

Since I the observer and I the observed are not two separate entities but one and the same person, and since I am ignorant, confused, imperfect and ill, the purity of mindfulness is sullied and its efficacy is reduced. Therefore in the early stages of the practice of mindfulness I cannot avoid the discriminative judgements characteristic of ambivalence, such as this is good, that is evil, this is pleasant, that is unpleasant, nor can I be free of preferential choice in favour of one dual against the other. I am caught in the stranglehold of isolative self-consciousness, which, by setting up an entity-I as an observing subject over and against an entity-me as an observed object, tears apart me the single person into two non-complementaries locked in conflict. Moreover, I am self-deceived into imagining that I am fully mindful and am clearly perceiving the truth about myself and the environment. If I do see the whole truth, I should have no cause ten years later to say, 'I was mistaken ten years ago'. Still more distressing is the experience of making the same confession at the end of a second, a third and even a fourth decade!

But how lovely in the dawn-light of salvation when at last I see that I do not and cannot know the whole truth about myself as long as I am confined to ambivalence and discriminative consciousness! The break-through comes on awakening to the fact that the self-centred passion to achieve the desirable not only holds me fast in the hard shell of the I-me duality but also constrains attentiveness to function fragmentarily, sullying the purity of mindfulness. Where there is no fragmentariness, mindfulness is pure, full and effectively transformative.

The release from the fragmentary functioning of discriminative consciousness depends upon the constancy and intensity of attentiveness. Here arises the problem of the wandering of the mind and distraction of attention. Even the great disciples of Jesus could not watch with him for an hour in Gethsemane but fell asleep.

Whither does the mind wander? It goes to where treasure lies. This treasure is but the tinsel of worldliness; my desires, longings and all that I want to grasp and enjoy. It also goes to where it would rather not go, but is forcibly dragged away by passions, or by what I fear and hate. In either case I am self-enclosed, in subjection to the perishing ephemeral, to sorrow and the bitterness of death. Possessions, ties of affection for family and friends, or the compulsion of bread-winning work or enslavement by ambition, prevent me from being fully attentive to the here-now, especially in its transcendent aspect. Hence the Buddha's invitation to come away from home to homelessness and live the holy life. And Jesus said to him who asked what he should do to inherit eternal life: 'Go thy way, sell whatsoever thou hast and give to the poor, and thou shalt have treasure in heaven: and come, take up thy cross and follow me.'[13]

My attention is seized by memories of pleasure or of pain; or by compulsive thoughts or pictures or tunes or by worry; or by external stimuli or the outburst of strong feelings; or by fantasies or plans. All of them feed and harden my self-centre, and in all such states I am isolatively self-conscious and unmindful.

Most, if not all, religious disciplines in the past have prescribed remedies for the wandering mind: deliberately bring back the mind to the matter in hand; turn away from temptation; fight evil; overcome the obstacles to spiritual progress or to the attainment of your goal; resist the dark powers within and without; resolutely follow your guru's instructions or your saviour's example.

Each of these remedies involves conflict, rigidity and confinement to duality. It prevents whole consideration since it rejects out of hand that which opposes me. It does not invite the possibility of transformation of the evil, of true healing and creative renewal. Above all, it negates the reality of mindfulness and choiceless attentiveness.

But there is a constructive way which is psychologically sound. It hinges upon resilience. If the wandering of the mind is not due to tiredness or exhaustion, I must observe and be clearly conscious of that to which the mind has wandered. Thus I maintain attentiveness, although the object of attention is different. By maintaining attentiveness without conflict I am learning ceaselessly, there is no wastage of psychical energy, and sooner or later the original object of attention may come

[13] Mark, 10.21.

into focus again. The resilient mind is ever fresh, vigorous, innocent and unharming. Though intensely sensitive, it can go through grievous experience and remain pure and unscarred. Such resiliency characterizes him who is free of a self-centre and hence of selfness. Free of partizanship, he can be fully attentive.

Whilst the dissolution of the self-centre enhances the power of attentiveness, the discipline of mindfulness fosters the ability to be fully attentive to the immediate factual here-now, which in turn dissolves the self-centre. This dissolution is a process like unto dying – dying transformatively. Whereas the wandering-mind condition is one in which there is mere oscillation between contrasting or opposting duals, or one in which I am helplessly pushed about hither and thither, this dying means being born into a new Life, into a more mature state with greater possibilities, with no returning to the old confinement.

Every transformative dissolution of selfness is a painful experience. The ignorant psyche prefers indolent comfort and clings to the security of the known and the established. This is contrary to creative Life. Hence there is pain each time Life bursts out into richer Life, which is inevitable where there is mindfulness and full attentiveness. It is like a succession of crucifixions together with the ascensions and resurrections during my single lifetime; and they take place right up to the supreme communion in which Transcendence realizes itself.

When, through perfect mindfulness (*sammā sati*), attentiveness (*cit*) is at its peak intensity, then all wanderings of the mind and fluctuations of attention,[14] personal volitions and intentions, impressions remaining unconsciously in the mind, and the present consciousness of past perceptions,[15] all vanish. The mind, emptied of all its clutter, is transparent and wholly unobstructive to Transcendence. It is the fully awake and enlightened Intelligence-mass,[16] God or Brahman as the Light of Lights. The Holy Ones who entered and abided in this state never argued – is it any wonder? – about the 'existence of God or Brahman'.

* * *

Since speech is the predominant form in which mindfulness is registered, let us consider the fourth precept in the Buddha's code of

[14] The *cittavrtti* spoken of by Patañjali in his Yoga-sutras, 1.2, and the *manaḥspanda* in the Śāṇḍilya Upaniṣad, 1.42.

[15] The *saṃkalpa* and the *vāsanās* spoken of in the Muktika Upaniṣad, Chapter 2.

[16] The *vijñāna-ghana* of the Subāla and the *prajñāna-ghana* of the Māṇḍūkya Upaniṣad.

moral conduct. The following is a slightly shortened and rearranged abstract of the original text:[17]

> Abstain from all speech that is lying, slanderous, harsh or rude; from all frivolous talk and vain or low conversation; from all wrangling disputation; from all speech that is tricky, deceptive patter and from droning out holy words for pay.
>
> All speech must be truthful, blameless, pleasant to the ear, lovely, reaching to the heart, refined or polished, dealing essentially with living religiously, deep, in season, and meaningful.
>
> The speaker must be faithful, trustworthy, a man of his word, a reconciler of those who are divided, an encourager of friendship, a peacemaker, an ardent lover of peace whose words make for peace.

It is little appreciated that the expression of by far the greater part of life is in speech forms. Thought, feeling, fantasy, desire, memory, knowledge, cognition, communication, concepts, percepts, comprehension, insight, experience, action and all our mental constructs, involve speech; they are all clothed in words. The dominance of speech in our daily life cannot be doubted. The profoundest insights need speech for their expression. The new born infant's first breath of life is accompanied by his first speech, a cry. AUM is the creative word of Hinduism, the *Ahuna-Vairya* of Zarathuśtrianism, the *ma'amar* or creative fiat of Elohim of Genesis, the *Logos* of Hellenistic theology, the *Word* of St. John's Gospel.

Magnificently does the Ṛg-vedic hymn[18] to Vāk, Speech personified as a goddess, present the height and depth of speech:

> 4. Through me alone all eat the food[19] that feeds them . . .
>
> 5. I make the man I love exceeding mighty, make him a sage, a *ṛṣi* and a *brāhman*.
>
> 6. I have penetrated Earth and Heaven.
>
> 7. On the world's summit I bring forth the Father: my home is in the waters, in the ocean. Thence I extend o'er all existing creatures, and touch even yonder heaven with my forehead.
>
> 8. I breathe a strong breath like the wind and tempest, the while I hold together all existence. Beyond this wide earth and beyond the heavens I have become so mighty in my grandeur.

[17] D., 1.4; M., 1.179/80.
[18] RV., 10. 125.
[19] The word of scripture.

Most significant is the sentence in the Avestā with regard to Zarathuśtra: 'He is eager to proclaim the Glory of Mazdā and His Eternal Law in songs of praise to us, so let him be blessed with sweetness of speech'.[20]

Unquestionably, I must be mindful of speech. The whole world talks unceasingly; only in deep, dreamless slumber the flow of words may come to rest. Observation shows that one of the most tiresome disturbances in everyday life is constant chatter – inconsequential, misinforming, misleading, mischievous, useless, confusion and trouble making, discourteous, unrefined, seductive, loud, blundering, frivolous, slandderous, malicious, evil-designing, lying, devilish chatter. The overwhelming bulk of the world's talk concerns food, sex, commerce; pleasure; horror, violence, excitements and gossip. This is not unnatural, since mankind as a whole lives – to use the symbolism of yoga – almost exclusively at the level of the three lower *cakras*, which are concerned functionally with sex and food and commerce. Few indeed are the words of peace and healing, of wisdom and beauty, creatively uttered by human tongue.

The Hindus have an excellent teaching here: if what is to be said is truthful, kind and useful, then say it; if it is not, silence is best. 'The godly man talks readily only about God': thus Meister Eckhart.[21] And St. Teresa says: 'How can your tongues be better employed when you are together than in praising God, Who has given us so much cause for it?'[22] The Buddha strenuously upheld the *ariyan* (noble) silence; if speech there must be, let it deal with the discipline of the holy life or with the *dhamma*, the teachings.

Mindfulness with regard to speech makes me increasingly sparing of speech, with consequent economy of energy. When the noisy leak of pointless chatter is stopped, the quiet well of understanding fills. Then conversation is a refreshing draught; at times, a healing stream. True conversation is a sensitive interchange between mature minds, rare and beautiful as a poem. And there are a few who can hold rich converse, simply by silent dialogue.

Ceaseless chatter proceeds in two ways: either it is spoken aloud or it is a silent flow in the mind. I can refrain from the former, but I am the helpless victim of the latter. It reels in tipsy fashion round the self: the

[20] Yasna, 29.8.
[21] *Meister Eckhart*, Vol 2, p. 104, translation by C. de B. Evans.
[22] St. Teresa, *The Interior Castle*, 6.6.14.

word 'I' occurs in almost every sentence whether spoken aloud or silently.

The dreamy condition, as fantasy or day-dreaming when awake and as dreams when asleep, affords a wonderful revelation of the state of the mind. I notice immediately that the fantasy life is disorderly. Hither and thither the silent chatter rushes wildly, driven by every sense stimulus from without, or by memory or desire from within. Sights, tunes, events, bits of conversation, thoughts, emotions, various indulgences (especially concerning food, sex, pleasure and sensational excitements), anxieties – the list is endless – all jostle each other.

The substance and form of the fantasies reveal past conditioning, how far desire and ego have been satisfied or frustrated, what has been repressed, what secret longings or ambitions are present. They indicate temperament, maturity or immaturity. They show whether the mind is vague and confused or perceptive and clear. They disclose biases, prejudices, preconceptions and assumptions.

Mindfulness exposes the cleavage between the hidden fantasy life on the one hand and the overt life of action and behaviour on the other. Fantasies reveal inward morality. Watch the fantasies of hate and anger – the terrible things one does to the hated one! The fantasies of lust for power, possessions, sex, personal superiority, success and for putting the world right! Watch, too, the fantasies of all the subtle forms of indulgence – artistic, religious, intellectual, sporting and exhilarating, planning out the lives of one's children and even of other people, wielding 'power behind the throne' in Church and State and society!

As I watch this ceaseless, silent chatter, which is speech diseased, and appreciate the vast area of the life-process covered by it, I see with increasing clarity the evil in the heart and the immaturity of the mind.

* * *

Nature brings the body to maturity in a couple of decades or so. Mine is the responsibility, shared by parents and teachers, to allow the mind to grow healthily to maturity.

The maturing of the mind is always outpaced by that of the body. Whether I can rise to the height or not has so much to do with the parental and home influence and with the social environment. It is the fact now, exactly as it has been throughout history, that the deterioration and downfall of a generation or of a whole civilization begins and proceeds apace when the parental influence ceases to maintain a virile and virtuous quality. The mothers of the world, as well as the fathers, fail. Discipline, law and order decline dangerously. Pleasure-lust and violence crack our moral backbone. May the Lord bless us with chastening catastrophe in good time, before we destroy ourselves altogether.

What if the parental influence and the environment were so unfortunate as to deprive me of any chance of mental maturity and spiritual flowering? Even so, granted that I am aware of a single spark of Transcendence somewhere, or if some heaven bestowed glimpse of Beauty or Love or Truth evokes an answer out of the depth of a bleeding heart to the call of Life, I can be fostered by the comfort of that divine blessedness. For within me lies the chastening power of mindfulness, which is not a mere observation-recording machine. As it shows me my true state in the immediate present, it keeps me attentive to the here-now. When I am inattentive to the here-now, I fall into self-centred self-consciousness and wallow in fear, desire and all the ills of selfness. Forgetfulness is a powerful ally of the devil; even a moment's unmindfulness could precipitate me into unhappy darkness.

For mindfulness to be effective, it must be desireless. Very difficult, but indispensable. Any desire, even the longing to serve 'Thy Will' only, is self-oriented; and thus self obtrudes upon the absolute Holy defiling the purity of mindfulness. In the early stages, the mindfulness I practise is cramped by all my mental constructs. And so I imagine I am efficiently mindful when in fact I am only a clumsy novice. As I outgrow my limitations the constructs change, till finally there is no construct, no image, but unrestricted pure mindfulness, which is pure insight, pure Awareness.

Such is the mindfulness which purges the heart of all moral defilements and cures the mind of intellectual defects such as bias, prejudice, preconception and assumption. The mind is then free of its ills. It is mature.

When there is non-attachment in mindfulness, then there is equanimity (*upekkhā*), necessary for that meditation which is communion. Hence I must not cling to the object of mindfulness nor let it cling to me. In other words I must remain completely free of any attachment, enslaved by the pleasant, and of any aversion, vanquished by the unpleasant. The same object, such as a member of the opposite sex – can be an object of attachment and also of aversion. When desire which arises for the attracting one is frustrated, or first gratified and later frustrated by the object of attraction or by circumstance, then it becomes a memory, a very powerful mental impression (*vāsanā*) which sinks deep into the well of the unconscious. It comes up into present consciousness when there is a stimulus – music, scenery, perfume, another person, a photograph, or a sudden memory – which throws one into a fantasy of violence or sorrow or self-pity. The embers of passion, still smouldering under an ash heap of inhibitory circumstance which prevents 'putting it right' or 'revenge' or 'happiness in the end', glow with the wind of stimulus in the present. If one is overpowered, there is a benumbing of sensitivity, a blinding of clear perception and a loss of power to see truth. The mind is dulled, loses zest and innocence. The sweetness of life turns to bitterness. How many, how very many, are thus battered! How heavy is the psychic atmosphere, grey with the despair and hopeless sorrow of millions! And each of those millions is me myself, you yourself, in different form!

This congealed memory , so intractable, is like a hard tumour in the psyche, needing treatment by the intensest mindfulness. Never refuse to face it. Keep mindful, most perseveringly, free from desire, fear, judgement, in short from everything which disturbs equanimity. Be as fully attentive as possible without *struggling* to fix attention upon it. Although the attentiveness may reach a white heat, the mind must remain calm and fully absorptive. When the psyche has touched the critical point, and full attentiveness is maintained, there is a sudden release. The imprisoned and dis-eased psychical energy of that congealed memory is freed. I am at ease. No more pain, sorrow, self-pity and a host of other afflictions. Nor is there elation or triumph.

There is, instead, the peace of God which passes understanding; and just a simple walking on, living the pure life. Within my heart, trust springs because a stir of inward awareness, inexplicable, is on the march towards vision. 'Tis Transcendence in action, not me. When the bounty of such experiencing, conjoined with the loving labour of purification has taken me to the edge of the divine dark, the Void is lighted up. The inexplicable becomes clear and simple without the intermediary of explanation. Childlike trust blossoms into Faith.

Within my heart, the springs of Compassion flow freely. This cannot happen were I not to overpass extremity – and die – and be raised up again. Spiritual alchemy of pure mindfulness!

* * *

It will be said, 'But there are many happy memories. Life would be intolerable if we did not treasure them and cherish them'. Yes, there are many happy memories. Yet life would not be intolerable without them. A memory is a dead fossil of the past, not the factual present. In strong contrast, if I am rightly attentive to the living here-now, I am immersed in actual happiness, not wasting my time with tombstones.

Consider. Why are we moved to tears by the happy memories of wonderful music or poetry, of nature or a baby's smile? Is it not due to associated memories of failure and misery spoiling those of deep joy and fulfilment? Memory leads to tears because we did not pay total attention to the immediate experience and understand it fully. There was an unworked out portion of that experience, a small or large debit account in connection with the memory of that experience. That memory can be deeply sunk in the mind. This debit is a knot, a sensitive spot in the psyche which hurts when the appropriate stimulus pricks it. So there are tears, although the stimulating source is wonderful or beautiful. Whatever is fully worked out leaves no possibility for tears.

* * *

The fruitive state of mindfulness is realized when mindfulness is ever present effortlessly, even in sleep,[23] and has become as natural as breathing. Now there can be perfect renunciation and relinquishment and I can put aside all that is ill. What does this mean?

It is little realized that grasping is dual. Attachment comes about because I seize the object desired; the root here is greed. Aversion springs up because I want to be free of that which I dislike or fear; here the root is hate. But there is just as much a binding relationship in aversion as in attachment. My psyche is merely reacting one way in attachment and the opposite way in aversion. This mere reacting is tied up with grasping; I grasp the object in the one case, and the object grasps me (or else there would be no reaction from me against it) in the other. The object and I are usually regarded as two separate entities. But actually, the object and I are comprised within a single whole situation. Only when I have transcended both attachment and aversion, that is, ceased from all grasping, is there right relationship between the object and myself. And then I am in the free state of poise and understanding.

He who is free from all grasping is the true Person, the one in whom all evil-mindedness is burnt out, the sinless second Adam who is the Son of his Father, the Enlightened One, the Jivanmukta. He is the egoless being. Since the context of religion is Transcendence, it is clear that the non-grasping or despiration of personality (the egoistic being with a

[23] M., 3.90. See also Maṇḍalabrāhmaṇa Up., 2.3.2.

limited self-centre, the source of ill) is indispensable for the release of the Person – the *puruṣa* of the Upaniṣads, the *puruṣottama* of the Gītā, the *uttara-puriso* of the Buddha, 'he that overcometh' of the book of Revelation.[24] The suggestion of de-personalization causes much heart-burning and excites fierce, hostile reaction from all those who have not understood the matter. In the *supreme* communion, the Person has no self-consciousness. After returning to worldly sense-mind functioning, there is a personality again with self-consciousness. The two states – supreme communion devoid of self-consciousness, and self-conscious separate personality – are made manifest through the one living organism. The repeated alternation and movement between these states during my single lifetime is, in innermost reality, the activity of Transcendence and not of an isolated me, a mortal entity.

Now we can see the deep significance of putting aside all that is ill. Because of my freedom from grasping, ill is unable to enter my being and find lodgement there. So it naturally falls away from me like a clod of earth which strikes a stone. But the analogy is deficient, for the clod of earth falls away in broken pieces, whereas ill is transformed into the Good by the Holy One. Thus we see that renunciation and relinquishment are not merely a casting aside or turning away but an activity of purificatory transformation by virtue of non-grasping. This is charity, *dāna, in excelsis*. This is the state of the yogi who has realized *pratyāhāra*.

Pratyāhāra is usually translated as 'the withdrawal of the senses from worldly objects'. Initially it is a withdrawal from grasping at all that I contact materially and mentally through the senses: hence attachment and aversion do not arise. Since the urge to seize or the desire to possess arises in the mind, *pratyāhāra* is essentially the mental act of renunciation (accompanied by physical relinquishment where necessary) of whatsoever arises in consciousness. Since arising (birth) necessarily ends in passing away (death), and since the entire becoming-process, moving as my own stream of consciousness tainted by my defilements, is the fundamental sorrow and the state of ill, *pratyāhāra* is the disengagement from all ill by not grasping at or clinging to it. This non-grasping, seemingly negative, is the positive putting aside of ill.

In my worldly state, all my thinking (silent talking) is conditioned by my sense impressions. By not grasping at these, *and* remaining intensely attentive, the silent chatter calms down and the mind awakes to a profounder mode of awareness. The conditioning by the sense activity is

[24] Rev., 2.7,11,17; 3.5,12. See also above, p. 23.

transcended, and transition from the physico-psychical to a psycho-spiritual functioning of the mind is effected. In the culmination of *pratyāhāra*, all conditioning by natural evolution and the socio-cultural heritage (including the Archetypal Ideas) is transcended and the supreme communion is realized. Thus we can appreciate another meaning of *pratyāhāra*, namely the re-absorption or dissolution of the world, that is, the world which I am conscious of as a becoming-process, the world of my mental constructs. This dissolution prepares the ground for *dhāraṇā*.

Whether any business in hand demanding attention is present or absent, the mind is often obsessed by a thought or feeling or sense-impression. The mind is a storehouse of *vāsanās* which are sources of pleasure or fear or hate. Either we turn to them for pleasure, like a child takes to sweets, or they seize us. Whichever way it happens, the thought or feeling repeats itself incessantly. Consequently, it is not possible to be fully attentive to what is actually present here-now. *Pratyāhāra* spells freedom from this invasion by past impressions.

When there is no sense-impress taking place in the moment, as when resting or on just waking up, and especially in deep meditation, the mind stays calm, empty of chatter. Now I am in a state of pure Awareness, open to the free inflow and outflow of Transcendence. Like Naciketas,[25] I am 'a dwelling open'. In this state, I am in harmony with *ṛta*, and uphold the eternal order inherent in the cosmos. This upholding is the meaning of *dhāraṇā*, the state in which one is firmly established in Brahman. And this meaning collects under its wings various other meanings: the concentrated mind, concentrated in the sense of fully conserved energy; right remembrance, namely of Brahman, Transcendence, embodied in all things. Then I can effectively carry out the meditations known as the *brahmavihāras*,[26] and be the instrument of peace and comfort. For this, I must be capable of silence and stillness of body and mind: hence the necessity for the grades from *yama* to *prāṇāyāma* as the foundation for *pratyāhāra* and *dhāraṇā*. Then indeed one sees the factual reality of the omnipresence of God, God not only as an untouched and ungraspable Other but also in constant (faithful) and complete relationship with all creation, ceaselessly suffusing it with divine influence.

But the mind has to be void of defilement, free of all speech, to know that this is true. The King speaks when I am speechless.

[25] Kaṭha Up., 2. 13.
[26] See below, p. 377 f.

'Cleanse my heart and my lips, O God, Who by the hand of Thy Seraph didst cleanse the lips of the prophet Isaiah with a burning coal from Thine Altar, and in Thy loving kindness so purify me that I may worthily proclaim Thy holy Gospel.'

* * *

Look steadily and endure fearlessly this purification with a burning coal. Then only do I learn continuously from the whole stream of consciousness as it flows past. So much of it is dear, pleasant and valuable, and I am so self-identified with it and crave for it, that to let it flow past and not to hold it and keep it feels like a burning coal. But let me take heed, and never be unmindful of the fact that the whole stream of consciousness is mortal, far from the light of truth, woeful. With right wisdom, then I put it aside, that is, I do not grasp at or cling to any object, person, situation, condition, memory, idea, or anything whatsoever, bodily or mental or spiritual.

By being truly mindful I see clearly that greed, hate and delusion all arise out of the living organism whilst I remain ignorant and inattentive. They give rise to misery and are the roots of evil. Just as I never grasp a hot ember after my first experience of the consequence of doing so, I refrain from grasping at any shape or body, or any feelings, thoughts, perceptions or states of consciousness however elevating or inspiring they may be. They come; they go. They are the ephemeral flux of the becoming process which is universal manifestation; transient reality; relative and conditioned; binding, and indeed bondage itself. But this flux is bondage itself only in so far as I try to grasp it. Experienced with perfect mindfulness, without grasping, the becoming-process is the shining garment of Transcendence, a divine pleasure which is unavoidable. Grasping cannot take place in relation to Transcendence, for the finite and mortal, the relative, cannot seize the immeasurable immortal, the Absolute.[27]

So with mind at ease, in vibrant poise, this truth of the nature of things is fully understood. It is clearly seen that all sense-impressions, fantasies, dreams and discursive thought are self-centred – and this keeps the psyche tainted. Not empty of self-rubbish, the activating of the inner depths of the mind is obstructed, and the beneficence of archetypal energies – the *ākāsic* forces – cannot flow through and irradiate the

[27] 'The Atman is unseizable' – Bṛh. Up., 3.9.20.

environment.[28] Hence, with right wisdom, put aside ephemeral things. Thus one slips out of the noose of the Lord of Death (Yama's noose) and one is free in the infinity of mind-space which is dimensionless.

In the early days of the practice of mindfulness, the observer-I does not see the observed-me at the identical moment that the me experiences a feeling or performs an act. There is a time-lag, in which there is a movement by the mind due to its conditioning. I am still confined within the bounds of discriminative consciousness.

There comes the stage when the time-gap closes. Time gives place to timelessness, the eternal now, for the mind is in vibrant stillness. This is the state of pure Awareness in which there is no separation between the I and the me. This is the state of pure attentiveness, momentarily, the state of meditation, the first sweet draught of the *unio mysticā*, just a flash of the *asaṃprajñāta samādhi*. Isolative self-consciousness is out; greed, hate and delusion are extinct. It is the peak point of perfect mindfulness.

On the lips of the Transcendent is a smile. Be wise, O my soul, and do not interpret it. The eyes of the Transcendent are as stars of blinding brilliancy shining out of the impenetrable dark. Be wise again: do not interpret. I only know that I must not preferentially choose the light against the dark. I myself am as nothing, for the NO-THING is me. Transcendence is Light-Dark, Life/other-Life; and also the Beyond/not-Beyond. Here-now, Transcendence IS, the aseity, *svayambhu*, knowing Itself, revealing Itself, Itself playing with Itself, the numinous ever-Unknown and Unknowable to me. The me, nevertheless, is IT embodied. Sacred, wondrous secret of eternal God!

And to me there is Joy and Bliss in my unknowing of Its transcendent self-knowing, *cit*, Its mystery-playing, *sad*, Its endless music of silent glory, *ānanda*, filling all solitude.

* * *

Whoso aspires, and dares, may realize the immeasurable. There is no authoritative instruction to give, no ideal to follow. There is no particular way to lay down. Yet, seek out the way – your own way. Every way which is a borrowed or a dictated way comes to a dead-end. But your own way – and you *are* a self-responsible, unique individual in reality – is the way which allows you continual emergence. Your own

[28] If we understand this we can understand one of the deep significances of the Mahāgosinga Sutta (No. 32) of the Majjhima Nikāya.

way is no other than your own mindfulness. It is the way of everlasting life, of sweet savour, without a moment of stagnation.

Mindfulness reveals that some of the most serious blocks are our own beliefs, especially our religious beliefs. Deep distress comes when cherished beliefs are seen to be illusions, tacit assumptions to be groundless and preconceptions to be unwarranted. One is most reluctant to relinquish the familiar intellectual and spiritual landscape, terrified to turn one's back upon what seemed safe ground and wing an uncharted flight into the trackless open. And this open seems to be nothing but an all-devouring emptiness, for all the hitherto familiar meaningfulness has vanished and there is not a sign in the heavens or in the earth to give a single indication of any *thing*. There is but the vast solitude of the nothing. The wings of the spirit are truly terrible, an invisible fire scorching every resource, a freezing chill petrifying head and heart and hand into immobility.

Now is the moment. Let go of everything – self, God, Master, values, knowledge, everything. Let them go absolutely, for now is the moment of the NO-THING. The whole of ever-dying time is not equal to this instant of poised eternity. It hurts, even as you were hurt when you were squeezed out of your mother's womb. And it hurts enough to wring out tears from the eyes of the soul. But tears must flow and wash away all vision-obscuring dust. In this state of revelation the heart wholly understands the Unborn, Unbecome, Unmade.

CHAPTER TWENTY-ONE
MEDITATION : THE HEART OF RELIGION

DISCURSIVE MEDITATION

To wing the uncharted flight in the trackless open! This is deep meditation, *samādhi*; this is contemplative prayer and the *unio mystica*.

The discipline of morality and religious observances, of the body and of the ethical conduct of body, speech and thought, and the purification effected and maintained through perfect mindfulness, transforms the whole being of the religieux. He whose psycho-physical organism is healthy and strong, whose sense functioning is pure and keen, whose mind is cleansed of defilements and is innocent, sensitive and alert, and whose heart is filled with strong peace and radiates love, he is well-fitted for communion.

The trackless open is 'the beyond' of ordinary religious parlance which is here-now within me in real fact. Its substance is the deepening intensities of awareness of the One Total Reality, which are, as it were, different worlds. The entry into each intensity is like a birth, and the changing into another is like a death followed by a rebirth. These births and deaths all take place within me the living being, and the entire process is one whole experiencing of the beyond.

When considering this process in terms of discursive thought and speech, it is essential to understand and emphasize the aspect of the series of deaths. Each death means a transcending of the previous state of consciousness through the renunciation of clinging to life and the relinquishment of the particular form through which it manifested. It is a solvent of a fixed embodiment which ambivalently holds pain-pleasure, sorrow-joy, evil-good. It releases me from a state of bondage and conflict into an integrated condition, into the holy state and into that voidness (*śūnyatā*) which has no characteristics. Each death contains, momentarily, the state of complete unconsciousness of the state which is being relinquished. It is the silence *per se*, in which an activity of transmutation takes place, which releases this-life awareness into other-life awareness. When the return journey is made back to everyday consciousness, the impression made by each other-life awareness on the existential psycho-physical being becomes hidden memory, which can be called up into discriminative consciousness on the return.

The activity of transmutation referred to in the above paragraph is the spiritual alchemy of Death, the other face of Life – Life in the sense in which mystics have spoken of Life Eternal, and the Chāndogya Upaniṣad in the affirmation 'Brahman is *prāṇa*'.[1] If Death meets any resistance in the mind, the transformations cannot take place and one falls from the contemplation of God, or falls asleep as did the disciples in Gethsemane. These transformations of the mode of awareness constitute the spiritual growth which culminates in the full flowering of the religiousness distinguishing man.

Perfect renunciation and relinquishment is the one part, creation the other part, of the activity of transcendent Love. Life/other-Life is the fulness of immortality, and Life-Death-Love-Immortality comprises the Action in Eternity of Transcendence. And this realizes itself through the individual being in that supreme communion which is the ultimate intensity of Awareness-Being possible for man. It is the peak point of meditation.

* * *

Even as out of thousands of talented men there arises one here, one there, who is the genius, so too the perfect communion is realized only through the few[2] – the poor, the peacemakers, the perfected Holy Ones. But the doors of the deathless are open to all who are willing to walk through the portals of death. The name of this walk is meditation, which begins in time and with human effort, and culminates in the timeless and the state of Grace in which there is divine ease.

There are two aspects to meditation. The first takes place in the worldly state. This is discursive meditation, a process or ritual of aspiration, feeling and thought clothed in words confined within the mortal ambit of discriminative consciousness. Here, 'I' am meditating. Emerging out of this confinement and immerging into the non-mortal infinite, there is present the other aspect of meditation, the perfect communion in which Transcendence shines with self-realization through me.

Meditation begins with establishing a calm state. Let the body be at ease, free of all strains in the pelvic and abdominal regions and in the muscles of the shoulders and arms, and especially of the neck which is the connecting link between the head (which contains the brain and all the sense organs) and the rest of the body. Let the back be erect, elastic: imagine the spine is like a spring. Let the head balance finely

[1] Loc. cit. 4.10.4.

[2] 'The Atman is to be realized only through the one whom the Atman chooses; to such a one that Atman reveals its own nature' – Kaṭha Up., 2.23; Muṇḍaka Up., 3.2.3.

on the neck and let the muscles around the eyes and the lower jaw be quite relaxed. This is essential for establishing my own gentle breath rhythm which will then effortlessly maintain itself without needing special attention. Let elastic ease pervade the entire body. This is the natural state of a healthy body. It is the happy and peaceful state, essential for meditation.

My breath rhythm is my own distinctive life rhythm, different in some degree or other from any other person's life rhythm. Life is universal. Whilst the breathing is rhythmic, I am in harmony within myself and with all around me, whether problems be present or not. Any two individual rhythms, however different from each other, can commingle harmoniously. My neighbour may be unrhythmic, out of tune with me. But if *my* stance towards him is right it will have a restorative effect on him.

The body at ease and the life rhythm flowing happily means that I am also at home in the world-body. Thus I am free in some measure from confinement within self's isolativeness and am alert and sensitive to the whole. Since the body is a psycho-physical organism, strains in the body betoken strains in the psyche also – fear, anxiety, repressions, frustrations, anger, depression, misery, self-pity and so on. Freedom from strains in the whole psycho-physical organism is necessary for meditation.

The state of ease can become habitual wherever one is. There is evidence for this: for example, in the experiences of remaining alert and poised when bombs are exploding around one during air raids, whilst actively doing what has to be done to put out fires or removing debris, seeing blood without fainting and hearing groans from the mangled ones without losing one's nerve, *and having no aftermath* of delayed shock or nervous upsets after any period of time.

* * *

Here we must note that the culmination of discursive meditation is the non-discursive state. This means that thought and imagination are pacified, stilled, and have given place to awareness-being. The consciousness process in the worldly mode of mortality is transformed into non-finite awareness in the mode of immortality. Speech silenced, oneself fully awake, not in a trance or self-hypnotized, true meditation is present.

The objective of discursive meditation is, therefore, to calm the whole psycho-physical organism and intensify attentiveness. In this state intelligence functions more freely and the power of insight grows as illusions and delusions are seen for what they are, till there is the deliverance out of evil into pure manhood.

* * *

There are scores of different forms of discursive meditation described in various books and in the scriptures of the world. Let the serious religieux beware of any appeal they may contain, intentionally or unintentionally, to selfness. There is nothing whatsoever for me – or for you – to grasp, attain, achieve, enjoy or anticipate for personal satisfaction. Grasping and achieving are the puerilities of the ill worldling, locked in the dungeon of sub-humanity. If this is not seen clearly and unreservedly, keep away from the fire of the spirit, for it will prove itself the fiercest fire of hell if the heart is impure and the motive is self-centred. Furthermore, meditation is not for having visions and auditions or private interviews with gods or demons, for gaining psychic powers or having trips to other worlds or expansive sensuous experiences, all of which are so attractive to the lunatic fringe and are so exploited by knaves. Visions and other experiences may take place; in which case be mindful, learn the lesson if there is one to be learned, be free of grasping, and make no vain display of it. Whoso cannot be sensible can never meditate.

It is often asked which is the best time to meditate and how often and how long should one meditate. Every moment lives within, and is, the mortal substance of eternity. There is no best nor worst time, then, for meditation or prayer, which is Transcendence thinking[3] through man. But I, poor mortal, am lost in the menacing wood of ignorance, and in my fear I am agitated. So for me there are opportune times to meditate, namely, when I feel moved to meditate and there is quietness around. As a means for disciplining a wayward or moody or sluggish organism, I may deliberately set apart a fixed time, such as on rising in the morning or before going to bed. The taming of the body and psyche has due place in disciplined living, for without such taming the training of the faculties and natural gifts with which I may be endowed becomes difficult or even impossible. As regards the frequency of discursive meditation, I respond as and when the spirit moves and circumstance allows, taking care not to let meditating become an emotional indulgence, nor

[3] See also above, p. 78.

to make a theatrical display in company and inflict an embarrassing situation upon those present. When I pray in secret silence, the still solitudes sing for joy.

If the body is unruly or the mind is restless, there are simple ways of inducing calm, such as counting breaths or repeating a word or phrase silently or audibly. But this induced calm is not the same as actually *being* calm. A tranquillizer is dope. The doped state is one of illness suppressed, not of health and vigour. When the mind is lulled into the quiet state there is diminished alertness, sensitivity and intelligence. Since the ability to let the body remain perfectly still for protracted periods of time is necessary for meditation, mindful observation of its fidgetiness is the cure. At first, when the body begins to stay at ease, the restlessness of the mind seems to increase alarmingly. Again, constant mindfulness; in due time there is calmness of mind. When the whole psycho-physical being is still and perfectly calm, I realize the meaning of the fact that I am no-thing. There is clear perception of the truth that whatever uprises, of necessity passes away. And I see the ending of everything. This emptying into the void is not a casting away into a pit for containing refuse. Because of calm and insight, it is seen as a restoration of everything to its pristine purity.

An oft-repeated *mantra* (that is, a phrase or word of power which, on occasion, may be used as a spell) is known as *japa*. It can be used to produce a calming effect. As used by members of various sects the world over, there is nothing transcendental about it. It is a technical means like a physical drug or psychological suggestion to produce a desired result. The Śāṇḍilya Upaniṣad (1.2) mentions *japa* as one of the ten religious observances (*niyamas*). The Yogatattva Upaniṣad[4] warns against the misuse of *mantras*. In the Tārasāra Upaniṣad,[5] Yājñavalkya teaches Bhāradvāja the right use of a certain *mantra* – *aum-namo-nārāyaṇāya* – which consists of eight syllables. Each separate syllable symbolizes aspects of Transcendence (Brahmā, Viṣṇu, etc.) or archetypal MIND energies. The meditator must be capable of being at one with these in consciousness, and not merely as mental constructs clothed in words. Then he can effectively use this *mantra* to realize supreme communion instead of being caught in the net of words and sensuous experiences.

Devotees may use the names of the Holy Ones or of God, or of archetypal MIND energies symbolized in the names of Archangels, or of

[4] Loc. cit. Verse 30.
[5] Loc. cit. 1.2; 2.1-4.

angels or *devas*, or of spiritual values or the *pāramitās*, or Excellences. As examples: Rāma, Kṛṣṇa, Śiva; God, Father, the Blessed Virgin Mary, Lord, Jesus; Yahoel, Adonai, Elohim; Kwan Yin, Avalokiteśvara, Bodhisattva; Love, Goodness, Wisdom, Truth, Peace. When the heart overflows to the object of adoration, the invocation of the name energizes the whole being. If at this time the mind is clean and free of personal desire (and this is the psychological correspondent of the bath or ceremonial ablution before entering the temple or sitting for prayer), the energizing will infuse calm throughout the organism. If the mind is not clean and free, the energizing may prove unfavourable and lead to conflict and ill sooner or later.

In discursive meditation, do not encourage the discoursing but let it quieten down. For example, use some of the Names of God as presented by Dionysius the Areopagite in his work on the Divine Names:[6] Goodness, Being, Life, Wisdom, Truth, the Ancient of Days, King of kings, God of gods. Or as in the Zarathuśtrian Ahuramazda Yaśt,[7] in Ahurā Mazdā's own words: I Who Am, the Shepherd, All-pervading, Supreme Righteousness, Wisdom, Almighty, Lord of Life, All-seeing, the Healer. And later on: 'O Zarathuśtra, here in my abode dwelleth the Good Mind, Perfect Holiness, Supreme Power, Pure Devotion, Wholeness and Immortality'. Or as in the recital by Kṛṣṇa in the Bhagavad-Gītā or by Śiva in the Tejobindu Upaniṣad[8] of what He is.

Each of these terms characterizing the divine being expresses man's own potentiality *in excelsis*. Each one of them is worthy of meditation. Take the name, or the quality, and let the mind dwell quietly upon it. At first the intellect will discourse analytically, starting with the simple dictionary meaning underlying my own mental construct of it. After a while let the discoursing come to rest, let attentiveness intensify and let the feeling mind reach *into* the quality or potentiality more and more sensitively, easily and effortlessly. This is meditation, communing, which means that I am becoming what I am meditating upon. I am not just acquiring information and remaining sub-human, which is about all that happens with a mere churning up of words. I am maturing in mind, which spells insight, compassion, purity, calmness and steadfast poise. Such sensitive meditating makes it possible to express the quality and to live virtuously, without conflict.

[6] *Dionysius the Areopagite on the Divine Names and the Mystical Theology*, translated by C. E. Rolt.

[7] Loc. cit. 13 ff; 33.

[8] Loc. cit. Chap. 3.

When the power of attentiveness reaches a peak of intensity, the flow of discursive thought-speech comes to its end and the discursive meditation changes into true meditation. It must be noted carefully that attentivenes does not diminish, so that one is moving towards sleep, but becomes more and more intense so that one moves towards full awakening, an indescribable awakening into the unimaginable 'beyond' – 'THAT from which speech and mind return not having attained' as said in the Upaniṣads.[9]

The Holy Ones themselves are a profound subject of meditation. Here it is essential to be well aware that when directing attention to the Teacher I am looking at my own mental construct of him. Whatsoever is called up in mind is an image, an idol, composed of sense impressions made into a finite pattern by my speech faculty. It tends to become a fixation. But wisdom lies in freedom from the tendency to fixation. So I learn from my meditation to refrain from clinging to my idea or image of the Teacher.

When I have grown the ability to drop all images, reality is present. A new kind of action starts up. Freed of obstructive images, the pure attentiveness directed to the unpictured Teacher is like a living seed in fertile soil. The warmth of fervour and the rain of love makes the 'Teacher' within my own being come to life. Vision or enlightenment and understanding arise and I see the truth in the sense that I am the truth. The kingdom of heaven is within : look within, thou art Buddha : *tat tvam asi*, THAT thou art. This happens when the discursive has changed into pure meditation.

[NOTE : The word 'I' is an awkward word to use in these paragraphs. It stands for the isolative self-consciousness of the separate individual, as in the context of discursive meditation or of an observing subject seeing an observed object apart from himself. And it is also used in those contexts, such as pure meditation or communion, in which the isolativeness of self-consciousness is transcended. In this latter context, the phrase 'there is a seeing or understanding' would be less misleading than 'I see or understand'. But the word 'I' is used because it is simpler to use a single word instead of an impersonal phrase.]

* * *

The transformation of discursive into pure meditation involves a remarkable change in the mind. Earlier it was said that mind may be regarded as a receptive-responsive sensitivity characterizing the living

[9] See above, p. 80.

organism. And later on it was suggested that MIND be regarded as a transcendent, universal energy, dimensionless, immeasurable and uncharacterizable, of which the psyche is the particular, distinctive and characterizable manifestation in each person. In pure meditation Psyche and Eros are in timeless union. There is a functioning of mind which for lack of words in any language may be called transcendent perception-feeling: an immeasurable, indescribable, universal 'sensitivity'. The change over is like a transmutation of psyche into MIND and of our ordinary sensitivity as we know it within the sphere of organic functioning and discriminative consciousness, *viññāṇa*, into transcendent sensitivity in the state of Awareness-Being, *ātman*.

Discursive meditations can help the release into this state and facilitate the entry and abiding in ease in 'the beyond'. The key to this lies in universalizing our ordinary psycho-mental sensitivities which are particular and limited, bound as they are within the confines of ambivalence, distinctions and discriminative consciousness, so that they transcend all measure and intensify into the measureless. This does not mean that one functions exclusively in terms of universality. It is, in fact, impossible to do so; and if, emulating the strange behaviour of Empedocles[10] in a modern form and situation, a man failed to be sensibly mindful in ordinary consciousness whilst crossing the street, a speeding lorry might very successfully despatch him into the universal.

Modern science tells us that the world is made up of minute atoms composed of infinitesimal electrons, protons and the like. The mind tries to picture these, and fails. I can picture a millimetre, a half of that, a quarter, and before long I give up trying to visualize an individual atom. The atom, like the universe, is 'the beyond' as far as my sense functioning is concerned. Abstract thinking comes to the rescue. The mathematician's skills give me information which, if correctly interpreted and subsequently verified by rigorous scientific experiments, tells me facts which cannot be known by sense experience alone. Through science and mathematics, then, I can know some facts about electrons composing atoms – and they are true since I can have sense-experience of electric shocks or atomic explosions – without ever seeing or smelling an atom, still less an electron.

Such knowledge owes much to the magic of speech; of words and the letters of the alphabet; of logic and reason; of concepts and philosophy. It usually evokes *reactions* of feeling: wonder, intellectual pleasure,

[10] The story has it that this sage of Acragas believed himself to be a god. As a final proof of his divinity he leapt into the crater of Etna, 'and was roasted whole' as remarked by one poet.

awe. Through meditation, such knowledge can become feeling, awareness which is being, communion. The same can happen through art. Thus art, philosophy, science, and indeed all living, is not merely 'tinged with religion' but is at-oned with religion.

My sense-apprehension of the world strikes me as far more real than cold mathematical formulae or intellectual abstractions about it. The colour and shape and perfume of a rose! How vivid! But rates of vibration, organic vapours producing olfactory effects, electrical phenomena – how vague!

But in the deeps of sensitivity, the aesthetic and the intellectual, feeling and pure rationality, merge into a not-two. Let the mind dwell quietly upon the rose – colour, shape, perfume. When the awareness becomes intenser and reaches its peak, descriptive consciousness and the naming process or analytic perception in terms of colour, shape and perfume changes into the pure awareness of rose-ness, without any loss but with utmost perfection of aesthetic fulfilment. All communion *is* supreme happiness – the non-descript positive of nirvana. (The negative statement concerning nirvana is extinction of greed, malevolence, etc., or the cessation of all grasping.) The realization of the 'ness' is the meaning of becoming the rose – possible only in that awareness which has transcended all thought and speech.

I can also start on the other road (if I am mentally endowed and equipped for it) and let the mind dwell quietly on the rose – molecules, vibrations, electrical and chemical processes. The marvel and mystery of Energy in action – creative action in eternity manifesting in time-space-matter. And the functioning of the intellect reaches that magical stillness in which it gives over to transcendent perception at-oned with transcendent feeling, whereupon there is that communion in which rose-ness is realized.

The word universe, and the statement that all life is one, cease to be impotent verbiage when such meditations culminate in the realization of the unitariness of the universe. It may be said that it is not difficult to condition the mind into a fixed belief in such unity. If you care to discover the truth, then practise, investigate and find out for yourself. But first there has to be the foundation of purity, morally and intellectually, in order to be able to enter such states of realization at all, and as the safeguard against being self-deceived by meditative practices. 'By their fruits ye shall know them.'[11] For where there is the fact of communion, fear and lust and violence are no more. No force for dis-

[11] Matt., 7.16.

unity emanates from him who has realized. There is only Love, invariably expressed in forms appropriate to the situation and the person. For the Holy One, the unity of the Total Reality is the simple fact. It is so natural to him that he has no necessity to *strive* to be in right relationship.

There are some unusual, little known forms of discursive meditation conducive to right relationship and unity.

Let the body be at ease, elastic, the spine erect and the head well poised. Let the breath-rhythm be established. Then let the mind, alert and sensitive, be keenly aware of the state of calm of the organism in harmony with its immediate environment. Maintaining the state of bodily and psychical calm, let the mind be aware, very generally, that most people in the longitude in which one is at the moment (say early morning) are probably having their breakfast or setting out for the day's work. Some may be doing other things, and thinking and feeling other thoughts and feelings.

Let the mind move slowly eastwards towards the lands where it is mid-morning, mid-day, afternoon and so on right round the globe back to where one is. At each station in this twenty-four hour circuit round the earth, let the mind feel very sensitively the different usual activities, bodily and mental, performed by people in their particular regions at that particular time.

In brief, if in a few minutes here at this very spot I compass the twenty-four hour living-process of mankind, it is seen clearly by the intellect and felt sensitively by the heart that at this single moment, and at every moment, all the deeds and thoughts and feelings of the human race are taking place. At this very moment feeding, procreating, dying, enjoying, sorrowing, warring, murdering, thieving, learning, discovering, beautifying, constructing, destroying, working, shirking, hating, loving – indeed everything is happening, is being thought and felt, is being expressed or frustrated, NOW, by someone, somewhere on this single earth.

Thus in each single moment of Earth's life is comprised the entire twenty-four hour life of the whole human race. I may extend this meditation to include all creatures and plants and everything that Earth is, and name it the Earth-Meditation.

It is necessary to remain poised throughout such meditations and maintain cool calmness together with warm sensitivity. Without deep feeling, cold intellect hardens me. Without crystal clear seeing, heated emotion unbalances me. In either case I am rendered ineffective, or become a liability to society. But if I am mindful, and do not let imagination run riot, then my sensitivity tells me truly the state of the world, and I absorb it into my own soul. The world is ill, in pain and sorrow, full of fear and violence and confusion. It is the thrall of ignorance not knowing the meaning and movement of Life and of the art of living in harmony with it. It is the slave of its greeds and passions, a clever and cunning slave sweating hard to wound and to destroy himself, to remain chained to the level of the beast, to remain immature in mind and never to realize manhood. Only because here and there in this sprawling darkness there shine a few lights, Love lives, Wisdom works, and there is Peace and Beauty.

To absorb all this calls for all the resilience and stability of the disciplined soul. This absorbing is the 'drinking of the cup of the world's evil and sorrow to the dregs'. Its poison has to be transmuted into ambrosia and nectar. At first it agonizes the soul. The agony must never be repressed, or else it will explode in some other situation even more painfully. No attempt must be made to explain it away by vain arguments or by consolatory chatter. I must remain very mindful, keenly observant. In time, any tendency to indulge in sentimental pity for suffering, or to react violently against evil, or to go through any emotional orgy, disappears. Instead, there is understanding. Compassion wells out and the mind remains poised and at peace. The compassionate and peaceful state is the state in which I can be most helpful with the action demanded by the situation.

When I am in this state, I am in right relationship with all the world and there is the realization of unity.

Throughout life, I am in relationship with things and situations, persons and ideas. Consider things. Here is the house and garden of which I am called the owner-occupier. How do I regard it? As *my* house? It was built over a generation before I was born, it housed several families before I came into residence, and will still be standing (unless it is deliberately destroyed) after I am dead, providing comfort for human beings. It serves me faithfully. The speechless rooms and furniture never raise their heads against me. The house and its contents fulfil their purpose in relation to me. I have a duty to them, namely to keep them in good condition, 'well' and 'happy'. They have an existence in their own rights. So the house is not my house in the possessive sense. It is not for me to dominate over it; it is not an object of my greed and vanity. It is home for the family and for all friends who come here. And 'home' means love, mutual consideration and care, respect and order, happiness and peace, and the cheer and beauty of life renewing itself. I am simply the trustee for the home, and also for all objects or property. So also in relation to the garden. It is not 'my' garden; it is the garden, the place of delight, Eden.

The wife is not my possession. She is the lady, mistress of the home and dispenser of bread, source of loving care and of grace, prime nurturer and educator of all under her wing, the quiet inspirer of the divine spirit, sleeping within, to awaken and to grow and to blossom into manhood. So too with children and friends, and with all people in the world.

Meditation brings to life and sustains right relationship with all things, including bombs, and all people, including enemies. A man may hate me, harm me. But if I mindfully maintain the poise and understanding, the forbearance, patience and compassion of the meditative state, I am not an enemy to that man; I do not hurt him; I am in right relationship with him and I uphold the fact that he is my fellow man. In the ripeness of circumstance, the power of wise love may transform his enmity into friendship towards me, *and towards several others.* The brotherhood of man is made real.

Non-grasping puts me in right relationship with ideas. Neither am I the captive of ideas, nor do I constrain another's freedom of mind with my ideas. Only in freedom of mind, in complete open-mindedness, is there right relationship with ideas. Then I see that just as this body which bears my name is a finite and temporal changing pattern emerging out of universal matter, 'my' ideas are swiftly changing patterns of universal mind manifesting itself through me. I have no proprietary rights over them. All ideas are fluid expressions of mind in action. Fixation of ideas, a rigid authoritarian creed or ideology betokens the disease of the mind. Then evil spreads, man suffers, and the scythe of death ultimately destroys the wild weeds.

Meditation salves the mind, for by meditation, the live transforming process which heals and renews can go on unhindered. The unity of Life is unbroken. Where there is no sundering of unity, there is no sin.

The key to right relationship and unity lies essentially in non-grasping, non-possessiveness, and non-obtrusion of self on things, persons and ideas.

THE MERGING

Transcendence I may not touch. But I may freely touch and love the Mother – Earth – with every cell of my being without incest. And as she thrills in response and remains the unstained virgin, the world sways and the stars swing the while I am in rhythm with the Body of Life.

As I walk mindfully over mountain paths and touch the rock's immobility, or listen to the singing streams, or soar over the peaks with a bird in fearless flight and breathe clean air in the clear expanse, I learn to reverence the Body of Life.

Seeing by the light of the soul invisible plumes of fire flaming to the zenith from the tops of trees and mountain peaks, I know that all is knit together in simple holiness by mysterious power. The whole universe interflows within itself. All make the One and the One is the all: an exquisite web of life in constant communion. All the world pours into me and I into it: an inter-fluence which is zest of creation; health of Body which is concretest Spirit; a marriage of Heaven and Earth. I am now the sacrificer and the sacrificed – in the state of worship – not 'me' – and there is revelation of God unto God through MAN stripped of selfness.

So there is nothing I lack, nothing I ask for: nothing to hold back: nothing to give but simply to be the point where the Eternal Giver is not prevented. The self unobtruding, nothing shrinks away from me. Bliss of Love! All Earth whispers its secrets. I cannot tell you what they are, for I cannot 'know' what I hear. I simply listen. But come if you care – with goodwill – the Mother stands beside us all – she beholds, and survives, the transforming of all the sons she begets – and if you are taken into the bliss of Love and are told her secrets, you too will have heard the truth, and become Truth as you ascend.

Sustained in that bliss of Love, the Earth-Meditation becomes the meditation of the whole body of Life. Then time flees not into an unknown fear-beset future but dances here-now. The spectre of death vanishes, the breach between time and space is healed, and the hitherto sundered Body and Mind are once again the Total Reality. And this is a state of Holiness, empty of all ill, enwrapped in Love's bliss.

So it is true that the signature of Transcendence is writ right through the deep! Returning from the silent void, I move through the measureless plenitude and re-enter the conditioned state of separate forms of mind and body. And I name them as before: gods and the divine hosts; mountains and seas; birds and fish and trees; and you my fellow-man; and Thou O God my Father. But whereas formerly in the fallen state ignorance and fear wounded these names, now Love exalts and sanctifies them. And I take no Name in vain for all Names are holy.

How strange that I, a speck of Man-dust, am the eyes and ears and brain through which Transcendence sees and hears and knows the wonder and the beauty of its own signs! MAN is indeed Transcendence thinking: creating, nurturing and enjoying: carefree, unwearied.

There are occasions when this creative thinking of Transcendence is suddenly very near. Verily it is inside myself although – awesome wonder! – I cannot think this SELF. Whereas creation by mortals is associated with toil and tribulation, *this* conceiving and bringing forth is free of all ill. But there is nothing to show for it in this world, apart from insight. Grace and transcendent beauty are immeasurable on these occasions when the Earth-Meditation becomes limitless. The mental atmosphere is intensely peaceful. Nature is quiet. Ease permeates everything. Body and mind are in harmony, awake and sensitive in unusual measure. It feels as if all the stars are propitious, and to this person here who is nothing a mystery is being revealed. I become intensely aware, not imaginatively but in the quiescence of thought, of the interplay of universal energies. In time, this awareness formulates itself as the ceaseless activity of interpenetrating energies weaving a pattern of withinness which is the force of destiny inside me the living existent, and an external pattern which is the power of fate acting upon me.

This destiny is, as it were, a web of consciousness: my mode of awareness of existence; characteristic of me; unique to me; not rigid; changing, in the sense of growing, into the all-light. It is, as it were, a hidden light of the soul with which the zodiac or the cosmos endows me. I have to be as the watchman, the keeper, the one who tends this light which is not an entity. Those who fulfil this trust realize liberation.

The pattern which is fate includes all destinies other than mine, and the pattern of fate for any other person includes all destinies other than his. The web of Life is indeed too complex to be comprehended by any man. Only by living selflessly in mutual trust, in love, can mankind survive and each of us fulfil his unique destiny without harming himself, without hindering others.[12] Without the overriding power of love, associated with the wisdom of the heart and the skill of the hand, we will never be free of the ills that afflict us. Any and every measure in any and every sphere of life is doomed to failure whilst we remain unloving. But with love, we can live as cooperative humans, as social beings.

The power of fate is a continuous challenge. If I am intelligent, I observe the situation intently and dispassionately in order to discover what is required of me, and what lessons I have to learn. If I do learn, and act accordingly, my destiny unfolds itself. If I fail to see the factual present, my lack of understanding puts me in conflict with fate and my destiny is only partially fulfilled. Nevertheless, the part that is fulfilled could well be complete in itself, as evidenced by the legacy bequeathed

[12] See also above pp. 240 ff., 309 ff.

to mankind by the genius of artists and poets and men of vision. Destiny is perfectly fulfilled in those whose lives reveal the true significance of the word human. And, in those lives, destiny and fate are free co-partners. If I am wise, I bring about the co-partnership; unwise, fate thwarts destiny and my life is a disharmony.

One of the profound lessons I learn on those occasions when the Earth-Meditation becomes limitless is how Transcendence works through me in this interplay of fate and destiny.[13] All one's potentialities, artistic or scientific or whatever they may be, are held within one's pattern of destiny. Transcendence manifests its transcendence by allowing this pattern to unfold in some. In others, Transcendence demonstrates its transcendence through denying the expression of their potentialities. If I care for Transcendence, I will see truly which way this pattern is going for me in the world – unfolding, or being denied expression – and in either case I will serve meekly and obediently, praise happily, and witness what wonders Love can do.

When self is wholly given to SELF, I live SELF-responsibly. So fate is not provoked to fury. The light of the soul, well tended, illumines the life in the world. Destiny is fulfilled.

Sensitive attentiveness to nature awakens me to my intimate relationship with the whole creation. As I feel and merge into the unity of the universe I am freed of that evil isolative consciousness which tears off me as a separate self from the rest of creation as the not-self. Peace reigns. And Love. And the mysterious open secret of the unbroken harmony of the All-Whole sustains me through all changes of fortune.

Without this, any attempt to realize supreme communion is void of substantial fact. The head may soar into the Heavens. But Transcendence cannot thrill through the heart and suffuse my whole being if my feet were not rooted in Earth. The Glory has to fill Earth and not suffer perpetual confinement in Heaven.

Mindful, meditative, Light and Love spread through me into this Earth and through all Earth unto the whole creation, by the Grace of Transcendence. When separate selfness has vanished, when All-Mother Nature contains the whole of me, when I am in the pure and blissful state of my nothingness which holds the plenitude, the Glory of God fills the worlds. Then, as I walk through the streets I know the solidity of brick and stone and metal even as I know the hardness of my own bone, and feel the flow of the river as the blood through my veins and the breeze as my breath.

And I know that all things and creatures are made of light and air

[13] See also above, p. 253.

and water and fire and earth; the elements; in the language of today, atoms, and a growing family of infinitesimals making up each atom. All is Energy. Primordial parent. And you and I and the countless worlds and all they hold are the progeny of this unknown parent, this mysterious power. An incalculable variety cohering in an unimaginable unity. So I love and reverence all nature, the feminine conjoint of God. And salute all as flesh of my flesh and bone of my bone.

And this-all answers me. Star and sky and cloud and wind, bird and tree and sea and earth, day and night, birth and death – all, all, speak truth, silent wisdom, and pour out bounty to me the mindful and meditative, harmless in my nothingness. Woe betides me in every unmindful moment, for the cloud of self obscures Reality's light. The Presence is banished and I am in darkness.

Mindful again, meditative, and the Presence is here again. But the Presence never was not here. It is omnipresent, eternal, immutable. It never fails. I am the one who falters and fails to breathe the everlasting truth. But now I know that Transcendence is all. Brahman is all. But beware of the error of saying that Brahman-realization is merely Nature mysticism, and of the greater error of dismissing the fact that Transcendence is all by calling it pantheism, or even less wisely, dangerous pantheism. Yes, Brahman is all, and I also know that my words cover the Truth with a veil of illusion – sad fate of all words and thoughts. Howbeit, let us use the gait of speech to enter into pure meditation and glimpse the unconditioned communion.

* * *

But there are thorns in my flesh – my defilements; and on my brow – memories of mortality blurring the vision of the immortal; and in my tongue – so my speech flows not in mellifluous silence.

Blessing is on me that I know this. Happy now, tremulous but fearless, I walk through the portals in the mansion of Death, Lord of the hidden Light. As I walk I am cleansed of my defilements. And the stones of my mind are changed into the knowledge of God and my speech is like honey gathered in the hives of Love's truth. 'Lovely is the Truth in the beginning, lovely in the middle, lovely in the end', said the Buddha. As I pass through the portals the Lord of the hidden light bestows on me the kiss of Life and holds me in his arms, safe. Immortality. No more me. Transcendence Alone.

* * *

With the body kept still and a gentle breath rhythm steadily maintained, attentiveness flows with increasing intensity as I 'set up mindfulness in front'[14] of me. There follows the expunging of hindrances to pure meditation : cravings for pleasure and self-indulgence; feelings of envy, jealousy, anger and violence; malevolence, states of fear, anxiety, depression, excitement, elation and self-conceit; thoughts and schemes for gain and self-aggrandisement, for dominating persons or situations, societies or nations and for fulfilling ambitions and desires.

After a while attentiveness slackens through various causes; bodily tiredness or fidgetiness, or insufficient mental stamina for sustaining full attention; the impact of sense stimuli, or the uprising into consciousness of unworked out residua of past impressions, the *vāsanās*; doubt or mental flurry or sloth or worry (expressed in such questions as 'Am I making any progress? Am I making a fool of myself?'); lack of serious-mindedness; lack of good sense and of genuine concern for Truth or Transcendence, and for living the religious life. Each such cause is a subject for mindful observation and examination.

When attention slackens it is wise to observe that to which the mind has wandered. If too tired, rest; if the circumstance has turned unfavourable, do what is appropriate to the changed situation – if fire has broken out, jump up and extinguish it.

The purging of the psyche means that the whole psycho-physical organism is calmed and made fit for freeing the mind of its conditioning and entering the profounder modes of awareness in which dormant potentialities of the mind become active. In the calm state, the tendency to observe and to relate everything from or to an isolated self-centre is reduced to a minimum.

Impartial, I can examine my mental impurities; prejudices, preconceptions, assumptions and biases; *fixed* ideas, beliefs, convictions, principles and ideals. When I see clearly that they hold the mind in bondage, the impurities dissolve. Delusive idealism gives place to true perception of what is actually present. This first denudation of the mind is indispensable for the awakening of intelligence.

The psyche pure, intelligence awake, the mind poised and attentiveness unflickering, all sense-functioning is pacified. Not dis-functioning, but functioning free of the limitations imposed by the conditioned mind and by confinement to discriminative consciousness. When sense-functioning is pacified, the mind is unified, not fragmentary. Thereupon the multitude of 'I-s' which plague me by their clamour, roguery, folly

[14] At the centre between the brows, the *ājñā cakra*.

and many other ills in everyday life, become a crystal clear unit. The attentiveness of the unified mind is the meaning of *cit*, in which *cittavṛtti*, the fluctuations of *citta* (mind) have ceased, and the *citta* is like the steady light from a flame in a windless place.

Sense-functioning pacified and attentiveness freed of the interpretive activity of the conditioned brain, *the flow of discursive thought and speech is silenced* and there is 'knowing' by being. Attentiveness intensifies to such a degree that it absorbs consciousness of self as a subject and of the not-self as a separate object of observation into itself. It becomes, as it were, a single intelligence-mass, the *vijñāna-ghana* of the Subāla Upaniṣad.

This is the movement through the first great portal in the mansion of Death-Lord. It is the first release out of bondage to ordinary sense functioning, speech and worldliness, the first free soaring into the trackless open *whilst I am bodily awake*.

* * *

Why is the Silence praised?

Consider its significance. First, by becoming free of the fragmentary mental functioning characterizing discriminative consciousness in which so much misunderstanding or disharmony between self and not-self can take place, I move out of restricted communication into free communion. Next, the hidden potentialities of the mind are stirred into life and begin to function. And third, this is the first actual realizing (making real) and not mere intellectual conceiving or verbal expounding, however lucid, of immortality.

Words represent whatever is cognized through the senses, or by logical intellection, or by feeling which has become sufficiently defined so as to become a communicable pattern by naming it. What the word represents is specific and measurable. Words belong to the state of limitation and finitude. Whatever is limited and finite has beginning and ending. This means that I am conscious of myself and my environment in terms of birth and death, of succession, of duality and multiplicity. I live as an ambivalent being and am conscious of life in terms of gain and loss, pleasure and pain and all the duals which produce constant conflict interrupted by ephemeral spells of a patched-up peace – compromise! a word so appreciated by so many! – holding the seed of murderous war in due time.

Therefore, to be conscious only in terms of specific sense images, of words and thoughts, of the known and the finite, and of succession and time, means that I am aware of existence in the mode of mortality. To walk through the first great portal of Death whilst bodily awake means that through me, awareness of existence in the mode of mortality has transformed into the mode of immortality. The first grade of communion, the first experiencing of pure meditation, the first state of supra-consciousness in which there is no self-centre and no isolative self-consciousness, is realized in this silence.

In this state there is equanimity, vibrant and firm; rapture; and an unusually peaceful joy and ease suffusing the whole being, not experienced in any worldly sensational pleasure, physical or cultural. In this, as well as in other states, various psychical phenomena may be experienced. Visions, auditions, bestowals of grace or revelations from so-called supernatural beings, 'stopping' of breathing, levitation, walking over water, moving through mountains, 'stroking the sun and moon with one's hand' – these and many others may take place. When the sense functions and speech are still and silent, obstructions to the play of energy in the deeps of the mind are in abeyance. The activity of this energy leaves impressions on the psyche. On emerging out of the silence, these formless impressions are structured into different forms. The shape and nature of these forms is determined mainly by one's own particular conditioning. If the strength or vividness of the impressions is great enough, one may be convinced that he has been through an actual physical experience.

In connection with this consider carefully that the fairies or angels or gods of different nations are always seen dressed in the national costume of the ladies and gentlemen of that nation, and even have the same hair styles; that the 'spirits' or 'supernatural beings' always talk the same language as the devoted recipient of such favour; that the Buddhist always sees or hears or receives a message from the Buddha or Buddhist sources, a Christian from Jesus or Christian sources, and so on. All these visions or apparitions are but projections out of one's own conditioned mind. In certain instances they make such a strong impression on the brain that one cannot distinguish between a physical seeing or hearing from the psychical impression of seeing or hearing which is as vivid and real as a physical experience. He who declares he saw or heard an angel honestly believes what he says. If he is lying deliberately, *he* knows it, and reaps the consequence. But the wise investigator does not equate belief, however honest, with actual fact. He keeps an open mind, well aware that all thought-forms are only pictures of truth, and not the reality itself.

Phenomena occur . Observe them, understand them and extract their significance if they have any. Then drop all the thought-forms and verbal constructs, and walk on. Whoever treasures them is liable to delusion; and also to obsession by vain conceits which, often enough, bring much unnecessary suffering. The wise religieux will watch his impressions and his reactions to them and not grasp them. Thus he will grow in self-knowledge and in freedom of mind.

In order to experience subtle and unusual psychical states, or to silence the constant, unbidden flow of discursive thought and speech, the unwise resort to the ways of Circe the enchantress, instead of treading the right road of purification, mindfulness and arduous practice. They take to drugs instead of religious discipline, sometimes in the name of scientific experimenting; they use compulsive methods, loathsome ascetic practices and indulge in short cuts to heaven or enlightenment, all of which in fact lead elsewhere, like the Gadarene swine driven by the demons within them into the sea. Keep clear of it all, keep clean, keep cool, and realize the comfort of the spirit. Never take leave of good sense.

All the great religieux and the true mystics have warned against indulging in phenomena and being entranced by them. And the Buddha, furthermore, expressly forbade his disciples to display psychic powers.

Maintaining equanimity and attentiveness after the pacification of speech and sense functioning, body and thought are tranquillized when the mind is rapturous. A hitherto hidden feeling sensitivity becomes active. Joy, clarity of mind, a growing aspiration towards Transcendence and an upsurging of psycho-spiritual energy are all present. Remaining unattached, without aversion or trepidation or self-conceit or attempting to grasp, the mind is free.

Relinquishing this joy, and with a corresponding release from sorrow,[15] one goes through another great portal in the mansion of the Death-Lord, and there is an abiding in perfect purity of equanimity and mindfulness. In this state one can 'look back into the past'. This is a review of preceding and succeeding body-mind states, as far as the ability of the reviewer enables him to do so. The reviewer need not be confined to a unidirectional time journey into the past. When the psyche is pure, the organism still, and the worldly speech and thought turmoil silent, awareness in terms of the unidirectionality of past, present and future time gives place to simultaneity. All time, multidimensional, is present here-now. In fact space and time become a space-time unity. My usual worldly mode of awareness, passing through this portal of

[15] The sorrow of not being in communion. See above, p. 151.

death, has undergone a remarkable transformation, and I can now be conscious of time like a whole chord of music instead of a succession of single notes. And also, just as I can play those single notes backwards or forwards, I can look backwards into the past from the now, or forwards from the past into the present.

This is not to be understood as a looking back into 'my' past lives in the popular reincarnational sense. It is a reviewing of the changing psychological states in this single lifetime, by means of an association technique unidirectionally in time, or by a comprehensive glance at all time. If the latter, its communication in speech is of necessity reduced to unidirectional terms. The awareness of the whole by a single glance finds expression in a phrase like 'As it was in the beginning, is now, and ever shall be'. The difficulty with such a phrase is that the words beginning, now and shall be, belong to the limited context of unidirectional time.

There is still another, and in some ways a more serious, difficulty. Awareness of space-time in its wholeness is not a functioning of discriminative consciousness which is specific to me. It is a functioning in and through the limited me of awakened and activated faculty of MIND, the universal and immeasurable. It transcends all 'I-am-I' consciousness. When this single glance of Totality takes place, the entire interaction of mentality-materiality (*nāma-rūpa*) is laid bare in the eternal here-now. Returning to ordinary discriminative consciousness using sense impressions, speech, three dimensional space and unidirectional time, the review backwards, associated with each conditioned state (*jāti*) of the 'I-am-I' consciousness, cannot go further backwards than the moment when the 'I-am-I' consciousness emerges. At the same time there is an overall awareness of the universal mentality-materiality process eternally present, in which unidirectional past time before 'my' birth is subsumed. If the two modes of awareness, the unidirectional and the whole, become confused in the mind of the reviewer, he may unwittingly present the review in terms of 'my past lives' in the reincarnational sense. This is clearly erroneous since the words I, me, mine or my, and the 'I-am-I' consciousness, have meaning and validity only within the limited context of the liftetime of the psycho-physical organism. If an eternal, immortal entity-I or self which persists through a series of bodily incarnations is postulated, this is an even greater error, for the simple reason that any discrete entity is limited, measurable and finite; it is of time and not the timeless, and therefore comes into specific being which is finite, and has an ending into non-being which has no name and form. Any entity is deathful and cannot be eternal or immortal.

This review backwards must not be equated with the association technique review by a man who, before falling asleep at the end of the day's work, examines what he has done and thought and how he has behaved during the day, or with the technique of the psychologist with his patient or with respect to himself. *This* review is carried out by one whose psyche is not in any ill state and whose mind is free of conditioning. It is carried out by using a power of perception which transcends perception through sense and formulation by speech. *It takes place during the silence of speech and thought, and the pacification of sense activity*. Because this is so, the meditator understands clearly how the transformation of the psychic state takes place, what the actual transformation is, and what is the nature and state of the mind of any person to whom he directs his attention. The Buddha repeatedly testifies – and so too does Jesus – that he knew by his own mind what was in the mind of the other person, that is, knew *directly* by his own pure mind and not by interpreting by the defiled or conditioned mind a gesture or action by the other person. Any shrewdly percipient man of the world can do the latter. Only the purified soul can do the former.

Thus it is that he sees how no one can escape his karma,[16] for the psyche is the receptacle of all the forces of thought, feeling, speech and action generated by him throughout his life. When this is clearly seen, he understands why the utter purification of heart and mind is indispensable for the fruition of man. Furthermore, he sees once and for all that morality in the true sense is rooted in a transcendent imperative deeply ingrained in his religiousness, and that its sanction is not flimsily related to compliance with, or defiance of, superficial social custom. True morality is intensely personal, personal in the meaning of one in whom evil-mindedness is burnt out.[17] It is the law of righteousness or holiness, a gift of grace from within, a meaning of the Zarathuśtrian Ashā, of the tablets written by the Lord himself which Moses brought down from the holy mount. Listen, carefree, to this merciful law of salvation and sing the Song of Life : and also obey, carefully, the law of the land, the king's writ, fearing judgement and the power of his wrath, and refrain from wrong doing.

This review unravels the tangled skein of memories and *vāsanās*. It is not a mere ploughing through a historical record. Each memory, each *vāsanā*, is seen with cool intellect and felt warmly with such intensity that it is fully worked out. Now there can be stainless purity of the psyche and order (*ṛta*) in the mind; self-knowledge; clear perception,

[16] See also above, p. 230 ff.

[17] See also above, p. 82 f.

insight and vision. For when I pass through this portal of death, I die to all worldliness. The beyond immerges into me. It moves and acts freely through me and there is the state of awareness of the Totality here-now free of intrusiveness by any isolative self-consciousness.

The psyche is now washed clean. The baptism by water. That by fire involves passing through another portal; and the body itself is changed. Transfiguration.[18]

SUPRA-CONSCIOUSNESS : PURE MEDITATION

The transformations of the mode of awareness must not be thought of as ascending or descending the rungs of a ladder. All physical similes are inadequate. It is perhaps less misleading to see these changes of consciousness as if they were varying intensities of light, the supreme communion being the intensity which is utterly transparent, not blinding but fully enlightening.

Various religious texts have, however, presented them as numbered stages. For example, Buddhist texts present them as four *jhānas* and four *samāpattis* culminating in the ninth stage named the Cessation. In the Hindu texts, the Upaniṣads speak of four *avasthās*; the Patañjali yoga presents a two-fold or four-fold or eight-fold classification according to the manner in which one views them. Christian mystical texts present a series of four: the prayer of Meditation, of Quiet, of Union and of Ecstasy. The essence alone is important: the peak is the one peak, however many or few the resting points may be on the ascent.

In my fallen or ignorant or unredeemed state I am not in communion. I am aware of existence in the mode of mortality, that is, of uprising-proceeding-ending in constant succession. This endless, unbidden and uncontrollable stream of births and deaths in my own consciousness during my single lifetime is the real meaning of rebirth for me the individual, for with every uprising (be it of a thought or thing or event or whatever it may be) I associate myself *in consciousness* with it. 'I' am born in it. When it is over 'I' am dead, and am born again with the very next feeling or event that has uprisen in consciousness. This is the meaning of *saṃsāra* the 'stream of births and deaths'. The Maitri Upaniṣad[19] affirms, '*saṃsāra* is just one's own *citta* (stream of consciousness) . . . By making mind all motionless, from sloth and distraction freed, when unto mindlessness (*amanībhāva*, the silent state which prevails when

[18] D., 2.133,134. Exod., 34.29,30,35. Matt., 17.1,2.
[19] Loc. cit. 6.34 (3 & 7)

fluctuating discursive thought is stilled) one comes, then that is the supreme state'. And the Śāṇḍilya Upaniṣad[20] declares, 'When the fluctuations of the mind cease, this cycle of births and deaths (*saṃsāra*) comes to an end'.

The mind is impure, dominated by desire; enslaved, bound to objects. I am in anguish within the sphere of mortality even when the forms of mortality are what my worldly understanding exalts as great or noble, as worthy or beautiful. For does not even the finest art or the sublimest philosophy, the most wonderful science or the profoundest theology, although holding within itself that creative Source which is eternal and immortal nevertheless remain a product of sense and discursive thought, doomed to the unidirectional process of beginning and ending, of birth and death in my own consciousness?

To cast off the fetters of mortality! In the communion with nature, in realizing that mankind's twenty-four hour daily life is a single moment of Earth's life, and especially in those silences when the tumult of the senses and thought calms down, there is a changed awareness of existence. The deeper the calm, the more intense is the awareness and the attunement with the rhythm of Life.

But even in those states when it feels as if I am rapt beyond the senses and pierce the heavens or dive through the deep of profundity, there is confinement to mortality as long as a Thou-and-I duality prevails; and then there is a falling away from the precarious poise of close proximity to the unseverable communion, back into the state of unlove and the cacophany of a worldly stream of consciousness.

Adam fell. So too did Yima, according to the Pishdadian legend, the earliest legendary history of Iran. But in the Ṛg-vedic tradition about Yama, there is no fall. Yama, it is taught, chooses death and abandons his body,[21] passes to 'the lofty heights above us and searches out and shows the path to many',[22] and exercises lordship over the highest of the three heavens.[23] He is the king of the dead.[24] He becomes the Master of death; he is not to be confused with *mṛtyu* the death-dealer.

Yama chooses death – that is he frees himself from all bondage to the sense life and worldly values. He grows to understand that the cycle of births and deaths is the stream of *saṃsāra* in his own moment to moment

[20] Loc. cit. 1.42.
[21] RV., 10.13.4.
[22] Ibid. 10.14.1.
[23] Ibid. 1.35.6.
[24] Ibid. 9.113.8.

consciousness, the stream which flows unbidden. He learns to observe this stream without reacting helplessly and unavoidably to it. The sense functions are pacified. Thus he remains poised and silent within himself, and is able to enter upon and abide in the profounder states of consciousness without falling asleep. There are energies present in the mind in these deep states: humility, feeling, perception, aspiration, a surge of love towards Transcendence, vigour, mindfulness and so on, but their content is far richer than the meanings of these words as understood by us in our confined ambivalent state. The mind is never a dead blank, an emptiness in the sense of an absolute vacuity.

Intensely attentive and contained (perfectly continent), Yama dies to the worldly mode of awareness. This is 'abandoning the body'. No longer isolatively self-conscious and caught in the conflict of duality, with senses and speech pacified and silent, he passes into the inner world. This inner world is not the world of exalted feelings, thought, visions and so on, all of which belong to the sphere of mortality, for in all of them one is aware in the mode of uprising-proceeding-dying. One is within time. But when bodily awake, speech, psychical reaction, imagination and all that comes within the confines of discriminative consciousness is quite still but vibrantly poised, there is no time-process of uprising-proceeding-dying (birth-death, *saṃsāra*). There is timeless Awareness-Being, the supra-consciousness.

This is Yama's mastery of death, his lordship of the highest of the three heavens.[25] This is the full *asaṃprajñāta samādhi* of the Hindu, the realization of the end of all ill or the 'touching Nirvana with the body' of the Buddhist. It is the actual condition of Revelation. This supreme communion wherein all birth-death is overleaped is the full experiencing and meaning of immortality. Time and space, the precondition for bodily being, pain-pleasure and stimulus-response, the touchstone of our psycho-physical life, and good and evil as we know them here – and all these are held within the mortal compass of discriminative consciousness – are all transcended, and you eat the fruit of the Tree of Life which stands in the self-same garden in which stands the Tree of the knowledge of good and evil. And that garden of Eden is your own psycho-physical being.

When supra-consciousness is realized through you, you have made real the Silence, for all the noise of the mental chatter which is the expression of your mortal awareness of an entity universe is stilled. Now you are the Awakened One, the Enlightened One, the Anointed One.

[25] cf. St. Paul's being caught up to the third heaven. See above p. 19.

Your mortal awareness of a space-time world is transformed into the immortal supra-consciousness of timeless reality. Well may you triumphantly cry, 'O Death, where is thy sting? O Grave, where is thy victory?' This entry into supra-consciousness is the meaning of 'And Enoch walked with God; and Enoch was not, for God took him' before the death of the person called Enoch; the meaning of Elijah being transported to heaven in a chariot of fire; the meaning of 'Be still, and know that I am God'. It is the meaning of both the Resurrection and the Ascension of Jesus; the meaning of his words 'And now I am no more in the world . . . and I come to thee', and of his great affirmation 'I and the father are one', which the Hindus before him expressed as 'Pratyagātman and Paramātman are one'.

This supra-consciousness is the meaning of that sentence in the Ṛgveda, 'We have drunk Soma and become immortal', and of those phrases in the Upaniṣads, 'realizing the Atman', 'knowing Brahman', 'becoming Brahman'. It is the meaning of the words in the Aitareya Upaniṣad of the eighth century B.C. that 'Vāmadeva having ascended aloft became immortal' – the Ascension is indeed a very ancient symbolical doctrine. This supra-consciousness was known to the Egyptian Initiates. It was the supreme Mystery which was kept secret in the Mystery cults of ancient civilizations. It was experienced four times by Plotinus and once by Porphyry. This supra-consciousness is the very heart of the enlightenment of the Buddha; it is the meaning of Nirvana here-now; it is the Kingdom of Heaven within you. It is the meaning of Eternal Life, of immortality, of God-realization or of union with God. It is the supreme religious experience.

This immortal supra-consciousness of timeless reality was realized here-now by the Great Teachers in India such as Prajāpati Parameṣṭhin, Kaśyapa, Bṛhaddiva, Satyakāma Jābāla, Naciketas, Ajātaśatru, Yama, Śāṇḍilya, Vāmadeva and Yājñavalkya – to mention only a few of the less well-known names – by Gotama the Buddha and several of his disciples, by Śrī Kṛṣṇa and several others. It was realized in other lands by Zarathuśtra, Lao Tze, Enoch, Elijah, Jesus, Plotinus and others. These men were the Holy Ones, rightly termed the Sons of God. They were supreme yogi-mystics. In them, love and wisdom, action and restraint had come to full flower.

In that supra-consciousness all that our sublimest thought and profoundest intuitions have grasped previously are as nought. There is no God there – the God of our conceptions. There is no time there, no space. You by virtue of having become the absolute good are united with the ceaseless creativeness of Transcendence with the as-it-is-in-itself-ness of existence. You, the within-the-self Infinite, are one with the Infinite which is the Universal Transcendent.

Whoso realizes such supra-consciousness is the embodied Revelation, the fount and source of religion. The immergence into supra-consciousness, which is the experience of the Silence, the Void, the Plenum, the Infinite, the Absolute, is the source-experience from which have emerged the deep teachings embodied in words like Brahman and Atman, Godhead and God, Eternity and Immortality, Nirvana and the Kingdom of Heaven, soul and spirit, and all other similar words which are current specie on the counters of theology and philosophy.

Once you realize supra-consciousness, you enjoy a permament awareness of the unity of all existence. You are always aware that you are not exclusively yourself but that you are in all things and all beings and they in you, and that you and the Eternal are in indissoluble union – 'Believe me that I am in the father and the father in me' as Jesus said; '*aham brahma'smi* – I am Brahman' as said in India. You are constantly awake to the fact that you are always in the presence of God. Then indeed you can truly live the unitive life and be a supreme influence for good, for that Good which is beyond the good and evil of ordinary life. Like all the Great Teachers, you are the Awakener of those who are ready to be awakened.

* * *

The practice of meditation and the knowledge and teaching regarding the deep states of consciousness culminating in the supreme communion antedates all the written records. The hymns of the Vedas, like the Qabalah, embody a great deal of this teaching, in code, with hints here and there which give some keys to this code. The metaphysics and the religious philosophy unavoidably involved in the attempt to preserve the knowledge of the discipline and the actual realizing of supreme communion – man's destiny, and one deep purpose of his existence – and to communicate this to the earnest, worthy seeker, is expressed in more straightforward intellectual terms in the Āraṇyakas, the religious treatises produced by forest dwelling anchorites which are to be studied *in solitude*, by a meditational rather than an intellectual process. The meditational process releases insight and nurtures wisdom; the mind is freed from conditioning and grows to maturity. The exclusively intellectual acquires knowledge; the mind is burdened rather than liberated and continues to suffer ill.

In the Upaniṣads – as also in other religious texts of all the religions – key teachings are given out. The central feature here is that they are fundamentally psychological. It must be emphasized, and fully appreciated, that the world's spiritual teachers were not immature psychologists – men who themselves were ill in psyche, deficient in perfect insight, *buddhi*. They had outgrown all imperfections; they were pure in heart and mind; and they were masters of the psychology of the mature and perfected mind. Such psychological wisdom cannot be acquired by mere intellectual study and experiment. It is realized in one's own person by purification, by accomplished communion and by finished action – the karma which is creative action in eternity.

And the heart of this creative action in eternity, for you and for me, is the pure meditation in which I die completely in each successive stage of meditation to all ill, unselfconsciously; immerge into deeper and deeper enstases of communion (*samādhi*), unselfconsciously and by Grace of Transcendence; and emerging out of supreme communion return to everyday discriminative consciousness, unselfconsciously and with Grace.

Then only is one the true psychologist even as a Homer or a Phidias, a Shakespeare or a Beethoven is the poet or sculptor or musician through whose genius Transcendence shines.

The Upaniṣadic Teachers chose as their psychological form the four states (*avasthās*) of waking, dreaming, dreamless slumber, and, *turīya*, the 'fourth', or simply, the transcendent. Dreaming and dreamless slumber must not be understood in their ordinary meaning which holds good when one is asleep bodily, but in terms of their psychological counterparts when one is clearly conscious in meditation.

In the waking state, *jāgrat*, common to all men, the religieux tries to be fully attentive and mindful (and *this* is his true wakefulness) of all his sense impressions and psychical functioning and his actions, whereas the worldling, concerned with the gratification of his desires and the pursuit of his ambitions, is unmindful.

Ordinary sleep comprises two states, the dreaming and the dreamless. Yājñavalkya points out to King Janaka[26] that the dream state is the intermediate state between the physically awake state and the state of being in the 'beyond' (in dreamless sleep). When bodily awake, a person experiences the limitations imposed by physical existence. His consciousness is outwardly cognitive as he sees all that is external to himself. But

[26] Bṛh. Up., 4.3.9 ff.

> 'When he goes to sleep he takes along the material of this all-embracing world, himself tears it apart, himself builds it up, and dreams by his own brightness, by his own light. Then this person becomes self-illuminated. There are no chariots (and other physical objects) there, no pleasures (etc.) there. But he projects from himself (out of his memory of sense experience) chariots (etc.) pleasures (etc.): he is the maker (of these images of objects and pleasures etc.)'

The Māṇḍūkya Upaniṣad starts with the affirmation that AUM (the supreme symbolic syllable) is all this. AUM is the past, present and future, and also whatever else there is beyond the threefold time. It then affirms that all this (the One Total Reality) is Brahman; and this Atman is Brahman. (In this context, translate Atman, in addition to its full meaning of being identical with Brahman, as also meaning the self, that is, you or I the microcosm reflecting the macrocosm. Atman, the transcendent Awareness, here suffers limitation and functions through each man as consciousness. In our present context, associate the word self or Atman with consciousness.)

This self has four 'quarters'. The first is called *vaiśvānara* because through each man in the ordinary waking state, Brahman-Atman experiences all-this as discrete objects, events, pleasures, pains and so on. Atman the universal suffers isolative self-consciousness through the ambivalence of the ill psyche or the fragmented mind of each self.

Yājñavalkya discloses[27] how a man projects the objects, pleasures, etc. of waking experience out of himself in the dream state. Here we see the Atman exercising its creative power in the limited form of imagination. A man has dreams in sleep, and fantasies or day-dreams when awake. If in the dream state in sleep he becomes conscious of the fact that he is dreaming, curious consequences may follow. He may fling aside the moral censorship and restraints of his waking state. If a woman is present in the dream he may immediately copulate with her (or try to do so), experience a bodily emission, and on waking up feel pleased or amused, or angry or depressed that it was not the real thing, or outrightly disgusted. If a hated one, or a feared creature (a tiger, say) is present, he will try to kill him in the dream to satisfy his passion for revenge or for ballooning his ego.

Thus a worldling is unmindful and unvirtuous in his dream state, whether in sleep or in waking fantasy. Hence Atman the universal is

[27] Bṛh. Up., 4.3.9 ff.

caged and darkened by imperfect man. In theistic terms, God suffers agony because of man's sin.

Now the Buddha taught in his discourse on Mindfulness of Body that he who is mindful in all his bodily actions, including sleeping,[28] is one who is acting in a clearly conscious way. In his conversation with Saccaka, a Jain, he declares categorically[29] that he the Tathāgata, falls asleep mindful and clearly conscious. And furthermore, he experiences in his sleep neither bewilderment nor non-bewilderment because the cankers (the *āsavas* or overflows of consciousness) connected with all defilements have been rooted out.

The purified man, of harmonized and peaceful mind, is no more the victim of dreams in his sleep, or of fantasies in his waking state. There is mental activity when he is sleeping, which is mindful and meditative. It is like a process of digestion, psychically, intellectually, of the psycho-mental activity which took place during the waking state. The answer to a question, the resolution of a problem or a penetrating insight into some abstruse investigation, comes up clearly in the mind on waking up. This digestion, in the symbolic terms of the yogic *cakras*, takes place at *maṇipūra*, the centre at the navel. With the undisciplined worldling it is all too often an indigestion rather than a digestion. In the case of the well-disciplined, what starts in *maṇipūra* is completed at *viśuddhi*, the throat centre, associated with prophetic speech.[30]

This digestion process, followed at times, though not always, by the flash of insight or by an inspiration, takes place in discursive meditation, properly conducted, and also through intense mindfulness. Since attention is turned inwards and becomes absorbed by the object of attention in such meditation, one is asleep, as it were, to the world around. When I do this, I am clearly conscious and mindfully asleep.

The Upaniṣads designated this meditative state as the *svapna* state, psychologically an advanced or superior counterpart to the *svapna* (dream) state when the body is asleep. For here in meditation I go through a similar kind of activity – namely, utilizing the material provided by sense experience, and the thought and feeling involved with such experience – as in ordinary dreaming, with this difference: in ordinary dreaming the controls are off; dreams are strange and confusing, and often mislead one into harmful action through the misinterpretation of their meaning; they are significant only in those far fewer

[28] M., 3.90.
[29] M., 1.249,250.
[30] See above p. 228 ff.

instances where there is right interpretation and some understanding of that which the unconscious is trying to convey to the conscious mind. In meditation, no controls are off. The attention follows where perception leads and extracts the essence. Moreover, whereas the thread is broken unpredictably in a dream and I am helpless to stop it from breaking or to make the dream come to 'the end of the story', I can, after a little practice, emerge out of meditation as and when I choose. Dreams are indicative of my confused ill-state. Meditation spells clarity and releases order.

The Nāradaparivrājaka Upaniṣad says[31] that one who meditates on the Atman in the *svapna* state as in the waking state is among the foremost of *brahmavādins*, the speakers on Brahman, or those who are fit to utter the Brahma-word.

It is necessary to exercise the utmost integrity and discrimination in the *svapna* state in meditation. Danger arises because of egoism, vanity, immaturity, lust for power and other defilements in relation to the inspirations or insights which emerge. Only a few of these are genuine. The rest are just ideas born of a fertile imagination, out of which detailed information is fabricated about spirit visions, invisible travels in immaterial worlds, confidential communications from great personages in heaven (or hell?) regarding the future of the world and the destiny of man and so forth, with all the solemn authority of self-arrogated prophets. The blind do lead the blind – the blind cannot see whether the self-appointed leader sees where he is taking them.

The meditative state energizes the whole psyche. In the quiet, a world of ideas spun out by imagination, an 'astral world', appears so lovely and attractive. But it is in fact a world of illusion. Underneath every flower there is a serpent coiled. The wise religieux observes all these alluring ideas and thought-forms very mindfully and refrains from grasping any of them. He will also meet with the horrible and terrifying, and with all kinds of seductive temptations. He must be free of aversion and fear, then, and maintain poise and purity.

If he stays intensely observant and free of all grasping, the denudation of the mind can proceed healthily, emptying it of everything that obstructs enlightenment. This denudation is one of the crucially important objectives of meditation. For when all my psycho-mental lumber is cleared out, the mind is illumined by the lamp of wisdom, which is other than all my mental constructs. The content of my psyche is like a

[31] Loc. cit. 5.5.

fire billowing out clouds of smoke. Wisdom is like the transparent clarity of invisible space on a cloudless day.

This is the third *avasthā* of the Upaniṣads, symbolized in the state of dreamless sleep, *suṣupti*, and named *prājña*. The dream state is associated with the unworked out impressions of the waking state. If attentiveness is complete in any experience in the waking state, that experience is fully worked out. There is no unworked out residuum which keeps disturbing the mind and is a contributory cause of dreams. One of the purificatory activities in meditation is precisely the refloating of these residua (*vāsanās*) out of the well of the unconscious in order to work them out fully. This is the exhausting or burning up of unworked out karma by the yogi. For the theistic mystic, the full recollecting, confessing and actual repenting (turning away for ever) from his sins enables God's loving grace to forgive him and restore him to his true state of holiness, of Man the Living Image of God.

Whether the experience and its impression is fully worked out or not, nature's beneficence grants us the healing state of dreamles slumber, the state of complete restfulness for the entire psycho-physical organism. Yājñavalkya tells King Janaka:[32]

> 'As a falcon, or an eagle, having flown around here in space, becomes weary, folds its wings, and is borne down to its nest, just so this person (*puruṣa*) hastens to that state where, asleep, he desires and sees no dreams.'
>
> 'This, verily, is that form of his which is beyond desires, free from evil, without fear. As a man, when in the embrace of a beloved wife, knows nothing within or without, so this person, when in the embrace of the intelligent Atman (*prājñenātman*, the Atman of unerring insight or perfect knowledge), knows nothing without or within.[33] That, verily, is his form in which his desire (*kāma* as the creative love-aspiration to the Supreme) is fulfilled, in which the Atman is his desire, in which he is without desire (*kāma* as worldly desires) and past sorrow.
>
> 'There. . . . he is not followed by good, he is not followed by evil, for then he has crossed beyond all sorrow of the heart.'

In this state which is nature's gift to all beings, objective consciousness which functions in the waking and dream states is absent. But here

[32] Bṛh. Up., 4.3.19, 21, 22.

[33] The distinction and separation between the without and the within is eliminated for there is no isolative, discriminative consciousness.

we are immersed in the unconsciousness of sleep. We return to the waking state recharged vitally, refreshed mentally. But we are not transformed into the state of the perfected Holy One. So the Atman is again caged in the empirical objective consciousness of the waking and dreaming states during the next day.

The religious discipline of purification and complete attentiveness enables one to pass through the portal of death and realize this third *avasthā* in pure meditation whilst bodily awake. Yājñavalkya declares this is the Brahman-world. In arriving here, the religieux passes through in ascending order, or is said to obtain, many worlds – and the word 'worlds' means states of consciousness in this and in all similar contexts in religious literature. Of him who realizes *suṣupti* in meditation, Yājñavalkya says:[34]

> 'The seer without duality becomes One, an ocean. This is the Brahma-world, Your Majesty.
>
> 'This is a man's highest path. This is his highest accomplishment. This is his highest world. This is his highest bliss. On a fragment of just this bliss other creatures live.
>
> 'If one is fortunate among men and wealthy, lord over others, best provided with all human felicities – that is the highest bliss of men.
>
> 'A hundredfold the bliss of men is the bliss of the fathers' world (i.e. state of consciousness) . . .'

Yājñavalkya proceeds, multiplying the bliss each time by a hundred, from world to world, culminating in the Brahman-world where one bliss is a million million times the highest bliss of men. The bliss of the Brahman-world is also the bliss of him who is versed in the Veda, who is without sin and who is free from desire.

Man, realizing bliss in states of communion in which all isolative consciousness is transcended, has ascribed bliss to the Supreme. Brahman is Being-Awareness-Bliss, *sad-chid-ānanda*: the Peace of God which passeth all understanding: Śiva the ever-blissful. All ascriptions to God are man's own supreme realizations in pure meditation.

The Māṇḍūkya Upaniṣad says[35] of this third quarter, *prājña*, that it is:

> 'The deep-sleep state, unified, just a cognition-mass, consisting of bliss, enjoying bliss, the mouth of consciousness (*ceto-mukha*).
>
> 'This is the Lord of all, the knower of all, the inner controller. This is the source of all, for this is the origin and end of all things.'

[34] Bṛh. Up., 4.3.32, 33.
[35] Loc. cit. 5,6.

This *prājña* state, realized when bodily awake, is a state of neither consciousness (discriminative) nor unconsciousness. Both are held in latency in this Awareness which is trans-consciousness or supra-consciousness. Move back to *taijasa* in the dream state and discriminative consciousness starts up again. So *prājña* is called *ceto-mukha*, the mouth of consciousness (discriminative). Mouth is a very appropriate word, for with the functioning of discriminative consciousness the speech faculty is in action again and I have stepped back into the world of differentiation. In the *prājña* awareness of undifferentiation, the unsundered holy (the unfallen, sinless Adam Qadmon), I am the lord of all (as protector, nurturer, Viṣṇu, the Son, *Tiphereth*) and the all-knowing one by virtue of holding in latency, in the mind, all that I will be conscious of discriminatively, on returning to sense-functioning and speech-thought activity. Hence this *prājña* state is called *prajñāna-ghana*, a cognition-mass or intelligence-mass, the source of all that I can discriminatively cognize when awake or dreaming, and the beginning and end of all things and beings, not in themselves but in terms of my perceptions and mental constructs of them as they uprise and pass out of the purview of my everyday life.

TRANSCENDENCE: THE BEYOND

The term Transcendence has been used in this book in the sense of Brahman, or the One Total Reality, the All. Transcendence embodied in me is not spoilt (not made *duḥ-kha, dukkha*, ill or evil), is not hurt or modified (that is, it is not subjected to any constriction) by the unfolding or infolding manifestation process which *I* experience and go through in terms of the waking, dreaming and dreamless sleeping (the *viśva, taijasa* and *prājña*) states, which are modifications of my *viññāṇa*, discriminative consciousness.

Transcendence meets itself when the fourth quarter, *turīya*, prevails unhindered in and through me the living existent.

That is the meaning – the live 'substantial' meaning – of Atman.

Turīya is Absolute. Dimensionless, indefinable, unknowable, unimaginable, inconceivable. Call this Absolute the Void. *Prājña* (in dreamless slumber, when bodily awake and in pure meditation), with *taijasa* (the dream-state) and *viśva* (in the waking state common to all), is the plenitude. In *prājña* this plenitude is held, as it were, in transparent, colourless solution. In *taijasa* and *viśva* it is precipitated into manifestation cognizable by discriminative consciousness through the functioning of senses, speech and the psycho-mental pattern-making activity of the mind.

Beyond the void-plenitude non-duality, no personal mind can conceive, no speech can express the *turīya*, the Absolute, in positive terms. Negative terms are used, only to stimulate sleeping Transcendence, the Immanent God, to set you or me alight with the light that never was seen on land or sea.

Speech and mind (*manas*) reach their quiescence and suspension in *prājña*. With their dissolution, their utter dissolution, you pass through the final portal in the mansion of Death. And then Death becomes one with the Lord, and *turīya* supervenes. Transcendence Alone is.

Death becomes one with the Lord! For now there is nothing more to which I could die in order that a transformation into something profounder could take place. 'My' mind is no more. Instead, MIND in its transcendence is present here-now. 'The Lord is in his holy temple'. I and the Father, *pratyagātman* and *paramātman*, are one.

Raikva the sage asked:[36] 'O Lord, how and by what means does this intelligence-mass, after moving upwards burn away its seat?' And the Lord answered: 'This intelligence mass burns up[37] . . . the four states (waking, dreaming, etc.), . . . virtuous and vicious conduct . . . the unmanifested, the imperishable. It burns Death. Death becomes one with the radiant Supreme. In the Supreme is neither existence nor non-existence, nor being/non-being. This is the exposition of Nirvana, this is the exposition of the Veda, yea this is the exposition of the Veda'.

And the means for this transcendent realization is the way of Silence, of which the Varāha Upaniṣad says:[38] 'Practise silence . . . practise silence . . . practise silence'. At each reiteration, attentiveness glows with these realizations: the I AM, *aham*, is the supreme Brahman, pure, non-dual Awareness, stainless and benign, beyond birth-death, happiness-misery; IT is the awake consciousness of the universe; IT is the Brahman that is the plenitude which has neither the relationships nor the differences existing in manifestation.

In this same Upaniṣad, as also in many others such as the Maṇḍalabrāhmaṇa, the Nādabindu, the Haṃsa and the Paiṅgala, the *gūdhasupti* (the secret sleep), and the states beyond mind (*manas* as we ordinarily know it), named *unmanī* and *amanaska*, are spoken of. The Varāha states[39] that the world is seen as a dream as one awakes to non-duality. In the dreamless state, the *prājña* quarter, he who is awake

[36] Subāla Upaniṣad, 15.
[37] Here follows a list of terms representing the functioning of the psycho-physical organism. 'Burns up' means completely transcends.
[38] Loc. cit. 3. 6-8.
[39] Loc. cit. 4.12-18,23.

is one who is liberated from the conflict arising in the state of duality and from the *vāsanās*. In the final stage, the *gūdhasupti* or secret yoga-sleep, there is the communion in which the separation between self and not-self disappears; and in this state where there is no second, no otherness, there is no fear. The Maṇḍalabrāhmaṇa says[40] that he who rises above (the fluctuations of) the mind to the state of *unmanī*, and thence to *amanaska* (the individual mind which has completely transcended all image making activity, that is, producing mental constructs) is one with Brahman. This *amanaska* state follows the complete pacification of sense-functioning.

The Śāṇḍilya Upaniṣad says that when the mind and the life-rhythm (*prāṇa*) are absorbed in an internal object (with intense attentiveness)[41] the state of Viṣṇu, which is void and not-void, dawns on him . . . (it is) of the nature of light, free of externals (limited characteristics) resplendent . . . the supreme truth . . . It brings about *unmanī* which causes the cessation of all fluctuations of the mind (of all intrusion of isolative self-consciousness) and one reaches the yoga-sleep.[42] For him, time does not exist. The thinking process having become perfectly still, one becomes, as it were, attentiveness itself – conscious of the *citta* – conscious of consciousness itself as it were, a transcendental counterpart of being mindful of mental states – the state of liberation from every constraint imposed by the conditioned mind. When the fluctuations of the mind cease the cycle of births and deaths comes to an end.

This ending of *saṃsāra* is coincident with pure meditation in seclusion (which is not possible without the preliminary indispensable basis of the purity of heart and mind), and with the establishment of an unchangingly peaceful life-rhythm (control of breath as it is called, *prāṇāyāma*). The fluctuations of the life-rhythm (disturbances of breath-rhythm which reflect corresponding disturbances of psyche and mind, of emotion and intellect) cease when, bodily awake and fully attentive, one clearly cognizes the *prājña* state which, for the yogi in meditation, corresponds to the dreamless slumber state in unconsciousness for the sleeping worldling.

Thus one is led to the fourth state, *turīya*. This is Transcendence itself – Nirvana – the beyond, the unitary wholeness in which all duality is integrated (and hence no conflict arises in mind and no ill is present),

[40] Loc. cit. 2.4; 3.1,2; 5.1.

[41] The *samprajñāta samādhi*, in which there is still the duality of self and the object of attention.

[42] Śāṇḍilya Up., 1.35. The Paiṅgala says (4.21) that in the *unmanī* state no conception of duality can enter, for the Brahman state is realized.

transcended, and held in subsumption in the One Total Reality in Awareness-Being-Bliss – the *asaṃprajñāta samādhi.*

The Māṇḍūkya Upaniṣad says of this *turīya* : not inwardly nor outwardly nor both-wise cognitive; not a cognition-mass; not cognitive nor non-cognitive; unseen; with which there can be no dealing; ungraspable, having no distinctive mark, unthinkable, that cannot be designated; the essence of certainty of the one Atman;[43] the tranquil, the benign; the non-dual.

In *turīya,* Transcendence realizes itself as the perfection of MAN-hood through you the living existent. Thereafter, the invisible, immortal, dimensionless 'centre' – the centre which is not me, nor mine – is the creative and enlightening source of Power working through all the states of the perfected Holy One. So he affirms *aham brahma'smi* – I am Brahman. But this *aham*, this 'I', is now the one and only transcendent I AM – the *ehyeh* pronounced by Elohim – affirming its eternal IS-NESS through the mouth of him whose lips have been touched by the eternal fire of LIFE, Brahman as *prāṇa*. Such is Atman-realization.

Let now the meaning of Atman be presented for consideration and deep meditation in the following way: When you yourself, utterly pure, still and silent, free of isolative self-consciousness, are the unresisting, sensitive nexus for the free inflow and outflow of Transcendence – then that is the meaning of Atman, the meaning of Brahman saying I AM. Not to be thus is the transcendental sorrow, *śoka*, the transcendental 'far from the Infinite', *dukkha*, the state of fallen Man, Adam in sin.

* * *

The inspiring utterances of the Great Teachers concerning the experiencing in supra-consciousness of Transcendence are pointers of light to the realization of supreme communion. They are part of the deep teaching of the scriptures showing what happens in the mind as the Immanence comes to full glory. As Jesus said: 'And now, O Father, glorify thou me with thine own self, with the glory I had with thee before the world was'.

In that supra-consciousness, the Immanent and the Transcendent become one. The manhood is lifted into unity with the Godhead. Thereafter, the Immanent within us, involving again into the human state, albeit the perfected human, is harassed, crucified, as it sheds its vestures of the divine splendour in the process of involvement. It is

[43] or, the absolute certainty of unitary Wholeness.

reduced to the limitations of body-mind and to the instruments of act and speech to tell of that ineffable light. But this experiencing of glorified Being and this telling of it, is indeed Revelation for those who have eyes to see and ears to hear. What is revealed is the unfolding and flowering of consciousness into supra-consciousness and its involving back again into ordinary everyday consciousness.

Revelation, rooted in the spaceless and timeless infinity of the eternal Silence, is of the very substance of religious fulfilment. It marks the fruition of the religiousness which essentially distinguishes man from all other species. It is the sign of the wholly purified and matured mind, the mind of the one become as a little child in the religious sense. Such a mind sees with the divine eye and understands the living Truth.

For centuries we have misinterpreted some of the great pages of the world's scriptures. But if we have at least some understanding of supra-consciousness – best of all the realization of supra-consciousness – we can go at least part of the way to remedy the harm done. Men and women suffer in life. The posture of world affairs is one of painful stress, almost presaging the destruction of life and values. The healing of the world, as of the individual, can come only through Religion. But the world of religion is itself in turmoil and in danger of eclipse, because the knowledge of the Heart of Religion has been forgotten by too many for too long. If this knowledge is reinstated in its proper place – the keystone of the arch – it will prove to be the power which makes all things new.

* * *

'Honour thy father and thy mother that thy days may be long upon the land which the Lord thy God giveth thee.'[44]

The significances of father: God as creative power; *Ḥokmah*; Energy; Eternity; the Sun; *puruṣa*; *prāṇa*.

The significances of mother: Nature; *Binah*; Matter; Time; Earth; *prakṛiti*; *ākāśa*.

Day is a symbol for clear consciousness or clear seeing of Truth, for enlightenment; land for the psycho-physical organism. The Lord is YHWH. God is Elohim. The verb 'giveth' is in the present tense, suggesting a continuous living process, not a single act once for all.

It is a man's divine destiny to be the living vehicle of Transcendence, if he really cares.

[44] Exod., 20.12.

The ancient wisdom had a teaching that the father principle – *Ḥokmah* or *puruṣa* – simply by virtue of its presence fecundated the mother principle – *Binah* or *prakṛiti* – setting in motion the universal becoming-process. The mother principle in action brings about differentiation: cosmos out of chaos, chaos meaning not disorder but a primordial quiescent order in which positive and negative forces, in balance, are waiting to be started up into action. The influence, the silent presence or glance, of the divine father gives rise to the interaction of positive and negative forces within the divine mother and the world-process is in being.

This is eternally so. There was not a particular moment in unidirectional time when the father directed a benign glance to the mother. *Ḥokmah* perpetually stimulates *Binah*, *puruṣa prakṛiti*, *prāṇa ākāśa*, God Nature. These are in the timeless conjugation which is still and silent. The interaction of positive and negative energies within the mother introduce motion, action, transformation, construction, disruption, birth, growth, decay, death and all that comes within the sphere of duality and mortality.

In the symbolic terms of *kuṇḍalinī* yoga,[45] Śiva resides in the thousand-petalled lotus, *sahasrāra*, at the top of the head, and Śakti, his consort, at the base of the spine. Śakti, psycho-spiritual energy, rooted in psycho-physical energy (the physico-chemical energy of the body) when stirred into activity by the yogi is made to ascend up the *suṣumnā nāḍī* the central canal through the spinal column and unite with her lord Śiva.

The first *cakra* at the base of the spine, *mūlādhāra*, which means root support, represents Earth. The Muṇḍaka Upaniṣad says:[46] 'Earth is the footing of the Lord'. In Isaiah[47] it is written: 'Thus saith the Lord, The heaven is my throne and the earth is my footstool: where is the house that ye build unto me? and where is the place of my rest?' The effects of *kuṇḍalinī śakti*, when aroused, can be either divine or demoniacal. The impure man is destroyed. Unbeknown to mankind, this energy finds expression in everyday life, as when a philosopher or artist or writer or speaker puts forth works and ideas. If his ideas, bearing the effects of his imperfection, moral and intellectual, influences men, either as mobs or as individuals, harm accrues, as amply testified in human history. Only he who is pure in mind and heart, living a simple and austere life, can safely handle *kuṇḍalinī*, the energy which sleeps

[45] See also above pp. 217, 228f.
[46] Loc. cit. 2.1.4.
[47] Loc. cit. 66.1. See also Acts, 7.49.

coiled up like a serpent[48] at *mūlādhāra*. Rightly utilized it leads to realization by Transcendence.

The fourth *cakra*, the heart centre, is *anāhata*, which means the place where the *munis*, the Holy Ones capable of silence of mind as well as of tongue, 'hear the sound which comes without striking two things together'. With *kuṇḍalinī* raised to *anāhata*, the *muni* hears the sound of the pulse of Life, Life in the non-biological sense. In tune with this sound, the yogi realizes true egohood, devoid of egoism and containing within itself the energy for transcending itself.

At *anāhata* the pacification of the sense-consciousnesses takes place. Pure meditation could begin here. Free of the conflict born of ambivalence, inward poise and equanimity (*upekkhā*) can be realized, and peace.

The fifth *cakra*, called *viśuddhi* which means made pure, is the throat centre. It is concerned with *mantric* sound, that is, with the use of the voice to produce deep psychical effects. Responsive to the realm of Transcendence, the yogi's prophetic speech, or gesture, awakens a sense and a longing for Transcendence in his listener. The *viśuddhi cakra* may be regarded as the source of the word of power, the *mantra*.

Whilst the intoning of the *mantra* or the use of audible, inspired speech is the external expression of the activated *viśuddhi cakra*, the yogi in this state is beyond the word, which means beyond finitude and mortality. He has passed through that portal of death which signifies the end of discursive thought and speech arising out of desire, confusion of mind and the conflict characterizing the ambivalent state. In *viśuddhi*, unified mind, in harmony with MIND, functions at its own level and in its own rights. There is freedom from isolative self-consciousness and the receptive-responsive sensitivity of the yogi functions at a peak.

At the sixth *cakra*, the *ājñā*, between the eyebrows and associated with the medulla, 'the command of the Teacher is received from above'. Because you yourself are Master and Learner, this command is heard from within. What is 'received from above' stimulates you and in response to it from within yourself there is enlightenment. Quiet, alert and sensitive, you learn the deep things beyond words and concepts. Going beyond ideation there is direct perception of the great archetypes. *Ājñā* represents insight into that Truth which is Transcendence. It is the divine Wisdom, the Teacher.

Finally, the Crown Centre, *sahasrāra* or the thousand petalled lotus,

[48] Consider in this connection the account in Exod. 7.10-12 of the casting of rods which turn into serpents by Pharaoh's magicians and by Moses and Aaron.

represents the integration of the other six *cakras*. It starts off a higher order altogether, as if a new octave of being and consciousness begins with *sahasrāra*,[49] the abode of Śiva. The transition from *ājñā* to *sahasrāra* represents the liberation out of all separate selfhood into Transcendence. Buddhist yoga regards *ājñā* and *sahasrāra* as a single Crown Centre. *Cakra* means a wheel. The Crown and throat centres are the front wheels, and the heart and navel centres are the rear wheels of the fiery chariot of the spirit in its ascent to Transcendence.[50] It is the realm of Divinity itself, of pure MIND, of All-Father Mind which is God.

In *sahasrāra* there is complete pacification of all sense-functioning, speech and thought, perception and feeling. One passes through the final portal of death. All self-obtrusiveness upon the world and all isolating differentiation between self and not-self is at an end. Holiness is realized. In this state of ineffable bliss there is nothing that one may call 'my' mind, for one has become empty and transparent, and MIND, the transcendent unknown energy, functions freely through you the unconditioned one.

* * *

In the usual cross-legged posture adopted in the practice of yoga, *mūlādhāra*, which represents the element earth, is in touch with Mother Earth. Man the microcosm is in sensitive relationship with Earth the macrocosm, earth to Earth. Similarly, Mother Earth the microcosm is in sensitive relationship with space, *ākāśa* the macrocosm. Also, the psychic energies emanating out of what we call matter and those which are concerned with man the living organism are in right relationship.

The spinal column is called *merudaṇḍa*. *Daṇḍa* means a rod; in this case, a living rod. Mount Meru is the mystical, sacred mount where the ultimate realization takes place, and the spinal column is the *daṇḍa* which leads to the Mount Meru of the individual, the point at which Transcendence touches the living being. In the cross-legged posture *merudaṇḍa* is upright, like a lightning conductor, and *sahasrāra* points to the celestial zenith. Even as Mother Earth is related to the celestial zenith, so is the yogi through *sahasrāra*.

The energy (*prāṇa*) of matter radiates out macrocosmically from Earth to Cosmos, and in the yogi, up microcosmically from *mūlādhāra* to *sahasrāra*. If you are well prepared, the energy of Transcendence

[49] The Sāṇḍilya Upaniṣad (1.48) mentions a twelfth centre. It is said that the brain itself is the seat of six centres besides the six below the brain.

[50] cf. Elijah being taken up to heaven in the fiery chariot.

responds through *sahasrāra* down to *mūlādhāra*, sensitizing, refining and transforming you. That is why, sitting properly, at ease, elastic, still and silent, heals the organism. If the basis of purity is present and the ascent to *sahasrāra* is accomplished in pure meditation, the finite self is at-oned with the Infinite. The wound of separation is healed. Benediction floods your being and spreads through you over the Earth.

Merudaṇḍa, in the worldling, is the tree of good and evil. In the Holy One, it is the Tree of Life. In the upward ascent from *mūlādhāra*, *śakti* releases herself out of the sphere of duality and conflict. At *anāhata* there is the first rapport with Transcendence, for it is the level at which the sub-human has changed, through purification, into the true human whose 'thought' is creative power in action.

At this point let us bend *merudaṇḍa*, as in the diagram below, making *anāhata* a pivotal base and moving the lower three cakras upwards to face the upper three.

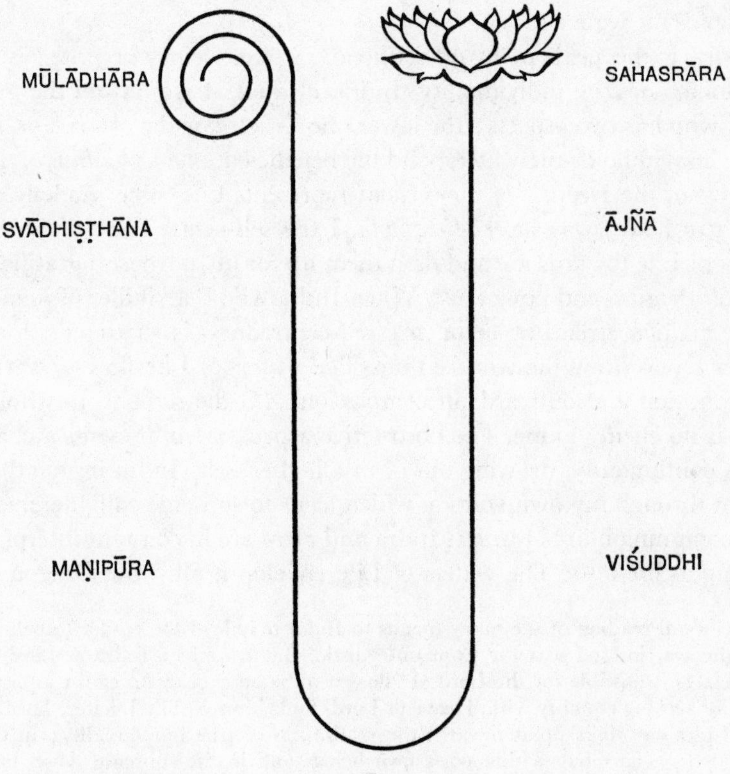

In the Ṛg-veda the universe consists of three parts – heaven, the mid-region or atmosphere, and earth. In man the microcosm, heaven is the cortical region of the brain, the mid-region includes the medulla and the cerebellum, and earth is the spinal column down to its base. Indra, the god who wields the lightning bolt with which he slew *ahi-vṛtra* the demon of drought, is the dominant deity of the mid-region. Noting the close proximity of the *ājñā* and *sahasrāra cakras*, the single Crown Centre of Buddhist yoga, and the victorious feats of the god, Indra's lordship lies by the heavenly region. So too, be it remembered, does that of Yama the Death-lord.

In the diagram, *mūlādhāra* faces *sahasrāra*. *Mūlādhāra* is dormant power. It functions in the worldly man in flashes of insight or genius, if he is gifted. The Yogi who has accomplished the uniting of *Śakti* and Śiva, can deliberately utilize this power for good whenever he wills to do so. *Svādhiṣṭhāna* represents the peak of egoistic self-assertion, especially through all expressions of sexuality, withholds spiritual fruition from the individual, and is the abode of *ahi-vṛtra*, the 'serpent who withholds the waters'.

Indra is the peak point of Selfhood as pure Being, or un-egoistic Egohood,[51] or true individuality. Indra, at *ājñā*, strikes at *ahi* the serpent, who has two aspects: the lower one as *vṛtra* or the obstructor, as one who withholds the waters; and the beneficient one as *budhnya*, the Dragon of the Deep. *Ahi* the serpent represents Life-force. As long as *ahi vṛtra* holds sway at *svādhiṣṭhāna*, I the self-centred one draw the forces of Life towards me and dam them up for my purposes: gratification of pleasure and power lust. When Indra who is a kindler of higher truth at *ājñā* strikes at *vṛtra*, my self-centredness is shattered. I no longer try to draw the world to me. The waters of Life flow upwards in aspiration and outwards in compassion. *Ahi* the serpent, in wholeness, is no enemy to me. The obstructive aspect, *vṛtra*, presents a challenge continuously, drawing out of my 'higher' self (Indra in me) that action through my own volition which leads to supreme enlightenment and communion in *sahasrāra*. Indra and *vṛtra* are in constant interplay as long as life lasts. The waters of Life envelop it all – the Dragon of

[51] A literal reading of the many hymns to Indra may lead the reader to believe that the warrior-god was far from un-egoistic. But consider: Indra is Lord of Heaven. Is it possible for the Lord of Heaven to be an egoist? An egoist aspiring to be, or seeking equality with, Heaven's Lord, finds himself, like Lucifer, Lord of hell. Indra's exploits point towards the realization of true individuality: in the finite sphere, harmony within one's own being; and in the supreme sense, harmony with the Totality.

the Deep encircles the whole world – and fertilizes the human so that he grows into the full flower of his humanity.

Transcendence alone has true creative power by virtue of which the unknown, new thing emerges out of No-thing. *Svādhiṣṭhāna* is associated with the genitals. The phallus in action, symbolized by the aroused moving serpent, is instrumental in generation. This serpent, *ahi vṛtra,* deceives me into believing I am a creator. In truth, I am just a procreator, for I am only an agent of continuity of the already existent and the known, namely, the human species. The unknown new has not emerged out of the transcendent No-thing because of my sexual activity. So too all that I produce of art or philosophy or anything which is a modification of the known or the past, is a procreation by me. The phallus has part rulership over all of it. Phallic delight[52] is the root of the pleasure and satisfaction, sensuous, aesthetic and intellectual, experienced in all such activity, in which the serpent's tail, as *ahi vṛtra*, plays full part.

Parental love, rooted in sexual love, could in rare cases become transmuted and open one's eyes to transcendent love, the love that Transcendence has for Totality, as manifested through the perfected Holy Ones. When this happens, it is coincident with the serpent's head, as *ahi budhnya*, coming into its own, that is, Indra exercising lordship at *ājñā*, the enlightened consciousness or pure intelligence. This stage is rightly symbolized by the serpent holding his tail in his mouth, for Transcendence never destroys anything, howsoever 'evil', but transmutes it – or else the transcendent nature of divine love would suffer obscuration.

Note the bodily positions and the functions of the nerve ganglions: the genitals and procreation; and the brain (Śiva's abode) and CREATION, when the supreme communion state of *samādhi* prevails. In *samādhi* the serpent is no longer the deceiver.

After Indra's lordship is the established fact, one is naturally celibate. The arising and the torment of the sexual drive and associated passions is over, for there is transmutation of procreative into creative energy and action. Woe betides him who enforces celibacy on himself, moved by power lust and egoism to gain the state of Indra's lordship at *ājña*. In the Temple of the Lord, no barter is possible.

[52] cf. 'By what do you acquire . . . bliss, delight and procreation?' 'By the generative organ.' Kauṣītaki Up., 1.7. 'Having obtained control over the generative organ by intelligence (*prajñā*) one obtains bliss, delight and procreation.' Ibid. 3.6.

Maṇipūra deals with the commerce of the psycho-physical life: food, daily work, experience, thought and social interchange. It 'digests' food for the psyche received through sense activity, experience and thought in the worldly context. Standing opposite to *maṇipūra* is *viśuddhi*. The functioning of *maṇipūra* purified and perfected is the functioning of *viśuddhi*: prophetic speech not common chatter; clarity of mind not confused thinking.

When I have seen the vision and begun to understand the trend of life and the meaning and purpose of human existence, *maṇipūra* gives over and obediently serves *viśuddhi*. So also *svādhiṣṭhāna* to *ājñā* and *mūlādhāra* to *sahasrāra*. Thus there is an end to conflict between the 'higher' and the 'lower' self. Instead, there is the harmony of cooperation through mutual stimulation between them. No higher self can come to fulfilment in the absence of the lower self, no lower self can ever find redemption without the inspiration and transmuting power of the higher self.

In the pure state, the *cakras* act as polar complementaries resting upon *anāhata*, the level of the HUMAN, as represented in the diagram. When that is realized, you are the *puruṣa*, the Person who is the true individual, one who fulfils the purpose of his existence. Transcendence has come home within you.

* * *

Kuṇḍalinī yoga is the way of Power. Keep right away from it until there is the foundation of perfect purity of thought, feeling, speech and action. Granting that purity is present, carefully test out whether you are gifted for treading that path. The best test is to make sure by means of lynx-eyed observation whether you have wisdom and love in harmony.

* * *

When Śakti is led right up to *sahasrāra*, she is blissfully united with her lord Śiva. Father and Mother are one. In this state you know the meaning of the words of Jesus after he had ascended:[53] 'All power (ἐξουσία) is given unto me in heaven and earth'. The united Śiva-Śakti return to *mūlādhāra*, completely purifying, refining and sensitizing the whole being. They ascend again to *anāhata*, transcendentalizing all the worldly functions represented by *mūlādhāra*, *svādhiṣṭhāna* and

[53] Matt., 28.18.

maṇipura and the work which falls to one's lot in everyday life, where they reside during the yogi's lifetime, for it is at the level of *anāhata* that one is in tune with mankind. At the time of the death of the yogi, Śiva-Śakti rise up to and through *sahasrāra*, and the end of the body takes place.

From *mūlādhāra* to *sahasrāra* is from Earth to Heaven. The Maitreya and Skanda Upaniṣads say: 'The body (of the pure Holy One) is the Temple of the Lord; the dweller in that temple is Śiva the ever-auspicious'. Hear again the words of Isaiah: 'The heaven is my throne and the earth is my footstool: where is the house that ye build unto me? and where is the place of my rest?' And the yogi answers: 'This pure body shall be thy house of Life, O Lord. Thy place of rest shall be *anāhata* whilst this body lives, and in its dying thou shalt enter thine own sabbath through the portal of *sahasrāra*'.

* * *

It may seem strange to couch the answer to the Hebrew YHWH in the language of an Indian yogi. But the Truth is one, its expressions manifold. God is one; but his garments woven in the roaring loom of time so variegated, that men have fought in hellish fashion like wild dogs fighting for meatless bones. Deliberately, therefore, have the expressions of Truth not been rigidly separated in this book. Are not the drops of sweetness from the vale of Kashmir as delicious as the vine clusters from Judah? Deliberately have some of the garments been used with a certain disregard of the stiff propriety demanded by the festive occasion. Would you really refuse to marry the queen of your heart because she happened to wear a purple hat instead of a silken veil when she walked up the aisle with her father? Yes? Then spend your wearisome years in the endless frustration of making love to a silken veil!

* * *

Whilst the Upaniṣadic Teachers present the whole range of consciousness as the four states, the Buddha presents the variations of the meditative state as four *jhānas* and four *samāpattis*,[54] and a final ninth state which is the culmination of the previous eight states.

[54] The Pāli *jhāna* is the Sanskrit *dhyāna*, a contemplative state. A *samāpatti* is an attainment, or a coalescence.

The first stage: Aloof (detached) from sense-pleasures and unskilled states of mind, one enters into the first *jhāna* which is accompanied by applied thought and discursive thinking, born of detachment. It is rapturous and joyful, and in this one abides.

The second stage: By the stilling of applied thought and discursive thinking, with the mind subjectively tranquillised and fixed on one point (or, with the inward heart serene and uniquely exalted), one enters into and abides in the second *jhāna* which is devoid of applied and discursive thought, is born of concentration and is rapturous and joyful.

The third stage: By the fading out of rapture, one dwells with equanimity, attentive and clearly conscious, experiencing in his own person that joy of which the ariyans say: 'Joyful lives he who has equanimity and is mindful', and enters into and abides in the third *jhāna*.

The fourth stage: By abandoning pleasure and pain, by the previous going down of happiness and sadness, one enters into and abides in the fourth *jhāna* which is free of pain and free of pleasure, and which is entirely purified by mindfulness and equanimity.

The fifth stage: By passing quite beyond all perceptions of form, by the going down of perception of sensory reactions, by not attending to perception of variety, by becoming aware that *ākāsa* is immeasurable, one enters upon and abides in the plane of infinite *ākāsa*.

The sixth stage: By passing quite beyond the plane of infinite *ākāsa*, becoming aware that consciousness is immeasurable, one enters upon and abides in the plane of infinite consciousness.

The seventh stage: By passing quite beyond the plane of infinite consciousness, becoming aware there is no-thingness (here-now), one enters upon and abides in that no-thingness.

The eighth stage: By passing quite beyond no-thingness, one enters upon and abides in neither-perception-nor-non-perception.

The ninth stage: By passing quite beyond the plane of neither-perception-nor-non-perception, one enters upon and abides in the stopping of perception and feeling. (This is called the cessation.)

In the first four *jhānas* there is a progressive denudation of some of the contents of the mind by the elimination of applied thought (*vitakka*), discursive thought (*vicāra*), rapture (*pīti*) and joy (*sukha*). There is freedom from bodily pain with the first *jhāna*, from mental grief with the second, from bodily pleasure with the third, and from mental joy with the fourth. During the earlier *jhānas* the whole body is 'drenched, saturated, permeated and suffused', as the Buddha tells Udāyin,[55] with rapture and joy. In the fourth *jhāna* there is only pure mindfulness and equanimity. The mind is now in the *ekaggatā*, the one-pointed, unified state; it is self-contained, functioning unfragmentarily.

When there is applied thought there is no sloth or torpor; by sustained discursive thought doubts are resolved; rapture dissolves hatred and joy dispels mental worry and restlessness, whilst pure mindfulness or concentrated attentiveness does away with greed.

Buddhaghosa in his Visuddhimagga (Chap. 3, Section 105),[56] gives a standard list of forty meditation subjects for mindfulness and concentration; it also deals with meditations in the exercise of wisdom. It must be clearly understood that the *jhānas* and *samāpattis* by themselves, rooted in mindfulness, giving rise to perfect poise, leading to ultimate enstasy, the cessation, in which separateness from the One Reality is transcended, are one moiety of the Holy Life. The other is wisdom, also rooted in mindfulness, leading to insight into the true or essential nature of things, that is, into their inward emptiness (*śūnyatā*), the void which is pregnant with the plenitude. But this wisdom and insight can come to flower only in the purified religieux, not in the worldling, even if he had genius. The integration of the two – the wisdom and the cessation – spell the realization of Nirvana.

In the first four stages the subject-object relationship prevails – the meditator and the subject of meditation. Where there is proficiency in the movement from one stage to the other there is no awareness[57] that 'I' am immerging into this particular stage as I go inward, or that 'I' am emerging out of it as I come back to ordinary sense-functioning and discursive thought and speech. The subject-object relationship of one in *jhāna* is qualitatively different from that of the worldling. The former is concerned with mindful observation in order to become purified in himself, to understand with insight, to grow in wisdom and transmute all Ill.The worldling sees with a conditioned mind in order to acquire intellectual comprehension, or to grasp something which he covets or to feed his ego or vanity; he is self-oriented, a preserver of Ill.

[55] M., 2.15,16.

[56] See Ñāṇamoli's translation p. 112. See also E. Conze, *Buddhist Meditation*, p. 14.

[57] M., 1.301,302; S., 3.235-238.

Meditation which leads to insight and wisdom is impossible if the mind is defiled, for it will always misperceive and misunderstand all that it observes or experiences.

The stilling of discursive thought distinguishing the transformation of the first into the second meditative state is of special importance, marking as it does the movement through the first portal of death, the first touch of the Silence.[58] The passage through the second portal takes one into the fourth stage. Because one has died to pleasure and pain bodily and mentally and to grasping after any kind of worldliness, the mind is pure, not only morally but also with respect to the functioning of intelligence. It can perceive and feel non-sensationally for its dormant inner sensitivity is awake, a sensitivity not restricted to form and finitude, but receptive to the impress of the beyond, the formless and the non-finite.

Now there can take place the dissolution of the barrier between self and not-self and between the conscious and the unconscious of worldly parlance. The pure, whole mind is not 'my' mind but the One Holy Mind, functioning unobstructed by my psyche, transparent and unresisting. Hence the stages beyond the fourth *jhāna* have no subject-object duality in restrictive finite terms. The Subject-Object now is the Infinite emerging into Self-Awareness through the finite me which is free of the shackles of isolative self-consciousness.

And it is this kind of transformed me which can 'put aside with right wisdom', once and for all, every shape, sensation, perception, volition and mental conformation which is generated and caught within the confines of discriminative consciousness, including discriminative consciousness itself. Which means that THAT, Transcendence itself, realizes its own free creative Living, 'sees' Truth and, through Wisdom, through the *prajñāpāramitā*, completely dispels ignorance and all discriminative consciousness. For discriminative consciousness can only be 'my' discriminative consciousness, whereas Transcendence is pure Awareness – *viññāṇaṃ anidassanaṃ anantaṃ sabbatopabhaṃ*, consciousness which cannot be characterized, endless, shining in every respect. When Transcendence takes over the whole of me, I do not get trapped in any beliefs and conceptions about Transcendence.

The word 'attainment' in connection with the fifth stage onwards is inadequate, even misleading. For with the 'going down of perception of sensory reactions, passing quite beyond all perceptions of form, becoming aware that *ākāsa* is immeasurable, non-finite', there is no

[58] See also above p. 343f.

meaning to the word attainment. The context of attainment is one of finitude, separate particulars, differentiation, comparison and so on. Since these no longer operate in the mind, there is no attainment. A dormant faculty, namely the capacity to be aware in terms of totality, infinity or unitary wholeness is now active, and in this context our vocabularies are inadequate. Therefore, whereas statements about the first four *jhānas* do lie within the framework of logical comprehension and formulation, the remaining stages cannot be presented in strictly logical form. The a-logical and a-rational eludes the net of precise definition.

What happens is that something like a coalescence of 'my' mind with totality takes place, reaching its fullness and peak intensity in the cessation. My body is alive, though it may appear to the ordinary onlooker like a log of wood, or dead.[59]

The entry and abiding in the profound states in meditation means restoration into the unitary wholeness of the One Total Reality, and the realization of the purity and freedom of the unselfed state. Time and again in his discourses the Enlightened One retails these states and associates liberation with the culminating state: '. . . and entering upon the stopping of perception and feeling and abiding in it, and having seen through unerring insight, the *āsavas* (the cankers, or overflows of consciousness) come to be utterly destroyed . . . (and) there is no other abiding that is higher or more excellent'. It marks the end of all Ill, *dukkha*. It is the perfect unselfing.

This, together with wisdom, means the realization of the Unconditioned. 'The goal of the holy life', said the Buddha,[60] 'is unshakeable freedom of mind'. The stopping of perception and feeling is the passage through the third great portal of death. It must be borne in mind that *this* perception and feeling which stops in the final stage is of a transcendental nature, quite different from the perception and feeling characterizing the daily life of the psycho-physical organism. In this connection, meditate upon the words of Avalokita, the Holy One, in the Heart Sūtra of the Prajñāpāramitā: 'Here, O Sāriputra, form is emptiness and the very emptiness is form . . . Here, all *dharmas* (ultimate essences) are marked with emptiness . . . therefore there is no form, feeling, perception, impulse, consciousness . . . no shapes, sounds . . . no objects of mind . . . no ignorance nor extinction of ignorance . . . no

[59] M., 1.296. See also Nādabindu Up., 52,53; St. Teresa, *The Interior Castle*, 6th Mansions: chap. 4, para. 17; chap. 5, para. 8.

[60] M., 1.205.

decay and death . . . no extinction of decay and death . . . no suffering, nor origination, no path, no cognition, no attainment and no non-attainment . . . Therefore, having relied on the perfection of wisdom, he dwells without thought-coverings. In the absence of thought-coverings he has not been made to tremble,[61] he has overcome what can upset, in the end sustained by Nirvana.'

Whilst this state persists, realized Transcendence is concretely manifested through that Being, the Holy One. This is the nirvanic state. Now one may begin to understand the meaning of 'the Tathāgata is trackless', and of the end of the Heart Sutra : '*gate gate pāragate pārasamgate bodhi svāhā* – gone, gone, gone beyond, gone altogether beyond, O what an awakening, all-hail !' The man who has no experience of pure meditation and of the beyond, would naturally call the above state one of vacuity or unconsciousness. For the pure man, the *puruṣa*, it is the full awakening, the perfect wisdom.

* * *

The experiencing of the immeasurable makes an impress on the living psycho-physical organism and actually changes it. That impress may step down into the limited forms of thought and speech, which invariably fall short of the actual experiencing for we are driven to represent the infinite in the figure of the finite. These forms are but pictures of the real substance. Only as you move through the deep states to your in-gathering into reality, you become free of bondage to the pictures.

The 'infinity of *ākāsa* and of consciousness', in which awareness functions in terms of the actual integration of space and time, stands for the non-differentiation of what we here call mind and matter. They are a one-energy when one's mind has coalesced into universal MIND : to use a suggestive phrase, when one 'vibrates in rhythm' with that energy. Some indications have been given above[62] of the interpretations given of the experiencing of this energy. In the scriptures they speak of nether worlds and upper worlds. So too have mystics, and poets.

When there is a genuine experiencing of these modes of awareness, by way of yoga or the Tree of Life symbols or the prayer or contemplative activity of the mystic, or in the symbolical terms of the Tibetan

[61] cf. Yājñavalkya's affirmation, 'The Atman. . . . does not tremble', Bṛh. Up 3.9.20.

[62] See pp. 66f., 96ff.

Bardo, there is a release of mental and spiritual power which can be used beneficently. In this connection let us briefly consider a remarkable practice distinguishing Buddhist religious discipline.

Among the forty subjects of Buddhist Meditation[63] are the Four Divine Abidings, the *brahmavihārā*: loving-kindness, *mettā*; compassion, *karuṇā*; gladness or sympathetic joy, *muditā*; and equanimity, *upekkhā*. The teaching is given sometimes in response to a seeker asking to be shown the way to union with Brahmā, the creator god of the world, and at other times as part of the training of the monk for living the holy life.

Right conduct in thought speech and action is the basis. Of the virtues, patience and forbearance are specially important. The meditator, having reviewed the dangers of hate in any form, having put aside pleasure lust and other impediments, and having calmed the mind, develops loving-kindness by strongly wishing, first for himself, ease, well-being and happiness, and freedom from enmity, injury and disturbance. When the mind glows with friendliness for himself, he directs this *mettā* to others: the teacher and those dear to himself; later on, with growing proficiency, to all others, including enemies; and finally, to the entire world. The usual formula in the texts[64] for this practice runs as follows:

> 'He dwells, having suffused the first quarter with a mind of friendliness, likewise the second, likewise the third, likewise the fourth; just so above, below, across; he dwells, having suffused the whole world everywhere, in every way, with a mind of friendliness that is far-reaching, widespread, immeasurable, without enmity, without malevolence. He dwells, having suffused the first quarter with a mind of compassion . . . sympathetic joy . . . equanimity . . . that is far-reaching, widespread, immeasurable, without enmity, without malevolence.'

If the Divine Abidings can be realized, it also means that the meditator can enter upon and abide in the profound modes of awareness. The two interdepend. When the mind glows with unlimited loving-kindness and compassion, all sense of otherness in relation to any person vanishes. Loving one's neighbour as oneself is a realized fact. In

[63] See Vism., Chap. 3, sections 104 and 105 for the enumeration of the forty subjects, and Chap. 11 for the full exposition of the *brahmavihārā*. See also Conze, *Buddhist Meditation*, pp. 118-133.

[64] D., 1.250 f.; M., 1.38,129,283,351; M., 2.195,207; M., 3.145 f.

these profound meditative states, one sees the light of the soul of one's neighbour and knows his destiny and fate.[65] Such a meditator is fit to be a teacher.

Not unnaturally, the unskilled practiser is deluded into believing that he is in a *brahmavihāric* state and is suffusing the world with love, when in fact he is merely going through a verbal ritual as he repeats to himself 'May all beings in the East (or any other quarter) be happy and free from ill . . .' Can I command or conjure or cajole the psyche to pour out compassion or to feel joy by a routine repetition of such words at a fixed time each day? Is there a real energy roused up thereby and an effective outpouring of loving-kindness realized? Or is the procedure a mere mumble of words as is the case with many a conventional, fashionable temple frequenter or church goer with his prayers and his rituals?

The answer lies in the living of the ethical life. If the daily life shines with harmlessness, truth, selflessness, and in short with abstention from evil thought, word and deed, the energy of the pure psyche leaps forward spontaneously with power and beauty in response to the impulsion of the mind when it prays with a fervent faith, 'May you be at ease and free from ill'. The warm feeling is efficiently canalised through the disciplined mind. If not for the environment, at least for the practiser there is psychological healing.

For the Holy One, the Divine Abiding goes beyond the psychophysical level and enters a transcendental state. If you, an individual, are pure, poised, beyond delusion, and intensely aware, you are a nexus for inflowing transcendent energy. You can give it special form such as compassion or peace and direct it wheresoever and to whomsoever you will. Even before full realization of MAN-hood, you can experiment and observe for yourself what happens. When the immediate circumstance is peaceful, and you are spontaneously urged to do so, be still and silent, breathing very calmly. You may, Grace granting, feel a mounting stir of an unknown energy thrilling through you, filling your being with blissful love and flowing out irresistibly into the world around you, a divine blessing. This is close kin to the *brahmavihāric* state, which in the Holy One functions at the levels of the deepest *jhāna* and in the infinity of *ākāsa-viññāṇa*. Stay perfectly still while experiencing this, and be particularly careful to remain unstained by pride and vanity after it is over. Above all, be quiet about it.

* * *

[65] See above pp. 339 f.

In my worldly state love is an infatuation, a being enamoured, a passion, an emotion, a delight, a pain, an intoxication, a madness. Is there love where there is envy, jealousy, possessiveness, exclusiveness, comparison, ambition, dependence, conditionality, sorrow, pining, increase, decrease, demand? But there are those unselfconscious moments when a magic thrills the heart and sweeps my whole being clean – and then there is no division between you and me. Indeed I do not see an other when I see you. Indeed there is no me that can prove to be an other. A little later, the spell is gone. But the flash of the vision stays as a memory of the beatitude of that which is beyond me, and lives in my soul as a flaming pointer to the reality of divine Love.

In the pure state, in mind-space which is *ākāsa* (which is both the limitless void and the conditioned fulness), and in the untrammelled awareness wherein is the transcendent energy which is creative action in eternity, the sacred mystery of Love is realized. So it becomes known here that Love was never born. Love never grows nor dies. Love IS. God – Transcendence – is the living Love that lights the flame of Life in the world and in me. Let me never cover Love with thought, memory. Eros has wings of gold. And if I let Love soar freely through all *ākāsa*, I die in ecstasy in every living moment of me the embodied Transcendence. And also, like Eros, I soar beyond the sorrow of dying in agony in every moment of clinging memory. Love, the Great Compassion, *mahā karuṇā* is actively present in the timeless infinite.

The Holy One loves. I the worldling sentimentalize; at best, I can touch romantic love at its finest. In the purified, holy state, I can let the power of Love heal and sanctify all through me as the instrument, whether it be in the form of the *brahmavihāras* or intercessionary prayer or any other chosen form.

I, here, know not what Love is and never can know. Seeking to know by thought or sensation – carnally – or seeing the semblance of Love, immediately banishes Love. Eros awoke when a drop of hot oil fell on him as he lay asleep, and disappeared. And Psyche suffered long agony.

Yet in truth Love is all around me, in me, and flows freely through me: infinite, invisible, one, peaceful, blissful, creative. If I love as the Holy One loves, all evil is overcome – no, not overcome, but transformed into eternal beauty by immortal love.

Love is Love – immediacy of eternity – timeless throb of the Unknown – blessedness of beatitude – the numinous no-thing – God.

* * *

Love makes wise. And Loving-Wisdom operating in the infinity of *ākāsa-viññāṇa* lays to rest in everlasting peace all the forms, concepts, dogmas, beliefs and objects of worship which my sense-mind functioning raised up since I first became dimly aware of the beyond. Reality IS. The energy or power of Transcendence is real, but unknown and unknowable. Its impress on me is interpreted in limited shapes, thought-forms. They make up the heavens and hells, the angels and demons, the gods and whatsoever else I put in words. They are real in so far as they are possibilities of consciousness. Born in the dawn of psychological time, they rule the thralls of ignorance and craving till the long night of the cosmos lays them to rest in the oblivion of sleep. But whoso is enlightened can go beyond them all. When I enter the state of the Loving-Wisdom of pure awareness all the gods and archangels and all the thought-coverings which are the mental constructs of the archetypal world are indrawn and resolved into their no-thing-ness.

Mere denial of traditional, conditioning beliefs in a psycho-spiritual cosmos, divine and demonic, cannot effect this resolution. The psyche has to go through a fiery baptism[66] as the mind is released into unconditioned freedom. With the twilight of the gods, the world is redeemed by Love and liberated by Wisdom. And benediction restores to Earth its pristine fragrance for now VIRTUE acts freely.

Perception and feeling, even of a transcendent order, still has thing-consciousness functioning. In ordinary everyday life we are atomistically conscious, that is, conscious in terms of separate particulars. In the infinity of no-thing, there is all-pervasive awareness[67] – field consciousness so to say. On atomistic consciousness and field consciousness is woven our own pattern of awarenes of the cosmic process. Perception belongs to atomistic consciousness, feeling to field consciousness. When Love-Wisdom resolves the pattern into no-thing, there is the sabbath day – rest, the primordial stillness where there is no motion.

Stay still now, for there is yet a slight oscillation, an inclining towards an unperceivable THAT and a withdrawing into a perceiving self.

[66] See Subāla Up., 15, quoted above p. 360. cf. Moses and the burning bush (Exod. Chap. 3). The distinctive, conditioned pattern (the 'bush') formed by the action of archetypal mind energies within the hidden depths of the psyche, exercises a binding influence on me as long as I am confined to discriminative consciousness. In the Holy One who can realize immergence into Transcendence, as did Moses, the bush lights up and the voice of God is heard as the burning goes on without consuming the bush; that is, the intensity of enlightenment enables the Holy One to realize the divine affirmation *ehyeh*, the ultimate I AM, in his own person.

[67] See also Varāha Up., 2.21.

There is a faint tremor of fear. Give way and in dark confusion you are flung back into limited self-consciousness. Stay still, neither perceiving nor not perceiving, for beyond this topmost Summit of Becoming is the Cessation, which is the end of the relative and conditioned, and which is the unconditional identity of the conditioned and the unconditioned, of the relative and the absolute. Such is the One Total Reality.

* * *

Unconditioned freedom of mind is realized when the psyche is emptied of all its obstructive contents. Thus the limited receptive-responsive sensitivity which is 'my' mind becomes non-finite. Universal MIND can then function without hindrance through the existential me.

The denudation of the mind by the pure man leads to the realization and manifestation by Transcendence of itself through the Holy One. Thereafter, his influence moves multitudes to live the good life. For the Holy One himself, this is now second nature. Free of striving, he is VIRTUE; he understands Reality because he is at-oned with it.

Now we can examine a problem in the Upaniṣads concerning the formulation of the One Total Reality. 'What is this Reality?' And the Teachers of the Upaniṣads answered: 'Brahman'. 'Who am I?' And they answered: 'Atman'. 'How did the world come into being?' 'Brahman became, and is, this-all (the world); and also, Atman became, and is, this-all'.[68] And then the great Teachers unequivocally affirmed the identity of Brahman and Atman.

But why two names for the one Ultimate Truth?

The Upaniṣadic answers were not arrived at simply by spasmodic intuitive flashes during odd moments of heightened sensitivity. The two words, Atman and Brahman, represent the experiencing of the one transcendent realization whilst it is actually occurring, and they represent *the mode of awareness functioning in the Holy One*, and not an objective perception or a subjective vision. So, the two basic questions concerning Reality and Self, posed by the intellect functioning within the confines of dualistic discriminative consciousness, are not, in fact, two separate questions, but are two different approaches to the one question: 'What is the whole fact, the supreme truth?' Looking outwards, inquiring objectively, investigating the 'not-self', the culmination is Brahman. Looking inwards, inquiring subjectively, investigating the 'self', the culmination is Atman. In either approach, the culmina-

[68] See also above pp. 85 f.

tion is realized only when discriminative consciousness is transcended, that is, when the Holy One is free of confinement within the subject-object duality.

The investigation is carried out not by means of scientific observation in the one case and of psychological analysis in the other, but by paying full attention to the changing modes of awareness of the nature of the not-self and of the self. Associated with the modes of awareness are the mental constructs, the *a priori* concepts such as space, time, substance, relation and causality, the archetypal spiritual and psychical energies symbolized in the *devas*, gods, *suras* and *asuras*, constructive and destructive or angelic and demonic forces, and so on. With respect to all these, the process of the inquiry in each case involves an *ascesis*, a putting aside of everything unessential, till in the supreme attentiveness there is only the unconditioned Reality defeating all description and with which there could be no dealing. In this *ascesis*, all beliefs, concepts, and in short all words and thoughts and the whole thinking and image-making activity becomes quiescent. The mind is no longer clamorous or confused. It is still, silent, rhythmically poised, totally attentive. This is the self-same condition in culmination, whether one starts with the question, 'What is Reality?' or with, 'Who am I?'

Through this complete denudation the psyche becomes utterly pure. Then the mind is perfectly transparent, sensitively and unresistingly open to Transcendence, and the state of union is realized. This state is the meaning of Truth, of Reality, in the religious context. Back in ordinary consciousness, it is seen retrospectively that the investigation, though appearing to start off, and to proceed for a while, in different directions, soon becomes the same movement. In the one case the personal self is integrated into the objective not-self, and in the other case the impersonal not-self is absorbed into the subjective self.

At the start, an ordinary thought process is at work. In time, discursive thinking subsides. Different modes of awareness operate as dormant faculties of mind begin to function. Whereas thought is a discourse *about* the object of thought which remains an 'other' to me, in the profounder modes of awareness the 'otherness' gives place to unity. The nature of the movement of these intensifying modes of awareness is more subjective and personalistic, if love and devotion predominate in the meditator, or objective and impersonal if wisdom and insight distinguish him. In culmination, however, all characteristics are transcended. The touch of love and the savour of wisdom merge into each other, and the 'ultimate' realized through the Holy One is

Awareness-Being, trans-personal and trans-conscious, One Total Reality. Hence the affirmation of the identity of Brahman and Atman.

The denudation of the psyche, like the treading of the Way, consists in the purification of mind and heart, the pacification of sense-functioning and discursive thought, the stilling of the wheel of imagination, and the putting aside of all conceptions, beliefs, convictions and archetypal images, for all of them veil Truth.

* * *

In the cessation of perception and feeling you are in rhythm with the creative pulse – the discontinuous throb which is Life/other-Life.[69] Each creation is new, not a reformulation or modification of the old. The creative pulse is non-repetitive. It has no continuity in our meaning of the word. We may say there is relationship by virtue of each pulse of creation being a complete transmutation of the previous pulse. ('Previous' is an inadequate word in the context of eternity.) In each new creation there is nothing whatsoever of the previous creation which is identifiable. How is it, then, that in everyday life, most things 'stay put' and are identifiable, which indeed enables us to live as we do? First we must bear in mind that we as we are understand *pro*-creation, biological and cultural, which is repetitive and true to type, with some modifications here and there, thus bringing forth the identifiable and that which is related to the known past. And next, that if any receptivity and capacity to respond to the creative pulse has at all begun to stir within us, it is so sluggish that we are aware of the actual discontinuity as a continuity, somewhat in the manner in which we are conscious of two pinpricks in sufficiently close proximity on the skin as a single sensation, or a small flaming object twirled sufficiently fast at the end of a wire appears as a continuous fire circle.

The Holy Ones in the state of the supreme communion in the ultimate enstasy possible to man found it so difficult to convey this adequately in olden days. Today it is a little easier; the advance in science and mathematics enables the mind to feel and to understand the difference between trans*formation* of the old material and trans*mutation* into the entirely new. The former is a manipulation or modification, the latter a creation. The former can be associated with causality, time and continuity, the latter is a-causal, timeless and discontinuous.

[69] See above, p. 186.

In attempting to convey the experiencing in transcendent awareness of this creative pulse of Life/other-Life in the forms of thought and speech there emerged the whole complex of ideas classed under karma – causality, retribution, reward, purgatory, hell, heaven, and the endless toil and moil of 'progress' in space and time – and under rebirth, variously termed re-incarnation, transmigration, metempsychosis, metensomatosis, palingenesis. The whole complex is ego-centred and revolves around the assumption of a permanent entity or immortal soul. Such doctrines and dogmas may have use in consoling the hurt heart or in encouraging the muddled mind to keep going a little longer. But their ethical and practical consequences have obstructed man's flowering. It is necessary to be open-minded, to learn afresh, to 'put aside with right wisdom' all that needs to be put aside. Freedom from all grasping is deathlessness.

During the cessation the body does not decay. The cessation is the arresting of death as disintegration. In cessation, attentiveness is total, in unison with the creative pulse of the here-now. In this state death is realized as other-Life. 'Death becomes one with the Lord' as the Subāla Upaniṣad says. Hence there is no fear, pain or sorrow associated with death as disruption.

Death itself is always other-Life in the actual creative pulse of Life/other-Life. It is because I myself am not totally attentive that I lose other-Life awareness. The timelessness – awareness in the mode of immortality – is replaced by time and I am conscious in the unidirectional mode of the succession of beginning-proceeding-ending, that is, of birth-death. The difference is a difference in *my mode of awareness*. The actual reality is for ever the dimensionless, timeless, discontinuous Life/other-Life creative pulse – an aseity, self-existent – and not a single line thread in time which *appears to me* to break now and again. Since I do not understand these breaks, these deaths seem so stark, fearful, mysterious, absolute, unanswerable.

In total attentiveness in timelessness, the 'interval' between pulses is not a gap or a break. There is no desire or fear or grasping present to interfere with and arrest the completeness of the attentiveness and thus change it from the state of unrestricted timelessness (im-mortality) to that of unrhythmic movement in time (mortality). There is no self-consciousness obtruding upon or obstructing Transcendence. This is one meaning of the saying that 'the yogi never sleeps'. Where there is desire or grasping, which inevitably introduces a fissiparous force, there is a gap or a break; and then there is the pain and sorrow of losing that which I wanted to hold on to and isolate for myself.

The paradoxical aspect of this situation is that on the one hand grasping prevents total attentiveness and on the other hand, not being totally attentive in the immediate present makes room for grasping. Whether I hold on to a dead past or grasp at a desired future, I am out of step with reality. So I fail to realize Death as other-Life.

In total attentiveness, which is always in the immediate HERE-NOW, there is no 'unknown', which belongs to a future, and there is full freedom from the 'known', which belongs to the past. Both 'known' and 'unknown' are enclosed in time, the context of mortality. When I am totally attentive, I do not, and cannot, think about myself, or of you or of anything as a separate particular. There is no scope for any sort of conditioned-mind functioning. Hence there is pure intelligence and action simultaneously present. This is the perfect Silence which includes all sound, and in which selfness is entirely precluded.

Whereas in total attentiveness there is the perfect synchronicity of psychological time[70] and chronological time, in the absence of total attentiveness there is a discrepancy between the two. Psychological time is invariably associated with desire and grasping, fear, anxiety, hate, ignorance and the compulsion of circumstance. Whoso clings to any memory, or harbours hate, or stays bound to any rigid picture of perfection, an ideal or an idol which he worships, banishes himself from the kingdom of heaven by maintaining a gulf between himself and the truth of the living present. The mind, trapped in psychological time, reacts against or in favour of whatsoever is presented by the world process in time and duality. This spells conflict which is a waste of energy and a perpetuation of the ill state. But when the mind remains still and silent, intensely watchful, it is in the timeless state, unshakeably poised and free. The things of time cannot prevail against the timeless. Peace and beauty supervene.

Clearly, the resolution of the problems and sorrows with which each man is beset in his daily life lies in total attentiveness. The ability to be fully attentive and the purity of daily living mutually interdepend. Both being present, the ambivalence of good-evil is transcended and VIRTUE acts unhindered through the pure and attentive one.

Death as pain and sorrow, as the wages of sin (the state of non-communion), and the absence of the synchronicity of psychological and chronological time are intimately inter-related. In total attentiveness there is that pure awareness in which psychological time is in perfect assonance with chronological time. This can also be stated as the extinction of psychological time and total freedom from the limitations

[70] See above, p. 212.

imposed on the mind by the ineluctable passage of chronological time. Then, whilst living *in* the world, the complete negation of the world as conceived by the unenlightened mind and the renunciation of all worldliness is realized without conflict.

* * *

In the house of Life is a door named Death. On the other side of it is bliss. If the door claims you the self – and ineluctably it will – you will never know that bliss. But if you, unselfed, swing that portal fearlessly with pure hand and heart, you are at-oned with bliss. And you know immortality.

* * *

Entering the Stillness and the Silence, Death is seen as the perfector and the consummator. Seeing this peacefully and fearlessly, I am filled with the wonder of creative renewal. Free of psychological time and the sorrow it holds, timeless eternity is realized in every moving flicker of time as I die wholly to time's beat whilst alive in the body. In this perfect rhythm is the dance of Life, the experiencing of the deathless state.

Death is not destruction nor annihilation. Death is the extinction of my illusion of continuity. So I see Death is other-Life, the non-finite non-being because of which there is no me repeated again. And I see that Death, Life's immortal and inseparable twin, offers the hospitality of Life – incomprehensible, silent containment by the Absolute in the unknown and unknowable eternity.

Austere? Then remember that for us who live as mortals there is only the way of Love and Understanding. Heart speaks to heart, noiselessly. Who loves, hears. Who listens, understands. So your tears can be wiped away ere they roll down. Even down here, in feebleness, to see and bear and understand the inconsolability of death is to be made deathless by Life and realize its benediction. This is Love, this is Freedom, this is Reality.

Deep in the womb of the timeless truth lies the certainty that we are not mere pawns of fate but the bearers of a divine destiny – the destiny to be MAN. It was there before the world was, hidden in the night of Sleep till the dawn of Awakening. And that golden Daybreak glowed with sweet and silent laughter when the still Mind spoke its wordless message promising redemption through enlightenment by Wisdom, peace through Compassion, freedom through that Beauty in which selfness is not.

Such is the Reality of Death. Let Death be. Power of transmutation! Restorer of union with Life Abundant! And the flow of this Life is the stream of Compassion, Wisdom, Truth, Purity, Goodness, Beauty – VIRTUE – Religion in fulfilment in every moment of daily life and work.

Thus it is that Death establishes me in my ALONENESS, even as Transcendence is the ALONE, the Life which is the creative pulse. Life never stands static. Nor does it move towards a goal. It writes on the edge of the Eternal Mind and laughingly erases the old word as it writes the new. The Eternal Mind itself is ever transparent, spacious, silent.

* * *

Watch the dying[71] of the Enlightened One, Lord of Compassion; the last gracious act ministering to the spiritual hunger of Subaddha; the last loving concern for the assembled *bhikkhus*: 'Has anyone here any doubt or misgiving regarding the Buddha, or the *dhamma*, or the path, or the method. Inquire freely, O *bhikkhus*'. And the last exhortation: 'Behold now, *bhikkhus*, I exhort you, saying, Decay is inherent in all compounded things; keep going without flagging'.

And then the journey for the last time through all the portals of death to the deathless unborn, unbecome, unmade. He enters into the four *jhānas* successively: dying to the realm of sense and the finite existent, into the infinity of *ākāsa* and *viññāṇa*: dying to that, into the no-thing, to neither-perception-nor-non-perception, and to the Cessation, touching Nirvana with the Body: Transcendence: Death the consummation and supreme fulfilment: the utter end of all ill: and this ultimate freedom of other-Life realized while still alive in the body!

Here, beyond the summit of all becoming, could have come the end of the body. The Infinite could have relinquished the finite, *viññāṇa* burning itself up through the channel in the head that leads to Brahman.[72] But if relinquished in this way, Compassion's claim cannot be met with effect when a suffering being calls upon the Name.

The Enlightened Love returns to the first *jhāna*. As he moves, the Unknown Absolute transcendentalizes the entire range of manifestation. What must the assembled *arahants* and *bhikkhus* have experienced! Their tongues are silent. But the living Holy Ones know.

In *this* first *jhāna* the whole body of the wisdom-religion (*buddha-dhamma*) is held in perfection as never before. The web of destiny embodied in Siddhattha Gotama is fulfilled as Buddha. Transcendence

[71] D., 2.148-156; and cf. above, pp. 204-7.
[72] Chānd. Up., 8.8.8 and Katha Up., 6.16.

will soon absorb that web. Fate will grow less harsh, her web more silken. And awhile, Earth will nestle in Heaven, sanctified.

The Light of Mind moves through the second and third *jhānas* on to the fourth, where it resolves into the quenchless light of perfect purity and equanimity. And there at the critical and central point of perfect humanhood, in unity with suffering mankind, he bequeaths to his race the final blessing – his own expiry! For thus he lives in our memory as long as our need calls on him, for the manner of his departure is still our manner – a last breath – a living link through dying! – so we feel no separation and fear, but only closeness and comfort.

The Buddha embodied the Supreme Beatitude in terms of transcendent Wisdom, the perfection of wisdom (*prajñāpāramitā*) which opens the door of deathlessness.

Who, now, is that Death-Lord, Lord of other-Life? He who can affirm: I WHO AM life immortal and also death; and being and non-being.

Listen! Look within! Keep going without flagging!

* * *

The Heart of Religion is the living of the religious life. It is the simple life, simple with the simplicity of creative genius. At first the genius learns the rudiments of his art, the rules of his craft and the errors he must avoid. In his maturity, a skilled master, his creative genius freely expresses itself. Simplicity marks his creations however complex their structure may be. So too is it with the religieux who realizes the supreme communion.

The simple religious life is the Life Beautiful, free of self-indulgence, fear and violence. Feeling, thought and speech, and all actions are pure, wise and compassionate, free of greed, hate and delusion.

The simple religieux asks nothing. He is in harmony within himself and with the world, a true individual. Selfless, he is awake. He is always mindful. Full of loving understanding, he is quiet. He refrains from everything unnecessary. So he does not disturb the peace or spoil the beauty of nature or of God.

The simple living of the religious life is to live in full communion in and with the world. Silent and still, it is the music of Transcendence and the pulse of Life for him who has ears to hear and eyes to see.

Always in communion, the religious man is the happy man; the intelligent man, the free man. He is the invisible focus through whom radiates all that Transcendence pours into him. He is VIRTUE. Exemplar of religious living, he is the Being through whom Transcendence has come to full self-realization as MAN, proving immortality through the mortal.

In this conjunction of Transcendence and man, the One Total Reality comes to blissful knowledge of its own infinitude, wholly embodied in all finites, and of its eternity vibrating in all moments everywhere – the moment of the galaxy is different from the moment of the earth, which again is different from the moment of a man or a flower. Here-now, the absolute is resolved into the relative, and the Holy One is absolved out of disjunction (the sinful state, *duḥkha*) into timeless conjugation within Transcendence, as Life and Death work in accord through his whole being.

The Holy One has no 'mind of his own' – that smoke-screen of mental obstructs. All separation, such as the conscious and the unconscious mind, is no more, for his receptive-responsive sensitivity is transparently open to Transcendence and the void is illumined by the light of Awareness-Being. Released from all bonds, cooled and pure, there is no resistance by the unified unconditioned mind to MIND's measureless power as it works through him, the unshattered, transmuting all that is drawn into that field of beneficence. He himself is then the Living Word,[73] Lord of Heaven in Earth, fountain-head of the liberating truth of religion that spells man's salvation, a focal point of creative action in eternity. Such is active supreme communion.

In this constant beatitude in which 'I am the I which has given up I', where mind is unshakably poised and free, ever still and silent, the senses are not only the cords of communion but also the channels of transmutative power. So when the Living Revelation looks at you at any moment he sees you as you actually are, and in that same instant, through his eye, the 'third eye', Transcendence sees itself in you as MAN. In this divine moment of truth, Grace touches you if your heart be quietly aflame with love and wholly open to the compassionate Holy One. That touch heals you. And in that healing is the creative renewal of all the world.

Such is the fulfilling of religious living, the Heart of Religion.

[73] See also, above, the last two paragraphs of Chapter 1.

BIBLIOGRAPHY

One learns best from the 'Book of Life', which each man writes for himself from moment to moment.

The reading of all other books can be fruitful only if the mind is at ease, open, attentive and meditative. It is hoped that although many titles had to be omitted for space reasons, the range covered by this list (divided into groups according to theme) will meet the special interests of the reader.

H. Bhattacharya, ed., *The Cultural Heritage of India*, vol. 4 (The Religions), Calcutta, 1956.
S. Dasgupta, *A History of Indian Philosophy*, 5 vols., Cambridge, 1952–1955.
M. Eliade (tr. by W. R. Trask), *The Myth of the Eternal Return*, New York, 1954.
E. O. James, *Comparative Religion*, London, 1938.
F. Max Müller, ed., *Sacred Books of the East*, 50 vols., Oxford.
Sir Monier Monier-Williams, *Indian Wisdom*, London, 1893.
S. Radhakrishnan, *Eastern Religions and Western Thought*, Oxford, 1939.
Indian Philosophy, 2 vols., London, 1927.
& J. H. Muirhead, *Contemporary Indian Philosophy*, London, 1936.
& others, ed., *History of Philosophy, Eastern and Western*, 2 vols., London, 1953.
P. J. Saher, *Eastern Wisdom and Western Thought*, London, 1969.
S. Spencer, *Mysticism in World Religion*, Harmondsworth, 1963.
R. C. Zaehner, *Mysticism, Sacred and Profane*, Oxford, 1957.

* * *

P. Freund, *Myths of Creation*, London, 1964.
Mr. & Mrs. H. Frankfort, J. A. Wilson & T. Jacobsen, *Before Philosophy*, Harmondsworth, 1949.
T. R. Glover, *The Conflict of Religions*, London, 1909.
G. W. Hegel, *The Philosophy of History*, English trans., New York, 1944.
A. Huxley, *The Perennial Philosophy*, London, 1946.
W. James, *The Varieties of Religious Experience*, London, 1902.
J. Mascaró, tr. and ed., *Lamps of Fire*, Cambridge, 1958.
J. H. Moore, ed., *Make-Believe*, London, 1973.
F. S. C. Northrop, *The Meeting of East and West*, New York, 1949.
R. Otto, *The Idea of the Holy*, English trans., London, 1925.
Mysticism, East and West, English trans., New York, 1957.
B. Russell, *Mysticism and Logic*, London, 1963.
History of Western Philosophy, London, 1949.

F. von Schlegel, *The Philosophy of History*, English trans., London, 1846.
Ueber die Sprache und Weisheit der Inder, (On the Language and Wisdom of the Indians), Heidelberg, 1808.
A. Schwegler, *History of Philosophy*, English trans., Edinburgh, 1871.

* * *

Sri Aurobindo, *Hymns to the Mystic Fire*, Pondicherry, 1952.
On the Veda, Pondicherry, 1956.
M. Blomfield, tr., *The Hymns of the Atharva Veda*, SBE vol. 42, 1897.
R. T. H. Griffith, tr., *The Hymns of the Atharva Veda*, 2 vols., Benares, 1895.
tr., *The Hymns of the Rigveda*, 4 vols., Benares, 1889–1892.
N. S. Sontakke and others, ed., *Ṛgveda-Saṁhita*, with Sāyaṇa's Commentary in Sanskrit, Text 4 vols., Indices 1 vol., Poona, 1933–1951.
P. Deussen, *The Religion and Philosophy of India*, vol. 1, part 1, *The Philosophy of the Veda*, Leipzig, 1894. Vol. 1, part 2, *The Philosophy of the Upanishads*, English trans., Edinburgh, 1905.
H. D. Griswold, *The Religion of the Rigveda*, Oxford, 1923.
A. Kaegi, *The Rigveda*, English trans., Boston, 1886.
A. B. Keith, *The Religion and Philosophy of the Veda and the Upaniṣads*, 2 vols., Cambridge, Mass., 1925.
A. Ludwig, *Der Rigveda*, 6 vols., Prag, 1876–1888.
A. A. Macdonell, *Vedic Mythology*, Strassburg, 1897.
History of Sanskrit Literature, London, 1928.
J. Muir, *Original Sanskrit Texts*, 5 vols., London, 1858–1870.
Max Müller, *Six Systems of Indian Philosophy*, London, 1902.
& H. Oldenberg, *The Vedic Hymns*, vols. 32 & 46, SBE., Oxford.

* * *

T. Aufrecht, ed., *Aitareya Brāhmaṇa*, Bonn, 1879; ed. and tr. by M. Haug, 2 vols., Bombay, 1863.
A. C. Burnell, ed. (in part) 1878, and by Oertel, with trans. and notes, in the Journal of the American Oriental Society, vol. XVI pp. 79–260, *Jaiminīya or Talavakāra Brāhmaṇa.*
Lindner, ed., *Kauṣītaki or Śānkhāyana Brāhmaṇa*, Jena, 1887.
R. Mitra, ed., *Taittirīya Brāhmaṇa*, 1855–1870, (Bibliotheca Indica); N. Godabole, Ānand. Ser. 1898.
A. Vedāntavāgīśa, ed., *Tāṇḍya Mahābrāhmaṇa, or Pancaviṁśa Brāhmaṇa*, Calcutta, 1869–1874 (Bibl. Ind.).
A. Weber, ed., *Śatapatha Brāhmaṇa*, Berlin, London, 1859; tr. by Eggeling in SBE, 5 vols.

* * *

H. N. Apte, ed., *Taittirīya Āraṇyaka*, Ānand. Ser., Poona, 1898.
R. Mitra, ed., *Aitareya Āraṇyaka*, Calcutta, 1876 (Bibl. Ind.).

* * *

P. Deussen, *Sechzig Upanishad's des Veda*, Leipsig, 1897.
R. E. Hume, tr., *The Thirteen Principal Upanishads*, Oxford, 1934.
J. Mascaró, tr., *The Upanishads*, Harmondsworth, 1965.
S. Radhakrishnan, tr., *The Principal Upaniṣads*, London, 1953.

* * *

The Bhagavad Gītā (The Song of the Lord). Various English translations are available, of which that by Charles Wilkins, 1785, is one of the earliest; modern translations by E. J. Thomas, S. Radhakrishnan, A. Besant and Bhagvan Das, J. Mascaró, Sri Aurobindo, K. Telang and several others.

* * *

G. Bühler, tr., *Sacred Laws: Āpastamba and Gautama*, SBE, Vol. 2, Oxford, 1879.
tr., *The Laws of Manu*, SBE, Vol. 25, Oxford, 1886.
J. Dowson, *Hindu Classical Dictionary*, London, 1928.
M. N. Dutt, tr., *Viṣṇu Purāṇa*, Calcutta, 1912.
C. C. Mukharji, tr., *Mārkandeya Purāṇa*, Calcutta, 1894.
H. Poddar, ed., *The Bhāgvata Purāṇa* (English trans.), 6 vols., Gorakhpur, 1952–1959.
H. H. Wilson, tr., *Viṣṇu Purāṇa*, 5 vols., 1864–1870.

* * *

K. N. Aiyar, tr., *Thirty Minor Upanishads*, Madras, 1914.
A. Avalon, see Sir John Woodroffe.
T. R. S. Ayyangār, tr., *Haṭhayogapradīpikā of Svātmārāma Svāmin*, Adyar, 1938.
tr., *The Yoga Upaniṣads*, Adyar, 1952.
A. Danielou, *Yoga: the Method of Re-integration*, London, 1949.
S. Dasgupta, *Yoga as Philosophy and Religion*, London, 1924.
An Introduction to Tantric Buddhism, London, 1950.
A. David-Neel, *With Mystics and Magicians in Tibet*, London, 1931.
M. N. Dvivedi, tr., *The Yoga Sūtras of Patañjali*, Adyar, Madras, 1934.
M. Eliade (tr. by W. R. Trask), *Shamanism*, London, 1964.
(tr. by W. R. Trask), *Yoga: Immortality and Freedom*, London, 1958.
B. K. S. Iyengar, *Light on Yoga*, London, 1968.
Rishabchand, *The Integral Yoga of Sri Aurobindo*, Pondicherry, 1959.
Sir John Woodroffe, *Shakti and Shakta*, Madras and London, 1929.
The Serpent Power, Madras, 1950.

* * *

Sri Aurobindo, *The Life Divine*, New York City, 1949.
E. B. Cowell and A. E. Gough, tr., *Sarva-Darśana-Saṁgraha of Madhavācārya*, London, 1914.
Sir Charles Eliot, *Hinduism and Buddhism*, 4 vols., London, 1921–1935.
M. Hiriyanna, *Essentials of Indian Philosophy*, London 1949.

C. Johnston, tr., *Vivekacūḍamaṇi and other Writings of Saṁkara*, Covina, California, 1964.

Swāmi Madhavānanda, tr. of Śaṁkara's *Vivekacūḍamaṇi, The Crest-Jewel of Discrimination*, Almora, 1952.

P. D. Mehta, *Early Indian Religious Thought*, London, 1956.

* * *

C. Bartholomae, *Die Gathas des Avestas*, Strasburg, 1905.

F. A. Bode, *Man Soul and Immortality in Zoroastrianism*, Bombay, 1960.

and P. Nanavutty, *Songs of Zarathuśtra*, London, 1952.

James Darmesteter, *Le Zend Avesta*, 3 vols., Paris, 1892-1893.

W. Geiger and E. Windischman, *Zoroaster in the Gathas and in the Classics*, tr. into English by Dastur D. P. Sanjana, Leipzig, 1897.

K. F. Geldner, *Avesta, the Sacred Book of the Parsis*, Stuttgart, 1886.

M. Haug, *Essays on the Religion of the Parsis*, Bombay, 1862, ed. by E. W. West, London, 1883.

I. J. S. Taraporevala, *The Gāthās of Zarathuśtra*, Text and translations into Gujarati and English, Bombay, 1947.

N. L. Westergaard, *Zend Avesta, or the Religious Books of the Zoroastrians*, Copenhagen, 1852–1854.

R. C. Zaehner, *The Dawn and Twilight of Zoroastrianism*, London, 1961.

Translations of the *Avestā* :

Anquetil du Perron, French, 3 vols., 1771.

Kleuker, German tr. of du Perron's French, 1781.

Spiegel, German, 1851–1863.

Bleeck, English tr. of Spiegel's German, 1864.

K. E. Kanga, Gujarati tr. of Geldner & Westergaard's Texts, 3 vols., Bombay, 1901–2.

* * *

W. Chan, *A Source Book in Chinese Philosophy*, Princeton, 1963.

K. K. S. Ch'en, *The Chinese Transformation of Buddhism*, Princeton, 1973.

Confucius, *The Analects.* Tr. by W. E. Soothill, London, 1937; by A. Waley, London, 1938.

H. G. Creel, *Confucius, the Man and the Myth*, London, 1951.

H. Dumoulin, *The Development of Chinese Zen*, tr. by R. F. Sasaki, New York, 1953.

C. P. Fitzgerald, *China*, London, 1935.

Fung Yu-Lan, *A History of Chinese Philosophy*, 2 vols., Princeton, 1952–3.

H. A. Giles, *Chuang Tzu: Mystic, Moralist and Social Reformer*, London, 1889 & 1961.

L. Giles, tr., *The Book of Mencius* (abridged), London, 1942.

E. R. Hughes, ed. and tr., *Chinese Philosophy in Classical Times*, London, 1941.

The Great Learning and The Mean in Action, London, 1942.

Lao Tzu, *Tao-teh-ching*; several translations available, by Giles, Old, Maurer, Mears, and others.
Treatise on Response and Retribution, tr. by D. T. Suzuki and Paul Carus, Le Salle, Illinois, 1973.
J. Legge, tr., *I Ching*, Dover edition, Toronto and London, 1963.
Lin Yutang, ed., *The Wisdom of China*, London, 1949.
A. Waley, *The Way and its Power*, London, 1934.
Three Ways of Thought in Ancient China, London, 1939.
R. Wilhelm and C. Jung, *The Secret of the Golden Flower*, tr. by C. F. Baynes, London, 1931.

* * *

Dīgha Nikāya, *Dialogues of the Buddha*, tr. by T. W. & C. A. F. Rhys Davids, 3 vols., Oxford, 1899–1921.
Majjhima Nikāya, *Middle Length Sayings*, tr. by I. B. Horner, 3 vols., London, 1954–1959.
Saṁyutta Nikāya, *Kindred Sayings*, tr. by C. A. F. Rhys Davids and F. L. Woodward, 5 vols., London, 1950–1956.
Anguttara Nikāya, *Gradual Sayings*, tr. by F. L. Woodward and E. M. Hare, 5 vols., London, 1951–1955.
Sutta Nipāta, *Woven Cadences*, tr. by F. L. Woodward, London, 1947.
Udāna, *Verses of Uplift*, and Itivuttaka, *As it was said*, tr. by F. L. Woodward, Oxford, 1948.
Vinaya Piṭaka, *Book of the Discipline*, tr. by I. B. Horner, 6 vols., London, 1949–1961.
Dhammapada, Several English translations available – by Radhakrishnan, Mascaró, Nārada thera, Buddhadatta mahāthera, and others.
Abhidhammattha-sangaha, tr. by Nārada thera, 2 vols., Colombo, 1956/7.
Nyanatiloka mahāthera, *Guide through the Abhidhamma-Piṭaka*, Kandy, 1971.
Buddhaghosa's *Visuddhimagga, The Path of Purification*, tr. by Ñāṇamoli bhikkhu, Colombo, 1956.
E. Conze, *Buddhist Meditation*, London, 1956.
Buddhism, its Essence and Development, Oxford, 1951.
Buddhist Thought in India, London, 1962.
in collaboration with I. B. Horner, D. L. Snellgrove, A. Waley, *Buddhist Texts through the Ages*, Oxford, 1954.
A. K. Coomaraswamy, *Buddha and the Gospel of Buddhism*, London, 1928.
and I. B. Horner present *The Living Thoughts of Gotama the Buddha*, London, 1948.
T. W. Rhys Davids, *Buddhist India*, London & New York, 1903.
S. Dutt, *Early Buddhist Monachism*, London, 1924.
Lama Anagarika Govinda, *The Psychological Attitude of Early Buddhist Philosophy*, London, 1961.
I. B. Horner, *Women under Primitive Buddhism*, London, 1930.
The Early Buddhist Theory of Man Perfected, London, 1936.
Ten Jataka Stories, London, 1957.

Christmas Humphreys, *Buddhism*, Harmondsworth, 1975.

ed., *The Wisdom of Buddhism*, London, 1960.

W. M. McGovern, *Manual of Buddhist Philosophy*, London, 1923.

T. R. V. Murti, *The Central Concept of Buddhism*, London, 1960.

Nyanaponika thera, *The Heart of Buddhist Meditation*, Colombo, 1956.

H. Oldenberg, *Buddha, His Life, His Doctrine, His Order*, tr. by W. Hoey, London, 1882.

F. Th. Stcherbatsky, *Buddhist Logic*, 2 vols., (Dover Edition), New York, 1962.

E. J. Thomas, *The Life of the Buddha*, London, 1949.

History of Buddhist Thought, London, 1933.

The Perfection of Wisdom, London, 1952.

* * *

E. Conze, tr., *The Prajñāpāramitā, the Large Sūtra on Perfect Wisdom*, London and Madison, 1961–4.

Selected Sayings from the Perfection of Wisdom, London, 1955.

Aśvaghoṣa's Discourse on The Awakening of Faith, tr. by D. T. Suzuki, Chicago, 1900. Another translation by Timothy Richard, London, 1961.

The Threefold Lotus Sūtra, the Saddharmapuṇḍarīka, tr. by B. Kato, Y. Tamura and K. Miyasaka. with revisions by W. E. Soothill, W. Schiffer and Pier P. Del Campana, New York and Tokyo, 1975.

Śāntideva, *Bodhicaryāvatāra*.

Śikṣāsamuccaya.

Sūtralamkāra, ed. and tr. into French by Sylvain Lévi, Paris, 1911.

The Lankāvatāra Sūtra, tr. by D. T. Suzuki, London, 1932.

Alberuni's India, tr. by E. C. Sachau, 2 vols., London, 1910.

S. Beal, *Buddhist Records of the Western World*, tr. from the Chinese of Hieun Tsiang (A.D. 629), 2 vols., London, 1906.

Life of Hieun -Tsiang, London, 1888.

L. C. Beckett, *Movement and Emptiness*, London, 1968.

Har Dayal, *The Bodhisattva Doctrine*, London, 1932.

Lama Anagarika Govinda, *Foundations of Tibetan Mysticism*, London, 1959.

His Holiness Tenzin Gyatsho, the XIVth Dalai Lama of Tibet, *The Opening of the Wisdom Eye*, Bangkok, 1968.

My Land and My People, ed. by David Howarth, London, 1962.

D. Snellgrove & H. Richardson, *Tibet*, London, 1968.

D. T. Suzuki, *On Indian Mahāyāna Buddhism*, ed. by E. Conze, New York, 1968.

B. L. Suzuki, *Mahāyāna Buddhism*, London, 1959.

G. Tucci, *The Theory and Practice of the Maṇḍala*, tr. by A. H. Brodrick, London, 1961.

W. Y. Evans-Wentz, ed., *The Tibetan Book of the Dead*, Oxford, 1957.

ed., *The Tibetan Book of the Great Liberation*, Oxford, 1954.

ed., *Tibet's Great Yogi Milarepa*, Oxford, 1958.

ed., *Tibetan Yoga and Secret Doctrines*, Oxford, 1960.

* * *

Hui-neng, *The Sūtra of Hui Neng*, tr. by Wong Mou-lam, ed. by Christmas Humphreys, London, 1966.

The Platform Scripture, The Basic Classic of Zen Buddhism, tr. by P. Vampolsky, New York and London, 1967.

Huang-po, *The Zen Teaching of Huang Po on the Transmission of Mind*, ed. and tr. by John Blofeld, London, 1971.

Record of Rinzai, tr. by I. Schloegl, London, 1975.

D. T. Suzuki, *Essays in Zen Buddhism*, 3 vols., London, 1928–1934.

* * *

Aeschylus, *The Tragedies.*

S. Angus, *The Religious Quests of the Graeco-Roman World*, London, 1925.

Aristotle, *Metaphysics*, Loeb Classical Library, London, 1933.

The Nicomachean Ethics, ed. and tr. by J. Warrington, London and New York, 1963.

R. Bultmann, *Primitive Christianity in its Contemporary Setting*, Eng. trn., London, 1956.

R. D. Casey, *The Excerpta ex Theodoto of Clement of Alexandria,* London, 1935.

Clemens Alexandrinus, tr. by W. Wilson, 2 vols., Edinburgh, 1867, 1869.

Cicero, *De Natura Deorum.*

De Senectute.

C. H. Dodd, *The Interpretation of the Fourth Gospel*, Cambridge, 1953.

J. Doresse, *Les Livres Secrets des Gnostiques d'Égypte*, Paris, 1958.

A. Dupont-Sommer, *The Essene Writings from Qumran*, Eng. trn., Oxford, 1961.

Euripides, *The Plays.*

T. Gomperz, *The Greek Thinkers*, 4 vols., Eng. trn., 1901–1912.

K. Grobel, trn. and commentary, *The Gospel of Truth*, London, 1960.

Homer, *The Iliad.*

The Odyssey.

Hesiod, *Works*, tr. by R. Lattimore & others, Ann Arbor (Michigan), 1959.

W. R. Inge, *The Philosophy of Plotinus*, 2 vols., London, 1918.

C. Kerényi, *The Gods of the Greeks*, tr. by N. Cameron, Harmondsworth, 1958.

T. Keightley, *The Mythology of Ancient Greece and Italy*, London, 1838.

H. D. Kitto, *The Greeks*, Harmondsworth, 1956.

Lucretius, *De Natura Rerum* (On the Nature of Things), metrical trn. by W. E. Leonard, London, 1916.

G. R. S. Mead, *Thrice Greatest Hermes*, 3 vols., London and Benares, 1906.

Fragments of a Faith Forgotten (reprint), New York, 1960.

Orpheus (reprint), London, 1960.

Pistis Sophia, London, 1896.

Gilbert Murray, *The Rise of the Greek Epic*, Oxford, 1934.
Five Stages of Greek Religion, London, 1946.
Plato, *The Dialogues*, tr. and ed. by B. Jowett, 5 vols., Oxford, 1875.
Plotinus, *The Enneads*, tr. by S. MacKenna, London, 1956.
Plotinus, Select Works of, tr. by T. Taylor; ed. by G. R. S. Mead, London, 1912.
Pythagoras, The Golden Verses of (etc.), selected and arranged by F. M. Firth, London, 1923.
R. Reitzenstein, *Poimandres*, Leipzig, 1904.
K. Schubert, *The Dead Sea Community*, London, 1959.
O. Seyffert, *Dictionary of Classical Antiquities*, revised and ed. by Nettleship and Sandys, London, 1906.
Sophocles, *The Tragedies*. (Various trans. available).
K. Stendahl, ed., *The Scrolls and the New Testament*, London, 1958.
E. J. Urwick, *The Message of Plato*, London, 1920.
G. Vermes, *The Dead Sea Scrolls in English*, Harmondsworth, 1962.
Virgil, *The Aeneid*.

* * *

J. Abelson, *Jewish Mysticism*, London, 1913.
G. H. Box and J. I. Landsman, *The Apocalypse of Abraham*, London, 1919.
M. Buber, *The Legend of Baal-Shem*, London, 1956.
I. Epstein, *Judaism*, Harmondsworth, 1959.
W. G. Gray, *The Ladder of Lights*, Toddington, 1968.
Moses Cordovero, *The Palm Tree of Deborah*, London, 1960.
R. H. Morfill & R. H. Charles, *The Book of the Secrets of Enoch* (The 2, or Slavonic, Enoch), Oxford, 1896.
E. Müller, *History of Jewish Mysticism*, London, 1956.
H. Odeberg, *3 Enoch or the Hebrew Book of Enoch*, Cambridge, 1928.
The Fourth Gospel, Upsala, 1929.
G. G. Scholem, *Major Trends in Jewish Mysticism*, London, 1955.
On the Kabbalah and Its Symbolism, London, 1965.
H. Sperling & M. Simon, tr., *The Zohar*, 5 vols., London and New York, 1933.
Sepher Yetzirah, The Book of Formation, by Rabbi Akiba ben Joseph, tr. by Knut Stenring, London, 1923.
C. Suarès, *The Cipher of Genesis*, London, 1970.

* * *

(The literature on Christian religion being so extensive, only a few titles are set down here).
The Bible
St. Augustine, *Confessions*, tr. by E. B. Pusey, London, 1949.
St. Thomas Aquinas, *Summa Theologica*, English trans. 12 vols., London, 1912–17.

Jacob Boehme, *Aurora* (1612); *Signatura Rerum* (1621); *The Supersensual Life* (1624); *Of the Divine Revelation* (1624). English ed. of Collected works by William Law, 4 vols., London, 1764–81.

C. Butler, *Western Mysticism*, London, 1922.

C. J. Cadoux, *The Life of Jesus*, West Drayton, 1948.

Of Cleaving to God (De Adhaerando Deo), Eng. trn., Oxford, 1947.

N. Cohn, *The Pursuit of the Millennium*, London, 1957.

Dante, *The Divina Commedia (Inferno, Purgatorio and Paradiso).* Several translations available.

'Dionysius the Areopagite', *On the Divine Names and the Mystical Theology*, tr. and introduction by C. E. Rolt, New York, 1920.

On the Heavenly Hierarchy and The Ecclesiastical Hierarchy, tr. by J. Parker, London, 1899.

Meister Eckhart, *Sermons and Tractates*, tr. from F. Pfeiffer's Collection by C. de B. Evans, 2 vols., London, 1947.

St. Francis of Assisi, *The Little Flowers*, tr. by T. Okey; *The Mirror of Perfection*, tr. by R. Steele, London, 1910.

Theologia Germanica, tr. by Susanna Winkworth, London, 1913. Another translation by W. Trask based on the German version by Joseph Bernhart, London, 1951.

C. G. A. von Harnack, *Dogmensgeschichte*, Freiburg im Breisgau, 1898. Reissue as *Outlines of the History of Dogma*, Boston, 1960.

Walter Hilton, *The Ladder of Perfection*, tr. by L. Sherley-Price, Harmondsworth, 1957.

F. von Hügel, *The Mystical Element in Religion as studied in St. Catherine of Genoa and her Friends*, 2 vols., Eng. trn., London, 1923.

St. Ignatius of Loyola, *The Spiritual Exercises*, tr. by A. Mottola, Garden City, New York, 1964.

R. M. Jones, *Studies in Mystical Religion*, London, 1909.

A. Jundt, *Les Amis de Dieu au XIV Siècle*, Paris, 1879.

St. John of the Cross, *The Ascent of Mount Carmel; Dark Night of the Soul*, tr. and ed. by E. Allison Peers, London, 1953.

Jan van Ruysbroeck, *The Adornment of the Spiritual Marriage; The Sparkling Stone; The Book of Supreme Truth;* tr. by C. A. Wynschenk Dom, ed. by E. Underhill, London, 1951.

Thomas à Kempis, *The Imitation of Christ*, tr. by C. Bigg, London, 1937 (Eleventh edition).

Brother Lawrence, *The Practice of the Presence of God*, London, no date.

V. Lossky, *The Theology of the Eastern Church*, London, 1957.

Jacques Maritain, *St. Thomas Aquinas, Angel of the Schools*, London, 1933.

D. Merezhkowsky, *Jesus the Unknown*, tr. by H. C. Matheson, London, 1933.

Johannes Müller, *Jesus as I see Him*, tr. by Hilda Bell, London, no date.

R. Payne, *The Holy Fire*, London, 1958.

E. A. Peers, *Studies of the Spanish Mystics*, 3 vols., London, 1927–1960.

Marguerite Porete, *Le Mirouer des Simples Ames*, *c.* 1300.

A. Poulain, *The Graces of Interior Prayer*, Eng. trn., London, 1910.
Benedict de Spinoza, The Chief Works of, tr. by R. H. M. Elwes, 2 vols., London, 1905/6.
Henry Suso, *The Life of the Blessed Henry Suso by Himself*, Eng. trn., London, 1913.
The Little Book of Eternal Wisdom, Eng. trn., London, 1910.
Tauler, *Twenty-five Sermons*, tr. by Susanna Winkworth, London, 1906, (new edition).
The Inner Way: Thirty Six Sermons for Festivals, Eng. trn., (3rd edition), London, 1909.
St. Teresa (of Avila), *The Life of St. Teresa by Herself*, tr. by J. M. Cohen, Harmondsworth, 1957.
The Interior Castle, Eng. trn., London, 1912.
E. Underhill, *Mysticism*, London, 1949.
ed., *The Cloud of Unknowing*, London, 1950.
tr., Nicholas of Cusa's *The Vision of God*, London, 1928.

* * *

A. J. Arberry, *The Koran Interpreted*, London, 1964.
Sufism, London, 1950.
trn. of Abu Bakr al-Kalabadhi's *The Doctrine of the Sufis*, Cambridge, 1935.
Farid Ud-din Attar, *The Conference of the Birds*, tr. by C. S. Nott, London, 1961.
H. A. R. Gibb, *Mohammedanism*, London, 1949.
A. Guillaume, *Islam*, Harmondsworth, 1954.
L. Massignon, *La Passion d'al-Hosayn ibn Mansur al-Hallaj*, 2 vols., Paris, 1922.
R. A. Nicholson, *The Mystics of Islam*, London, 1914.
Studies in Islamic Mysticism, Cambridge, 1921.
Rumi, Poet and Mystic, London, 1950.
Margaret Smith, *Rabi'a the Mystic*, Cambridge, 1928.
Al-Ghazzali the Mystic, London, 1935.

* * *

J. Krishnamurti, *Commentaries on Living*, 3 vols., ed. by D. Rajagopal, London, 1959–1965.
Freedom from the Known, ed. by Mary Lutyens, London, 1970.
The Only Revolution, ed. by Mary Lutyens, London, 1970.
Emily Lutyens, *Candles in the Sun*, London, 1957.
Mary Lutyens, *Krishnamurti, The Years of Awakening*, London, 1975.

* * *

H. Bondi, *Cosmology*, Cambridge, 1960.
and W. B. Bonner, R. A. Lyttleton, and G. J. Whitrow, *Rival Theories in Cosmology*, London, 1960.
H. J. Campbell, *The Pleasure Areas*, London, 1973.
F. J. Capra, *The Tao of Physics*, London & Berkeley, 1975.

P. Dirac, *The Principles of Quantum Mechanics*, Oxford, 1958.
Lectures on Quantum Mechanics, New York, 1964.
Lectures on Quantum Field Theory, New York, 1966.
L. De Broglie, *Matter and Light*, The New Physics, New York, 1939.
M. Duquesne, *Matter and Antimatter*, tr. by A. J. Pomerans, London, 1960.
A. S. Eddington, *Space, Time and Gravitation*, Cambridge, 1920.
The Nature of the Physical World, Cambridge, 1928 & 1932.
Science and the Unseen World, London, 1929.
The Philosophy of Physical Science (The Tarner Lectures, 1938), Cambridge, 1939.
A. Einstein, *Relativity: The Special and General Theory*, tr. by R. W. Lawson, London, 1920.
J. B. S. Haldane, *Science and Life*, London, 1968.
A. Hardy, *The Biology of God*, London, 1975.
W. Heisenberg, *The Physical Principles of Quantum Theory*, tr. by C. Eckart and F. Hoyt, Chicago, 1930.
Physics and Philosophy, London, 1959.
F. Hoyle, *The Nature of the Universe*, Harmondsworth, 1963.
Of Men and Galaxies, London, 1965.
M. Laue, *Das Relativitätsprinzip*, Braunschweig.
G. Lemaitre, *L'Hypothèse de l' Atome Primitif*, tr. by Betty & Serge A. Korff, New York, 1950.
J. R. Oppenheimer, *Science and the Common Understanding*, London, 1954.
Max Planck, *The Philosophy of Physics*, tr. by W. H. Johnston, London, 1936.
The Universe in the Light of Modern Physics, tr. by W. H. Johnston, London, 1937.
M. Polanyi, *Personal Knowledge*, London, 1958.
E. Schrödinger, *What is Life?*, Cambridge, 1944.
Mind and Matter (The Tarner Lectures, 1956), Cambridge, 1958.
C. Sherrington, *Man on his Nature*, Cambridge, 1940.
C. H. Waddington, *The Ethical Animal*, London, 1960.
W. Grey Walter, *The Living Brain*, Harmondsworth, 1961.
Lyall Watson, *Supernature*, London, 1974.
H. Weyl, *Raum – Zeit – Materie*, Berlin, 1918.
Philosophy of Mathematics and Natural Science, Princeton, 1949.
A. N. Whitehead, *Religion in the Making*, Cambridge, 1926.
The Interpretation of Science, Selected Essays, ed. by A. H. Johnson, Indianapolis, N.Y., 1961.
J. Z. Young, *Doubt and Certainty in Science*, Oxford, 1951.

GLOSSARY

(Listed in Sanskrit alphabetical order)

S=Sanskrit P=Pali A=Avestan Gk=Greek H=Hebrew

aum (S) The sacred sound (word).
abba (Aramaic) Father.
akem (A) Bad.
agni (S) Fire; the god of fire.
attan, or *atta* (P; Skt. *ātman*) The manikin soul as a permanent entity as postulated in the animistic theories of the 6th & 7th century B.C. in N. India; oneself, yourself, himself.
atyāśramin (S) An ascetic of the highest degree.
anattā (P) Devoid of ultimate reality; without abiding entity.
anāhata (S) The fourth centre of psychic energy; associated with the heart.
anicca (P) Impermanent; relative, not absolute.
anguttara (P) Graduated according to a consecutive series of numbers.
antevāsin (S) A pupil who dwells near or in the house of his teacher.
amanaska (S) The condition of the quiescence of intellection or discriminative perception, when the mind is still and silent but awake.
amanībhāva (S) As for *amanaska*.
ameretāt (A) Immortality.
arahant (P) One who has realized the supreme worthiness, *nibbāna*, perfection.
avatāra (S) Manifestation or incarnation of deity on earth.
avasthā (S) State or condition.
avidyā (S; Pali, *avijjā*) 'Ignorance' in the sense of the non-realization of supreme communion or of the eradication of all ill.
ash (H) Fire (cosmic).
ashah (H) The feminine aspect of cosmic fire; the Woman (Gen., 2.23).
ashā (A) Divine Law and Order, Righteousness, Truth, Holiness.
aśvattha (S) The sacred tree.
aśvamedha (S) The horse sacrifice.
astam (S) Home.
asatya (S) Untruth, the unreal.
asaṁprajñāta samādhi (S) The supreme communion or *samādhi* wholly free of isolative self-consciousness and of an object of attention.
asura (S) is a term with opposite meanings: evil spirit, demon; Spirit, God.
aham (S) I.
ahi (S) A snake; the serpent of the sky.
ahuna-vairya (A) The Will of the Lord.

* * *

ākāśa (S; Pali, *ākāsa*) Mind-space, sky, clear space; the subtlest of the five elements, the others being earth, water, fire and air.
ācārya (S) Teacher.
ājñā (S) The centre of psychic energy between the eyebrows.
ātman (S; Pali, *attan*) The ultimate reality, identified with Brahman. In some Upaniṣads pictured as a manikin soul.
āthar (A) Fire (of the Spirit).
āditya (S) Son of Aditi; belonging to the Ādityas (a class of gods); divine.
ānanda (S; P) Calm, peace, bliss.
āraṇyaka (S) A book containing the meditations of a forest-dwelling sage.
āśrama (S) A hermitage or retreat; a station of asceticism or mortification.
āsana (S) Any yogic bodily posture.
āsava (P) Exudation, overflow; intoxicant, canker.

* * *

itivuttaka (P) Thus said.

* * *

uttara (P) Beyond, further.
udāna (P) Inspired utterance.
unmanī (S) The state of the mind when its conditioned interpretative activity is at rest.
upāya (P) Means, method.
upekṣā (S; Pali, *upekkhā* or *upekhā*) Equanimity, perfect poise born of mindfulness; indifference.
$\sqrt{}$*uṣ* (S) To burn.
urvā (A) Soul.

* * *

eka (S) One; alone, only; single.
ekāgratā (S; Pali, *ekaggatā*) One pointedness of mind; the unified state of mind.
eksousia (Gk. ἐξουσία) Power, means, authority to do a thing.
evātmānaṁ (S) Precisely (*eva*) that *ātman*.

* * *

karuṇā (S; P) Compassion.
kalyāṇa (S) Beautiful; blessed; prosperous.
kāma (S; P) Desire, lust, love; Eros.
kuṇḍalinī (S) The mysterious energy said by yogis to be coiled up and stored at the base of the spine.
kṣatra (S) Dominion, sovereignty, power (human or supernatural).
kṣatriya (S) A member of the military or reigning order.

* * *

khandha (P; Skt., *skandha*) Aggregate, mass, all that is comprised under.

* * *

gata (S; P) Gone.
gamaya (S) Lead me; make me go to.
garo-demāna (A) The house of Songs; the Heaven of the Zarathuśtrians.
guru (S) Spiritual preceptor.
gūdhasupti (S) Secret (mysterious) sleep.
geush (A) Ox (typifying the Creation).
gevurah or *geburah* (H) Judgement, punishment.
gṛhapati (S) House-lord.

* * *

cakra (S) Wheel; in *kuṇḍalinī* yoga, a whirling centre of psychic energy.
citta (S; P) The 'heart', mind; intelligence; attention.
cidātma (S) Pure Intelligence, the essence of Mind; unconditioned attentiveness.
cinmātra (S) Consisting solely of thought.
ceto-mukha (S) The 'mouth' of thought.
ceto-vimutti (P) Freedom of mind.
chela or *chelo* (Gujarati, derived from Skt., *cit*, an attendant or friend.) A disciple; a scholar or pupil.

* * *

japa (S) The repetition of a word or phrase in order to produce a result.
jarā (P) Old age; decrepitude.
jāgrat (S) The waking state; the first of the four states of consciousness as presented in the Upaniṣads.
jāti (P) Existence, life; birth or rebirth; rank, caste; a conditioned state.
jīvanmukta (S) He who is liberated whilst living.
jñāna (S) Knowledge; especially the higher or spiritual knowledge which is the fruit of meditation and insight.
jhāna (P; Skt., *dhyāna*) A deep state of attentiveness in which the mind becomes still and silent.

* * *

tat or *tad* (S) 'That'. (*tat tvam asi*=THAT thou art).
tadasmi (S) That am I.
tadvanam (S) The longing or intense aspiration for THAT.
taṇhā (P) Craving.
tapas (S) Warmth, heat; religious austerity, fervour.
tamas (S) Darkness; heaviness; inertia; ignorance; illusion.
tashā (A) Architect.
tiphereth (H) The sixth *Sephira*; beauty, harmony, balance; the 'Lesser Countenance'; the Son.
turīya (also *turya*, S) The fourth; the state of the Supreme Communion; Transcendence, Brahman.
tṛṣṇā (S) Thirst (especially for sensation); avidity.
taijasa (S) Originating from or consisting of light (*tejas*); brilliant; associated with the second meditative state (the 'dream' state).

tov (H) Good (this is the usual translation, 'good' being regarded as that which is established, secure, but obstructing new creation and change, even though the change could lead to growth or true progress).

* * *

daṇḍa (S) Rod, staff; punishment.
dāna (P) Gift; charity; munificence.
dīgha (P) Long.
din (H) The power of God mainly manifested as stern judgement and punishment.
diva (S) Heaven; radiance, brilliance.
dukkha (P) Suffering; the ill state; absence of ease; unsatisfactoriness, anguish. No English word covers the same ground as *dukkha* does in Pali.
duḥkha (S) Pain, hardship, misery, suffering; far from the Infinite, or, the Infinite made bad or evil through constriction into the finite.
daeva (A) Evil-doer; demon.
deva (S and P) A deity or divine being; a man of excellence or very high rank such as a brahman, king, prince.
dyaus (S) Heaven; sky, day.

* * *

dhamma (P) Doctrine; right or righteousness; condition; phenomenon; mental object or pure idea; the truth, or wisdom, as taught by the Buddha; norm; thing. *dhammā* (plural) Things, mental objects, states of mind.
dharma (S) Established order, rule, duty; virtue; justice; religion; the upholding of the eternal order (*ṛta*) of things.
dharmakāya (S) The truth-body.
dhāraṇā (S) Holding or supporting (the Law, *ṛta*); maintaining a state of consciousness in deep meditation.
dhyāna (S) Profound abstract meditation; paying full attention to.

* * *

nāma-rūpa (S; P) Name-shape; informing principle-form; mind-body or psycho-physical organism.
nāos (Gk. ναός) The dwelling of a god; temple.
nikāya (P; S) Assemblage, class, group; collection.
nitya (S; Pali, *nicca*) Permanent; eternal; absolute.
nididhyāsana (S) Profound and repeated meditation.
nibbāna (P; Skt., *nirvāṇa*) The blowing out or extinction of all defilements of mind; the *summum bonum* of human existence; the supreme bliss; transcendence.
nirmāṇakāya (S) The body of transformation; the body of the Buddha as visible on earth.
niyama (S. P) Restraint, self-control; religious observance.
neti (S) Not this.

nephesh (H) The vital principle, the lowest of the three grades of the soul.
neshamah (H) The moral consciousness, the highest of the three grades of the soul.

* * *

√*pat* (S) To master, to rule; to fall down or apart.
pati (S) Husband, master, sovereign lord.
patnī (S) Wife, mistress, sovereign lady.
paṭicca-samuppāda (P) 'Arising on the grounds of (a preceding cause)'; causal genesis; dependent origination; conditioned co-production.
paṭipadā (P) Means of reaching a goal; path; method; practice.
paññā (P) Wisdom; perfect insight.
para or *pāra* (P) Beyond; on the further side of.
param (S) Beyond, final, supreme.
paramātman (S) Ultimate essence of Being, or Reality.
pāra (S) The further shore; the utmost reach or fullest extent.
pāramitā (P; S) Excellence, perfection.
pīti (P) Emotion of joy, delight; rapture.
pāpa (P; S) Evil, wrong-doing, sin.
punabbhava (P) Again-becoming.
punarjanman (S) Rebirth.
pubbenivāsa (P) Former habitation.
pūrva (S) Being before or in front; former, prior; eastern.
pṛthivī (S; Pali *paṭhavī*) The earth or wide world; the earth element; extension, breadth.
puruṣa (S) Man, person; the soul or spirit animating a man.
puruṣottama (S) The highest person; the Supreme Being.
prakṛti (S) Original or primary substance; primordial Nature (distinguished from *puruṣa*); Śakti, energy personified as a goddess.
prajñā (S) Wisdom; perfect insight. (Characterises the purified mind).
prajñā-pāramitā (S) The excellence or perfection of wisdom.
pratyagātman (S) The individual soul.
pratyāhāra (S) Drawing back, withdrawal, abstraction (non-attachment to or aversion) from the objects of sense.
prājña (S) The pure intelligence associated with the third *avasthā*, that of *suṣupti* (deep sleep), in meditation.
prājñenātman (S) The intelligential *ātman*.
prāṇa (S) Life-energy in all its grades, from pure spirit to densest matter; breath; vitality.
prāṇāyāma (S) Control of – that is, not squandering – life-energy, biological, psychical, spiritual.

* * *

phala (S; P) Fruit; result.
phassa (P) Contact.

* * *

bāj (A) A Zarathuśtrian hymn of praise.
bindu (S) Drop, globule, spot, point.

buddhi (S) Pure intelligence; wisdom; unerring insight; faultless perception. (Characterises the stainless mind).

budhnya (S) Coming from or belonging to the depths.

bodhi-sattva (S) One whose essence is perfect knowledge; *-satta* (P) A being destined to attain perfect enlightenment or buddhahood.

brahmacariya (P) Living the holy life.

brahmacarya (S) The state of a chaste student living the religious life.

brahman (S, neuter gender) Prayer, the sacred word (of the Veda as opposed to *vāc* the word of man); a text or *mantra* used as a spell.

brahma (S) The one self-existent Spirit; ultimate reality; the absolute.

brahmaputra (S) Son of Brahmā (the creator god).

brahmabhūta (P) Become *brahma*; a divine or most excellent being.

brahmavihāra (P) A divine abiding (in meditation); a way to union with Brahmā.

* * *

bhakti (S) Devotion, worship, ardent love for God.

bhava (S; P) Coming into existence, birth, production, origin; becoming, (form of) rebirth, a 'life', (state of) existence.

bhikkhu (P) Almsman, mendicant, a Buddhist monk.

bhikkhunī (P) Almswoman, female mendicant, a Buddhist nun.

bhūta (P) Living being; animate Nature; (plural, *bhūtāni*, inanimate Nature, the elements [earth, air, etc.] usually enumerated as *mahābhūtāni*).

* * *

magga (P) The path of good and moral living and the way to salvation.

majjhima (P) Middle, medium, moderate.

manana (S) Thinking, reflecting, considering.

mantra (S) Sacred word or phrase; prayer or song of praise; Vedic hymn, sacrificial formula; incantation, charm, spell, magical formula.

maṇḍala (S) Disc, circle, anything round; a map of the cosmos, a cosmogram; (it is also) a psycho-cosmogram (a kind of 'horoscope', different from the zodiacal horoscope).

manas (S) Mind (in its widest sense as applied to all the mental powers).

maṇipūra (S) The third centre (*cakra*) of psychical energy associated with the navel.

manuṣya (S) Human being.

manuṣyaputra (S) Son of man (mind).

maraṇa (P) Death; dying.

mahā (S; P) Great, large.

mahātmā (S) Great soul; great being; a perfected holy man.

mahāvākya (S) A great saying (such as *tat tvam asi*=THAT thou art.)

māyā (S) Extraordinary or supernatural power; wisdom; illusion, unreality; trick, deception; magic.

muditā (P) Sympathetic joy; love expressed as joy in the (spiritual) progress and fulfilment of others.

muni (S) A saint or sage or seer who has realized the silence, or an hermit who has taken the vow of silence.
mūlādhāra (S) The first centre of psychical energy, associated with the base of the spine.
mṛtyu (S) Death, dying; the god of death (Yama).
metanoia (Gk. μετάνοια) After-thought; repentance; a turning away from.
mettā (P; Skt., *maitri*) Amity, loving kindness, friendliness.
medha (S) Any sacrificial ritual; offering, oblation.
merudaṇḍa (S) The spinal column.
mainyu (A) Twin.

* * *

yama (S; P) Restraint; a great moral rule (*niyama* being a minor rule); (name of the) ruler, and judge, of the dead.
Yamarājñah (S) King Yama (who attained lordship over the highest of the three heavens.)
√*yuj* (S) To yoke or join; to concentrate the mind and realize union with the Universal Spirit.
yogi (S) One skilled in yoga. (The term yoga should not be restricted to the practice of bodily postures only).
yogeśvara (S) Prince of yogis; a title bestowed on Yājñavalkya.

* * *

raa (H) (usually translated as) evil. It is the disrupting by creative energy of an outworn form in order that there may be progressive growth.
rajas (S) 'coloured or dim space', the sphere of clouds; (also) 'the whole expanse of heaven or sky' divided into an upper and lower stratum; gloom, darkness, impurity; the darkening quality, passion, disturbed or disturbing motion.
√*ram* (S) To delight, make glad, to play, to enjoy.
raḥamin (H) Compassion; the sixth Sephira; another name for Tiphereth.
ṛta (S) Sacred or pious action or custom, divine law, faith, divine truth; the eternal order of things.
ṛṣi (S) A singer of sacred hymns; an inspired sage.
ruaḥ (H) (literally, spirit). The intellectual faculty, the middle of the three grades of the soul.
rūpa (S; P) Shape; form; appearance.
rocanā (S) Pleasing, lovely.

* * *

loka (S; P) Free or open space; the world or universe; a region or country. In connection with meditation, attaining or entering a specific *loka* stands for a particular state of consciousness.

* * *

vānapraśtha (S) A forest-dwelling sage or hermit.
vāsanā (S) The unworked out part of impressions remaining unconsciously in the mind; the present consciousness of past perceptions.

vicāra (P) Turning over a subject for thought in one's mind.

vijñāna (S) The act of discerning, of right judgment; science, doctrine; worldly knowledge; comprehending.

vijñāna-ghana (S) Pure knowledge; nothing but intelligence.

vijjā (P) Knowledge; art; secret science; higher knowledge; revelation.

vitakka (P) Initial application of thought to a subject for thought; reflection.

vidyā (S) Knowledge, scholarship, philosophy; knowledge which is realization by completely seeing the truth.

vidha (S) Form.

viññāṇa (P) Discriminative consciousness.

virāga (P) Dispassionateness; indifference towards; waning; purifying; emancipation.

viriya (P) Vigour, energy, effort, exertion.

viśuddhi (S; Pali, *visuddhi*) Brightness, excellence; purity, virtue, holiness.

visarga (S) Discharge; liberation; cessation, end.

viśva (S) All-pervading, all-containing; whole, entire, all.

vṛtra (S) A foe, harasser; the demon of drought slain by Indra.

vedanā (P) Feeling; sensation.

vaiśya (S) A man who settles on the soil; peasant, agriculturalist, trader.

vaiśvānara (S) Relating or belonging to all men; omnipresent, general, common; known or worshipped everywhere.

vohu-mano (A) The Good Mind.

* * *

śakti (S) Strength, skill, efficiency; active power or female energy of a deity (especially of Śiva).

śabda (S) Word, sound, tone.

śāstra (S) Scientific or canonical work; scripture; compendium of any branch of learning.

śūnya (S; Pali, *suñña*) Empty, devoid of reality, unsubstantial, phenomenal.

śūnyatā (S; Pali, *suññata*) Emptiness; the void; freedom from lust, ill-will and dullness.

śoka (S; Pali, *soka*) Anguish, grief, sorrow, affliction.

* * *

sat (S) Actual, real; existent; good, virtuous.

sati (P) Memory; mindfulness; self-possession; alertness; conscience, self-consciousness.

satta (P) A living being, creature, person.

satya (S) True, real, actual.

saṁkhāra (P) Confection, preparation; mental pattern produced by prevailing causes; predisposition; a mental aggregate, a 'put together'.

saññā (P) Conception, idea, notion; sense impression and recognition.

sambodhi (P) Highest wisdom, enlightenment, awakening.

saṁsāra (S; P) Wandering through a succession of conditioned states (the 'round of existences', the faring on); the worldly life.

samādhi (S; P) The perfect meditative state when the still and silent mind is free of all isolative self-consciousness.

sambhogakāya (P) 'Body of enjoyment'; one of the three bodies of the Buddha.

saṁprajñāta samādhi (S) The meditation in which there is an object of attention.

samāpatti (P) A meditative state of coalescence with (entering upon and abiding in the infinity of) *ākāsa* and *viññāṇa*, No-thing, and neither consciousness nor unconsciousness.

saṁyutta nikāya (P) The collection of texts entitled Kindred (bound by ties of relationship) Sayings.

sarva (S) All, every, everyone.

savitṛ (S) A Vedic sun-deity that shines by night as well as by day.

sahasrāra (S) The seventh centre (*cakra*) of psychical energy, known as the thousand-petalled lotus, associated with the brain.

sīla (P) Moral practice; code of behaviour; Buddhist ethics.

sukha (P) Happy, agreeable, blest.

sura (S) A god, divinity, deity.

surā (P) Intoxicating liquor.

suṣupti (S) Dreamless sleep; the third *avasthā* in meditation.

suṣumnā (S) The central canal in the spinal cord.

sūtra (S) Thread, cord; an aphoristic rule; a manual consisting of strings of such aphoristic rules.

sephira, plural *sephiroth* (H) (Literally) the numbers 1 to 10, associated with the realm of the ten divine emanations in which God's creative power unfolds.

spenta (A) Holy.

sphoṭa (S) Sound (conceived as eternal, indivisible and creative; the eternal and imperceptible element of sounds and words and the real vehicle of the idea which flashes on the mind when a sound is uttered).

sphoṭāyana (S) Name of a grammarian quoted by Pāṇini, 6.1.123.

svapna (S) The dream state; the second *avasthā* in meditation.

svādhiṣṭhāna (S) The second centre (*cakra*) of psychical energy, associated with the genitals.

* * *

haṭha (S) Force; violence; a forced meditation. Haṭha-yoga is a yoga attended with bodily restraints.

hiraṇyagarbha (S) Womb or embryo of gold. Name of a cosmogonic power of Brahmā; also of intellect conditioned by the aggregate.

hṛdaya (S) The heart (or region of the heart as the seat of feelings and sensations), soul, mind (as the seat of mental operations); the heart or interior of the body; the heart or centre or core or essence or best or dearest or most secret part of anything.

haurvatāt (A) Perfection; health; wholeness.

INDEX

For clarity in the small type used for this index, most diacritical marks have been omitted. The correct Sanskrit spelling will be found in the text and glossary.